Texts in Computer Science

Series Editors

David Gries, Department of Computer Science, Cornell University, Ithaca, NY, USA

Orit Hazzan , Faculty of Education in Technology and Science, Technion—Israel Institute of Technology, Haifa, Israel

More information about this series at http://www.springer.com/series/3191

David Parsons

Foundational Java

Key Elements and Practical Programming

Second Edition

 Springer

David Parsons 🆔
The Mind Lab
Auckland, New Zealand

ISSN 1868-0941   ISSN 1868-095X (electronic)
Texts in Computer Science
ISBN 978-3-030-54520-8   ISBN 978-3-030-54518-5 (eBook)
https://doi.org/10.1007/978-3-030-54518-5

This Springer imprint is published by the registered company Springer Nature Switzerland AG
The registered company address is: Gewerbestrasse 11, 6330 Cham, Switzerland

To my parents, gone but not forgotten.

Preface

In the Spring of 1996, I attended the Object Technology conference at Christ church College, Oxford. The excited buzz around the "new" Java language at this conference got me curious, and a few months spent getting up to speed with the syntax convinced me that it was worth trying out as a teaching language. After overcoming some hurdles, including getting a teaching lab upgraded from Windows 3.1 to Windows 95 so we could run Java, I taught a class of student volunteers at what is now Southampton Solent University the basics of Java in 1997. From this experience I wrote the first edition of "Introductory Java" which was published by Letts Educational in 1998. In 1999 I left academia to spend some years in industry, training and consulting in Java. This gave me a whole new perspective on the language as a professional tool, and the second edition of "Introductory Java" was published in 2003. By 2012 I was back teaching various programming languages in academia, but also continuing to deliver Java training for commercial clients and felt that a completely new book was needed to address all the changes in the language over the intervening decade. Hence the first edition of "Foundational Java: Key Elements and Practical Programming" was almost a completely new book with a new focus and a new publisher, covering Java up to version 7.

Fast forward to 2020 and the many accumulated changes to Java since version 7 had reached a point where I felt that Foundational Java needed a significant update, hence this second edition. It has grown out of more than 20 years of teaching Java both to students and to professionals across the world and reflects a wealth of experience and insight. I have had a great journey with Java, and I am grateful for the opportunity to share my Java knowledge with readers of this book.

Overview and Goals

The second edition of "Foundational Java: Key Elements and Practical Programming" guides the reader through all the core features of Java, and some more recent innovations, in a way that builds skills and confidence though tried and trusted stages, supported by exercises that reinforce the key learning points. Using this book, the reader is introduced to all the most useful and commonly applied Java syntax and libraries and is provided with many example programs that can provide the basis for more substantial applications.

Integral to the book is the use of the Eclipse Integrated Development Environment (IDE) and the JUnit testing framework. This ensures maximum productivity and code quality when learning Java. However, the fundamentals of using the Java compiler and run time are also explained to ensure that skills are not confined to one environment. In addition, coverage of the Ant tool ensures that the reader is equipped to automatically build, test and deploy their applications, including simple web applications, independent of an IDE.

Organization and Features

The book is organized into 20 chapters that cover various levels of Java (see "Suggested Uses" for further information). Each chapter covers a discrete topic and includes scaffolded exercises that build skills in a step by step fashion. I have experimented in the past with teaching Java using an "objects first" approach but experience has shown me that it is better to cover the language fundamentals before addressing object-oriented concepts, so this book follows an "objects later" philosophy.

The key features of this book are that it

- Meets the needs of both students and professionals.
- Provides both introductory and intermediate coverage
- Has been completely updated, including Java 14
- Uses the Eclipse IDE, the most popular open source Java IDE, but also explains how Java can be run from the command line
- Makes unit testing one of its key themes, integrating the JUnit 5 testing framework to emphasize the importance of unit testing in modern software development
- Includes coverage of the Ant build tool
- Comes with code examples and exercises throughout
- Is accompanied by a full set of PowerPoint presentation slides that have been road tested with classes
- Builds on three previous volumes and a set of classroom training materials that have been refined and developed as Java has continued to evolve.
- Includes some important illustrations in color.

Target Audiences

This is primarily an undergraduate textbook. It can be used for basic introductory courses or for intermediate classes. From that perspective it has been structured as a teaching text that breaks into weekly topics that build upon one another. It is also a book suitable for professional software developers who need to pick up Java from previous experience in other tools or languages. The materials have been tried and tested in commercial training courses for professional software developers over a period of 15 years. The choice of intermediate topics has been driven by customer requirements. All these topics have been requested by clients in various courses.

Suggested Uses

The book has been structured in such a way that it breaks easily into weekly topics. There is a core set of chapters that can be used as an introductory course, in a single semester, and a further set of chapters that can be used for intermediate study, for follow-on, longer or double weighted courses. It contains exercises throughout, designed to reinforce learning about the topics covered in each part of the chapter. The final exercises at the end of each chapter draw together the key aspects that have been covered, which are also reiterated in chapter summaries.

Foundational Java can be used for courses of different lengths and levels by using it in three different ways. The first 12 chapters, listed below, cover the core knowledge of Java, and provide a solid basis for an introductory course on object-oriented programming with Java. These fit easily into a 12-week semester, providing 11 weeks of teaching material (Chap. 1 is just an introduction) and opportunities for revision and reflection.

1. The Java Story
2. Compiling and Running Java Programs
3. Data Types, Arithmetic and Arrays
4. Control Structures
5. Creating Objects
6. Creating Domain Classes
7. Objects Working Together: Association, Aggregation and Composition
8. Inheritance, Polymorphism and Interfaces
9. Exception handling
10. Unit Testing with JUnit
11. Exploring the Java Libraries
12. The Collections Framework and Generics.

The following four chapters, listed below, are more intermediate, and provide more specialized coverage of Java; interaction with external connections to files, databases and build tools, as well as introducing multithreading. These are useful in longer semesters, or courses that require intermediate level study.

13. Input and Output Streams
14. Automatic Building and Testing with Ant
15. Java and the Database (JDBC)
16. Multithreading.

The final four chapters are specific to building applications with a graphical user interface or connecting to a web server and provide optional coverage for courses that have requirements for this type of programming. They provide additional resources and flexibility for longer or broader courses.

17. Building GUIs with the JFC Swing Library
18. Event Driven Programming
19. Dialogs and Menus, Models and Views
20. Java Web Servers and the HttpClient.

Supplemental Resources

Several supplemental resources are available from the book's website at http://www.foundjava.com

Resources on the website for students include

- Downloadable source code for all the examples in the book
- Downloadable source code for solutions to selected exercises.

Additional resources for instructors include

- A complete set of PowerPoint slides
- Downloadable source code for solutions to all exercises (on request to the author).

A Note About the Code

Source code in the text appears in a Courier font to mark it our clearly from the surrounding text

```
Java source code appears in this font
```

Due to the page width, it has often proved necessary to break lines of code in places where the original source code (which can be downloaded from the website) would not have a line break.

In most cases the line breaks have been inserted so that they do not affect compilation. For example, this code statement appears in Chap. 3.

```
double mean =
  ((double)intArray[0] + intArray[1] + intArray[2])
  / intArray.length;
```

This is, in fact, a single statement, even though it is broken across three lines of text. A single statement in Java is terminated by a semicolon, and line feeds do not, in most cases, affect the way the code works. However, in a very small number of cases it has not been possible to break lines within the margin constraints of the book in such a way that their workings are unaffected. If in doubt, or if you are having problems with compiling or running code, please refer to the original source code files.

Auckland, New Zealand   David Parsons

Acknowledgements

It is difficult to acknowledge all the individuals who have contributed to this book, because my experience of Java has been so long and broad. I am grateful to many authors of courseware from my various past employers; The Object People, BEA Systems, Valtech, IBM and Software Education Associates. The experience of teaching from material authored by others, however good or bad it is, provides new perspectives and understanding that goes way beyond what if possible when only teaching from your own perspective.

I am also grateful to Wayne Wheeler at Springer-Verlag London Ltd., who gave me the opportunity to bring this new edition of the book to publication.

Contents

The Java Story

1

Java is now well established as one of the world's major programming languages, used in everything from desktop applications to web-hosted applications and enterprise systems, and embedded in devices such as mobile phones and Blu-ray players. Its virtual machine (a core feature of the Java runtime platform, which we will explore later) also supports a family of related languages including Scala, Groovy and specialized versions of Ruby and Python. However, its beginnings were relatively humble and obscure, until it came to wider attention via the web in 1995. Within a year it had become "the next big thing" in software. Interest in the language was quite remarkable, considering that it only existed in beta test versions. In many ways, it was a question of being the right product at the right time, its popularity riding on the explosion of interest in the Internet and World Wide Web in the mid-1990s.

1.1 A Brief History of Java

Java was never intended to be quite what it became. It grew out of a project at Sun Microsystems to build the "Star7," a special type of Personal Digital Assistant (PDA) that was intended to control all the electronic devices in the home. For the system to work, it needed to be built with a language that could be used on various pieces of hardware, from televisions to toasters. The language that drove the Star7 was called "Oak" (named after a tree outside the window of its main designer, James Gosling), but attempts to sell the technology to various potential customers, such as digital TV set top box manufacturers, fell through. Eventually, it was decided to sideline the hardware development and promote the language itself on the Internet as a tool for providing online multimedia. This led to development of a program that would run on the Internet using the HTML (Hypertext Markup Language) pages that provided the basis for the World Wide Web, which had begun to achieve widespread popularity in 1993 due to "Mosaic", the first graphical web

© Springer Nature Switzerland AG 2020
D. Parsons, *Foundational Java*, Texts in Computer Science,
https://doi.org/10.1007/978-3-030-54518-5_1

browser. This program was the "WebRunner" web browser, later renamed "Hot-Java." Unlike the other browsers that existed at that time, HotJava was able to run small Java programs (known as "applets") within its window, adding dynamic content to the largely static text and images that had previously been possible. The first-ever applet showed "Duke" (the Java mascot, a sort of extracted tooth with a red nose) waving, establishing a strong and abiding image of Java as a language for writing animated web pages, though in practice it was much more than that. And the Java name? It changed from Oak only because there was already a registered trademark of that name. Java is named after the strong Java coffee popular in the United States, though many other names were considered including "Neon", "Lyric", "Pepper" and "Silk."

Since those early days, Java has matured into an industrial strength language, with different editions for desktop, server and portable/embedded device development, and a huge number of Application Programming Interfaces (APIs) for different kinds of application. From humble beginnings it has become one of the key technologies of global software development. Since Oracle's takeover of Sun Microsystems in 2010, Java has become an Oracle technology, but is still free to use for development purposes and is also available as an open source project, the OpenJDK.

1.2 Characteristics of Java

Java is in many ways a conservative language in that it was built on the successes of its predecessors while attempting to overcome many of their limitations and problems. It was designed to be "jargon-compatible" with a set of criteria that sum up what was "good" for a modern programming language back in the mid-1990s. Its designers reasoned that such a language should be

- Simple
- Object-oriented
- Distributed
- Robust
- Secure
- Architecture-neutral
- Portable
- High-performing
- Multithreaded
- Dynamic

It is, perhaps, a tribute to the success of Java that many of these characteristics, which were cutting edge at the time, are now de facto requirements for many programming languages. What follows is a brief outline of each of these features.

1.2.1 Simple

Nobody wants to program in a language that makes life more difficult than it already is. James Gosling said that Java is "C++ without the knives, guns and clubs". C++, the language developed by BjarneStroustrup in the 1980s as an object-oriented extension to the C programming language, is very popular and powerful but has many features that, like weapons, are very dangerous in the wrong hands (perhaps any hands). Java has much in common with C+ +, but a good deal of arms limitation has been applied. One major simplification in Java is the way that memory is managed, using largely automatic processes rather than requiring the programmer to do this. Simplicity is, however, a relative term!

1.2.2 Object-Oriented

The object-oriented approach to programming has become so common that to use a non-object-oriented language is now the exception, rather than the rule (though it has to be noted that functional programming has become popular in recent years, so some additions have been made to Java to also include some aspects of functional programming). However, this was not the case in the early 1990s, when the two main object-oriented languages, C++ and Smalltalk, were still regarded as a very new approach to programming. In an object-oriented language, instead of having data on one hand and processes on the other, the two are "encapsulated" together to provide objects that have both state (data) and behavior (processes). By tying the two together, we make it easier to model the behavior of the real-world things that we are trying to reflect in software. Much of this book is concerned with the concepts and application of object orientation.

1.2.3 Distributed

If computing is anything these days then it is distributed, since most computers are connected to a network and probably to the Internet. There is a trend toward making the machine on the desk (or in the hand) less important and the network that it is connected to more important, by providing software and other resources via the network (or the cloud) rather than storing everything locally on a hard disk. For enterprises this makes a lot of sense in terms of control, economy and organization. Therefore, any new language must provide the facilities to write systems where programs are distributed across many computers. Java is designed for network programming and can easily work with common Internet protocols such as HTTP (Hypertext Transfer Protocol) and FTP (File Transfer Protocol), providing libraries for network data streams, web services and various other aspects of distributed computing.

1.2.4 Robust

A robust program is one that does not behave unpredictably or fail due to pro-grammer error. By automatically taking on some tasks such as memory manage-ment, Java simplifies the task of the programmer, allowing more robust code to be written. It is also very strict about using the correct data types, meaning that it is difficult to deliberately corrupt the data in a program to, for example, introduce a virus.

Perhaps the most significant aspect of Java in terms of robustness is that it removes the concept of the "pointer" from code. A pointer is a mechanism for directly accessing memory, and many languages allow a programmer to allocate and manipulate a block of memory directly. Although this is a powerful feature, it is also a dangerous one if not managed correctly. Manipulating memory that has not been correctly allocated can crash a program, while failing to free up memory that has been finished with leads to "memory leaks" where a program can eventually run out of memory space to run in. Java has only "references" to objects, not pointers to the memory they occupy. Since programmers cannot directly access memory, they cannot wrongly manipulate it. In addition, since the programmer cannot directly allocate memory, it is not their responsibility to free it up either. That task is undertaken by the garbage collector, an aspect of the Java system that automatically recovers memory from objects that are no longer needed.

1.2.5 Secure

As well as programmer error, programs are vulnerable to deliberate sabotage. Security systems built into Java ensure that the code, once written, is not easy to tamper with. This is particularly important for a language that is used to write programs that are distributed widely over networks.

1.2.6 Architecture-Neutral

One of the most important aspects of Java (perhaps the most important) is that it is a "write once, run anywhere" language. In other words, it does not matter which type of computer you write Java code on or run the resulting programs on. The programs are written and run just the same. This is achieved by combining two different approaches to converting program source code into a runnable program. Most languages prior to Java were either compiled or interpreted. A compiler converts the entire source code of a program into an "executable", a program targeted to run within a specific operating system. In contrast, an interpreter converts the source code into runnable code one line at a time while the program is running. This is much slower than running a compiled program, but the same piece of source code can be run on different interpreters that are designed for different operating systems. Since an interpreted program can only be run when the interpreter is present, there is an extra overhead when using such programs; two pieces of software (the program and the interpreter) are needed rather than just one.

Java draws on both approaches by being a combination of both a compiled and an interpreted language. The Java compiler does not convert the source code into an executable for a specific environment. Rather, it compiles into "byte code". This byte code can then be run on any hardware that has a Java Virtual Machine (JVM), a relatively lightweight piece of software that interprets the byte code to run on a specific computer. For example, the same Java byte code can be run on a Windows PC, a Mac or a Linux machine with no changes to the original program. In this way, the amount of interpretation required is reduced to the absolute minimum to allow the same byte code to run on different systems (Fig. 1.1). The only proviso to this is that virtual machines for earlier versions of Java will not be able to run code written for later virtual machines that have additional features. Another thing to be aware of is that each platform needs to have its own virtual machine, so that there are, for example, different virtual machines for Windows, Mac and Linux.

1.2.7 Portable

Part of Java's architecture neutrality is based on portable definitions of how big different types of data are. In many languages, there is no specific definition of how much storage an integer, say, takes up in relation to other types such as "short" or "long" integers. One of these might be 8 bits long on one machine and 16 bits on another. In Java the storage sizes of all types of data are specified so an integer, for example, is always 32-bits long. Java types are also always signed, meaning that they can contain both positive and negative numbers. Though there are some features that allow certain operations on unsigned integers.

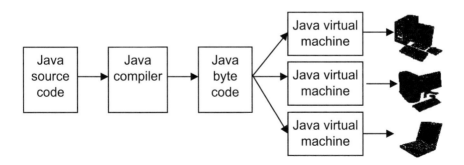

Fig. 1.1   The Java virtual machine allows the same byte code to be run on different platforms and operating systems

1.2.8   High-Performing

Execution speed can be a potential problem for Java. Because the byte code has to be interpreted, Java programs generally run more slowly than equivalent programs written in languages that are compiled. To overcome this problem, several strategies have been adopted. Just-in-time (JIT) compilers have been developed that speed up the interpretation process, and "native" compilers have also been written. In other words, the architecture neutrality is sacrificed in order to run the programs more quickly. A native compiler produces an executable that only works on a specific type of machine. This can be useful for developers who want a system that compiles and runs quickly for testing purposes or who know exactly where their programs will be deployed. The same source code can always be recompiled into portable byte code using a normal Java compiler if required. Another development was the "Java chip" a hardware virtual machine (a slightly less virtual machine perhaps) built into a chip. This is much faster than running byte code with software, and Java chips can be embedded in all kinds of electronic devices. Work on improving Java compilers is ongoing, though much of the optimization of code is done by the virtual machine rather than the compiler.

1.2.9   Multithreaded

Since many operating systems allow multithreading (where more than one process can be going on at any one time), it is useful if a language can take advantage of this. By building syntax for multithreading into the language, Java makes it easier for programmers to write multithreaded programs that are more efficient than single-threaded programs (where only one thing can be happening at any one time). Even where the operating system itself is not multithreaded, Java code can be written that uses multiple threads of control.

1.2.10   Dynamic

A Java program can dynamically change the resources it is using at runtime. This is useful in a distributed environment because it means that the program can be flexible in terms of size and behavior. It is also easy to write programs that use many different objects because it is easy for them to locate each other at runtime, even when they are in different places.

1.3   The JDK and the JRE

Java installations come in two forms. To develop Java software, you need the Java Development Kit (the JDK) which includes all the necessary tools for writing Java programs, in particular the Java compiler ("javac"). However, if you only need to run, rather than develop, Java programs then you only require the Java Runtime

Environment (JRE), which includes the Java Virtual Machine and supporting libraries but no compiler or other development tools. Both types of downloads are publicly available from the Oracle Java website (and through the OpenJDK), but to use this book you must have the full JDK. If you are using a Java Integrated Development Environment (IDE), then the necessary tools may already be included in that application, but to use the Eclipse IDE, as described in this book, a separate JDK must be installed.

1.3.1 Java Versions

Java first appeared for public consumption as version 1.0 in 1995. There were several minor modifications before its first major revision to Java 1.1 in 1996. Perhaps the most significant change between these two versions was to the event handling mechanism for user interfaces. Events are typically things that the user does such as pressing a button with the mouse or selecting an item from a menu and the way this was handled in version 1.0 was very inflexible, so major improvements were made with version 1.1. Java 1.2 (introduced in 1998) made more significant changes, including the introduction of the Collections Framework (a library of objects based on data structures that can contain other objects), and the original user interface library, the Abstract Windowing Toolkit (AWT), was made part of the much larger and more powerful Java Foundation Classes, including the Swing GUI libraries. At this point Java was also split into three editions (as described in the following section). Version 1.3 in 2000 mainly focused on updates to existing Java features rather than adding many new features, though sound support was considerably improved. Version 1.4 in 2002 focused largely on performance and security improvements, but also introduced support for XML processing, the NIO (new input/output) libraries for more efficient handling of IO, including network socket communication, and improvements to many other existing libraries.

Java version 5.0 in 2004 was a major upgrade to Java, introducing several important new features. At this point, the version numbering also changed in style, so that in addition to the internal version number (version 1.5) there was an external version number, 5.0. Cynics might argue that the timing and content of this update to Java was a consequence of Microsoft introducing its new C# language which also had a number of these new features. However, many of them, such as generics (which enables the type of objects in a collection to be specified), had been developed in the background for some years. In addition to generics, important new features of Java 5 included annotations, which make it easier to work with application frameworks such as the JUnit test framework, and autoboxing, which makes it easier to put simple data types into a Java collection. Java 6 (2007) saw some language features that had previously been available as external libraries, such as web services and Java to XML Binding, integrated into the standard Java distribution. Update 10 of Java 6 was a major update in terms of changes to the JRE, making it much easier to distribute Java applications by reducing the minimum footprint of the deployed JRE.

Java became open source in 2006, which was a significant change in approach for Sun Microsystems who had until that point had complete control over the development of the core Java language. Another significant change took place in 2010, when Sun Microsystems was acquired by Oracle Corporation. The first major version of Java delivered under Oracle's ownership was version 7 in 2011, though several features originally planned for Java 7 were eventually deferred until Java 8. In parallel with the Oracle version of Java, the OpenJDK Community also made their version of Java 7 available.

Java 8 was quite a significant update to the Java language, particularly in its responds to the increasing popularity of functional programming with the introduction of lambda expressions. This programming style also underpinned some interesting updates to the date and time API. Oracle introduced Long Term Support (LTS) for Java 8, which meant that many organizations remained using Java 8 for a long time (LTS support lasts 8 years) instead of upgrading to each new subsequent release, particularly because the release schedule changed significantly after the Java 9 release.

Perhaps the main change that came with Java 9 in 2017 was the introduction of modules (Project Jigsaw), a major change to the way that large systems could be modularized. This is particularly useful when adding features from newer versions of Java to legacy systems.

Changes in Java 10 (March 2018) were mostly behind the scenes improvements to the platform, and impacted little in at the coding level, but type inference for local variables provided for some new coding styles. However, the introduction of the "var" keyword to optionally replace the declared data type of local variables did not imply that any underlying changes were being made to the type system. From Java 10 onwards, the release schedule changed so that instead of having major releases every few years, with point release updates in between, Oracle Java versions would be released every 6 months (in March and September each year), with LTS versions every 3 years. Updates to the Open JDK normally follow 6 months behind.

Java 11, an LTS released in September 2018, was perhaps the most notable for changes in web-based programming, with the introduction of the HttpClient and the removal of the old Applet and Web Start features that were no longer viable web components due to security issues. Those parts of the Java Enterprise Edition (Java EE) that had been bundled with the JDK for some time were also removed.

Java 12 (March 2019) introduced a preview version of a "switch" expression, providing an alternative to the existing "switch" statement. Preview features were introduced into Java to provoke developer feedback based on real-world use. This feedback can lead to it either becoming permanent in a future Java SE Platform release or being removed. Around same time that Java 12 was released Oracle changed their licensing arrangements, requiring some types of users to pay a subscription fee in order to use Oracle's version of Java. However, Oracle Java remains free to use for development purposes and the OpenJDK continues to provide a free open source option.

For Java 13 (September 2019), perhaps the most obvious change from a programming perspective was a preview of Text Blocks, which allows multiline strings without any escape characters. There was also a revision of the switch expression, updating the preview changes in Java 12. Under the covers, the garbage collector and the Socket APIs received significant updates in their implementations.

Java 14 (March 2020) brought some additional escape characters to the Text Blocks preview, confirmed the switch expression syntax and introduced a more informative NullPointerException message among other things. Perhaps the most interesting new feature was a preview of "records" which simplifies the creation of classes that just contain data fields through the java.lang.Record class. A record automatically takes care of standard methods such as constructors, accessors, "equals", "hashCode" and "toString".

Java 15 (September 2020) mostly focused on improvements to some underlying implementations, but also included a second preview of changes to the "instanceof" operator, making it easier to test the type of an object in the context of larger expressions, as well as Text Blocks coming out of preview mode into permanent status.

All the code in this book has been tested with Oracle Java version 14. Some of the simpler examples will still work with much earlier versions. However, where syntax examples depend on a minimum version of Java to run, these have been indicated in the text.

1.4   Java APIs

As well as the core Java syntax, which consists of the basic keywords and some fundamental libraries, there are also many Java application programming interfaces (APIs). These provide libraries to allow the development of specialized applications such as Internet programming and rich client interfaces (using Swing or Java FX). Some of the more specialized libraries (often known as the Java extensions) are not provided with the standard edition of the JDK. At the introduction of JDK 1.2 in 1998, Sun categorized Java technologies within the "Java 2 Platform", organizing the large number of new features being introduced by providing different versions for different types of application–the Java 2 Standard Edition (J2SE), the Java 2 Micro Edition (J2ME) and the Java 2 Enterprise Edition (J2EE). At this point, the "JDK" prefix for the Java Development Kit was dropped in favor of "J2SE." With the release of version 5 in 2004, the "2" was dropped and these editions were then known as Java Standard Edition, (Java SE), Java Enterprise Edition (Java EE), and Java Micro Edition (Java ME). All the core libraries, along with the libraries necessary for desktop application development, are in the standard edition (Java SE), the version that we use in this book. Those that specifically apply to small or embedded devices and the Internet of Things are provided with the Java Micro Edition (Java ME), while those that relate to client server programming (servlets, JavaServer Pages, Enterprise JavaBeans, etc.) are part of the Java Enterprise Edition (Java EE), which became Jakarta Enterprise Edition (Jakarta EE) in 2018. Most of these libraries are beyond the scope of this book, but they provide many powerful programming features for various types of software applications.

1.5   Summary

Java is a mature and popular language that is used across the world for all kinds of applications. To program successfully in Java, we need to understand object-oriented concepts and then apply them to Java objects, which have their own peculiarities. It is, however, worth the effort because Java can be more rewarding than any other programming language. Its rich syntax and wide-ranging APIs mean that it can be used for all kinds of programming, from writing a command line utility to building a distributed client server system or a complex multithreaded real-time system. After the initial hype surrounding Java had died away, it matured into a major programming language supporting a huge software industry. Although to some extent Java is becoming a legacy language, no doubt it will continue to evolve and be providing programmers with the tools for coding a host of applications in all kinds of contexts for many years to come. Even if Java itself eventually fades away as a programming language, its influence is such that knowledge of Java can be extremely useful in learning the new generations of languages that have followed it.

Compiling and Running Java Programs

2

In this chapter, we meet our first Java applications. These short programs consist of classes that contain some simple code that displays output on the screen. The main purpose of this chapter, however, is to gain an understanding of the Java compiler and runtime environment and learn how to use packages and the classpath. In the early examples, we will be exploring how to use Java from the command line to help gain a deeper understanding of what is going on. At the end of the chapter, we introduce the Eclipse Java Integrated Development environment (IDE), where many of the low-level processes are taken care of for you.

2.1 Java from the Command Prompt

For our first couple of examples, we will be compiling and running our Java code from the command prompt rather than using an integrated development environment (IDE) for Java like Eclipse, Apache NetBeans, or IntelliJ IDEA. At first glance, this may seem a rather tedious and pointless exercise, when an IDE makes much of the process of editing, compiling and running code relatively easy and transparent. However, it is useful to at least get some idea of what is happening in the background when you use a Java IDE to understand what happens when code is compiled, how it is run, and how packages and the Java classpath relate to the file system. Having an awareness of these issues can help you to solve problems if you get into difficulties using an IDE, or when you want to take code you have written in an IDE to use in another context (e.g. when you need to deploy your applications so they can actually be used). To open the Command Prompt in Windows, simply type "cmd" into the search box at the bottom of the screen. You should see the Command Prompt app appear in the window. You can then click on this to open the Command Prompt. On a Mac, you will need to open the Terminal app, which is usually in the utilities folder of the Finder.

© Springer Nature Switzerland AG 2020
D. Parsons, *Foundational Java*, Texts in Computer Science,
https://doi.org/10.1007/978-3-030-54518-5_2

2.1.1 Setting the Path to the JDK

Before you can run any of the tools in the JDK from the command prompt, you need to ensure that the "path" environment variable includes the JDK's "bin" folder, where the programs you need, including "javac" and "java," reside. On Windows systems, the default installation location for the Oracle JDK "bin" folder is usually something like (*but not exactly*):

```
C:\Program Files\Java\jdk-14\bin
```

If you are using the OpenJDK, you can unzip the downloaded archive into a folder of your choice so the path will depend on where you extracted it to.

Make sure that you are locating the "bin" folder from the JDK, not the JRE, since the JRE does not include the compiler, or the other developer tools we will look at later. The path can be set either permanently as an environment variable or temporarily in a command window. In a command window, you can set your path to include the JDK tools by using "set path", for example:

```
set path=C:\Program Files\Java\jdk-14\bin;%path%
```

Including the reference to %path% is not essential but will append any existing path settings you already have. Setting the path from a command window does not change the system path, and only applies as long as that command window is open. Alternatively, you can set the path permanently in your system settings. To do this in Windows, you need to open the "Settings" dialog (from the gear wheel on the Windows side menu), search for "Path" and then choose the option to edit your environment variables. This will open the "System Properties" dialog with the "Advanced" tab selected. Press the "Environment Variables" button. You should see the "path" listed as one of the system variables. Select this variable and edit it. Add the path to the Java "bin" folder at the beginning of the list, separated from what follows by a semicolon, then press "OK."

Note
Changes to the path in the System dialog will not affect any command windows that are already open. A new command window will need to be opened to reflect changes to the path. We also have to be aware of the "classpath" variable, but this will not need to be set for the initial examples to work.

2.2   A First Java Program

Like almost every other first example program, our first Java application simply displays a message on the screen. Although it is very basic, it still introduces several important aspects of Java code that will be explored in detail later. It shows how to write a *class* in Java, used here simply as a program entry point. Classes have other roles in Java, but to get a program to run, you need a class that contains a "main" *method*, as we do in this example. A method is an operation that the class can perform. In the case of the "main" method, the operation is to act as a program entry point. In this example main method, another class from the Java libraries ("System") is used to print a message on the console. There is a lot more to learn about classes, but we will defer these discussions until later examples.

The source code of our first application (which you can enter into any basic text editor) is

```
public class MyJavaProgram
{
  public static void main(String[] args)
  {
    System.out.println("My Java Program Running!");
  }
}
```

This may seem a rather complex set of code just to print a simple message, but it includes several key features of Java. We will explore each part of the code as we work through the example.

2.2.1   The MyJavaProgram Class

The first line of code declares the class.

```
public class MyJavaProgram
```

No Java code can be written that does not belong to one class or another. This particular class is called "MyJavaProgram" but the class name is not important here, it is something decided by the programmer. The naming convention for class names is sometimes called *Pascal Case*, which simply means that the name begins with an upper case letter, and any embedded words (like "Java" and "Program" in our example) also begin with an upper case letter. The "public" prefix means that the class can be visible to all other classes, even those that are not in the same *package* (a file directory or folder) and is how most of our classes are declared. If we omit this prefix, the class will only be visible within its own package. For the moment, we are not specifying which package this class is in, so it will be put into the unnamed default package (which is in fact the current folder). We will look at packages in more detail in the next example.

The MyJavaProgram class must be saved in a file called "MyJavaProgram.java", preferably with the same mix of upper and lower case letters. Calling the file by the same name as the class is required for public classes and makes life much easier when we want to find a class later, since only one public class may appear in a ".java" file. It is essential that the file extension is ".java" because it is required by the Java compiler (at least it is by the Oracle JDK compiler).

Note

When you save the file, make sure that the text editor you are using is saving in plain text format, not some other format like rich text format (RTF) which is, for example, the default file type for Windows WordPad. Also ensure that the editor does not add another extension such as "txt" to your file, which Windows Notepad will do by default (to avoid this if you are using Notepad, put quotes around the filename when you enter it into the "save as" dialog).

The *body* of the class (the code that it contains) is surrounded by braces (curly brackets {}). Everything between the opening and closing brace belongs to that class. This is known as *scope*; the class contains everything that falls within its scope (i.e. appears between the two braces). In this example, the only thing that is in the scope of the class is a method called "main". The "main" method is a special method that allows a class to act as an entry point to a program.

2.2.2 The "main" Method

The main method is always the first to be executed when a class is run on the Java Virtual Machine, and a program must have at least one class with a main method in order to run at all. A program can have more than one class with a main method, but only one of them would be used as its entry point (others might be there, for example, purely for testing purposes, not meant as part of a larger system). The method is declared "public," which means that it is part of the public interface of the class, and also "static," a term we will explore properly later, but it enables us to run the main method directly using the name of the class. Its return type is "void", meaning that it does not return any value.

```
public static void main(String[] args)
```

Its parameter list (**String[] args**) is always the same, and means that we can, if we wish, send one or more strings of text to this method as parameters. Although the name used to refer to these strings can be anything we like, it typically appears as "args" or "argv" (because they are "arguments"). The square brackets ([]) indicate that this is an *array*, which will also be explored later. In practice, we rarely use this facility of passing String objects to the main method, but later we will see an example of how it may be used in order to understand why it is there.

2.2.3   Output with the System Class

To test our programs, it is useful to be able to output information direct to the console (the standard text output window). In Java, we can do this by using "System.out". Note that System begins with an upper case letter because it is the name of a class but begins with a lower case letter as it is an object. We will look at this distinction in a lot more detail later, but for now just be aware that "System.out" enables us to print text to the console by using the "println" method. The code that does this in our example is this single line in main:

```
System.out.println("My Java program running!");
```

"System.out.println" takes a string of characters as a parameter and prints it on the screen before adding a line feed. In addition, we will see later that any type of data can be passed to "println" for display. A similar method is "print" which also writes text to the screen but does not add the line feed, so any subsequent output would appear on the same line. We could therefore have written the following to print a line without a line feed:

```
System.out.print("My Java program running!");
```

Since this program only outputs a single line of text, this would not make any difference to this example.

2.3   Compiling Java

As described in Chap. 1, Java source code must be converted to byte code by the Java compiler. This byte code is written into ".class" files, which can then be run using the Java virtual machine. When we start to use an integrated development environment to write our programs, there will be various tools to allow you to do this. For the moment, however, we will learn how to use the Java compiler ("javac") from the command line.

For the first example, you will need to ensure that you have a command window opened in the same folder as your source code. You will also need to make sure that the "bin" folder of the JDK is included in your system path.

The source code must be compiled using the "javac" compiler. You can check if the compiler is on the path by simply typing "javac" at the command prompt. You should see a long list of options beginning something like this:

```
C:\>javac
Usage: javac <options> <source files>
where possible options include:
-g                      Generate all debugging info
-g:none                 Generate no debugging info
-g:{lines,vars,source}  Generate only some debugging info
```

However, if the "javac" command is not recognized, then this means there is a problem with your path settings that must be corrected before you can go any further.

If "javac" is on the path then you can compile your source code into a ".class" file (bytecode) to produce (for this example) "MyJavaProgram.class". Simply add the name of the source file after "javac" on the command line.

```
javac MyJavaProgram.java
```

You must use the full filename, including the ".java" extension. The Oracle Java compiler is not case-sensitive, but it is good practice to use the correct mix of upper and lower case, since many Java tools *are* case-sensitive. The compiler will either successfully compile the Java source file into byte code (in which case the system will simply display the next command prompt) or, if there is some error in your program, display compiler error messages. When the file successfully compiles, it will create a class file called "MyJavaProgram.class" in the same folder as the source code.

2.4 Running Java

Once the class has been compiled, it can be run on the virtual machine using "java *class name*," in this case:

`java MyJavaProgram`

When running a Java class, you do *not* add a file extension, just the name of the class itself. The virtual machine is case-sensitive and requires the correct mix of upper and lower case letters. The Java runtime must be able to find this file on the classpath, but by default, the classpath is the current folder. As long as we are working within a single folder, the classpath will not cause us any problems.

If you are using a different Java compiler or runtime, then the detail of the process may be a little different, but the same things are happening, namely, that the source file is compiled into a class file that is then run on the virtual machine. When run, the program displays the following on the screen:

`My Java program running!`

Control then returns to the command prompt from which the application was run. Figure 2.1 illustrates the sequence of compiling and running your code. Within the JRE, there is a class loader, which brings the byte code of the required classes into memory, and then the byte code is interpreted by the Java Virtual Machine to run on the specific operating system platform on which it has been deployed.

Exercise 2.1
This exercise simply walks through the steps in the first example.

- Enter the MyJavaProgram class source code into a text editor.
- Save it in a file called MyJavaProgram.java (make sure it is saved as a plain text file with the correct extension).

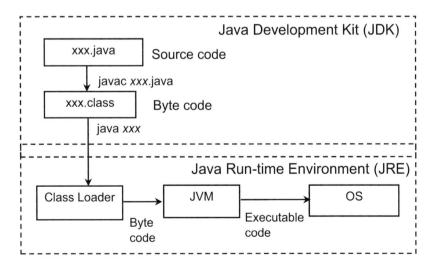

Fig. 2.1 The sequence of compiling and running Java code

- From the source code folder in a command window, compile the class using the "javac" compiler.
- If necessary, fix any errors, and continue to compile and edit your code until it compiles successfully.
- Once you have successfully generated a compiled ".class" byte code file, run the program by using the "java" runtime.

2.5   The Java Classpath

The Java classpath is what the Java compiler and virtual machine use to find compiled .class files (byte code). By default, the classpath is the current directory, which is why our example program ran without us being aware of the classpath. The JVM was able to find the required class file in the current folder. However, we cannot always work with everything in one folder, so we need to understand how the classpath works. Since the classpath is closely linked to Java packages, we also need to understand what packages are for and how they work.

2.5.1   Packages

All Java classes are placed in a package, even if it is the default (unnamed) package. Packages are a way to organize our classes, and a package typically contains a set of classes that are related together in some way. All the classes in a package are put into the same folder, and it is the folder pathway that gives the package its name. Package names consist of one or more folder names, separated by periods, all in lower case. Classes have a *simple name*, which is the name of the class itself, and a *fully qualified name*, which includes the package name. For example, the System class is in a package called "java.lang," so its simple name is "System," but its fully qualified name is "java.lang.System". Because the package name maps directly onto the structure of the file system, it appears in a folder called "lang" which itself is in a folder called "java".

Note
The actual folders do not have to be created in advance. The Java compiler can create these as required. It is only the compiled byte code that needs to be in the named folder; the source code can be anywhere.

We use packages to give a class its "namespace". This is useful because it means that a class in one package can be distinct from another class that has the same class name but is in a different package. For example, if I write a BankAccount class, it is probably not the only class of that name in the world, but I can make it unique by putting it into a uniquely named package. A common convention for naming packages is to base them on a URI (Uniform Resource Identifier). Since URIs are unique names, based on Internet style domain names, using them as the basis for package naming helps to keep package names globally unique. Package names are often created from *reverse URIs*, where we change the order of the main part of the domain name. For example, if I have a domain called "foundjava.com", then the reverse URI would be "com.foundjava". From that starting point, various sub-folders can be used for different projects and applications, so I might have a package called "com.foundjava.chapter2" for the example code used in this chapter. If my package name is "com.foundjava.chapter2" then if I put a "BankAccount" class into that package, then the fully qualified class name will be "com.foundjava. chapter2.BankAccount", giving it a different fully qualified name than, for example, "com.bigbank.system.BankAccount" because although the class name is the same, the package name is different. This is an important aspect of component reuse in Java, because it means that we can combine classes from many different sources without worrying about name clashes.

To place a class in a specific package, we use a "package" statement that must appear as the first line of code in the file. Note the package name is in lower case, with the folder names separated by periods. Numbers can be included but not as the first characters of any of the folder names in the package (only letters and numbers are valid characters). If "MyJavaProgram" is put into a package called "com.-foundjava.chapter2" then the package statement will look like this:

```
package com.foundjava.chapter2;
public class MyJavaProgram
{
  // etc.
```

2.5.2 Compiling into a Package Folder

Once we put a class into a package, it needs to be compiled so that the byte code ends up in the correct folder. This is easily achieved by using the "-d" (directory) option on the java compiler. This option is followed by space, then a directory name, and another space. It ensures that the compiled class file will automatically be placed into the correct package folder underneath the one you specify (it will create the required folder structure if it does not already exist). For example, we can use the period (".") to specify the current folder:

```
javac -d . MyJavaProgram.java
```

If you compile using this option, you should be able to see that the directory structure has been created for you, and the compiled class file is in the correct folder. The original source file is, of course, still in its original folder, since it is only the byte code that must be in the correct package structure in order to be located by other units of code.

To run our updated Java application, we need to understand how packages are related to the Java classpath, an environment variable that, like the path, may be set in the operating system and defines where Java bytecode (i.e. compiled classes) may be found by the Java compiler and virtual machine. This is important because when you compile or run Java code, it is very likely to rely on other classes and libraries. These can only be located if they are on the classpath. The classpath can be set from the command line, i.e.

```
set classpath=list of classpath entries
```

or by system-wide configuration, which will vary depending on your operating system.

By default, the classpath includes all the Java libraries and the current working directory. This is why our first example ran without specifying a package, as we compiled and ran it from a single directory.

To set the classpath correctly, the first directory used in the package name (in this example "com") must be beneath a directory specified in the classpath. For example, if our classpath is something like the following:

```
set classpath=c:\code
```

then the package directory structure "com\foundjava\chapter2" must appear inside "c:\code". The classpath does not include subdirectories that are part of packages, only the ones above them (Fig. 2.2). Be aware that the classpath relates only to compiled class files, not to Java source code.

Note
The sample code for this book (downloadable from the website) is arranged in subdirectories that match the default structure of an Eclipse project, with source code in a "src" folder. Eclipse will by default put the compiled byte code in a "bin" folder, though for any new project these folders can easily be changed.

Exactly where you set the classpath varies between operating systems. In Windows systems, for example, it can be set, like the path, through the system environment variables dialog. Alternatively, we can enter the "set classpath…" line at the command prompt, but this must be done each time we open a new command window. Whichever way we choose to do it, packages must be defined in conjunction with the classpath to enable running Java programs to find the necessary classes at runtime.

When you set the classpath, it can have multiple entries, separated by semi-colons. When setting the classpath from the command line, we can also refer to

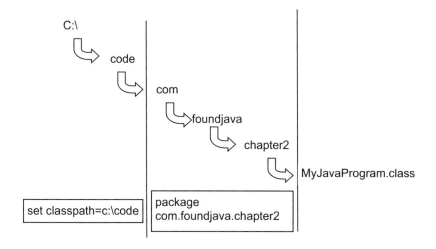

Fig. 2.2   The relationship between packages and the classpath

existing system classpath settings by including %classpath%, as we did with the
"path" example earlier in this chapter. For example, we could set the classpath to
include existing settings, "C:\code" and the current directory (indicated simply by a
period), like this:

```
set classpath=%classpath%;c:\code;.
```

2.6   Comment Syntax

Comments are not code and are ignored by the compiler. They are used to document code for human readers. There are three styles of comment that can be used in
Java. One is the old "C" style syntax:

```
/*
 * Anything between the
 * slash-asterisk and asterisk-slash
 * is a comment
 */
```

This type of comment should be avoided in Java in favor of Javadoc comments, which we will introduce in a moment.

There is also a syntax for single line comments, using two forward slash characters:

```
//single line comments
```

This type of syntax (which comes from the C++ programming language) is easier to use for short comments in the body of the code, because it does not need any other character to indicate where the comment ends. The end of the comment is automatically taken to be the end of the line on which it appears.

The third type of comment is used by Javadoc, the automatic class-documenting tool that works with Java code (we will look at Javadoc later in this book). The important thing to note is that the first characters of the comment block have two asterisks following the forward slash, instead of the single asterisk used with "C" style comments.

```
/**
 * Anything between the
 * slash-asterisk-asterisk and asterisk-slash
 * is a documentation comment
 */
```

The Javadoc tool uses this type of comment when generating HTML documentation. (Javadoc ignores "C" and "C++" style comments). It is good practice to have a Javadoc comment before each class that you write, and any methods that are interesting enough to need some explanation.

Exercise 2.2

This exercise simply draws together the steps in the previous example:

- Make a copy of your MyJavaProgram class.
- Rename both the class and the file "MySecondProgram."
- Add an appropriate package statement to the top of the source file (use the reverse URL convention for the package name).
- Add a Javadoc comment block immediately above the class declaration, and a single line comment within the body of the main method.

- Change the message in System.out.println so you can be certain which class you are running.
- Compile the class with the –d option to create the package folder structure.
- Set the classpath on the command line (or as a system variable).
- Run the program (remember you need the fully qualified class name).

2.7   Using the Eclipse Integrated Development Environment (IDE)

In our first example, we used the basic tools of the JDK from the command line. Although this is helpful in understanding the role of the compiler and the Java runtime, and the classpath, it is not a very productive development environment. For the rest of this book we will be working with the Eclipse IDE (Integrated Development Environment). This can be freely downloaded from the "eclipse.org" website. The same IDE can be used for developing code in different languages and comes in several different versions for different types of software development. The version use for the example in this book is the "Eclipse IDE for Java Developers". Installing Eclipse is very easy. You only need to download the installer file and run it. When the installer starts up it will show a list of language options, so you should choose "Eclipse IDE for Java Developers" (Fig. 2.3).

The Eclipse installer should automatically locate a JVM (assuming you already installed the JDK, which includes the JVM, for the command line activities from the first part of this chapter). You may need to configure the path to the JVM and where you want Eclipse to install (Fig. 2.4), then the installation will complete.

Fig. 2.3   The option to choose the Eclipse IDE for Java Developers in the Eclipse Installer

Fig. 2.4 Selecting the
existing JDK location and the
new Eclipse installation folder

2.7.1 Creating a New Project

When the IDE starts, it will ask you to specify a workspace, which is simply a disk
location where your project data will be stored. You can either accept the default or
point it to a new location (this can always be changed later). When the IDE appears,
it will initially appear something like Fig. 2.5 (other versions may look slightly
different). If a "Welcome" tab appears first, simply close it to see the main editor
view. The IDE window is divided into four main areas, within which various tabbed
panes may appear. On the left is the explorer area, where you can view your files in
various ways. In the center is the code editing area, and at the bottom there is a
tabbed area that can show things such as errors, program output, etc. On the right,
there are several other possible views such as the outline that will show details of
the class currently being edited. Since there are many different windows and tabbed
panes that can be shown or hidden, and the layout of these within the frame can be
changed at will, we will not explore the general screen layout any further as
customization means that individual users' IDE screens will vary widely. In
addition, there are several different perspectives that can be viewed with the IDE.
The perspective shown in Fig. 2.5 is the Java perspective (as can be seen from the
button in the top right-hand corner of the screen), but there are a number of other
perspectives that can be used when working with Java code, including the debug

perspective. If you need to restore this default perspective layout at any point, select "Window" → "Perspective" → "Reset Perspective…".

In this section, we will recreate the "MyJavaProgam" code within Eclipse, which should give you some impression of how much more efficient it is to use an IDE than to program from the command line. The first step in using Eclipse is to create a new Java project; select "File" → "New" → "Java Project" from the main menu bar. You will see a "New Java Project" dialog displayed like that shown in Fig. 2.6.

In the example in Fig. 2.6, the project name "My Java Project" has been entered. There are several ways that a new project can be configured, but in this worked example we will just accept the default settings and press the "Finish" button. You will then see a dialog asking you if you want to create a file called "module-info.java" (Fig. 2.7). Modules were introduced with Java 9 as a way of breaking down larger Java systems into separate modules. In Fig. 2.7 the module name "com.foundjava.examples" has been entered but the name of the module is up to you. General practice is to use the same reverse URI style as package names, and use the same name for the module as the main package within it, but this is a convention rather than a requirement. When you click "Create" you will see that it

Fig. 2.5 The initial screen when loading the Eclipse IDE with the default window layout

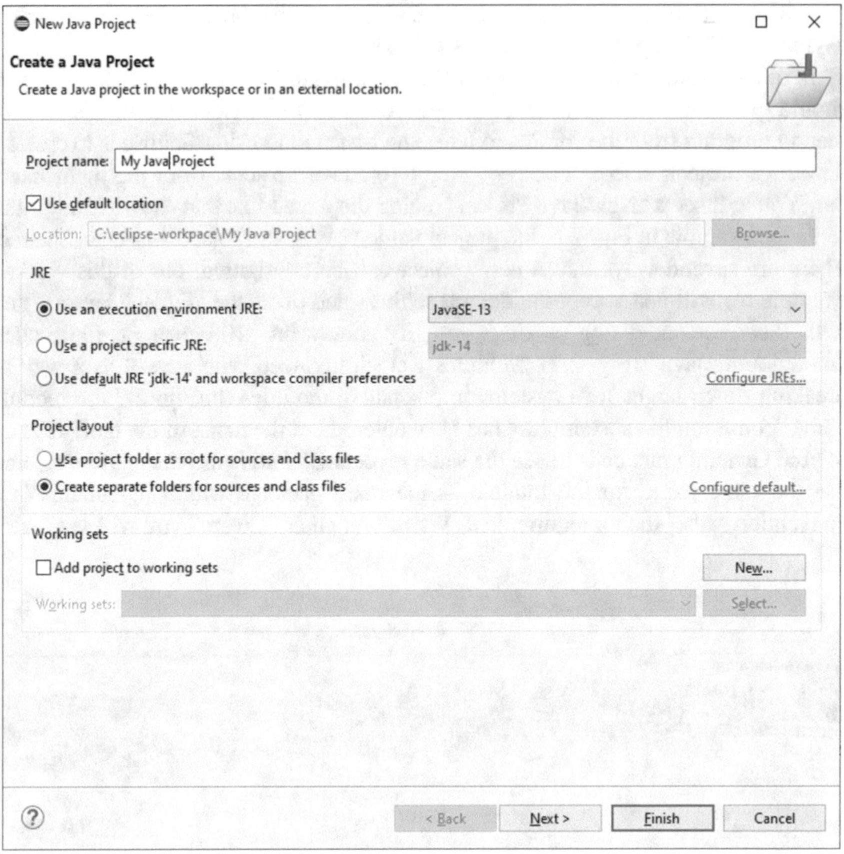

Fig. 2.6 The "New Java Project" dialog in Eclipse

creates an empty "module-info.java" file in your project. We will return to modules, and what goes into this file, later in this book.

Once the project has been created, you should add a new Java package to it. As we saw from our first example, it is not essential to use Java packages in order to get a simple class to compile and run, but it is important to use packages for any meaningful Java development, since we cannot sensibly continue to put every class we write into a single folder. From now on, we will put all our Java examples into suitable packages.

2.7.2 Creating a New Package

To create a new package, right-click on the project name that appears in the "Package Explorer" pane on the left of the screen and select "New" → "Package"

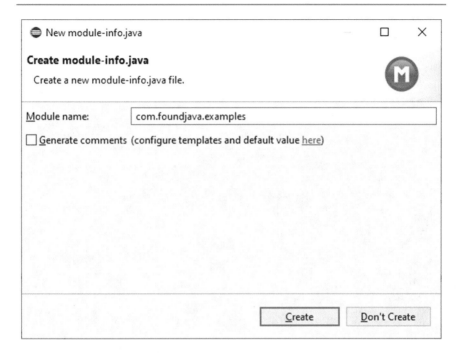

Fig. 2.7 The "Create module-info-java" dialog in Eclipse

from the pop-up menu. You should see the "New Java Package" dialog (Fig. 2.8). In the example in Fig. 2.8, the package name "com.foundjava.chapter2" has been entered. Remember the package naming conventions; all lower case, cannot begin with a number, no punctuation characters, with periods between sub-package names. Eclipse will display a warning if you try to name a package incorrectly. If the source folder is not correct (it should be the "src" folder of your project), you can browse to it. Click "Finish" to create the package.

2.7.3 Creating a New Class

Once the package has been created, we can add a new class to it. Right click on the newly created package and select "New" → "Class". You should see the "New Java Class" dialog (Fig. 2.9).

In the example in Fig. 2.9, the name of the class has been entered ("MyJavaProgram"). Note also that the checkbox has been selected to create a stub for the "main" method. This will save you from having to type it into the editor manually.

Once you click "Finish" the source code should appear in the IDE as shown in Fig. 2.10. Eclipse will have automatically added the names of the package and the

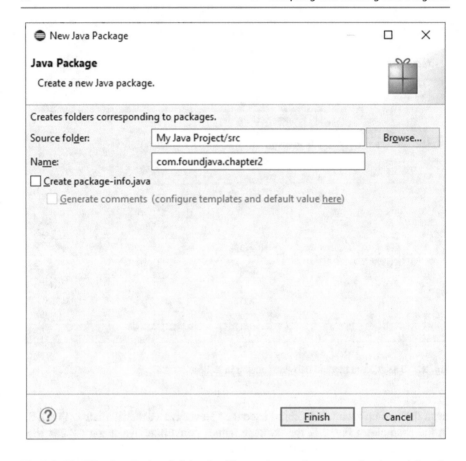

Fig. 2.8 The "New Java Package" dialog. It will warn about package names that do not follow the correct naming conventions

class into the source file, some empty comment blocks (which can be edited or removed) and the stub of the main method, leaving you only to add the required code to the main method.

2.7.4   Editing Code in Eclipse

As in our previous example, we will simply add a "System.out.println" entry to the body of the main method. Even here, Eclipse can give you some assistance. Figure 2.11 shows a pop-up window of context-sensitive code options that could apply to the "System" class (you can see "out" as one of the options in the list). This window will often appear when you type a period after the name of a class (or object, as we will see later) or you can press CTRL-spacebar to invoke the options

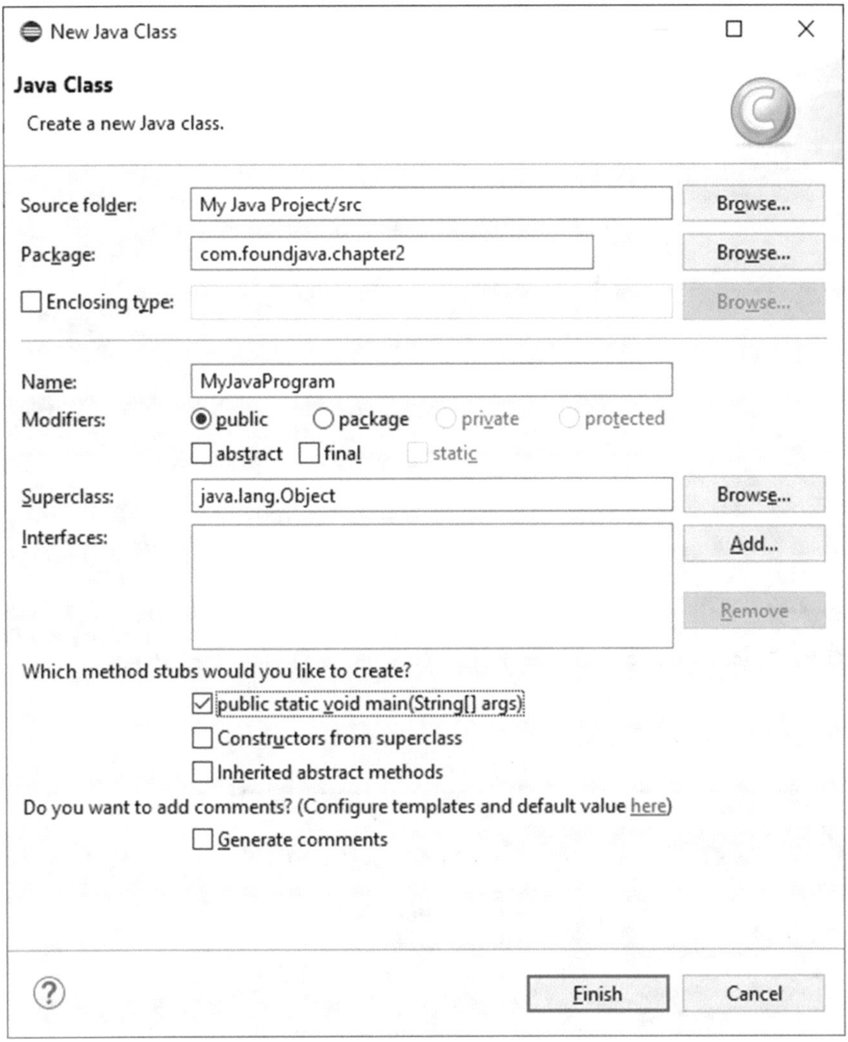

Fig. 2.9 The "New Java Class" dialog in Eclipse. In this example, the checkbox has been selected to generate the stub of a "main" method within the class

directly). You can scroll up and down this list and select the entry you require (with the mouse or the Enter key) as an alternative to typing it in.

Figure 2.11 also shows some other features of the Eclipse IDE. Note the red circle with the white "X" on the left of the editing window. This appears to the left of any line that is not syntactically correct and is dynamically updated (though its behavior can sometimes be misleading as the dynamic updating can get out of sync

Fig. 2.10 The Eclipse IDE after the class has been created. Note the project, package and class shown in the "Package Explorer" pane on the *left,* the generated code in the *center*, and the "Outline" pane on the *right* where an outline of the class and its methods is shown

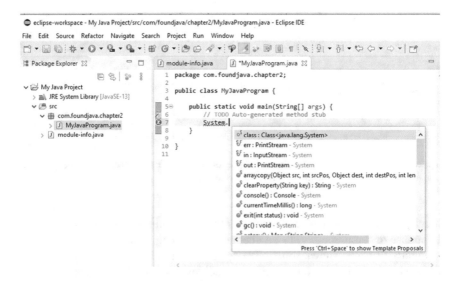

Fig. 2.11 Eclipse providing a context-sensitive pop-up list of suggested code options after a period has been typed into the source code or CTRL-spacebar has been pressed

in complex programs). Note also that the tab at the top of the editing window has an asterisk to its right. This means that the current file has unsaved edits.

Figure 2.12 shows some further features of the red and white error indicators on the left of the editing window. In this example, the final semicolon has been deliberately left off the end of the line. Information about errors can be seen in two places. If you hover over the red error indicator with the mouse, a pop-up message will appear (as can be seen in the editing window in Fig. 2.12). Further, a list of current errors and warnings across all the code in the project can be seen in the "problems" pane at the bottom of the IDE. However, you should note that this list is only updated when a file is saved; it is not updated dynamically like the error indicators in the source code editor. There is a good reason for this, which is that Eclipse automatically compiles a Java source code file when it is saved. In fact, there is no explicit "compile" step when using Eclipse, so "save" is effectively the same as "compile". The "Problems" pane only shows errors that appear in compiled code, not in unsaved edits. Note that error symbols also appear on the tab of the editing pane and in the Package explorer.

Fig. 2.12 A syntax error being indicated both in the source code editor and the "Problems" pane

2.7.5 Compiling and Running Code in Eclipse

Having no explicit "compile" step but having error indicators in the editing pane that are dynamically updated can be potentially misleading. For example, in Fig. 2.13, the error has been corrected (the marker has gone from red to gray) but the file has not been saved (note the asterisk in the tab of the editing pane). This means that the updated file has not yet been compiled, which is why the error message still appears in the "Problems" pane. This can cause confusion when you are working with multiple files. You may have corrected errors in one source file, but not saved (and compiled) it. This means that there may be other errors appearing because code in other files is still reliant on the previously saved (but wrong) version. The basic message is, as soon as you make changes to your code, save the file to compile it.

Once your file is correct, complete and saved, it can be run. To run a class with a "main" method, right-click on the class in the Package Explorer window, and then select "Run As" → "Java Application" from the pop-up menu. Alternatively, you can use the green "run" button on the toolbar at the top of the IDE, which will run whichever class is currently at the front of the editing window (not likely to cause any confusion at the moment when we only have one class being edited). Figure 2.14 shows the output from the program displayed in a new "Console" tab that will appear at the bottom of the screen. Note that when you are running code in Eclipse, the classpath (actually a module path) to your own classes is automatically

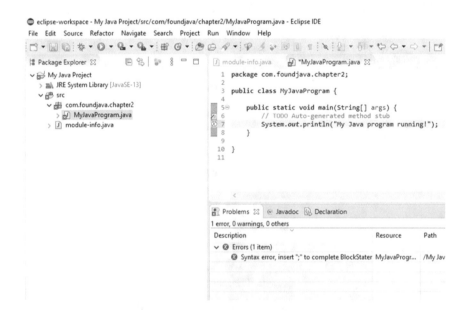

Fig. 2.13 Corrected code in the editing pane. Unlike the source code editor, the "Problems" pane only updates when files are saved and automatically compiled

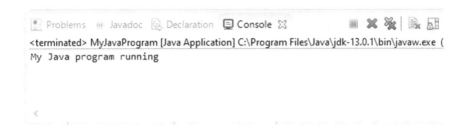

Fig. 2.14 Output shown in the "Console" pane at the bottom of the screen

set, so you do not have to worry about it. However, in some later chapters, we will have to look again at classpath settings, even within the context of Eclipse.

Exercise 2.3

- Create a new Eclipse project, including a module-info file.
- Add a new package to the project.
- Add a new class containing a "main" method to the package.
- Add multiple lines to "main" using "System.out.println" to display text in the output console.
- Once your program has been successfully run, change the "println" statements to "print" statements and observe the change in the output.

2.8 Summary

This chapter outlined the basics of using the tools provided with Java to compile and run code. We saw how the source code of Java class is structured, how it can be compiled using the "javac" compiler (provided with Oracle's Java Development Kit or the OpenJDK) and how it can be run on the Java Virtual Machine from the command prompt/terminal. We have seen how Java code is put into packages, and how these packages relate to the Java classpath, which it is necessary to set for the Java runtime to locate compiled code. The chapter also described how the same process of editing, compiling and running code can be done much more easily using the Eclipse Integrated Development Environment (IDE), which also provides many other useful facilities such as assisting with automatic code generation and highlighting errors. We also saw how Eclipse can automatically put classes into Java modules that may contain multiple packages.

Data Types, Arithmetic and Arrays

3

In this chapter, we introduce Java's primitive data types, arithmetic operators, String concatenation and arrays. With these basic components, we can begin to build some useful programs. Along the way we look at some important concepts relating to how Java handles combinations of different data types, including promotion and casting.

Java has two groups of data types: primitive types, which include integral and floating-point numbers, characters, and Boolean values and reference types, which include arrays, classes and interfaces. In this chapter, we begin by examining the primitive types, and later in the chapter we introduce arrays.

3.1   Java Primitive Data Types

To begin this chapter, we meet the Java primitive data types. These are the simple types used to store numbers, characters, and Boolean (true/false) values. For most of this book, we will be dealing with classes and objects. However, Java, like most other programming languages, also has a set of built-in simple data types that represent characters and numbers. Each has a specified size in terms of bits (binary digits) and, therefore, a specified range of possible values. A byte, for example, is always 8 bits long, so its maximum positive value is 127, which is the binary number 1111111 (7 bits) with 1 bit reserved for the sign (+ or −) (Fig. 3.1).

Unlike some other languages, Java does not have unsigned data types, which means that all of them (apart from "char," which is designed to contain characters rather than numbers) can contain both positive and negative numbers. In addition, there is a "boolean" type, which can only contain the values "true" or "false". The available types are shown in Table 3.1. It is important to note that all primitive data type names are in lowercase. This differentiates them from other data types which use other naming conventions. For example, we have already seen that class names are written using Pascal case.

© Springer Nature Switzerland AG 2020
D. Parsons, *Foundational Java*, Texts in Computer Science,
https://doi.org/10.1007/978-3-030-54518-5_3

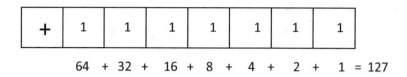

$$64 + 32 + 16 + 8 + 4 + 2 + 1 = 127$$

Fig. 3.1 The Java "byte" data type is 8 bits long

Table 3.1 Java data types

Stores	Data type	Can contain	Range
Signed integers	byte	8-bit integer	From −128 to 127
	short	16-bit integer	From −32,768 to 32,767
	int	32-bit integer	From −2,147,483,648 to 2,147,483,647
	long	64-bit integer	From −9,223,372,036,854,775,808 to 9,223,372,036,854,775,807
Signed floating-point numbers	float	32-bit floating-point number	Large numbers with decimal points
	double	64-bit floating-point number	Very large numbers with decimal points
Boolean value	boolean	True or false	
16-bit character (positive values only)	char	Single character from the Unicode character set	Numeric range from 0 to 65,535

3.1.1 Literals and Variables

A literal is a specific immutable (i.e., fixed when a program starts running) value that appears in code. Literals can be numbers, characters, Booleans or Strings. The Java compiler infers data types from literals. For example, a whole number is assumed by the compiler to be of type int, whereas a literal floating-point number is assumed to be a double. In general, these assumptions area worth following through in your own code, so that you should use int types to represent whole numbers and double types to represent floating-point numbers, unless there is a good reason to choose one of the other data types. One example of this would be storing a timestamp in milliseconds. In Java, this type of value is usually stored in a variable of type long, because the storage size of an int is too narrow. There are only two possible literal values for a boolean; "true" or "false". A character literal is surrounded by single quotes, and a String by double quotes (unlike the other examples, a String is not a primitive type, but nevertheless can be assigned using a literal).

```
10          // an int
45.5        // a double
true        // a boolean
'a'         // a char
"string"    // a String (not a primitive type)
```

Literals alone are not of much use for programming. Programs also need to store data of different types and sizes in memory that can have dynamically changing values at runtime. To do this, we must declare variables of the appropriate type. A variable is simply a name given to a memory location that will be used to store a specific type of data, which can change in value (but not type) over time. To store a 32-bit integer, for example, we need to declare an "int" with a name. A variable must also be initialized (set to an initial value), preferably when it is declared. This is done with the "=" (assignment) operator, for example,

```
int intValue = 0;
```

This declares "intValue" to be the name of a memory location that is large enough to store a 32-bit integer, with an initial value of zero. The naming convention commonly used for variables is Camel (caMel) case, where the name starts with a lowercase letter, embedded words begin with uppercase, and no underscores are used. You can see that the example above ("intValue") uses Camel case. The only difference between Pascal case and Camel case is whether the first letter is in upper or lower case.

If a variable is being locally declared in a method (such as "main"), then it must be specifically initialized. If you simply declare a variable without initializing it, you will only get a warning from the compiler. However, if you attempt to refer to an uninitialized variable in other parts of the code, you will get a compiler error.

Variables can be reassigned to new values after they have been declared, and can be assigned the value of some other variable, for example,

```
// reassign intValue to a different literal
intValue = 5;

// assign one variable to the value of another
int anotherIntValue = intValue;
```

Multiple variables of the same type can also be declared in a single statement, separated by commas, for example,

```
int myVar1 = 0, myVar2 = 0;
```

3.1.2 Literals and the Compiler

When we assign variables to literals, there are some issues with the compiler that we must watch out for. For example, a literal whole number is assumed by the compiler to be an "int", so this line of code is fine.

```
int myNumber = 9; // int is default whole number type
```

However, we could not do the following assignment because the value is a little too large to fit into an "int" variable:

```
int myBigNumber = 2147483648; // won't compile
```

Changing the type of the variable from "int" to "long" is only part of the solution:

```
long myBigNumber = 2147483648; // won't compile
```

This still causes a compiler error, because the literal value given cannot be an "int", but the compiler assumes that a literal whole number is an "int". Therefore, we must add an "L" to the end of the literal so the compiler will treat it as a "long" data type rather than an "int":

```
long myBigNumber = 2147483648L;
// will compile (L or l = long)
```

The "L" does not have to be in upper case, but a lower case "l" looks too much like the digit "1" so the upper case letter is much easier to read.

A similar situation occurs with floating-point numbers. The following variable assignment is fine because a double is the default type for floating-point literals.

```
double d = 3.5;
// will compile - floating point literals are doubles
```

This, on the other hand, will not compile, because a float has a smaller storage capacity than a double:

```
float f = 4.56; // won't compile
```

Again, the solution is to use a letter suffix to change the type of the literal, in this case an "F" or "f" to indicate that this should be treated as a float by the compiler:

```
float f = 4.56F; // will compile (F or f = float)
```

While some of this might seem obscure, the main thing to take from it is that whenever you declare numeric variables, you should work on the basis that "int" and "double" are the default types to work with. Only use one of the other types if you have a good reason to do so, such as needing to save memory in very large arrays.

That way, you are less likely to come up against typing problems between variables and literals.

Note

Floats and doubles are not suitable for some floating-point calculations such as financial transactions where precise values are required. For these purposes, you should use the BigDecimal class.

3.1.3 Boolean Variables

Boolean variables are very simple since they can only be assigned the values "true" or "false". These values can be assigned as literals (which must be all in lower case) or they can also be assigned the result of an expression that returns a Boolean value.

```
// assigning booleans
boolean isFull = true;
isFull = false;
```

3.1.4 Unicode Characters and Escape Sequences

A "chartypes" variablecan hold a single 16-bit character from the standard Unicode table (an extension of the old 8-bit ASCII table). A char can be assigned using a literal in single quotes:

```
char myChar = 'c';
// assign the literal character 'c' to a char variable
```

It can alternatively be assigned the Unicode value of the character:

```
char myOtherChar = 99;
// assign the Unicode value of 'c' (99)
```

The maximum Unicode character value is 65535. This is much higher than the maximum possible value you can store in a "short", even though a short is also 16 bits long. This is because a "char" variable does not store negative numbers, since the Unicode table only contains positive values, so no space need be set aside to store a sign.

A "char" variable may contain one of the "escape sequence" characters (control characters and other special characters) that are preceded by the backslash (\). Although these may appear to contain two characters, they still represent single "chars." This is because the escape sequences are also referencing numbers in the Unicode table. For example, "\n" represents the new line character (Unicode number 10). The escape sequences are shown in Table 3.2.

Table 3.2 Escape sequence characters

Backspace	\b	Horizontal tab	\t
Single quote	\'	Double quote	\"
New line	\n	Carriage return	\r
Form feed	\f	Backslash	\\
Octal Unicode character value	\xxx	Hexadecimal Unicode character value	\uxxxx

Most of these are applicable to formatting output. Note that since the backslash is the escape character, it must have its own escape sequence to be usable in another context (for example in a Windows file path).

Here are a couple of simple examples. First, we assign the tab escape sequence character to a char variable:

```
char tab = '\t';
```

Escape sequence characters can also be embedded in String literals, as in this example:

```
String quotation =
    "Java is C++ \"without the guns, clubs and knives\"";
```

If we were to display this String in the console, we would see:

```
Java is C++ "without the guns, clubs and knives"
```

3.1.5   Variable Scope

Before moving on, there is one more important thing to understand about variables, which is their scope. You may recall that the body of a class, and the body of the "main" method, are surrounded by braces {…}. These braces define the scope of those elements of code. When you declare a variable, its scope is defined by the block of code, defined within braces, that it appears inside. Variables cannot be used in code until after they have been declared and cannot be used outside of the scope within which they were declared.

```
{
    int myVariable = 3;
    // can use 'myVariable' now
}
// 'myVariable' is now out of scope and can't be used
```

The usual convention in Java is to declare variables as close to the point of first use as possible. However, because of scope requirements, this may end up being some distance away from the first use of the variable. In the example above, we would have to declare "myVariable" outside the scope of these braces in order to access it after the closing brace, for example,

```
int myVariable = 0;
{
   myVariable = 3;
   // can use 'myVariable' now
}
// 'myVariable' is still in scope and can be used
```

Note

If we do not have a specific value that we want to use to initialize a numeric variable, the normal convention is to set it to zero.

Exercise 3.1 Here is a "main" method containing some random fragments of code that assign variables of different types. It contains several deliberate errors relating to literals and scope. Fix these errors by applying your knowledge of the various concepts that have been introduced so far in this chapter. The method contains some braces that serve no useful function; they are simply there to enable you to demonstrate your understanding of scope. In making your changes, do not change any of the data types; change only the values or the way they are expressed.

```
package com.foundjava.chapter3;

public class DataTypesExercise {
   public static void main(String[] args) {
      long myBigNumber = 2147483648;
      float myFloat = 4.56;
      boolean isFull = False;
      char myChar = -1;
      {
       byte myByte = 127;
      }
      String filePath = "com\javabook\chapter3";
      System.out.print("Value of myBigNumber = ");
      System.out.println(myBigNumber);
      System.out.print("Value of myFloat = ");
      System.out.println(myFloat);
      System.out.print("Value of isFull = ");
      System.out.println(isFull);
      System.out.print("Value of myChar = ");
      System.out.println(myChar);
      System.out.print("Value of myByte = ");
      System.out.println(myByte);
      System.out.print("Value of filePath = ");
      System.out.println(filePath);
   }
}
```

3.2 Arithmetic and Other Operators

In the previous section, we looked at the primitive data types available in Java, including several different types of number (int, double, etc.) and saw a few examples of how to assign values to variables of these types and display them. In this section, we see how variables can be used in arithmetic statements and some associated issues related to the processing of different data types in an expression.

Most programs use numeric variables to do arithmetic, even if this is no more complicated than keeping a count of something. Arithmetic in Java can be done with five *operators*: the four familiar arithmetic operators that are common to most programming languages, plus a remainder operator.

Add	+
Subtract	−
Multiply	*
Divide	/
Remainder	%

3.2.1 Arithmetic Statements

All arithmetic statements in Java have the same format, namely, that a variable on the left of an assignment (=) operator is made to equal the result of an arithmetic expression on the right:

```
variable = expression;
```

The arithmetic expression will use a combination of operators and *operands*, the values that are being operated on. These may be both variables and literals. Some examples (assuming that the size of a class of students must be an integer) might be:

```
double netPay = grossPay - deductions;
double distanceInKm = distanceInMiles * 1.6093;
double perimeter = height * 2 + width * 2;
int numberOfGroupsofFour = classSize / 4;
int studentsNotInGroupOfFour = classSize % 4;
```

When writing expressions that contain more than one arithmetic operator you need to be aware of "order of precedence", that is, which part of the expression will be evaluated first? There is a standard table for this that applies to virtually all languages, but the most important part is this:

() parentheses

have a higher order of precedence than

*/% multiply, divide and remainder,

which have a higher order of precedence than

+ − add and subtract
Consider this example:

```
int result = 4 + 2 * 3;
```

Since the multiplication will be executed before the addition, the result would be 10. If this is not what we want, we can use parentheses to change the order in which parts of an expression are evaluated. To force the addition to be executed first, we can write

```
int result = (4 + 2) * 3;
```

As you would expect, this gives the result of 18, since the addition is now performed before the multiplication. If two operators of the same precedence (i.e., add and subtract, or multiply, divide and remainder) appear in the same expression, then they are evaluated from the left to the right. For example,

```
int result = 10 * 3 / 2;
```

will evaluate the multiplication before the division, giving the answer 15. The remainder operator works quite simply, as we can see from this example:

```
int numberOfGroupsofFour = classSize / 4;
int studentsNotInGroupOfFour = classSize % 4;
```

If the value of the "classSize" variable happened to be 21, "numberOfGroupsOfFour" would contain 5 (the result of dividing 21 by 4) while "studentsNotInGroupOfFour" would contain 1 (the remainder from dividing 21 by 4).

An integer remainder is usually known as a "modulus," but since we can also use this operator with floating-point data types, it is not strictly speaking a modulus operator.

3.2.2   Increment and Decrement Operators

There are simple operators to increment or decrement a variable by one. The most used is probably the "++" operator that adds one to a variable, like this:

```
int counter = 1;
counter++;
```

In this example, the integer variable "counter" would be incremented to hold the value "2". We can see that the increment operator is simply shorthand for

```
counter = counter + 1;
```

There is also a decrement operator, which logically enough is "−−" and subtracts one from a variable:

```
counter--;
```

This is shorthand for

```
counter = counter - 1;
```

3.2.3 Prefix and Postfix Operators

The previous examples of the increment and decrement operators both used "postfix" notation (i.e. the "++" or "−−" appears after the variable). We may also use "prefix" notation (the operator appears before the variable):

Postfix notation:	counter++	Or	counter--
Prefix notation:	++counter	Or	--counter

This makes no difference if the operator is not used as part of a larger expression but can be significant if it is. If one of these operators is used in prefix notation, then the operator will execute before the rest of an expression, but if postfix notation is used, then it will be executed afterward. For example, if the value of our "counter" variable is to be assigned to another variable in the following expression:

```
int counter = 1;
int currentCount = counter++;
```

The value of "x" will be 1, because the increment operator (which adds 1 to "counter") will be evaluated after the assignment of the value of counter to "x" (postfix notation). With prefix notation, where the increment takes place before the assignment, the value of "x" will be 2:

```
int counter = 1;
int currentCount = ++counter;
```

To avoid confusion, the increment and decrement operators will not be used as part of larger expressions in this book, and the postfix notation will be adopted in all cases.

3.2.4   Assignment Operators

The increment and decrement operators are appropriate only when we need to add one to, or subtract one from, the existing value of a variable. However, we also have shorthand for changing the value of a variable by arithmetic on its existing value. In this syntax outline, "*?*" means any one of the five arithmetic operators:

In general terms:	var = var ? n
Can be replaced with:	var ? = n

Therefore, to add two to "myVariable," we could replace:

```
myVariable = myVariable + 2; with: myVariable += 2;
```

Variables can be decremented similarly, so to subtract two from "myVariable," we could write

```
myVariable -= 2;
```

Similar examples for the other operators might be

```
myVariable = myVariable * 2; is equivalent to myVariable *= 2;
myVariable = myVariable / 2; is equivalent to myVariable /= 2;
myVariable = myVariable % 2; is equivalent to myVariable %= 2;
```

3.2.5   Promotion and Type Casting

When Java performs calculations on mixed data types, a process of *promotion* takes place. In this process, the operands belonging to *narrower* data types (i.e. smaller in terms of maximum storage) are widened to the *broader* type automatically. For example, if we have an int and a long in an arithmetic expression, the int value will automatically be converted to a long. If we have both floats and doubles in a calculation, the floats will be converted to doubles, and so on. Since this is an automatic process, you may wonder why we need to know about it, but this should become clear as we work through some examples.

Not all conversions between data types are automatic. Sometimes we need a variable of one type but have something a bit different. Values that are returned from methods are not always exactly of the type that we want, so we sometimes need to convert them using a technique called "type casting." This allows us to convert from one type of number to another compatible type or from one object type to another. This is often required where we need to put a value into a smaller or less precise type than the current one. The compiler prevents accidental loss of data or precision by not allowing larger types to be assigned to smaller ones, so it will not, for example, allow you to assign a double value to a float variable (which is smaller), even though the actual value assigned at runtime might easily fit into a float. Type casting is a way of signaling to the compiler that we are prepared to risk this type conversion. The syntax is

```
(type we want) value we've got
```

For example, we might have a double value that we want to convert to a float. If "doubleValue" is of type double, we can cast it to type float like this:

```
float floatValue = (float)doubleValue;
```

Although this might seem a bit obscure, it is quite a useful technique, particularly when we are working with objects rather than primitive data types, as we will see in later chapters.

3.2.6   String Concatenation

Before moving on from looking at operators and type conversions, it may be appropriate to look briefly at String concatenation. This is the process by which various data types (including other Strings) can be joined onto a String to make a larger String of characters by using the "+" operator. Implicit in this process is a type conversion that takes other data types and converts their values to String data. In fact, this data conversion is what happens whenever you display a variable using "System.out.println". Whatever the original type of the variable, its value is converted to a String of Unicode characters before it is displayed.

In this example, we declare and assign an "int", and then concatenate its value with a String:

```
int myVariable = 99;
System.out.println("The value of myVariable is " + myVariable);
```

This code will print "The value of myVariable is 99" in the console. You can also use the "+ =" operator as a shorthand for concatenating Strings, rather like the assignment shorthands we have already seen used with primitives, for example,

```
String greeting = "Happy birthday";
String message = greeting += "Mr. President";
System.out.println(message);
```

The important thing to bear in mind with String concatenation is that it is using the "+" operator in a different way to how it is used in addition. It only works for concatenation when at least one String is being used in an expression. For example, here we use the "+" operator with "System.out.println" but only use "char" data types:

```
System.out.println('a' + 'b' + 'c');
```

Instead of getting "abc" printed in the console we will get 294, since the operator will add the Unicode values of the characters together (i.e. 97 + 98 + 99).

In contrast, this will print "abc" because the first character is a String (note the double quotes), not a char:

```
System.out.println("a" + 'b' + 'c');
```

3.2.7 Bitwise Operators

The bitwise operators (AND, OR, XOR), shown in Table 3.3, can be applied to integer types at the bit level, and control what value results when two bits are operated on at a given position in the two operands. In most cases, these do not impinge much on Java application developers. There is, however, one exception to this, which is the bitwise OR operator (the "|" character). At the bit level, this operator takes two bit values and, as can be seen in Table 3.3, provides the result of "1" as long as at least one of the two bits being operated on is a "1." This operator is used in some library components in Java as a way of combining different config-uration values. For example, as we will see in Chap. 17, the bitwise OR operator can be used to combine bold and italic font styles together.

Exercise 3.2 In this exercise, we use some of the arithmetic operators. You can also use String concatenation when displaying the results. Do not forget to choose the appropriate data types for the variables. The currency unit used here is the Simoleon (§), as used in The Sims series of games from Electronic Arts.

- Create a class with a main method.
- In the main method, calculate the hydrogen fuel consumption of a fuel-cell car that just cost §72 to fill up to the top of the tank at §1.80 a liter after going 390 km since it was last filled to the top with fuel.
- Display the number of Kilometers traveled per liter.
- Display the number liters used per 100 km.

Table 3.3 The bitwise operators with examples of results from operating on 2-bit values

bit1, bit2	& (AND)		(OR)	^ (XOR)
0, 0	0	0	0
0, 1	0	1	1
1, 0	0	1	1
1, 1	1	1	0

3.3 Arrays

Earlier in this chapter we noted that an array of String objects appears as an argument to the "main" method. In this section, we look at how arrays can be used to hold a collection of values. An array consists of a fixed number of elements that all have the same name but a different index number, which appears in square brackets. The elements in an array are always indexed from zero upward. Figure 3.2 shows that the elements of an array containing four values would be numbered from zero to three.

We have already seen an example of an array being referred to when we declare a "main" method:

```
public static void main(String args[])
```

"args" refers to an array of Strings that can be passed to a program when it starts running. However, in this section, we will see how to create and manage our own arrays within the main method.

An array can contain either primitive types or objects of a single data type, specified when we declare the array. Arrays themselves are reference types, and are declared differently from primitive types, as we will see when we look at the syntax for creating them. Arrays have a fixed size, and are bounds-checked, which means that trying to access an index beyond the upper or lower bounds of the array will cause a runtime exception (i.e. the code will compile but it will fail when it runs). Arrays are not very flexible; for example, they cannot be dynamically resized, but they are an efficient way to store a collection of data of a single type.

3.3.1 Declaring Arrays

The array passed to "main" is already defined for us as a parameter, but if we want to use other arrays in our classes, then we must declare them. An array reference is declared by putting empty square brackets after the name of the data type that we wish to store to indicate that this is an array rather than a single value. For example, to declare an array to store values of type int, we would write:

```
int[] myArray;
```

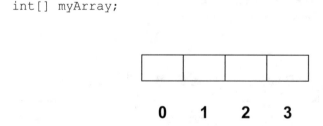

Fig. 3.2 Array index numbers start at zero

Array objects are created like other objects by using the keyword "new", followed by the data type to be stored and the size of the array that we want. The array size appears in square brackets; for example, this creates an array that can hold three "int" values.

```
myArray = new int[3];
```

We can combine declaring the reference and creating the array into a single line. Note that the square brackets appear twice, once to say that the reference is to an array and again to set the size of the array:

```
int[] myArray = new int[3];
```

This means that the array has three elements, named "myArray[0]", "myArray[1]" and "myArray[2]". Because the array index numbers start at zero, there is, of course, no "myArray[3]."

Creating an array of a primitive type will set the value of each element to its default. For example, each of the "int" values in "myArray" will be initialized to zero.

3.3.2 Initializing Arrays

We can assign different values to the array elements by using index numbers in brackets to indicate which array element is being accessed. For example, this array will contain integer values representing the average monthly rainfall in millimeters in Auckland, New Zealand, from January onward:

```
int[] monthlyRainfall = new int[12];
monthlyRainfall[0] = 74;
monthlyRainfall[1] = 81;
monthlyRainfall[2] = 86;
//etc...
```

Assigning the initial values to an array one at a time can be pretty tedious for a large array. An alternative is to use an initializer block. Where you assign a new array reference to a number of comma-separated values surrounded by braces. For example, this array is initialized with 12 integer values representing the average monthly rainfall over a year.

```
int[] monthlyRainfall =
{74,81,86,93,100,116,126,111,93,80,84,91};
```

The size of the newly created array will automatically match the number of values you have provided. In the example above, the array will have 12 elements. It is important to note that an initializer can only be used with a newly declared array reference. You cannot reassign an existing reference to an initializer block.

3.3.3 Accessing Array Data

The data in an array element can be updated or retrieved using the index number. For example, we could update the last element of the rainfall array and supply a new value:

```
monthlyRainfall[11] = 92;
```

Similarly, we can retrieve the value from any element in the array and assign it to a variable of a compatible type:

```
int augustRainfall = monthlyRainfall[7];
```

Or include an element of an array in output:

```
System.out.println("March rainfall was " +
    monthlyRainfall[2]);
```

Attempting to access an array element using an index number which is out of range will lead to an exception at runtime (an exception will halt program execution at that point). For example, the following line will not cause a compiler error but will fail when we try to run the program, since a 12-element array only has indices in the range 0–11:

```
monthlyRainfall[12] = 92; // exception at run time
```

Arrays can only store values of the type specified by the reference and these types are checked at compile time. For example, if we tried to assign a literal double to an element of our array, it would fail to compile:

```
monthlyRainfall[0] = 74.3; // compiler error!
```

3.3.4 The Array "length" Field

Arrays have a public "length" field, which can be useful to know to help avoid going beyond the bounds of the array. As we will see in a later example, the "length" field can be used to control a loop.

```
System.out.println(monthlyRainfall.length);
//'12' printed in console
```

3.3.5 Multidimensional Arrays

Java also supports multidimensional arrays, which are declared using multiple pairs of brackets. For example, this fragment of code relates to a two-dimensional array that contains two names for each month in the year (short and long versions).

```
String[][] monthNames = new String[12][2];
monthNames[0][0] = "Jan";
monthNames[0][1] = "January";
monthNames[1][0] = "Feb";
...
monthNames[11][1] = "December";
```

3.4 Precedence, Type Casting and Promotion by Example

To explore some of the concepts we have introduced in this chapter, we will work through the following example:

- We will create an array of type int with three elements, containing different integer values.
- Using the arithmetic operators, we will calculate and print out the mean average of the three values.

We are going to start with a deliberately naive implementation, which is intended to show the importance of understanding order of precedence, casting, and promotion in Java. Here is the declaration and initialization of an array of type int containing three values. If you work out the mean average of these three values you will see that it is four and a third, so as a floating-point number it will be about 4.3 ("about," since the 3 will be recurring).

```
int[] intArray = {3,4,6};
```

Here is a deliberately simplistic solution to calculate the mean average, adding up the three values and dividing by three:

```
int mean = intArray[0] + intArray[1] + intArray[2] / 3;
System.out.println(mean);
```

What happens if we run the program? The answer comes out at 9, which is a long way from 4.3. Hopefully you will have noticed that the default order of precedence will not give the result that is needed. Because the division has a higher order of precedence than the addition, the third element in the array (which has the value 6) is being divided by 3 before the two additions are performed. To fix that problem, we can put parentheses around the additions to ensure they are executed before the division:

```
int mean = (intArray[0] + intArray[1] + intArray[2]) / 3;
System.out.println(mean);
```

This is an improvement, as we now get the answer "4," which is closer to what was expected but still not the correct answer. Of course, we do know that we need to get a floating-point number as the result, so we should change the data type of "mean" to be "double" rather than "int":

```
double mean =
    (intArray[0] + intArray[1] + intArray[2]) / 3;
System.out.println(mean);
```

This is a further improvement, since the result now comes out as "4.0" which is clearly a floating-point number, but where is the ".333...."? As you may have worked out by now, the problem is that all the operands in the expression are integers. This means that the result of an expression using only integers will give a result which is also an integer, which in this case is truncating the floating-point value that we want. A quick and dirty fix might be to turn the "3" that we divide by into a literal double ("3.0"). This will have the effect of promoting the other operands to doubles as well.

```
double mean =
    (intArray[0] + intArray[1] + intArray[2]) / 3.0;
System.out.println(mean);
```

This is much better. We now get the correct result of 4.333333333333333 (or at least as correct as we are going to get trying to represent a third using floating-point arithmetic on a primitive type). However, using that literal is not good coding practice, since it is an example of a "magic number", a literal value that appears in a program without a clear origin. Here, the magic number represents the number of elements in the array, so it would be better to use the "length" field of the array:

```
double mean =
(intArray[0] + intArray[1] + intArray[2]) / intArray.length;
System.out.println(mean);
```

Unfortunately, we have now lost the double value that was triggering the promotion of the operands, so we are back to getting "4.0" as the answer. Now, we need to trigger the promotion to double in another way. We can do this by casting one of the operands (it can be any of the four) to type double. In this example, we cast the first operand to type double.

```
double mean =
((double)intArray[0] + intArray[1] + intArray[2]) / intArray.length;
System.out.println(mean);
```

Finally, we get the correct result without a magic number. You could, of course, cast more than one operand but there is no point, since promotion does that for you.

This example demonstrates not only that issues such as precedence, casting, and promotion need to be considered carefully when working with primitive data types, but also that code needs to be carefully tested to check that the result we are getting is, in fact, correct. In the next chapter, we will introduce code that can make selections, enabling us to, for example, write test code that can check if a result is, or is not, correct. In Chap. 10 we will introduce the JUnit testing framework so that all program outputs can be validated.

Exercise 3.3 This exercise involves doing some arithmetic on numbers stored in arrays. Distances expressed in kilometers will be converted to their equivalents in miles and nautical miles. One kilometer equals 0.62 miles and 0.54 nautical miles.

1. Create a new class with a "main" method.
2. In "main," create and initialize an array of type "double" containing the values 0.62 and 0.54 (representing the conversion multipliers).
3. Create and initialize an array of type "int" containing the values 2, 5 and 10 (representing distances in kilometers).
4. For each element in the integer array, calculate and display the equivalent distances in miles and nautical miles. Use String concatenation to add text labels to make the output understandable.

3.5   Summary

In this chapter we have seen the various data types available in Java and differentiated between primitive types, which include numbers, characters, and Boolean values, and reference types such as arrays, and how variables of these types can be declared and initialized. The Java arithmetic operators were introduced, and code examples showed how they can be used in arithmetic expressions. Our examples of order of precedence, promotion and type casting have shown how important it is to be aware of the way that Java manages the relationships between different data types, and how we can write code to make explicit data type conversions to ensure that our programs generate the correct results. The chapter also demonstrated how Strings (which are referencetypes) can be concatenated together and how arrays can be used to group together related data into a single structure that can be accessed by a zero-based index. The syntax for declaring and initializing arrays was examined, including arrays that have multiple dimensions.

Control Structures

4

In this chapter, we look at the main control structures in Java that enable selection and iteration. For selection, we cover "if-else", "switch", "break" and "continue" statements, and the ternary operator. As well as covering the "switch" statement that has been in Java from the beginning, we cover the switch expression introduced in Java 14. For iterating over code, we explore the "while", "do-while" and "for" loops. We see how "for" loops can be used to iterate through arrays, including the array of Strings that is passed to the "main" method.

In the context of control structures, it is worth noting that although Java has no unstructured "goto" statements, "goto" is a reserved word, precluding it from being used for anything else.

4.1 Making Selections

The code examples we have seen in previous chapters have been sequences of Java statements, but sometimes we also need to make selections, to choose between more than one possible course of action. This can be done using "if" statements.

4.1.1 "if" Statements

An "if" statement consists of courses of action and a condition, which appears in parenthesis after the "if". A condition is an expression that returns a value of type boolean, and which course of action is taken depends on whether that boolean value is true or false. One course of action may be, in fact, to do nothing.

© Springer Nature Switzerland AG 2020
D. Parsons, *Foundational Java*, Texts in Computer Science,
https://doi.org/10.1007/978-3-030-54518-5_4

"if" statements look like this:

```
if(condition)
{
  // do this
}
else
{
  // do this instead
}
```

The "else" part is optional. If the condition is false and there is no "else" part then no code in the conditional statement will be executed.

The code after "if" or "else" can be a single statement or a block of multiple lines. If it is a single statement then using braces is optional, as shown here:

```
if(condition)
  // do this single line of code
```

However, it is always safer to use braces around the statement to avoid confusion if, for example, you add further lines of code later. Here, without braces, the second line will not be part of the "if" statement

```
if(condition)
  // do this single line of code
  // add a line here… oops! Not part of the "if"!
```

Here, all lines of code within the braces will be regarded as part of the "if" statement:

```
if(condition)
{
  // do this single line of code
  // add a line here… still part of the "if"!
}
```

These statements can also be nested inside each other to any level, so that an "if" or an "else" statement can contain other "if" statements, as shown here:

```
if(condition)
{
  // statements
}
else
{
  if(condition)
  {
    // statements
  }
  else
  {
    // statements
  }
}
```

4.1.2 Expressing Conditions with Relational and Boolean Operators

When writing any kind of conditional statement, including both "if" statements and the loops covered later in this chapter, we need to express conditions that compare values (variables, literals or other expressions) using relational, equality and inequality operators. The symbols used in Java are shown in Table 4.1, along with some examples of how they might be used in an "if" statement.

The relational operators can only be used with numeric primitives (including "char" data), whereas the equality and inequality operators can be used with any data type (including reference types such as "String"). The operator that can cause the most errors when writing code is the equality operator ("=="). This is because it can easily be confused with the assignment operator, which is a single "=" character. The assignment operator is never used to compare values, only to assign them to variables.

All these expressions return either "true" or "false". To evaluate more complex conditions, we can use Boolean operators to combine multiple relational or equality expressions. The Java implementations of the three Boolean operators (AND, OR, NOT), along with some examples, are shown in Table 4.2.

Table 4.1 Relational and equality operators

Condition	Operator		Example
Equal to	==	Equality	if(temperature == 100)
Not equal to	!=	Inequality	if(grade != 'F')
Less than	<	Relational	if(sales < target)
Less than or equal to	<=		if(engineSize <= 2000)
Greater than	>		if(hoursWorked > 40)
Greater than or equal to	>=		if(age >= 18)

Table 4.2 Boolean operators in Java

Boolean operator	Java operator	Meaning	Example
AND	&&	Return true if both sides of the expression are true	`if(age > 4 && age < 16)`
OR	||	Return true if at least one side of the expression if true	`if(timeElapsed > 60 ||` `stopped == true)`

NOT	!	Return true if the expression is false or vice versa	`if(!drawingChanged)`
			`// assumes "drawingChanged"`
			`// is a boolean variable`

The "not" operator ("!") can be confusing because it returns true if the expression is false. For example, the expression "if(!drawingChanged)" in the table will be true if "drawingChanged" is false, i.e. if the current drawing has not been changed then "not drawing changed" is true. We often find this operator being used to test boolean "flag" variables that indicate when something has happened. The "not" operator is matched by the ability to do a test for true, for example, "if (drawingChanged)" is an equally valid expression, as long as "drawingChanged" is a Boolean value.

Note

The && and || operators in Table 4.2 are the "lazy", or "short circuit" versions of these operators, which only evaluate as much of a condition as they need to. For example, if the left-hand side of an AND expression is false, there is no need to evaluate the right-hand side as well because both sides of the expression cannot be true. Similarly, if the left-hand side of an OR condition is true, there is no need to evaluate the one on the right because only one side needs to be true. There are also Java Boolean operators that force evaluation of the complete expression. These use single character operators instead of double, i.e.

& AND operator (full evaluation)

| OR operator (full evaluation)

However, you are unlikely to need these operators very often.

4.1.3 Using Selection: The CoinExample Class

The code in our first example includes a selection using an "if" statement. This selection is based on using a randomly generated number to represent a coin being flipped and landing on either heads or tails.

In order to represent the flipping of the coin, we need to randomly generate a value. A simple way of generating a (pseudo) random number is to use the Math class, which (like the System class) is available as part of the standard Java libraries. The Math class has an operation called "random" that returns a random double value greater than or equal to 0.0 and less than 1.0. In the code, we assign the return value from this operation into a local double variable:

```
double randomNumber = Math.random();
```

Having got this value from the Math class, themethod then uses an "if" statement to choose whether the coin is showing heads or tails. If the random number is less than 0.5 then the coin is set to "heads", otherwise it is set to "tails". Of course, from the point of view of the program it makes no difference whether we use "less than" or "greater than", since either way we get a 50/50 chance (more or less).

This is the complete example:

```
package com.foundjava.chapter4.examples;

public class CoinExample
{
  public static void main(String[] args) {
// generate a random number in the range >=0.0 and <1.0
    double randomNumber = Math.random();
// use the random number in an 'if' statement to
// display the face of the coin
    if (randomNumber < 0.5)
    {
      System.out.println("The coin shows heads");
    }
    else
    {
      System.out.println("The coin shows tails");
    }
  }
}
```

One possible output from running this program is

```
The coin shows heads
```

The other possible output is

```
The coin shows tails
```

4.1.4 The DieExample Class

This next example does not add anything new to our knowledge of Java syntax but shows how some of the various techniques that we have already introduced, random number generation, arithmetic operators and type casting, may be used in combination. More importantly, it leads into an example where we use an "if" statement to test the results of our code.

The DieExample class is similar to the CoinExample class but can generate six different possible values rather than two (representing the six faces on a die). To get a random number in the appropriate range (1–6), we use both arithmetic and type casting. First, we generate a random number between zero and one using the "Math. random" methodmethod as we did in the CoinExample class. Then we multiply it by six and add one:

```
double randomNumber = Math.random();
randomNumber *= 6;
randomNumber++;
```

This will give us a floating-point number (a double) greater than or equal to 1 and less than 7. The number generated is a double, but we can cast it to get an integer, ignoring any fractional part of the number (a crude but adequate approach):

```
int dieValue = (int)randomNumber;
```

This gives a random integer in the range one to six. Here is the complete example

```
package com.foundjava.chapter4;

public class DieExample
{
  public static void main(String args[])
  {
// generate a random number in the range >=0.0 and <1.0
    double randomNumber = Math.random();
// to get a number in the range 1 to 6, we need to
// multiply the random number by 6 and add 1
    randomNumber *= 6;
    randomNumber++;
// to convert this value into an integer we cast it
    int dieValue = (int)randomNumber;
    System.out.println(dieValue);
  }
}
```

The output from this program can be any integer in the range 1–6.

Exercise 4.1

- Create a class with a "main" method
- In "main", generate a random integer between 1 and 10 (inclusive).
- Work out of the random number is odd or even.
- Using an "if" statement, write an appropriate message to the console that displays both the random integer and whether it is an odd or an even number.

4.1.5 Writing Test Code

Now that we have seen how to write code that can make selections, one useful application is to use it to test the results of our Java programs. Writing a test is basically about comparing the answer you expect with the answer the code gives you. While code that generates random numbers is not the easiest thing to test, we will see how we might begin to create some test code for our simulated throw of the die.

We expect the result will always be an integer in the range 1–6. Since Java's typing will ensure that the result is an integer, we only need to check the range. We can do this with an "if…else" statement. Note how we use the Boolean "&&" (AND) operator to check a compound condition; that the value is at least 1 and no more than 6.

```
if(dieValue >= 1 && dieValue <= 6)
{
  // OK message
}
else
{
   // error message
}
```

Here is the complete class.

```
package com.foundjava.chapter4;

public class DieTestExample
{
  public static void main(String args[])
  {
// generate a random number in the range 0.0 to 1.0
    double randomNumber = Math.random();
// to get a number in the range 1 to 6, we need to
// multiply the random number by 6 and add 1
    randomNumber *= 6;
    randomNumber++;
    // to convert this value into an integer we cast it
    int dieValue = (int)randomNumber;
    if(dieValue >= 1 && dieValue <= 6)
    {
       System.out.println("Valid die value: " + dieValue);
    }
```

```
    else
    {
       System.out.println
          ("Error. Expected value between 1 and 6 but was "
           + dieValue);
    }
  }
}
```

This type of test is necessary to find coding errors. For example, we might have accidentally typed "randomNumber += 6" instead of "randomNumber * = 6". This is a runtime error, not a compiler error, and would lead to the test failing and making us aware of the problem. Although this is a small and limited example, it demonstrates the idea that tests should be written in code, rather than being done manually (by, for example, running the code and checking the numbers being generated by looking at them). Writing tests in code means that the same tests can be run repeatedly without human intervention. In large systems, this helps us to run regression tests, where we can check if adding new code to a system has caused errors in any existing code due the interactions between them. In Chap. 10 we will look at the JUnit testing tool that can make the process of writing and running tests very easy.

4.1.6 "switch" Statements

Because an "if" statement can only handle a maximum of two different courses of action, it can be rather ponderous to check all the possible different states of a single variable. When a selection is based on a single (whole number) variable that can have many different values, and those values can be expressed as literal numbers, then a switch statement can be useful. The switch statement looks like this (note that there is no semicolon after the closing brace):

```
switch(variable)
{
  case literalvalue1 : // some code here
       break;
  case literalvalue2 : // some code here
       break;
// etc. for as many cases as need to be handled
  default:
// default code to handle cases not already dealt with
}
```

The variable being checked must be of type int, char, short or byte (or String since Java 7). You cannot use a long value or any floating-point types (these restrictions are related to underlying implementation structures within the Java bytecode). Each case is a specific value that the variable being tested may have. The default clause is used if the value passed to the switch does not match any of the specified case values. This, like the "else" part of an "if" statement, is optional. The "break" clause is important because it sends control to the end of the "switch" statement without evaluating any other cases, otherwise the rest of the cases will also execute. This may seem rather odd but allows us to use a single response to more than one possible value. For example, we could use it to check for both cases of a character if we were parsing a string of characters and were not concerned about whether they were upper or lower case:

```
switch (aChar)
{
  case 'a' :
  case 'A' : // my code here
    break;
  case 'b' // etc…
```

Since the case for "a" has no break clause, if "aChar" contains an "a" then control will drop through to the next case ("A") and that code will be executed.

4.1.6.1   A "switch" Example: The Dice Man

In Luke Reinhart's book "The Dice Man", the main character in the story begins to run his life by throwing a die to determine his actions. In this example, we do something similar. The die is thrown, and then we check its value and display a message telling us what to do. Because a die has six possible states, we would have to use six "if" statements to decide how to respond to it. In circumstances like this, we might be better off using a "switch" statement.

This "Dice Man" program uses a switch statement to look at the state of the die. The "default" clause covers any case where the number passed to the switch statement is out of range.

```java
package com.foundjava.chapter4;
public class DiceMan
{
  public static void main(String[] args)
  {
// "throw the die"
    double randomNumber = Math.random();
    randomNumber *= 6;
    randomNumber++;
    int dieValue = (int)randomNumber;
    String instruction = null;

// the die value is used to display an instruction (slightly
// modified version of the Dice Man's first throw of the
die!)
    switch (dieValue)
    {
      case 1:
        instruction = "forget the whole affair";
        break;
      case 2:
        instruction = "wait until the party on Saturday";
        break;
      case 3:
        instruction = "do what Arlene says";
        break;
      case 4:
        instruction = "have a platonic relationship";
        break;
      case 5:
        instruction = "follow your emotions";
        break;
      case 6:
        instruction = "go to Arlene's apartment tonight";
        break;
      default:
        instruction = "not a valid throw of the die";
    }
    System.out.println(instruction);
  }
}
```

This is the output similar to that achieved by the Dice Man.

```
have a platonic relationship
```

Note that it would be wise to read the book before following this philosophy of decision-making. It does not have a happy ending.

4.1.6.2 "break" and "continue"

The use of "break" in a switch statement is not the only context in which this keyword can be used. In fact, it can be used anywhere in a Java code block and always moves execution to the end of the current block (i.e. the next closing brace). There is another keyword, "continue", that has a similar function. However, the difference is that "continue" takes control back to the beginning of the current code block rather than the end. These keywords can be useful in, for example, searching and sorting large arrays to make the process more efficient by short cutting unnecessary parts of the process. Some readers familiar with such things might have noted that "break" and "continue" act rather like structured "goto" statements.

Exercise 4.2

- In a "main" method, generate a random integer between 1 and 13 to represent the possible values in a suit of playing cards.
- Use a "switch" statement that applies cases to your random integer
- If the random number is 1, print out "Ace" to the console
- If the random number is 11, print out "Jack" to the console
- If the random number is 12, print out "Queen" to the console
- If the random number is 13, print out "King" to the console
- The default case should simply print the random integer to the console.

4.1.7 The "switch" Expression

You may have noticed that the switch statement has a couple of limiting features. For example, it cannot return a value, so in "The Dice Man" code above we had to assign a value to a pre-declared variable and set its value in each "case" statement. The "break" syntax is also rather clumsy and potentially error prone. To address these issues, a new switch *expression* was released in Java 14. So, what is the difference between a statement and an expression? Basically, a statement manages the flow of control of code, while an expression provides a value. The example below uses a switch expression as an alternative syntax to the Dice Man switch statement previously introduced. In this example there are several features to note:

- The switch expression returns a value—a String in this example.
- "yield" is used to return a value from a specific case
- Matching to multiple values is done by simply putting the cases in a comma separated list (cases 5 and 6 in this example)
- There is a semicolon after the closing brace of the expression

```
String action = switch (dieValue)
{
  case 1:
    yield "forget the whole affair";
  case 2:
    yield "wait until the party on Saturday";
  case 3:
    yield "do what Arlene says";
  case 4:
    yield "have a platonic relationship";
  case 5, 6:
    yield "follow your emotions";
  default:
    yield "not a valid throw of the die";
};
System.out.println(action);
```

Instead of using the colon operator and just yielding a value, there is also an alternative syntax using the arrow operator, where an expression can be put on the right-hand side of the arrow. In our example the expression just the String being returned but it could be a more complex expression.

```
String action = switch (dieValue)
{
  case 1 -> "forget the whole affair";
  case 2 -> "wait until the party on Saturday";
  case 3 -> "do what Arlene says";
  case 4 -> "have a platonic relationship";
  case 5, 6 -> "follow your emotions";
  default -> "not a valid throw of the die";
};
```

Finally, both "yield" and the arrow operator can be used together, where an expression consists of multiple lines (enclosed in braces). "yield" must be used to specify the return value of the multi-line expression.

```
action = switch (dieValue)
{
  case 1 -> {
    System.out.println("Die value " + dieValue);
    yield "forget the whole affair";
  }
  case 2 -> {
    System.out.println("Die value " + dieValue);
    yield "wait until the party on Saturday";
  }
  case 3 -> {
    System.out.println("Die value " + dieValue);
    yield "do what Arlene says";
  }
  case 4 -> {
    System.out.println("Die value " + dieValue);
    yield "have a platonic relationship";
  }
  case 5, 6 -> {
    System.out.println("Die value " + dieValue);
    yield "follow your emotions";
  }
  default -> {
    System.out.println("Die value " + dieValue);
    yield "not a valid throw of the die";
  }
};
```

Note that the switch expression is likely to develop further in future versions of Java to allow more options for pattern matching. Also note that the introduction of the switch expression does not mean that the switch statement is being replaced, just that another coding option is being provided.

4.1.8 The Ternary Operator

This operator is a shorthand "if-else" statement that can be used when a condition is used to select a value to be returned rather than managing the flow of a program. The syntax is

expression ? *value1* : *value2*

If the expression is true, then the first value will be returned, otherwise the second is returned.

In this example, a ternary operator is used to return the String "even" if a number does not have a remainder when divided by two. If it does have a remainder then the String "odd" is returned.

```
String result = x % 2 == 0 ? "even" : "odd";
```

There is no requirement to use ternary operators since the same affect can be achieved with an "if...else", but some developers might prefer the brevity of the code.

4.2   Iteration

In the first part of this chapter, we saw how methods could be written that included selections between more than one possible course of action. Examples used both "if" and "switch" statements. We will now see how to write code that iterates, meaning that it can repeat a section of code more than once. Each pass through the repeated code is a single iteration. Iteration can be achieved in three slightly different ways:

1. "while" loops
2. "do...while" loops
3. "for" loops

In each case, there will be a condition that allows the loop to terminate. Which one to use depends on several factors and we often find that more than one will meet our requirements, but we must be aware of their differences in order to use them correctly.

4.2.1   "while" and "do...while" Loops

These loops are very similar in that both execute while a given condition is true, but there is one key difference between them. The "while" loop tests for a precondition, which is to say that the condition is evaluated at the beginning of each loop. In contrast, the "do...while" loop tests for a post condition, where the condition is evaluated at the end of each loop. This means that the "do...while" loop executes at least once, whereas the "while" loop may not execute at all (if the condition is already false). A "while" loop executes zero or more times whereas a "do...while" loop executes one or more times. Which one you choose in a given application depends entirely on the context, but the sensible default choice is probably a "while" loop, which always checks the condition before executing any code.

The "while" loop has the following syntax:

```
while(condition)
{
        // statement(s) here...
}
```

Similarly, the "do...while" loop has this syntax

```
do
{
  // statement(s) here…
} while (condition);
```

Note the semicolon that must follow a "do...while" loop. Do not put a semicolon after the condition at the beginning of a "while" loop, or you will get an endless loop within which nothing happens (the semicolon will separate the "while" from its associated actions so they cannot be executed).

4.2.1.1 A "do...while" Example

The next example program demonstrates a "do...while" loop that simulates the throwing of a die until it shows a 6. As in a previous example we generate a random number in the range 1–6, but this time we do so within a loop so the die can be "thrown" multiple times until its value is 6. It makes sense to use a "do...while" loop here because we need to go through the code at least once in order to generate a value for the "die". However, it would be trivial to change the example to use a "while" loop, since the initial dice value is set to zero, so a "while" loop would also execute at least once.

```
package com.foundjava.chapter4;

public class GameStarter
{
  public static void main(String[] args)
  {
    int dieValue = 0;
// loop until throwing the Die gets a six
    do
    {
// generate a random number in the range >=0.0 to <1.0
      double randomNumber = Math.random();
// to get a number in the range 1 to 6, we need to
// multiply the random number by 6 and add 1
      randomNumber *= 6;
      randomNumber++;
// to convert this value into an integer we cast it
      dieValue = (int)randomNumber;
      System.out.println("You have thrown a " + dieValue);
    } while (dieValue != 6);
// confirm the die value is six
    System.out.println("Well done, you can start the game");
  }
}
```

A sample test run produced this output, but of course this will change each time the program is run:

```
You have thrown a 1
You have thrown a 4
You have thrown a 6
Well done, you can start the game
```

With the syntax we have covered so far, it is difficult to provide good examples of selecting between a "while" or a "do...while" loop. However, we will see many examples later in the book where we will be selecting one or the other depending on the requirements of the code.

4.2.2   "for" Loops

Like "while" loops, "for" loops have a condition that controls the iteration of the loop. In addition, they have initialization and update actions built into the syntax. This makes them very useful where an index value is used within the body of the loop. A "for" loop has three principal elements:

1. The initialization action, executed once before the loop begins
2. The terminating (while) condition—the loop executes while this condition is true
3. The update action that takes place at the end of each iteration.

The format is

```
for(initialization; 'while' condition; action)
{
      // some code here
}
```

Note that the three parts of the statement following the word "for" are enclosed in brackets and separated by semicolons.

Any or all of the three sections can be left empty. This, for example, would be an endless loop:

```
for(;;)
{...
```

However, if we are not using all three sections then we would be better off using a "while" loop. A "for" loop should be used only when its initialization and update sections are needed, otherwise it makes the code more complex than it needs to be. An endless "while" loop is, for example, more readable.

```
while(true)
{...
```

4.2.2.1   Iteration with a "for" Loop

Our first example of a "for" loop provides an example of how an incremented index number can be useful within the loop. It is a class that displays some characters from the Unicode character set. The 16-bit Java "char" character is big enough to represent all the international characters in the Unicode set, but for most purposes, programs written for English-language readers need only to use the basic printable characters in the ASCII (American Standard Code for Information Interchange) table. The ASCIITableViewer class described here displays the (reliably) printable characters in the ASCII character set. The main method uses a "for" loop to display the printable characters from the ASCII table. These fall in the range 33–126, so the loop looks like this:

```
for(int i = 33; i < 127; i++)
{
// etc.
```

This means that the integer "i" is declared with the value 33. The terminating condition is a "while" condition; the loop continues while the value of "i" is less than 127. Each time round the loop, "i" is incremented by one ("i ++"). This happens at the end of the loop. The output from the program shows both the ASCII (Unicode) value of a character and the character itself. Since the loop is counting integers, we can display this directly as the ASCII value. To display the character, we cast the (32 bit) integer value to a (16 bit) char type.

```
char character = (char)i;
```

This cast is necessary so that when we pass the "char" variable to the "println" statement, the character itself is displayed rather than its ASCII value. The following statement displays both the value and the character:

```
System.out.print(i + ": " + character + '\t');
```

Notice that the escape sequence character '\t' is used to put a tab stop between each pair of values. The literal String (": ") included in the statement is important. Remember that using the "+" operator with only numeric variables (i.e. without a String) is interpreted as addition by the compiler. If there are no Strings being concatenated, as in this example, the "+" operator will add the values together, not what we want!

```
System.out.print(i + character + '\t');
// will not give the required output!
```

Because we are displaying the output tabbed across the screen, we will soon run out of space and need to move on to the next line. In the program, this is handled by an "if" statement that works out if there are nine number/character pairs on the current line (this value can easily be changed to give different line lengths). If there are, it forces a line feed using the ' \n ' escape sequence for a new line character. The arithmetic that calculates this uses the remainder operator. Bear in mind that the first character we are displaying has the value 33, so we ignore the first 32 characters by subtracting 32 from the current value of "i" (the variable that is being incremented by the "for" loop). If the resulting number can be divided by 9 with no remainder, then we must be on the ninth character of the current line, so a new line is needed. Note the use of parentheses to ensure that the subtraction takes place before the remainder by changing the precedence:

```
if((i - 32) % 9 == 0)
{
  System.out.println('\n');
}
```

This is the complete class.

```
package com.foundjava.chapter4;

public class ASCIITableViewer
{
  public static void main(String args[])
  {
    System.out.println("ASCII character table" + '\n');
// the 'for' loop counts from 33 to 126, the range of the
// reliably printable characters in the ASCII table
    for(int i = 33; i < 127; i++)
    {
// convert the integer to a 'char' using a cast
      char character = (char)i;
// display the ASCII number along with its character
// then add a tab
      System.out.print(i + ": " + character + '\t');
// if there are 9 characters on a row, add a line feed
      if((i - 32) % 9 == 0)
      {
        System.out.println('\n');
      }
    }
  }
}
```

The output from this program is

```
ASCII character table
```

```
33: !  34: "  35: #  36: $  37: %  38: &  39: '  40: (  41: )

42: *  43: +  44: ,  45: -  46: .  47: /  48: 0  49: 1  50: 2

51: 3  52: 4  53: 5  54: 6  55: 7  56: 8  57: 9  58: :  59: ;

60: <  61: =  62: >  63: ?  64: @  65: A  66: B  67: C  68: D

69: E  70: F  71: G  72: H  73: I  74: J  75: K  76: L  77: M

78: N  79: O  80: P  81: Q  82: R  83: S  84: T  85: U  86: V

87: W  88: X  89: Y  90: Z  91: [  92: \  93: ]  94: ^  95: _

96: `  97: a  98: b  99: c  100: d 101: e 102: f 103: g 104: h

105: i 106: j 107: k 108: l 109: m 110: n 111: o 112: p 113: q

114: r 115: s 116: t 117: u 118: v 119: w 120: x 121: y 122: z

123: { 124: | 125: } 126: ~
```

You could modify this program to print out any subset of the Unicode table (or indeed all of it) by simply changing the start index value and the termination condition. For example, you could print out the characters in the braille character set by modifying the "for" loop as follows:

```
for(int i = 10240; i < 10495; i++) {
```

However, the ability of your machine to display various characters from the Unicode table will vary depending on what fonts have been installed.

4.2.2.2 "for" Loops and Arrays

"for" loops are frequently used to loop through an array. We can use the index value in the "for" loop to access elements of the array and use the array's "length" field to control the loop iteration. For example, here is a "for" loop that iterates through two arrays, the array of integers representing average rainfall that we introduced in the previous chapter, and another array that contains the names of the months of the year. Note how the same index variable has been used to access both arrays. We use two separate arrays here, rather than a single two-dimensional array, because arrays are strictly typed. We cannot put Strings and integers into the same array.

```
package com.foundjava.chapter4;
public class ArrayForLoopExample
{
  public static void main(String[] args)
  {
    String[] monthNames =
     {"January","February","March","April","May","June",
      "July","August","September","October",
      "November","December"};
    int[] monthlyRainfall =
     {74,81,86,93,100,116,126,111,93,80,84,91};
    System.out.println("Average monthly rainfall");
    for(int i = 0; i < monthlyRainfall.length; i++)
    {
      System.out.println(monthNames[i] + ": " +
        monthlyRainfall[i] + "mm.");
    }
  }
}
```

Here is the output from running the class:

```
Average monthly rainfall
January: 74mm.
February: 81mm.
March: 86mm.
April: 93mm.
May: 100mm.
June: 116mm.
July: 126mm.
August: 111mm.
September: 93mm.
October: 80mm.
November: 84mm.
December: 91mm.
```

4.2.2.3   Iterating Through the Array Passed to "Main"

In the previous example we knew that there were 12 elements in the arrays, because they were initialized in the same piece of code. This is not always the case, which is why using the "length" field is so useful. For the next example we will use a "for" loop to iterate through the String array that can be passed as a parameter to "main". The parameter we always use with "main" is an array of Strings, which may or may not be empty

```
String[] args
```

The size of this array depends entirely on how many Strings are passed to it from the command line or IDE when the program is run, so we need to use the "length" field to control a loop that iterates through this array, because when the code is compiled we do not know how long the array will be at runtime. In this example, we use the parameter to "main" to display any Strings that are passed to the class when it is run.

```
package com.foundjava.chapter4;

public class MainArrayLoopExample
{
  public static void main(String[] args)
  {
    for (int i = 0; i < args.length; i++)
    {
        System.out.println(args[i]);
    }
  }
}
```

Of course, to test this piece of code we need to have some way of passing Strings to the "main" method. If you are running the program from the command line, the Strings are added to the invocation of the class. If you want any of your Strings to contain spaces, they must be put into double quotes, as with "some strings" in this example (note that this would need to all be entered as one line at the command prompt):

```
java com.foundjava.chapter4.MainArrayLoopExample hello I am
"some strings"
```

When running the class from within Eclipse, you send parameter Strings to "main" using the "Run Configurations" dialog. Select "Run" from the main menu bar and choose "Run Configuration…" from the menu. This will show the "Run Configurations" dialog (Fig. 4.1). In this dialog, select the class from the list on the left, and then click on the "Arguments" tab. If you can not see the class in the list, try running it first without any arguments. In this tabbed pane you can enter as many Strings as you like in the "Program arguments" area. These will be passed to the "main" method as an array when the class is run.

Regardless of whether you run the class from the command line or from within Eclipse, the output will be

```
hello
I
am
some strings
```

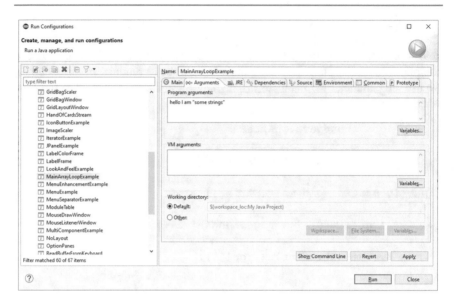

Fig. 4.1 Using the "Run Configurations" dialog in Eclipse to pass arguments to the main method of a class

Note that each String appears on a new line as they are each displayed by a separate call to "System.out.println" within the loop ("some strings" is a single String because of the double quotes).

The kind of data usually sent to "main" tends to be optional configuration data such as file names or "flags" that change the behavior of a program (like the parameters to the "Javadoc" document generator that we will look at later in this book). In a later chapter, we will see an exercise that makes more practical use of a parameter passed to main.

4.2.2.4 Multiple Initializations and Actions
Before concluding this chapter, there is another feature of "for" loops that may be useful to know, which is that the initialization and action sections of the "for" statement can contain lists of values, separated by commas. Here, for example, three variables ("letterCount", "upperCount" and "lowerCount") are initialized, and they are all updated at the end of each iteration. This may be a somewhat contrived example, but it uses multiple counters to display characters from different parts of the Unicode table, in this case the lower and upper case letters of the Latin alphabet.

```
package com.foundjava.chapter4;

public class MultiValueForLoopExample {
  public static void main(String[] args)
  {
    for(int letterCount=1, upperCount=65, lowerCount=97;
    letterCount<=26; letterCount++, upperCount++,
    lowerCount++)
    {
      System.out.println("Lower case: " + (char)lowerCount +
        " Upper case: " + (char)upperCount);
    }
  }
}
```

The output will appear as follows

```
Lower case: a Upper case: A
Lower case: b Upper case: B
Lower case: c Upper case: C
Lower case: d Upper case: D
Lower case: e Upper case: E
Lower case: f Upper case: F
Lower case: g Upper case: G
Lower case: h Upper case: H
Lower case: i Upper case: I
Lower case: j Upper case: J
Lower case: k Upper case: K
Lower case: l Upper case: L
Lower case: m Upper case: M
Lower case: n Upper case: N
Lower case: o Upper case: O
Lower case: p Upper case: P
Lower case: q Upper case: Q
Lower case: r Upper case: R
Lower case: s Upper case: S
Lower case: t Upper case: T
Lower case: u Upper case: U
Lower case: v Upper case: V
Lower case: w Upper case: W
Lower case: x Upper case: X
Lower case: y Upper case: Y
Lower case: z Upper case: Z
```

Exercise 4.3
Create a new class with a "main" method. In "main", take the following steps

1. Create and initialize an array containing the integers 1, 2, 3, 4, 5, 6, 7, 8, 9 and 10.
2. Use a "for" loop to print out the contents of the array
3. Add a "while" loop that prints out the contents of the array in reverse order
4. Add a "do...while" loop that iterates forward through the array. Inside the loop, add an "if" statement so that only even numbered values from the array are printed.

This exercise is virtually guaranteed to give you ArrayIndexOutOf BoundsExceptions, which are caused by attempting to access an element of the array that does not exist. Sorting out these problems will help you become familiar with the way that both loops and arrays work in Java.

4.3 Summary

In this chapter we have seen how Java's control structures are used for selection and iteration. We looked at various types of selection syntax, including "if" and "switch" statements, and introduces the relational and Boolean operators that are used in the conditions that control "if" statements and loops. We also saw the ternary operator, which provides a shorthand way of writing simpleSimple selections that return a value. In the context of switch statements, we discussed the "break" keyword and compared it with the behavior of the "continue" keyword. We also saw the syntax options in the recently introduced switch expression, which unlike a switch statement can return a value and includes syntax such as the "yield" keyword (to return a value) and the "arrow" operator to invoke an expression. Examples of different kinds of loop were illustrated, including "while" loops, "do... while" loops and various configurations of "for" loop, which are particularly useful for iterating through arrays. Code examples also showed how the Math class can be used for random number generation, and how an array of Strings can be passed to the "main" method of a class at runtime, either from the command prompt or via the "Run Configurations" option within Eclipse.

Creating Objects

5

We have already seen that Java has both primitive types and reference types. We spent some time looking at primitive types in Chap. 3, but also introduced Strings and arrays, which are both reference types. Reference types include all kinds of classes, including user-defined types (such as BankAccount, InsurancePolicy, Customer, etc. created for use in specific applications), collection classes like Lists, data classes that group multiple pieces of related data together like those that handle dates and times, and many more. Reference types are more complex than primitives, which just represent a single value, and are accessed through a reference to a specific area of memory.

In this chapter, we will begin by looking at the basic mechanics of objects; how they are created, how we can call their methods, and how they are handled in memory. We will explain the distinction between a class and an object and begin to interact with some simple objects from the Java libraries and explore some of their constructors and methods.

5.1 Classes and Objects

A class has several different roles in Java. In previous examples, we have seen that classes can provide us directly with methods that we can utilize in our programs. For example, the System class can be used to display output on the console, and the Math class can be used to generate a random number. We have also seen many examples of classes being created in order to act as the entry point for a program by containing a "main" method. Both roles are useful, but an even more important role of a class is to act as the specification for a type of object. In other words, the class describes an object type in terms of its attributes (the data fields that it contains) and its operations (the methods that it makes available).

© Springer Nature Switzerland AG 2020
D. Parsons, *Foundational Java*, Texts in Computer Science,
https://doi.org/10.1007/978-3-030-54518-5_5

Individual objects are instantiated (created) from a specific class, and many objects can be created of the same class, for example, there may be many different Strings in a single program, but all of these are members of the String class.

Recalling what we have covered previously, when we declare a variable of a primitive type, we declare the type and name of the variable and assign a value to it, for example:

```
int myVariable = 0;
```

We have seen from examples of using arrays that creating a variable of a reference type is somewhat different, as it requires the "new" keyword. However, there is still a declaration of the data type and the name of the array, for example:

```
int[] myArray = new int[5];
```

Creating objects follows a similar pattern; we still need to specify the type of the object, which is defined by its class name, and the name of the variable that we will use to reference this object. The object itself is created by calling a special method of the class called a constructor.

5.1.1 Object Creation—Constructors

The job of a constructor is to construct objects of a specific class. Constructor methods have the same name as the class to which they belong so that, for example, the Constructors for class "String" are also called "String". Like arrays, objects are created by using the "new" keyword, though the syntax is different since arrays do not have constructor methods. To create a new object, first declare a reference variable of the required type, and then invoke the constructor method after the "new" keyword. For example, we can construct a new Object:

```
Object myObject = new Object();
// myObject is an Object, Object() is the constructor
```

The "Object" class is provided as part of the Java libraries. You may wonder what the point of an "Object" is since it does not represent any particular kind of object, and on the whole you would be right. We do not often find a need to create instances of Object but is it useful to do so when looking at simple syntax examples.

Of course, there are many other types of object that can be created. We could, for example, create a new String object:

```
String s1 = new String(); // s1 is a String (an empty one!)
```

Some constructor methods can accept parameter arguments. For example, we can create a new String object by passing it a literal String as a parameter:

```
String s2 = new String("Hello"); // s2 is another String
```

You will notice that these are different ways of creating Strings from the simple assignment to a literal that we have used before, but it makes it clear that String is in fact a reference type, not a primitive type. When we assign String references to literals the compiler creates String objects from these literals.

```
String s3 = "Hello";
// same effect as String s3 = new String("Hello");
```

The String class has several different constructors, which vary by the types of parameters that are passed. This feature, where more than one version of a method exists, but each version has a different list of parameter arguments, is known as *overloading*, and is a common feature of constructors as well as other types of method.

An object reference needs to be initialised, but it need not always reference an object. An alternative is to initialise it to "null", which is a Java keyword used for a reference that does not currently point to anything:

```
String customerName = null;
```

This is particularly useful where, due to scope, we need to create a reference to an object in a different part of the program to where the object will be created.

5.2   Classes and Methods for String Data

Methods are operations that an object can perform. They are invoked using the "." (dot) operator. When we invoke a method of an object the method name is always followed by parentheses. These parentheses are used to list any parameter arguments that are used by the method:

```
objectName.methodName(parameter arguments)
```

If there are no arguments being passed, then the parentheses will be empty. In this section, we will look at some of the methods available for objects that represent String data.

5.2.1 The String Class

As we have seem from previous examples, a String is simply a string of Unicode characters (letters, numbers, spaces or other symbols), which may vary in length from no characters (a "null string") to whole sentences or even documents (for example, an XML document could be represented by a String). String characters are indexed from zero, like an array (Fig. 5.1).

Strings in Java are also "immutable", meaning that they cannot be changed once created. Therefore, most of the methods available for Strings are concerned with querying the current state of the String such as its length, searching for elements within the String such as characters or substrings, or performing comparisons between different Strings.

All objects have methods to provide their behavior. The next example program shows a few of the methods provided for objects of the String class, listed in Table 5.1 (there are many more not listed here). In this table, the "original String" refers to the String that the method is being called upon. The "length" method is not passed any parameters, so the parentheses are empty when it is called. However, the other methods used in this example all take at least one parameter argument. Some of these methods are overloaded so they will work with either single characters or Strings being passed as parameter arguments.

The following class shows some of the methods of the String class being used with a String object containing a very simple HTML document. Here is the content of the String, formatted with line feeds and indents to render it more readable.

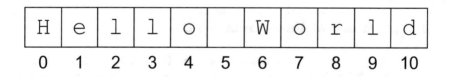

Fig. 5.1 Strings contain Unicode characters that are indexed from zero, like an array

Table 5.1 Some methods of the String class

Method	Purpose
length()	Returns an integer representing the number of characters in the String
contains(...)	Returns "true" if the character or String passed to the method is matched inside the original String, otherwise returns false
startsWith(...)	Returns "true" if the character or String passed to the method is matched inside the original String, otherwise returns false
indexOf(...)	Returns the index (as an int) within the original String of the first occurrence of the specified character or String (returns-1 if not found)
lastIndexOf(String)	Returns the index (as an int) within the original String of the last occurrence of the specified character or String (returns −1 if not found)
substring(int, int)	Returns another String that is a copy of the part of the original String between the two indices provided

```
<!DOCTYPE html>
<html>
  <head>
   <title>My HTML Page</title>
  </head>
  <body>
    <h1>Welcome to my page</h1>
    <p>This page is written in simple HTML<p>
    <p>
      Since HTML files are just text markup, they can be
      contained in Java String objects
    </p>
  </body>
 </html>
```

Since HTML browsers discard white space, we can represent this page as a single String in Java. Note that in the actual code the whole String needs to appear on a single line, without the line feeds that are used below to fit the text onto the page. Although this example program does not perform any practical function, it shows how Strings can be processed using their methods. The kind of processes demonstrated here could be used to, for example, extract data from a web page, check the document type being used or identify elements to be used when attaching stylesheets.

```
package com.foundjava.chapter5;

public class HTMLStringExample
{
  public static void main(String[] args) {
    String HTMLString = new String(
      "<!DOCTYPE html><html><head><title>My HTML Page
</title></head><body><h1>Welcome to my page</h1><p>This page is
written in simple HTML<p><p>Since HTML files are just text
markup, they can be contained in Java String ob-
jects</p></body></html>");
    System.out.println("String length: " +
      HTMLString.length());
// length of the whole HTML page
    System.out.println("Has level 1 headings: " +
      HTMLString.contains("h1"));
// check for level 1 headings
    System.out.println("Has level 2 headings: " +
      HTMLString.contains("h2"));
// check for level 2 headings
    System.out.println("Has a DOCTYPE: " +
      HTMLString.startsWith("<!DOCTYPE"));
// check that the page has a DOCTYPE of some kind
    System.out.println("Position of the \'!\' " +
      HTMLString.indexOf('!'));
// result is 1, because the first index is zero
    int startIndex = HTMLString.indexOf("body");
// result is first char of "body"
    startIndex += 5;
// go past the rest of the characters in the tag
    int endIndex = HTMLString.lastIndexOf("body");
// result is first char of "body"
    endIndex -= 2;
// go back to remove the first character and the leading '<'
    String bodyContent =
      HTMLString.substring(startIndex, endIndex);
    System.out.println("Body content " + bodyContent);
  }
}
```

When the program is run, the following output is displayed:

```
String length: 239
Has level 1 headings: true
Has level 2 headings: false
Has a DOCTYPE: true
Position of the '!' 1
Body content <h1>Welcome to my page</h1><p>This page is writ-
ten in simple HTML<p><p>Since HTML files are just text
markup, they can be contained in Java String objects</p>
```

5.2.2 Long Strings and Text Blocks

In the previous example, it was suggested that the HTML String used in the code should appear on a single line, but this does not make the HTML code very readable. For example, we might want to add tab and newline characters so that the code is readable when printed. In order to make the source code, as well as the output, readable we might need to split the String into many lines and concatenate them all together. We could write the declaration of the String something like this:

```
String HTMLString = new String(
  "<!DOCTYPE html>\n" +
  "<html>\n" +
  "\t<head>\n" +
  "\t\t<title>My HTML Page</title>\n" +
  "\t</head>\n" +
  "\t<body>\n" +
  "\t\t<h1>Welcome to my page</h1>\n" +
  "\t\t<p>This page is written in simple HTML<p>\n" +
  "\t\t<p>Since HTML files are just text markup,
   they can be contained in Java String objects</p>\n" +
  "\t</body>\n" +
  "</html>");
```

This works perfectly well but is rather a clumsy solution. Since Java programmers do find themselves from time to time having to handle strings of source code (such as HTML or SQL) there is a "Text Block" feature (first previewed in Java 13) that uses triple quotes to enclose a block of formatted, multi-line text. Using this feature, we could replace the declaration of the formatted String above with the following:

```
String myLongString = """
  <!DOCTYPE html>
  <html>
    <head>
      <title>My HTML Page</title>
    </head>
    <body>
      <h1>Welcome to my page</h1>
      <p>This page is written in simple HTML<p>
      <p>Since HTML files are just text markup,
      they can be contained in Java String objects</p>
    </body>
</html>
""";
```

Both versions provide the same output, as shown below, but the Text Block version is much easier to write and maintain.

```
<!DOCTYPE html>
<html>
  <head>
    <title>My HTML Page</title>
  </head>
  <body>
    <h1>Welcome to my page</h1>
    <p>This page is written in simple HTML<p>
    <p>Since HTML files are just text markup, they can be con-
tained in Java String objects</p>
  </body>
</html>
```

Note
*The version of the text block shown above is the preview version as provided in
Java 14. It is possible that it may not be supported in subsequent versions of Java.*

5.2.3 String Builders

In our previous coverage of the String class, we discussed the fact that Strings are
immutable (cannot be changed once created). Methods of a String that might at first
glance appear to change the String (e.g. "toUpperCase", which returns an upper
case version of the original String) simply create new String objects that have a
different state; the original String remains unchanged. However, sometimes it is
useful to be able to directly change an existing String of characters. The class that
enables you to do this in Java is the StringBuilder class. TheStringBuilder constructor creates a StringBuilder with a default capacity of 16 characters, plus the
length of any String argument passed to the constructor, but it will automatically
resize itself if necessary.

```
StringBuilder eventLogger = new StringBuilder();
// no arguments - capacity will be 16

StringBuilder eventLogger = new StringBuilder("Errors:\n");
// an argument of length 8 - capacity will be 24
```

We can find out the current capacity of a StringBuilder with the `capacity`
method, e.g.

```
int capacity = eventLogger.capacity();
```

The main operations on a StringBuilder are to change the contents of the String it
contains by appending or inserting extra characters. To append extra characters to
the end of a StringBuilder we use one of the overloaded `append` methods, for
example,

```
eventLogger.append("more text");
```

To insert characters, we use the "insert" method, which takes two parameters: the position to make the insertion, and the string of characters, for example:

```
eventLogger.insert(0, "new text")
```

The following example, which is somewhat contrived, demonstrates the "capacity", "append" and "insert" methods by showing how a StringBuilder can be changed over time. Here, we simulate an event log having errors and warnings added to it as they occur. The StringBuilder is initially created containing the label "Errors:", and its initial capacity is displayed, then the label "Warnings" is appended. After that, error and warning messages are appended onto the end of the StringBuilder or inserted into it by acquiring the appropriate index values and then adding new messages in the correct position. At the end the new capacity of the StringBuilder is displayed.

```
package com.foundjava.chapter5;

public class StringBuilderExample
{
  public static void main(String[] args)
  {
    // Create a new StringBuilder
    StringBuilder eventLogger = new StringBuilder("Errors:\n");
   // The initial capacity of the StringBuilder is 16
   // plus the length of the String argument
    System.out.println
      ("Initial capacity " + eventLogger.capacity());
  // Add more String data
    eventLogger.append("Warnings:\n");
  // Add a warning to the log - easy as it comes at the end
    eventLogger.append("Fridge wrong colour\n");
  // Add an error - a bit harder as we must
  // insert it before the warnings
  // Find the first character index of the "Warnings" string
  // to add an error before it
    int errorIndex = eventLogger.indexOf("Warnings:");
    eventLogger.insert(errorIndex, "Fridge on fire\n");
  // Print out the whole StringBuilder
    System.out.println(eventLogger);
  // Print out the final capacity (longer than when it started)
    System.out.println
      ("Final capacity " + eventLogger.capacity());
      }
 }
```

This is the output from this program. Note how the capacity of the StringBuilder increases as we append and insert extra data.

```
Initial capacity 24
Errors:
Fridge on fire
Warnings:
Fridge wrong colour
Final capacity 102
```

5.2.4 String Buffers

The StringBuffer class provides the same interface as the StringBuilder but is potentially less efficient since it is thread-safe (i.e. it only allows single threads to access it at any one time). When we are not using multiple threads, the String-Builder is a better option because it does not carry the unnecessary overhead of thread management in situations where this is not required. We explore multi-threading in Chap. 16.

5.2.5 The "toString" Method

One of the methods that is common to all objects in Java is the "toString" method, which returns a String representation of an object. The default implementation of this method can help us to understand how reference types are handled in memory. The examples that follow take advantage of the "toString" method to analyze the behavior of some reference types.

Here, we create an Object, get the results of the "toString" method from that object and then display the result.

```
Object myObject = new Object();
String myString = myObject.toString();
System.out.println(myString);
```

In fact, we do not have to call "toString" explicitly if we want to print out any type of object. If we put an object reference into a "System.out.println" statement, "toString" gets called implicitly to display the object, so the code above could be written more simply as:

```
Object myObject = new Object();
System.out.println(myObject); // toString called implicitly
```

You may find the results of this rather strange when compared to printing out String objects, which simply display the text they contain. The output will be something like (but probably not exactly)

```
java.lang.Object@36d64342
```

What does this represent? It is actually a combination of the name of the class, and a value derived from the memory address of the object itself (actually the *hash code* of the object, which is an integer derived from the memory address and displayed as a hexadecimal number). The class name is java.lang.Object; in other words the Object class is in the "java.lang" package. The remainder of the output is the hash code, preceded by the "@" symbol. If you create two new Objects, you should see from their displayed values that they have different memory addresses, which of course is necessary, you cannot have two different objects sharing the same memory address. Being able to demonstrate this role of a reference will clarify the content of the following section.

Note that the actual addresses displayed when you run this type of code will vary for each execution. Do not expect your output to look the same as some of these examples.

Note
Since the hash code is not actually the memory address of the object, it is possible that two hash codes could be the same, depending on how the hash code is calculated, so not all objects will necessarily generate unique hash codes

Exercise 5.1

- Create a class with a "main" method.
- In "main", create a new String object that contains lower case letters.
- Create another String object that contains upper case letters.
- Create a StringBuilder object that contains the first String converted to upper case.
- Append a lower case version of the second String to the StringBuilder.

Exercise 5.2

- Create a class with a "main" method.
- In "main", create three objects using the Object constructor.
- Print out all the objects using "System.out.println"—note that their hash codes should appear different.
- Print out the hash code of one of the objects using the "hashCode" method. Note that it looks different from the one generated by "toString" because that is the hexadecimal representation of the same value.
- Use the "Integer.toHexString" method to convert the hash code of one of the objects to hexadecimal. You should see that the value looks the same as the one generated by the "toString" method.

5.3   References and Memory

One important feature of Java is that it does not use pointers to memory but uses references instead. A reference is very much like a pointer, in that it does access an area of memory, but does not expose access to that memory in the same way as a traditional pointer. A reference cannot be used to, for example, remove something from memory or access and manipulate memory addresses directly. Nevertheless, we need to have some understanding of the way that references relate to computer memory in order to handle them correctly.

So far, we have seen that we can create new objects, and these objects will have different memory addresses. We can also use assignment operators with objects. If you use assignment with primitive types, values are copied from one variable to another, for example:

```
int var1 = 5;
int var2 = 9;
var1 = var2;
var2 = 10;
```

In this piece of code, we start with two separate integer variables with different values. When we assign the value of "var2" to "var1", the value of "var2" (9) is copied into "var1". Then we change the value of "var2" to 10. "var1" remains unaffected by this and retains the value 9. All very straightforward. With reference types, life is a bit more complicated, since the assignment operator acts on the references, not on the objects they are pointing to. For example, we might create two objects, using references called "a" and "b". Initially these two references point to different areas of memory:

```
Object a = new Object();
Object b = new Object();
System.out.println(a);
System.out.println(b);
```

Running this piece of code might give you output something like the following; as you would expect, two different memory locations.

```
java.lang.Object@19821f
java.lang.Object@addbf1
```

What happens if we use the assignment operator with these object references?

```
a = b;
```

If these were primitive types, the value in "b" would be copied to "a". With reference types, only the address of the reference is copied, so if we print out the two references again, we end up with something like:

```
java.lang.Object@addbf1
java.lang.Object@addbf1
```

What happens is that both references end up pointing to the same object. This has implications for object state and for memory management. To show what this means for object state, we will create a slightly different example using String-Builders. Unlike the behavior of "toString" when used with an Object, the "toString" method of a StringBuilder returns the current characters in the String-Builder, so this will be useful for seeing what happens when we redirect references to other StringBuilder objects.

This fragment of code creates two StringBuilder objects and then prints out their current contents:

```
StringBuilder word1 = new StringBuilder("First");
StringBuilder word2 = new StringBuilder("Second");
System.out.println(word1);
System.out.println(word2);
```

As you would expect, the console output would show:

```
First
Second
```

What happens if we assign the first reference to the second? From the earlier examples using the Object class, you should expect them both to refer to the same object, and indeed this is what happens. This fragment of code assigns "word1" to "word2" so that both references point to the second object:

```
word1 = word2;
System.out.println(word1);
System.out.println(word2);
```

When we print out both StringBuilder references they both display "Second":

```
Second
Second
```

Now that both references are pointing to the same object, they can both change its state. For example, we can call the "reverse" method (which reverses the order of the characters in the StringBuilder) using one of the references, in this example "word1" (though we could also have used "word2").

```
word1.reverse();
System.out.println(word1);
System.out.println(word2);
```

Because the single object that both references point to has been changed, the output from running this code would be

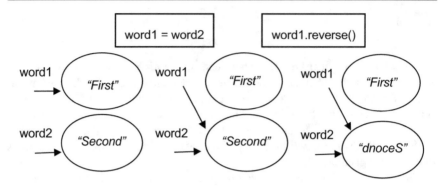

Fig. 5.2 The effects of redirecting object references

```
dnoceS
dnoceS
```

This is obviously something we should be aware of if we redirect references to objects. Figure 5.2 shows the state of the objects over time. First, the two references point to different objects, then they point to the same object, then the state of that object is changed using a method one of the references.

5.3.1 Garbage Collection

There is a further issue with what has happened in Fig. 5.2, which is that the object containing "First" is no longer referenced by anything. It has therefore become a "garbage" object in memory which needs to be cleaned up. In some programming languages the programmer is responsible for freeing up memory when objects that have been created are no longer required. This can have some unfortunate side effects if errors are made when coding. On the one hand, an object may be removed from memory by one part of the program when it is still needed by some other part of the program. This will result in an exception occurring at runtime when the program tries to access the object that no longer exists. On the other hand, the programmer may fail to write code that removes objects from memory once they are finished with. This can lead to an ever-increasing number of "lost" objects in memory, taking up space that may be needed. This is known as a "memory leak" and if the program runs long enough it will run out of memory. To overcome these problems, Java takes over the management of memory by providing an automatic *garbage collection* mechanism.

In Java, an object that you no longer require cannot be deleted manually. If you have finished with an object, then the only action you can take is to redirect any references that currently point to it to other objects, or to "null", or simply let the references fall out of scope. Objects that are no longer being referenced are then eligible for automatic garbage collection by the Java runtime. In Fig. 5.2 the StringBuilder object ("First") that is no longer referenced will be garbage collected if the memory it is taking up is needed by the program. The garbage collector is part of the runtime system which runs automatically in the background when the JVM needs more memory to continue executing. The garbage collector only runs when it needs to free up memory. You cannot force it to run, though there is a "gc" method on the System class that lets you suggest that it might like to do some garbage collection, though it may not actually do any.

```
System.gc();
```

Depending on how long a program runs for and how much memory it uses, the garbage collector may never run at all. Over time, Java's garbage collection mechanism has become increasingly sophisticated so that it works very efficiently.

5.3.2 Object Equality

The "==" and "!=" operators (equality and inequality) can be used with objects, but it is important to understand that they compare the references, not the objects that are being referenced. The equality operator (==) returns "true" only if the two references being compared point to the same object in memory. The actual state of the objects themselves is not relevant. Figure 5.3 shows the behavior of the equality operator in relation to object references. On the left of the figure, two StringBuilder objects (referenced by "word3" and "word4") have identical state (they contain the same characters), but because they are separate objects, comparing their references means they are not equal. On the right of the figure, two references point to the exact same object. In this case the equality operator will return "true".

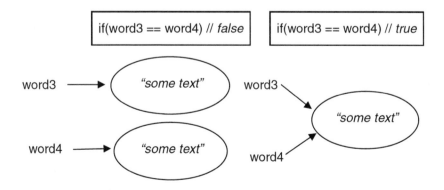

Fig. 5.3 The behavior of the equality operator when used with object references

The following code fragment shows this example. The first part of the code will display the message "Objects are not equal". After both references have been assigned to the same object, the second part of the code will print out "Objects are equal":

```
StringBuilder word3 = new StringBuilder("some text");
StringBuilder word4 = new StringBuilder("some text");
if(word3 == word4)
{
  System.out.println("objects are equal");
}
else
{
  System.out.println("Objects are not equal");
}
word3 = word4;
if(word3 == word4)
{
  System.out.println("objects are equal");
}
else
{
  System.out.println("Objects are not equal");
}
```

Note

Do not try this example with String objects. If you create two Strings from the same String literal, the compiler will only create a single String and direct both references to it. This is because Strings are immutable, and therefore cannot be altered by any of the references that point to them, making it safe to use the same String object for multiple references.

5.3.3   String Concatenation and Memory

One final thing to be aware of while we are looking at garbage collection is that, because all operations on Strings return new Strings, concatenation can generate a lot of work for the garbage collector. In the following piece of code, three Strings are concatenated, but one of the references is reused:

```
String greeting = "Hello";
String name = "World";
greeting = greeting + " " + name; // result is "Hello World"
```

The result of this process can be seen in Fig. 5.4. A new String has been created containing the required text, but the original String referenced by "greeting" is now garbage. When dealing with large amounts of String manipulation, see if you can reduce the amount of work for garbage collector by, for example, using String-Builders instead of Strings.

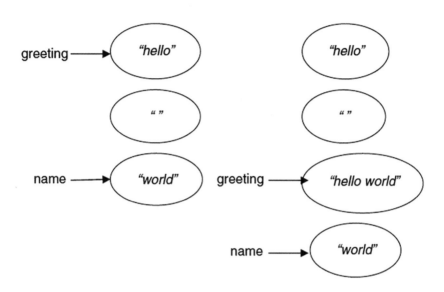

Fig. 5.4 String concatenation can create extra work for the garbage collector

5.4   Java Library Packages

The many Java classes provided in the runtime libraries are in various packages containing groups of classes that have similar roles. For example, all the classes that allow us to create graphical user interfaces are in one set of packages, whereas all the classes for handling input and output are in another.

The classes we have seen already, such as String, come from the default Java package "java.lang", so the full name of the String class is in fact "java.lang. String". However, so far we have not had to concern ourselves with the package names of the classes in our examples because "java.lang" is such a fundamental package in Java that we are able to refer to classes from this package directly without referring to "java.lang" at all.

However, this is not the case for any of the other packages. For example, one of the Date classes in Java (which represents both a date and a time) appears in the "java.util" package (which contains various utility classes). Its fully qualified name is therefore "java.util.Date". Since it is not in "java.lang", to use it in our code we need the fully qualified class name for both reference declarations and constructor calls. To create a new Date object, then, we would need to write:

```
java.util.Date date = new java.util.Date();
```

This class is a good example of why packages are important, because there is another Java Date class called "java.sql.Date", for working with database dates. Without the package name it would be impossible for the compiler to know which of the Date classes we wanted to use.

Note
The java.util.Date class is still available in Java, but the old date and time classes were superseded in Java 8 with a new set of classes in the "java.time" package. However, since using these newer classes require an understanding of various code features that we have not yet introduced, we will leave coverage of them to a later chapter and work with java.util.Date in the meantime

5.4.1 Importing Classes

Although it is perfectly acceptable to use the fully qualified name of a class (including its package name) in code, it can lead to rather complex-looking programs. A neater alternative to using the fully qualified name is to *import* the required classes. Importing means we only need to state the package name of a class once, rather than every time we refer to it.

We do this with an "import" statement at the beginning of the code (following the package statement), followed by the name of the package and the name of the class we want to import. The Date class is in "java.util", so the import statement to use this class reads:

```
import java.util.Date;
```

The import statement provides, at both compile time and runtime, a general route for locating classes so that we can, in this example, simply refer to "Date" in our code rather than "java.util.Date" every time we want to use it. Here is a very short example class that imports the Date class, creates an object of the class and then prints the date object on the console.

```
package com.foundjava.chapter5;

//import the definition of the 'Date' class from java.util
import java.util.Date;

public class DateExample
{
  public static void main(String[] args)
  {
//the default 'Date' constructor sets the object to the current
//date and time
    Date today = new Date();
//we can display a Date object because it has a 'toString'
//method, which is implicitly called here
    System.out.println("The date and time is " + today);
  }
}
```

When the "toString" method is called on a Date object, it displays the date and time of its creation, using a default format, so the output from this program will be something like

```
The date and time is Sun Mar 01 14:58:08 NZDT 2020
```

The actual output will, of course, depend on the date, time and time zone of the program's execution.

5.4.2 Wild Cards and Multiple Imports

You can have as many import statements as you like at the top of your class, between the package name and the class declaration:

```
package xxxx;

import …;
import …;
public class …
```

You can either import the individual class names or use the "*" wildcard to include all the classes from a package. For example, we might want to use two different classes from "java.util", the Date class and the Formatter class, which can be used to format the output of numbers, dates, etc. Using the wildcard, the import statement could look like this:

```
import java.util.*;
```

Alternatively, we could import the two classes separately.

```
import java.util.Date;
import java.util.Formatter;
```

It is better to specify all your imports separately, because in a class that imports many other classes, it is hard for someone reading the code to know easily where an individual class has come from if wild cards are used. By specifically naming each imported class, it is easy to see which package they belong to.

In this short program we create a Date object and a Formatter object. One of the methods of the Formatter is "format", one version of which takes as its parameter arguments a format String and the value to be formatted (in our example a Date object). There are many ways of specifying the format String for a Date, but Java includes a few simple ones that are preceded by the characters "%t". This example uses the format character "R", which displays a formatted time using the hours and minutes of the 24-hour clock.

```
package com.foundjava.chapter5;

import java.util.Date;
import java.util.Formatter;

public class ImportExample
{
  public static void main(String[] args)
  {
    Date myDate = new Date();
    Formatter myDateFormatter = new Formatter();
    myDateFormatter.format("%tR", myDate);
    System.out.println(myDateFormatter);
  }
}
```

The output from this program will be something like this:

```
06:10
```

Table 5.2 shows the set of format Strings that can be used for common date and time formatting, though note that there are also specific date and time formatters for the newer classes in the "java.time" package that we will look at in Chap. 11.

5.4.3 Modules, Packages and Sub Packages

You may recall that when we first created our Java project Eclipse added a "module-info.java" file, which was initially empty, but included the name of the module that we chose for our own classes ("com.foundjava.examples"). Since Java 9, Java itself has been divided into multiple modules. The main advantage of this

Table 5.2 Common format Strings for Date objects

Format String	Output Format
%tR	Time formatted for the 24-hour clock as hours and minutes, e.g. 12:00
%tT	Time formatted for the 24-hour clock as hours, minutes and seconds, e.g. 12:00:00
%tr	Time formatted for the 12-hour clock as hours, minutes and seconds plus AM or PM, e.g. 12:00:00 AM
%tD	Date formatted as day month and (short) year, e.g. 01/01/20
%tF	Date formatted as (long) year, month and day, e.g. 2020-01-01
%tc	Date and time formatted as day, date, time, zone and year, e.g. Wed Jan 01 12:00:00 EDT 2020

division of a system into separate modules is that only the modules that are required by an application need to be deployed with that application for it to work, rather than the whole Java Runtime Environment (JRE). For those working with legacy systems it also makes it possible for different modules to use different versions of Java, enabling some newer features to be used in one module of a system without breaking dependencies on older versions that code in another module may have.

The packages we have used so far ("java.lang" and "java.util") both come from a module called "java.base". Since this module contains all the core packages of Java, we do not need to do anything for our code to access this module. There is a relatively small number of core Java packages in this module, which use the "java" folder and have one subfolder in the package name:

- java.io
- java.lang
- java.math
- java.net
- java.nio
- java.security
- java.text
- java.time
- java.util

There is also one "javax" (extension) package, "javax.net", which provides classes for networking applications.

In addition, there are many sub packages. For example in Chap. 11 we will be introducing some classes from the "java.time" package, which provides an updated set of date and time classes to replace the original date and time related classes from "java.util". The "java.time" package has a number of sub packages, including "java.time.format", which contains classes to print and parse dates and times.

Import statements in Java only apply to a specific package, they do not include any sub packages. Therefore if we wanted, for example, to use classes from both "java.time" and "java.time.format" in a program, then we would need to import from both packages (wildcards have been used for this example, but specific imports would be preferable).

```
import java.time.*;
import java.time.format*;
```

Note

There is on one extension package, which has a package name beginning with "javax" in the "java.base" module, but there are many in other modules. Many of these packages relate to the enterprise and micro editions of Java but there are also some in the standard edition, such as the javax.swing package (from the "java. desktop" module) that we will look at in Chap. 17.

5.4.4 Managing Imports with Eclipse

Eclipse has some useful tools that can help you with your import statements. These can be accessed from the "Source" menu, which is on the main tool bar and can also be accessed from the pop-up menu which appears when you click the right mouse button in the code editor window. One of the options under "Source" is "Add Import". If your cursor is positioned over the name of a class that needs to be imported, then Eclipse will create the import statement for the required class. A more general option on the Source menu is "Organize Imports". This will import all the required classes for your source file. In addition, if you have already imported classes using a wildcard, Eclipse will resolve these imports into the individual classes that you have used.

You must be aware, however, of some possible unwanted side effects of using the import tools. One problem is that some class names appear in more than one package. If this is the case, Eclipse will provide a dialog like that shown in Fig. 5.5, listing all the available classes of that name in their different packages. You need to be careful because the default choice will be the first one in alphabetical order, which may not be the one that you want. In Fig. 5.5 you can see that the default Date class that has been selected is "java.sql.Date", not the one we have been using, which is "java.util.Date". Check this dialog carefully if it appears and ensure that you have chosen the correct class.

The other side effect to be aware of is that you may have added an import to your code, and then perhaps temporarily commented out or removed the code relating to the class to which that import referred. If you use the "Organize Imports" option, Eclipse will remove any import statements that are no longer being used. If you then reintroduce the class that was removed or commented out, then the import will have gone, and you will need to add it again.

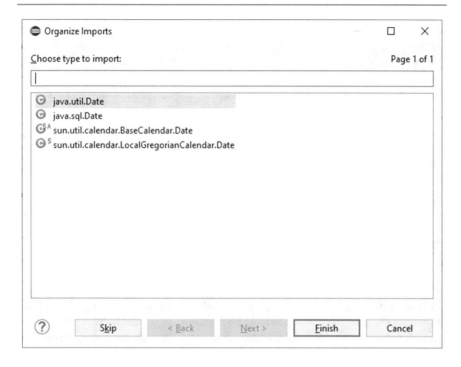

Fig. 5.5 The "Organize Imports" dialog appears if there are multiple classes that have the same name

Exercise 5.3

- Create a class with a "main" method.
- In "main", create a new Date object (from the "java.util" package). Use the necessary "import" statement.
- Create a String object that contains the same date by explicitly using the "toString" method of the Date class.
- Create another string object that contains the same date converted to upper case.
- Display the message "Today's date is…." followed by your upper case string using a single "System.out.println" statement.

5.5   Using Javadoc

As we have started to use the classes in the Java libraries, you will no doubt want to find out more about these classes, and others, and how they can be used. All of this information is made available in the Java documentation, which can be viewed

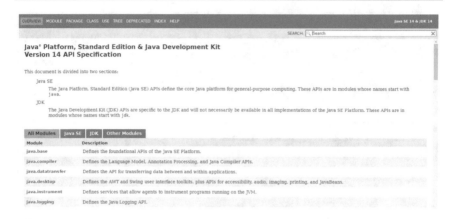

Fig. 5.6 The index page of the Javadoc documentation for Java 14

online at "https://docs.oracle.com/en/java/javase/" or downloaded from the Oracle Java site (it is a separate download, not included in the JDK) and viewed as local HTML pages. This documentation has been created using the Javadoc tool, which generates documents from Java source code and Javadoc style comments. The whole of the JDK is now modularised, so you will find all the packages appearing in modules. The most important module to become familiar with is java.base, because it contains all the foundational APIs.

If you choose to download the documentation rather than reading it online, the folder structure includes a "docs" folder. Inside this is an "index.html" page that you can open in a browser (Fig. 5.6). This has links to all the other documentation pages.

5.5.1 Viewing Javadoc in Eclipse

As well as viewing the Javadoc as a set of external pages, it is integrated into Eclipse. You can see context sensitive documentation just by hovering the mouse pointer over a class or method name (Fig. 5.7).

If you move the mouse pointer onto the pop-up, a menu bar will appear at the bottom which includes options to view Javadoc in a "Javadoc View" tab in the window at the bottom of the screen, or open up the Javadoc in a new tab in the code editor window.

If you do not want to be dependent on having an Internet connection to the online Javadoc, you can link Eclipse to a locally downloaded version. To do this, select "Preferences" from the "Window" menu. Then within the "Preferences" dialog, select "Java" and then "Installed JREs". In the right-hand pane select the JRE that you are using (there may only be one) and then press the "Edit" button. This will take you to the "Edit JRE" dialog, where you can select the current

```
public class ImportExample
{
    public static void main(String[] args) {
        Date myDate = new Date();
        Formatter myDateFormatter = new Formatter();
```

> **java.util.Formatter**
>
> An interpreter for printf-style format strings. This class provides support for layout justification and alignment, common formats for numeric, string, and date/time data, and locale-specific output. Common Java types such as byte, BigDecimal, and Calendar are supported. Limited formatting customization for arbitrary user types is provided through the Formattable interface.
>
> Formatters are not necessarily safe for multithreaded access. Thread safety is optional and is the responsibility of users of methods in this class.
>
> Formatted printing for the Java language is heavily inspired by C's printf. Although the format strings are similar to C, some customizations have been made to accommodate the Java language and exploit some of its
>
> Press 'F2' for focus

```
    }
}
```

Fig. 5.7 Context–sensitive Javadoc appearing in Eclipse

Javadoc location, then press the "Javadoc Location…" button, which will take you to the dialog where you can select the path to the archive (you need to point to the original archive, not an extracted folder). Once you have added the path to the archive, make sure you add the path "docs/api" to the "Path within archive" field. Figure 5.8 shows the various dialogs that are involved in this somewhat complicated process.

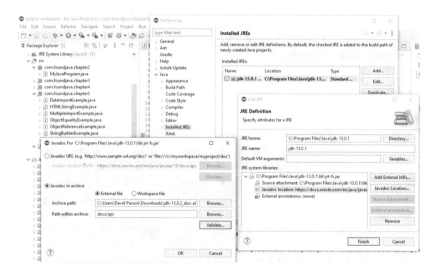

Fig. 5.8 Adding Javadoc into the Eclipse environment

Exercise 5.4

- Create a class with a "main" method.
- The Point class within the "java.awt" package represents the "x" and "y" coordinates of a point in a two-dimensional space. In "main", create a new java. awt.Point object using thezero arguments constructor. Add the necessary "import" statement.

Note

If the "module-info.java" file included when you first created the project is empty, your code will fail to compile, with the error "The import java.awt cannot be resolved". This is because in the module system the "java.awt" package is in a separate module called "java.desktop" that is not loaded by default. There are two easy fixes to this:

1. *Manually add "requires java.desktop"; to your module-info file*
   Or
2. *Right click on your Eclipse project and select "Configure"- > "Create module-info.java". This will create a new "module-info" file with all the required entries. It will also add all the packages in your project as "exports". This means that any other code that used your module could access the classes in these packages.*

- Print the Point object on the console using "System.out.println"—what are its "x" and "y" coordinate values?
- Change both of its coordinate values and print it again (see the Javadoc for details of which methods can be used to do this).
- Why do you think the "x" and "y" fields of Point objects are publicly accessible?

Exercise 5.5

For reasons best known to the designers of Java, the Date class has a "getTime" method that returns (as a long integer) the number of milliseconds that have passed since January 1, 1970 in Greenwich Mean Time (GMT). We can use this to calculate the current time by using the divide (/) and remainder (%) operators. It is not the easiest way of displaying the time (the newer classes in the "java.time" package provide a much simpler solution), but serves as a useful arithmetic exercise. To save you getting out the calculator, the following figures are required:

- there are 86,400,000 ms in a day
- there are 3,600,000 ms in an hour
- there are 60,000 ms in a minute

Use these to write some code that will tell you the current time.

5.6 Summary

We began this chapter by looking at the creation and use of some objects and methods related to String data (Strings, StringBuilders, StringBuffers and the "toString" method). This was followed by some important issues regarding the way that objects are referenced in memory when programming with Java, and the way that some operators work with objects. The Java garbage collector, which handles the removal of unwanted objects from memory, was also introduced. Again, String objects were discussed, in the context of String immutability and concatenation.

The latter part of the chapter concerned itself with issues of how objects from packages other than "java.lang" can be used in Java applications, by using various ways of importing classes, and being aware of modules and the role of the "module-info.java" file.

The chapter concluded with a brief introduction to the Javadoc documentation that can be viewed online or downloaded and viewed in a browser (as well as being integrated into Eclipse) to support you in Java programming. Being able to reference the Javadoc is an essential tool when working with Java, and we will refer to it regularly in the rest of this book.

Creating Domain Classes

6

In the previous chapter we created objects of some of the commonly used classes in the Java libraries, including Strings, Dates and Points. However, in order to build useful software, we need to go beyond these generic library classes and reflect the concerns of our own application domains. In this chapter, we will begin to explore how we create new domain classes that can represent the objects of interest to us in our own applications.

6.1 Object Orientation and Domain Objects

Object-oriented programming is based on a simple premise, that as human beings we think of the world around us as being made up of objects, and that software can be made up of objects too. Of course, it is not quite that simple. Although we can look at real-world objects to help us understand the key concepts of object orientation, we must also realize that objects in software have their own characteristics. In this chapter we will begin by looking at objects and their relationships in the real world and then see how these ideas can be applied to the task of programming.

A real-world object is something we perceive as having a unique identity (my ruler, that pencil etc.) and an existence that can be described in terms of what it is (a blunt HB pencil with a chewed rubber on the end) and what it does (it draws and it rubs out). In *Zen and the Art of Motorcycle Maintenance*, Robert Pirsig draws a diagram of his motorcycle that includes both its components and its functions as different aspects of the same object (Fig. 6.1).

We notice some other things about objects too. We find that individual objects are not so unusual that they do not have a lot in common with other objects of a similar type. For example, we can recognize all kinds of rulers as being of type "ruler", even though they may be different lengths, have different measuring scales and be made of different materials. We also note that objects are not much use on

© Springer Nature Switzerland AG 2020
D. Parsons, *Foundational Java*, Texts in Computer Science,
https://doi.org/10.1007/978-3-030-54518-5_6

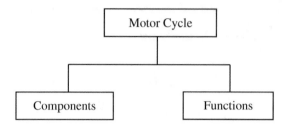

Fig. 6.1 A motorcycle object includes both its components and its functions

their own. A ruler, to be useful, must interact with other objects (such as people and pencils) in order to measure, or to draw a line.

To explore these ideas further we will use the example of a clock, which has the advantage of being an object that spans the gap between the real world and programming. As well as being surrounded by clocks of different types in our everyday lives, we are also frequently bombarded by clocks in software, since they appear in a quiet corner of many applications. First, we will look at some aspects of "real-world" clocks.

6.1.1 Clock Objects in the Real World

Take a clock and describe it. It might be a wall clock with a round face and three hands. Say it has a white face, with black hour and minute hands and a red second hand. This is all descriptive about what a clock is, or its "state". Some aspects of a clock's state will not be so obvious to us. In a battery-powered clock for example the level of charge in the battery does not become evident until the clock stops. The state of an object is represented by its attributes, or *fields*.

It also has "behavior" which is what the clock does. The most important (possibly only) behavior of a clock is to tell us the time. Other possible behaviors of clocks might include telling us the date or sounding an alarm. State and behavior are very closely related, as we can see if we consider that the state of the clock at any one time includes the time that it is displaying. Similarly, the behavior of an alarm clock that allows it to ring is related to its state of ringing. The behaviors that an object can perform are known as its operations, or *methods*. Figure 6.2 shows a class diagram using Unified Modeling Language (UML) notation that shows some attributes and operations of a clock object. In this kind of diagram, a rectangle is divided into three, with the top section containing the type of the object (the class name), the middle section the names of the fields and the bottom part the names of the methods.

Fig. 6.2 UML class diagram
of a clock, with some fields
and methods

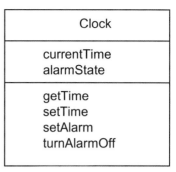

6.1.2 Encapsulation and Information Hiding

An object "encapsulates" both state and behavior by drawing them together into a cohesive whole. This encapsulation brings together the public interface of an object (the face it presents to the outside world) with private elements that go to make up its inner representation. Part of this drawing together of an object's state and behavior is the ability to hide much of the inner workings of an object. We need to see the face of the clock, but we do not need to know how it works. We might need to interact with it in other ways, such as changing the battery or winding a clockwork mechanism on an antique clock, but we still do not need to know how it works internally to use it. This characteristic of objects is called "information hiding" and helps to simplify the building of software systems because it hides what we do not need to know, allowing us to focus on the important aspects of an object's character. Thus, an object shows the world only that which the world needs to see. This is rather like a company or other organization that has some parts of its operation that provide its public image, for example, an online shopping website, and other parts that provide purely internal services such as company intranets, supply chain management systems, etc. (Fig. 6.3).

6.1.3 Object Identity

We are able to recognize that two objects that appear the same have a different identity. If we stand next to a production line watching hundreds of identical clocks go by, we know that they are all individual objects. It may be that the internal state of all these clocks is the same. For example, analogue clocks and watches (i.e. those with hands) are typically sold with the hands pointing at ten past ten to show the maker's name. Even so, we know that they are different objects because they occupy a different space at any one time. We also know, however, that all these clocks are of the same type, they belong to the same *class*. On one level, then, classifying objects means recognizing that all identical objects belong to a single class.

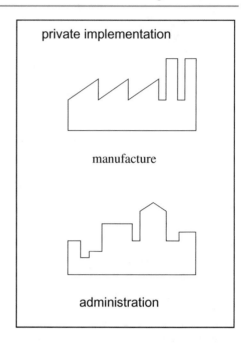

Fig. 6.3 Information hiding means that we only need to see the public interface of an object, not its internal implementation

6.2 Creating New Classes

Having introduced some concepts from the real world, we will now bring our focus back to Java programming. Building object-oriented systems means creating classes that will reflect the specific concerns of different application domains. In this section, we will work through an example class representing courses offered by a training company. The "Course" class is not meant to represent a specific delivery of a course, rather it defines a course about a practical subject that can be offered multiple times in different locations by different trainers.

Although it is not really helpful to think of classes as just data holders, because the methods of an object are its most important feature, it is helpful to start out this way to see how a class is put together, particularly in Eclipse. The UML class diagram in Fig. 6.4 shows that the Course class has three fields: the name of the course, the duration of the course (in days) and the price (per person). Later we will add the methods.

In past examples, we have seen how to create a class with a "main" method, but a class that is to act as a domain object does not have a "main" method, since it represents a type of domain object rather than an entry point to a program. Therefore, to create a "Course" class in Eclipse we would uncheck the option to create a "main" method (Fig. 6.5).

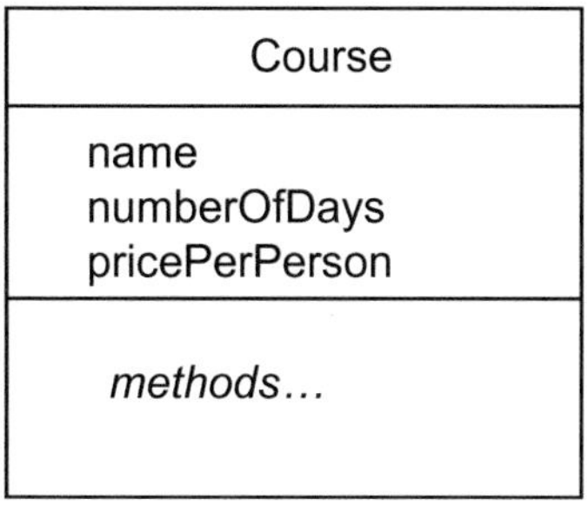

Course
name numberOfDays pricePerPerson
methods…

Fig. 6.4 The fields of the Course class

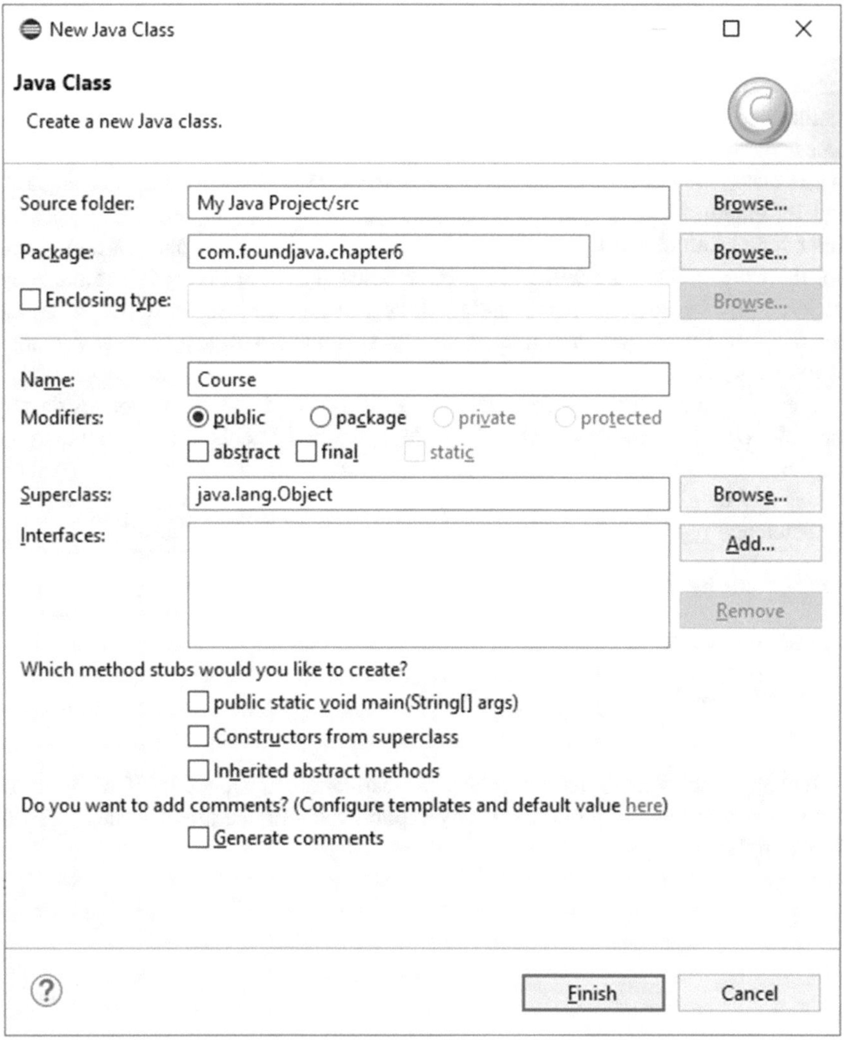

Fig. 6.5 Creating a domain class in Eclipse (without a main method)

As we saw in the previous chapters, where we created classes containing "main" methods, a Java class is declared by using the "class" keyword, followed by the name of the class (which by convention uses Pascal case) and the opening brace of the class definition. Classes that are generally visible to other classes are also declared "public". The beginning of the class definition for Course, generated by Eclipse, therefore looks like this (creating a class with no "main" method will generate just an empty class body):

```
public class Course {

}
```

6.2.1 Adding Fields to a Class

Inside this class body, we will start by adding the data fields. Unlike the "main" method, which has public visibility, fields are usually marked as "private". This access modifier specifies that the data fields are only accessible from within objects of the class; they are not visible to other objects. This is part of the encapsulation and information hiding that we introduced earlier in this chapter. We protect the inner state of an object from being arbitrarily changed by other parts of a program. For the Course class, we will add the three fields shown in Fig. 6.4. The fields are declared private, and the "name" field will be a String, the "numberOfDays" an int, and the "pricePerPerson" a double. A private attribute is still visible to any method of the same class, so any method of a Course will be able to access these fields.

Field declarations are added directly to the body of the class, not inside any method. Unlike variables declared inside a method, fields do not have to be explicitly initialized. When an object of the class is created, each of the attribute values will be given the default value for that type; zero for numeric types and null for reference types (such as Strings). Boolean fields default to "false".

```
public class Course
{
   private String name;
   private int numberOfDays;
   private double pricePerPerson;
}
```

Although fields have default values, we can assign other values if we wish, or simply aid the readability of the code by explicitly stating the initial value of a field, for example,

```
public class Course
{
  private String name = null;
  private int numberOfDays = 0;
  private double pricePerPerson = 0.0;
}
```

6.2.2   Adding Methods to a Class

Having added the fields to the class, we need to provide some methods so that other parts of our code can interact with Course objects. The simplest types of methods are the "getters and setters", which let the fields be accessed in a controlled way. The methods of a class also appear inside the class body, but these are usually declared with "public" visibility because they provide the public interface for the object.

First, we will look at the creation of a "getter" method that allows the name of a Course object to be accessed. A getter method needs to return a value to the code that called the method. "return" is Java keyword that is required in any method that returns a value (i.e. when the return type of the method is not "void", which means that no value is returned). The "return" keyword is followed by the name of the primitive value or object being returned, which in this case is the "name" field. Any method that returns a value must include the type of that returned value as part of its declaration. In this case, a String is being returned, so the method definition begins with this type, followed by the name of the method and the parameter list parentheses. There are no parameter arguments to this method, so the parentheses are empty:

```
public String getName()
{
  return name;
}
```

Note
A return statement is the last line of a method that is executed, even if it is not the last line of code in the method. Lines that occur after a return statement will be ignored. Occasionally we can use this approach to short circuit the execution of a method, rather as we can do with a "break" statement.

The second method we will add is the matching "setter" that can set the value of the "name" field. In order to do this we have to pass a String parameter argument to the method, containing the name to be set, so the type of this parameter must be provided, along with a local name that will be used to refer to this parameter in the body of the method. The local name of the parameter can be same as the name of the field, but if this is the case, the reference to the field must be preceded with the keyword "this", to specify that it refers to the field in "this" object, not the local parameter. The return type of the method is "void", meaning that it does not return any value. Here is the method:

```
public void setName(String name)
{
    this.name = name;
}
```

Note

The use of "this" to disambiguate the field and the local parameter names is something that the compiler will not be able to assist you with. It is perfectly legal to write the method like this:

```
public void setName(String name)
{
    name = name;
    // assigns the value of the local parameter argument "name"
    // to itself and does not set the field value!
}
```

However, the effect of this is to ignore the field of the object and simply set the value of the parameter to itself. Something to watch out for!

The creation of getters and setters is such a basic requirement that Eclipse provides a tool to generate these methods from fields. Simply select "Generate Getters and Setters" from the "Source" menu. This will display the dialog in Fig. 6.6. This dialog will list all the getter and setter methods that have not already been created for the fields in the class. In Fig. 6.6 the getter and setter for the "name" attribute have already been written manually, so only methods for "numberOfDays" and "pricePerPerson" are still available for selection. Note that the new methods will be added at the current cursor position (this is indicated in the dialog) so make sure that you have positioned your cursor in the right place before generating these methods.

If we write or generate getters and setters for all the fields of the Course class, the code will look like this:

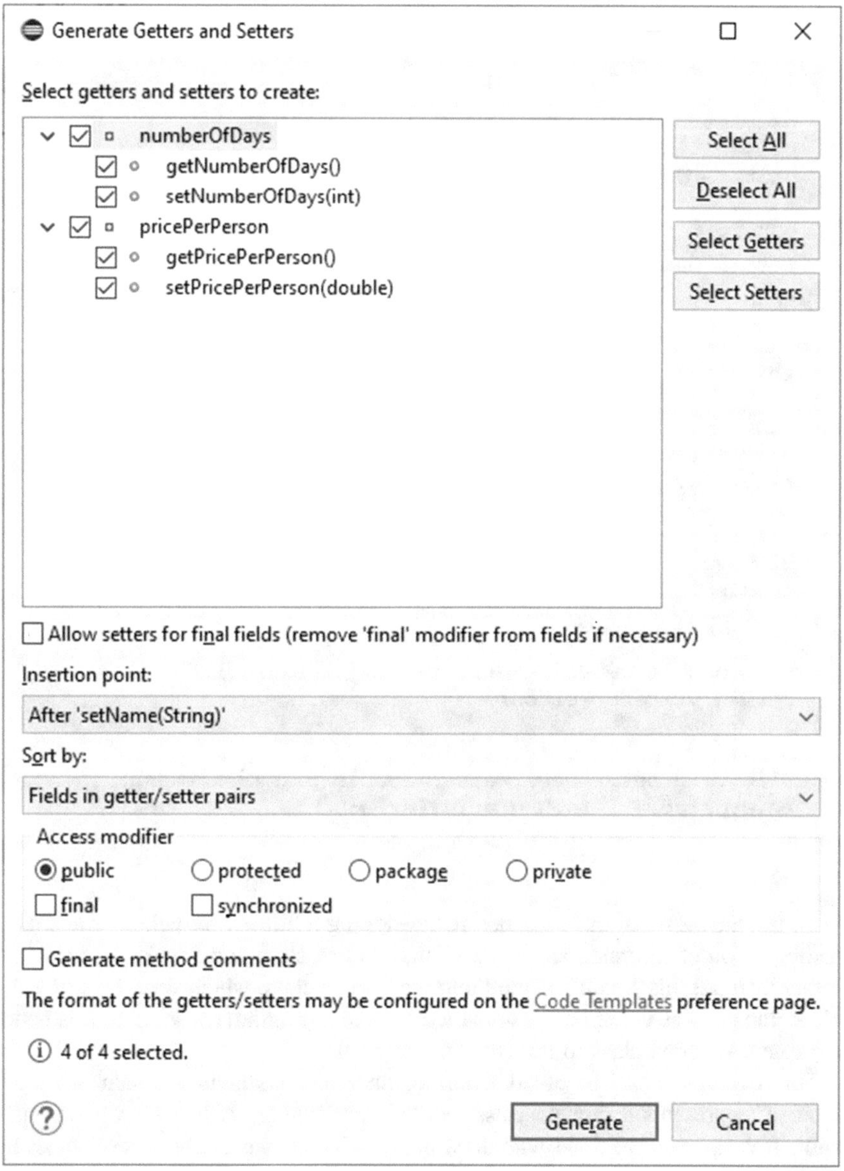

Fig. 6.6 Selecting methods to be generated from fields in the "Generate Getters and Setters" dialog

```java
package com.foundjava.chapter6;

public class Course
{
    private String name;
    private int numberOfDays;
    private double pricePerPerson;

    public String getName() {
    return name;
}

public void setName(String name) {
    this.name = name;
}

public int getNumberOfDays() {
    return numberOfDays;
}

public void setNumberOfDays(int numberOfDays) {
    this.numberOfDays = numberOfDays;
}

public double getPricePerPerson() {
    return pricePerPerson;
}

public void setPricePerPerson(double pricePerPerson) {
    this.pricePerPerson = pricePerPerson;
}
}
```

To test the basics of this class before developing it further, we will need a "main" method in order to create an object of the Course class and invoke its methods. Rather than put this "main" method into the Course class, which would confuse the role of the class as being both a domain class and a program entry point, it is better to create a separate class to host the "main" method.

This example class is called CourseRunner and contains a "main" method. "Course" represents a domain class, but "CourseRunner" is just a program entry point. Just as we have done with Java library classes, we create a new object by calling the constructor method and use the "dot" operator to invoke a method of the object.

```
package com.foundjava.chapter6;

public class CourseRunner
{
  public static void main(String[] args)
  {
    Course javaCourse = new Course();
    javaCourse.setName("Java");
    javaCourse.setNumberOfDays(3);
    javaCourse.setPricePerPerson(1000.0);
    System.out.println(javaCourse.getName() +
          " course lasts " + javaCourse.getNumberOfDays() +
          " days and costs " + javaCourse.getPricePerPerson());
  }
}
```

The output from this program is:

```
Java course lasts 3 days and costs 1000.0
```

6.3   Constructors

One thing you may find strange from the previous example is that we were able to create a new Course object by calling a constructor, but we never defined a constructor method. This is because there is default (zero arguments) constructor available for each class. Any class that you create will have this default constructor available. This is useful, but its limitation is that the default constructor cannot explicitly initialise the state of a new object, since it does not take any parameter arguments.

To overcome this limitation, we can create our own constructors, and these constructors can take parameter arguments. For example, we might want to create a constructor that can take three parameter arguments to set the initial values of the three fields. This can be added to the class body like the getters and setters we have already added. The constructor, unlike other methods, has no return type specified (the actual return type is always an object of the class). It always has the same name as the class, so the "Course" constructor will also be called "Course". In this example constructor, the three parameter arguments are specified, and in the body of the method the fields are set to equal the parameter values.

```
public Course(String name, int days, double price)
{
  this.name = name;
  this.numberOfDays = days;
  this.pricePerPerson = price;
}
```

A perhaps unexpected side effect of this is that if you add this constructor to your class, you will find that the CourseRunner class no longer compiles, because the following line now has an error:

```
Course javaCourse = new Course();
```

This problem is caused by the fact that the default constructor is only available if you do not specify any of your own constructors. Now that we have created a constructor method, the default one will no longer be usable.

6.3.1 Overloaded Constructors

Fortunately, you can have more than one constructor, overcoming the problem of losing the use of the default constructor. This is possible using the technique of overloading, which we have seen previously, where the same method name can be used with different combinations of parameter arguments. It works by providing multiple implementations of the method, each one having a different combination of types and/or numbers of parameter arguments. We may want to have a zero arguments constructor as well as the one that takes three parameters, to give users of the class more options about how they create new Course objects. To illustrate this possibility, we add another constructor that takes no parameter arguments. This constructor sets the values of the fields to some reasonable defaults.

```
public Course()
{
  this.name = "Unnamed Course";
  this.numberOfDays = 3;
  this.pricePerPerson = 1000.0;
}

public Course (String name, int days, double price)
{
  this.name = name;
  this.numberOfDays = days;
  this.pricePerPerson = price;
}
```

We can now create objects using the parameterised constructor. The correct version of the constructor is called based upon its signature.

```
Course c = new Course("C#", 2, 1500.00);
```

6.3.2 Chaining Constructors

An unfortunate side effect of adding an additional constructor in the example above is that we have some rather ugly duplication of code between the two constructors, each of them assigning values to the three fields. Having duplicated code like this is an ongoing maintenance problem and is best avoided. The danger with duplicated code is that over time it gets updated in one place but not another. The solution to this problem is to use a technique called constructor chaining, which is where one constructor calls another constructor of the same class in order to implement its functionality. The syntax for doing this uses the "this" keyword, but in a slightly different way to how we have seen "this" being used before. In the case of constructors, you can call one from another using the following approach.

```
public Course()
{
    this("Unnamed Course", 3, 1000.0);
}

public Course(String name, int days, double price)
{
    // initialisation code using parameters…
}
```

The use of "this(…)" calls another constructor with matching parameter arguments, so the zero arguments constructor will call the three-arguments constructor, removing the code duplication and making the class more robust in the context of future changes.

6.3.3 Internal Encapsulation in Constructors

It is important that a class should not expose its objects' state (i.e. its fields) directly to clients, so we have used private fields, encapsulated within the class, but also provided a set of "getter" and "setter" methods through which an object's state can be manipulated. Although we have not yet gone beyond simple getting and setting of field values, the implementation of these methods can protect an object's state from being made inconsistent. Because these methods may include functionality over and above the simple getting and setting of values, it is a good idea to use the getters and setters even within the class itself, as in this version of the three-arguments constructor.

```
public Course (String name, int days, double price)
{
    setName(name);
    setNumberOfDays(days);
    setPricePerPerson(price);
}
```

This internal encapsulation becomes important if, for example, we add some guard conditions to the setter methods to prevent them being set to inappropriate values. For example, we might restrict the value for the "numberOfDays" attribute to a positive integer in the range 1–10 or apply some other business rule about how many days a course should be able to last. Here is a slightly updated version of the method that ensures that the "numberOfDays" can only be set within the range 1–10. Values outside that range are ignored.

```
public void setNumberOfDays(int numberOfDays)
{
  if(numberOfDays >= 1 && numberOfDays <=10)
  {
    this.numberOfDays = numberOfDays;
  }
  else
  {
    // do not accept the parameter value
    // should probably throw an exception (see Chap. 9)
  }
}
```

By restricting our access to the "numberOfDays" field to within the setter method only, we can ensure that this conditional code is always applied when the field value is set, even from within the class itself.

Note
In this example we are simply ignoring the parameter value if it is outside the acceptable range. Unfortunately, this does not help to signal the problems to the code that sent the unacceptable value. In Chap. 9, we will see how to throw an exception if this kind of problem occurs, so that knowledge of what has happened can be propagated to other parts of the program.

6.4 Access Modifiers

As we have seen from our examples so far, access modifiers are used to control access to classes, constructors, fields and methods. As a general guideline, attributes are marked as private, and classes, constructors and methods marked as public, but this is by no means a universal rule. For example, not all methods should be public. Take a class that represents a bank account. It may have a "setAccountBalance" method. This may be useful inside the class, but it is probably not sensible to make

Table 6.1 Visibility modifiers

Visibility modifier	Meaning
Public	Visible from anywhere that has access via the classpath
Private	Accessible only within the class itself
<default> (no modifier keyword used)	Visible within the class and also throughout the package
Protected	Visible within the class, throughout the package, and to subclasses in other packages

it public. External changes to an account's current balance should only be made through a valid transaction, not arbitrarily. Therefore, we sometimes find that we write methods for internal implementation only and these will be marked as "private"

Occasionally, fields are public. There are several reasons why this might be the case. One is that they are *final* fields. Since a field marked as "final" in Java cannot be changed once its value has been set, there is no danger in exposing it as a public field. For example, the Math class (which we have used to generate a random number) has a public field called "PI" (representing the value of π), which cannot be changed. The Point class has the fields "x" and "y", which are public partly as a result of being "legacy" code from a very first version of Java, but also (due to some subsequent changes) enable us to retrieve the values of the fields as integers, when the "get" methods return them as doubles. This is an interesting variation on overloading, since normally overloading can only be done by parameter lists, not by return types. This means that we cannot differentiate two methods of the same name by the return types. The public fields in the Point class give us a kind of workaround to that issue which at least may save us from doing an unnecessary cast from a double to an int.

So far, we have only discussed "public" and "private" access, but there are four visibility modifiers in Java, including the less used (but sometimes useful) "default" and "protected" visibilities. Table 6.1 summarizes the four visibility modifiers. We will see some examples of applying the "default" and "protected" modifiers in the following chapters.

6.5 Javadoc and Code Comments

In the previous chapter, we saw how Javadoc documentation for standard Java library classes can be downloaded and linked to Eclipse. We can also use the Javadoc documentation tool to create our own documentation, since it is shipped with the JDK (you will find the "javadoc" application in the "bin" folder of the JDK installation). Documentation of your own classes will be created as set of hyperlinked HTML pages, using the same structure and formatting as the standard Javadoc. When you generate documentation with Javadoc, it extracts the basic information about classes such as the names of their fields and methods. We have already introduced the syntax for writing block comments that will be included in the Javadoc.

```
/**
 javadoc comments to explain your classes and methods
*/
```

There are a number of symbols that we can use inside these comment blocks to help increase the amount of information included in the generated Javadoc, for example, some HTML tags (such as the simple "<br/>" for a line break or "<hr/>" for a horizontal rule) and certain keywords preceded by the "@" character, including:

`@author`   (to show the author's name)
`@version`   (to show the version number of the class)
`@param`   (to give an opportunity to explain the meanings of the parameters to a method)
`@return`   (to show the return type of the method)

Most of these can be generated automatically by Eclipse where they are relevant. Simply place the cursor in an element of code and select "Generate Element Comment" from the "Source" menu. This will add a comment block and the relevant "@" tags, to which you can add additional explanatory text.

There are many other aspects of Javadoc syntax not covered here, but there is complete information available on the Oracle website.

The complete Course class follows, including several Javadoc-style comments. This detailed Javadoc style of commenting is not used beyond this chapter, but you can of course use it in all your code if you wish. Even without any of this syntax, Javadoc can create some useful documentation from your classes such as details of constructors, fields and methods.

```java
package com.foundjava.chapter6;

/**
 * The Course class represents a training course definition,
 * not an individual delivery of the course
 * @author David Parsons
 *
 */

public class Course
{
  private String name;
  private int numberOfDays;
  private double pricePerPerson;

/**
 * zero arguments constructor
 */
  public Course()
  {
    this("Unnamed Course", 3, 1000.0);
  }

/**
 * Parameterized constructor
 * @param name The name of the course
 * @param days The length of the course in days
 * @param price The cost of the course per person
 */
  public Course(String name, int days, double price)
  {
    setName(name);
    setNumberOfDays(days);
    setPricePerPerson(price);
  }

/**
 * @return The name of the course
 */
  public String getName() {
    return name;
  }

/**
 * @param name The name of the course
 */
  public void setName(String name) {
    this.name = name;
```

```
  }

/**
 * @return The length of the course
 */
  public int getNumberOfDays() {
    return numberOfDays;
  }

/**
 * @param numberOfDays The number of days the course lasts
 */
  public void setNumberOfDays(int numberOfDays) {
    if(numberOfDays >= 1 && numberOfDays <=10)
    {
      this.numberOfDays = numberOfDays;
    }
    else
    {
      // do not accept the parameter value
      // should probably throw an exception
    }
  }

/**
 * @return The price of the course per person
 */
  public double getPricePerPerson() {
    return pricePerPerson;
  }

/**
 * @param price The price of the course per person
 */
  public void setPricePerPerson(double price) {
    this.pricePerPerson = price;
  }
}
```

6.5.1 Creating Javadoc in Eclipse

To generate your own documentation from within Eclipse, you must set up the
output folder location where the files will be generated (this must be a different
location from your standard Javadoc download). To do this, select "Properties"
from the "Project" menu option on the main menu bar. This will show the
"Properties" dialog (Fig. 6.7). Select "Javadoc Location" from the list of options on
the left of the dialog, and then browse to your chosen output location to set the
"Javadoc location path". However, be careful not to choose any folders with spaces

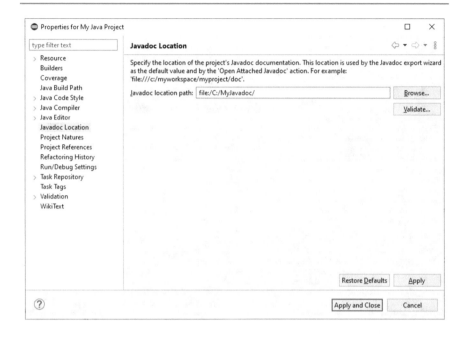

Fig. 6.7 Setting the Javadoc location in the project's "Properties" dialog

in the name or this can cause problems. You can press the "Validate" button to ensure that Javadoc can be written to that location.

To generate Javadoc, select "Generate Javadoc" from the "Project" option on the main menu bar. This will open the "Javadoc Generation" dialog (Fig. 6.8). In this dialog, you can either just click "Finish" or configure the output using this dialog and those that follow (using the "Next" button). Since you can regenerate your Javadoc as often as you like, you can always experiment with these settings and change the output configuration later if you want to.

Note
If the path to "javadoc.exe" is not automatically found by Eclipse, you will need to configure the path by pressing the "configure" button by the "Javadoc command" text field, then browse to the "javadoc.exe" file in the "bin" folder of your JDK installation.

When you click the "Finish" button on the "Generate Javadoc" dialog, the documentation will be generated in your chosen output folder. If you navigate to that folder you will be able to open the "index.html" page in a web browser. Figure 6.9 shows part of one of the HTML pages generated by Javadoc being viewed in a browser.

Fig. 6.8 The "Generate Javadoc" dialog. The Javadoc command can be found in the "bin" folder of your JDK installation

6.5.2 Running Javadoc from the Command Line

If you want to run javadoc from the command line, rather than from within Eclipse, you simply type "javadoc" at the command line followed by the name of a Java file, e.g.

```
javadoc Course.java
```

This example assumes that the Java files are in the current folder. You can generate Javadoc for all the classes in a folder by using a wildcard, for example,

```
javadoc *.java
```

You should find that the HTML pages are written by default to the same directory as your source file(s). Again, you can load the "index.html" file into a

Fig. 6.9 Sections of one of the HTML pages generated by Javadoc being viewed in a web browser

browser to see the documentation. To get the fullest information possible written by Javadoc, we can add a few options, preceded by hyphens, to the "javadoc" command, for example,

```
javadoc -private -author -version *.java
```

The first option ("-private") ensures that all attributes and methods, whether private or public, are written to the output files. The other options ("-author" and "-version") ensure that any "@author" and "@version" entries also appear in the file. To see all the possible options (there are many), simply type "javadoc" at a command prompt and they will be listed.

Exercise 6.1

- Create the Course class with its attributes, methods and constructors
- Create a separate test class with a main method that creates an instance of the class and exercises its methods
- Add a "maximumParticipants" attribute with appropriate getters and setters
- Add a new constructor that takes account of your new attribute
- Modify your "setMaximumParticipants" method to ensure the consistency of the object state
- Update your main method to test your new constructor and methods
- Generate some Javadoc for your class

6.6 Types of Method

Not all methods are just simple "getters" and "setters". Indeed, if they were, classes would be very boring. Other types of methods that are useful include calculations, more complex queries than field-related getters, and commands. Examples of calculation methods on the Course class might be calculating discounts, profit margins, etc. Course queries might relate to past or future deliveries of the course (since the Course class does not itself represent a course delivery—this would require further objects). Commands are anything of the "do this" variety, for example, a class might be asked to write its course outline to file.

Figure 6.10 shows a UML diagram that includes some possible methods for the Course class over and above its getters and setters. There is another class in this diagram, the "CourseDelivery", with some suggested fields. These two classes are associated, meaning that an object of one class can communicate directly with objects of another (this is indicated by the solid line between the two classes). The asterisk symbol means "many", i.e. one course can have many course deliveries associated with it. We will look at association in more detail in the next chapter.

Exercise 6.2
Add a new method to the Course class with this signature:

```
public double discountedCostPerPerson(int percentDiscount)
```

You do not need to add any new fields to the class to get this to work, since it only needs to base its calculation on the existing "costPerPerson" field.

This method should calculate how much it costs for a participant to enroll in the course if a special offer discount is applied. Note that it takes an "int" value as a parameter argument and returns a "double" value (calculated inside the method).

Use some code in a "main" method to try out your "discountedCostPerPerson" method and then regenerate your Javadoc.

Exercise 6.3
This is a design exercise, rather than one that asks you to do any coding. You can draw your suggestions using UML class diagrams.

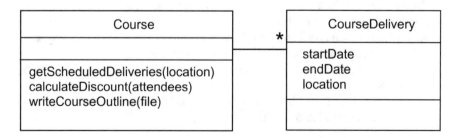

Fig. 6.10 Further methods of the Course class, and an association with many CourseDelivery objects

- What might a more complete design for the CourseDelivery class look like?
- What other attributes might it have?
- Currently the diagram in Fig. 6.10 shows no methods. What methods, apart from getters and setters, might be appropriate for a CourseDelivery?
- We have suggested the Course and CourseDelivery classes might be associated. Can you suggest other classes, that might be relevant to this domain, which could be associated with either the Course or the CourseDelivery classes?

6.7   Class Reuse

In our development of the various features of the Course class, we have seen how object-oriented programming enables us to model the real-world objects of a domain in software. Another of the advantages of encapsulation in an object-oriented language like Java is code reuse. In Chaps. 3 and 4 we saw more than one example where we simulated the throwing of a die by generating and manipulating a random number. In each case we had to repeat the same code. If we can encapsulate this code into a "Die" object, we can easily reuse it in multiple applications that require this functionality; a single Die class can be used to create many Die objects. In this section, we will look at a "Die" class that encapsulates the code for generating a random integer between 1 and 6. Inside the class, there is the implementation of a method. The signature of this method (its visibility, its return type, its name and its parameter list) is

```
public int roll()
```

From this we can see that the method has public visibility (can be accessed by any other objects), it returns an "int" value to the code that calls this method, it is called "roll", and it takes no parameter arguments (the parentheses are empty).

Inside the method, the generation of the random number and the arithmetic are the same as our previous examples of simulating the throw of a die. However, the last line of the method returns a value to the caller of the method. In this example, the value that is returned is the integer representing the value of the die. This is the complete class:

```
package com.foundjava.chapter6;

public class Die
{
  public int roll()
  {
    double randomNumber = Math.random();
    randomNumber *= 6;
    randomNumber++;
    return (int)randomNumber;
  }
}
```

Now we can create as many Die objects in client code as we like, without needing to duplicate the implementation. In this example, two Die objects are created and "thrown"

```
package com.foundjava.chapter6;

public class DiceRoller



{
  public static void main(String[] args)
  {
    Die die1 = new Die();
    Die die2 = new Die();
    int diceTotal = die1.roll() + die2.roll();
    System.out.println("Total of 2 dice is :" + diceTotal);
  }
}
```

One major advantage of encapsulating code into objects like this is that we can modify the implementation of an object's methods without affecting any of the code that uses the object provided that the behavior remains the same. We might, for example, replace the rather clumsy implementation that generates a random integer using the Math class by using the java.util.Random class instead. This class has the useful method "nextInt" which generates a random integer rather than a floating-point number, as "Math.random" does. In addition, the method can be passed a parameter to specify the upper limit of the range of random numbers to be generated. The following implementation of the Die class's "getRoll" method uses an object of the Random class to more easily generate a random integer in the range 1–6.

```
package com.foundjava.chapter6;

import java.util.Random;

public class Die {
  public int getRoll()
  {
    Random randomNumberGenerator = new Random();
    int randomNumber = randomNumberGenerator.nextInt(6) + 1;
    return randomNumber;
  }
}
```

This kind of code change, where we improve the design of a method without affecting its behavior, is known as refactoring, and is a useful technique for ensuring the quality of code is as good as it can be.

6.8 Static Fields and Methods

From the examples we have seen so far, it should be clear that we can write a class from which many different objects can be created; there is one class but there may be many objects of that class. When a Java program starts running, all the required classes for that program are loaded into memory by the Java classloader, so they can be used to create dynamic objects at runtime. However, in addition to being the source for creating objects, classes exist in their own right, and they too can have fields and methods that belong to the class, rather than the objects. The advantage of a class's fields and methods is that they can be accessed and used even if no objects of that class have been created. One context in which this is useful is in writing methods that do not need any object state in order to work. With these methods, the response would always be the same regardless of which object (of that type) received the message. In such cases, it is more appropriate for the class to have the method. This type of method is like a traditional function in a non-object-oriented language, where parameters are provided to the function and it returns a value, without needing to access any object fields.

One example could be an ExchangeRate class with methods that provide information about different currency conversions. Since this information is global, and not dependent on the state of any objects, it would reside in the class itself. An ExchangeRate class might be able to tell us, for example, the exchange rate between two different currencies without any individual ExchangeRate objects needing to be created.

A simple example of a static field from our Course example would be one that tracks how many objects of the Course class have been created. This field is much better placed in the class than in individual objects. First because it is still possible to access the field even if no objects have been created yet, and second because the value only needs to be maintained in one place, inside the class. If it was an object field, its value would have to be updated in every single object of the class, every time a new object was created.

Fields and methods that belong to the class are marked as "static". Here is a static field that could be added to the "Course" class, to count how many courses have been created. Apart from the keyword "static" it is just like declaring an object field.

```
private static int numberOfCoursesCreated = 0;
```

To make sure this value incremented when a new object is created, we could add to this value in the constructor:

```
numberOfCoursesCreated++;
```

As long as we have chained our constructors together, we should only need to do this in one place.

6.8.1   Static Methods

Static fields are usually accessed by static methods (i.e. if the field belongs to the class then so should the methods that access it). Here is an example of a static method that returns the value of the numberOfCoursesCreated field:

```
public static int getNumberOfCoursesCreated()
{
  return numberOfCoursesCreated;
}
```

Again, this is just like declaring a normal method apart from the addition of the "static" keyword. Here is part of the Course class including the static field and method and an updated constructor.

```
public class Course
{
  private static int numberOfCoursesCreated = 0;
  private String name;
  private int numberOfDays;
  private double pricePerPerson;
// constructor
  public Course(String name, int days, double price)
  {
    setName(name);
    setNumberOfDays(days);
    setPricePerPerson(price);
    numberOfCoursesCreated++;
  }
  public static int getNumberOfCoursesCreated()
  {
    return numberOfCoursesCreated;
  }
//...etc.
}
```

6.8.2 Invoking Static Methods

Static (class) methods should be invoked using the class, not an object. Note how the class name "Course" is being used here, not the name of a Course object:

```
int courses = Course.getNumberOfCoursesCreated();
```

Actually static methods can be also invoked by an object, as it does not cause a compiler error to do this, but it does not help the readability of the code so you will get a warning from Eclipse if you try it. On the other hand, you cannot invoke object methods using a class.

6.8.3 Static Final Fields

The nearest thing to a constant in Java is a static final field. The "final" keyword means that the field's value cannot be changed once it has been assigned.

We might, for example, add a static final field to the class to store the name of the training company. Since this data should not change dynamically, it is marked as final, and since there is no point repeating it in every object, it is static; it exists once in the class. Since it cannot be changed, it can be made public, since there is no need to encapsulate it behind getter and setter methods. The naming convention for constant values in Java is to use all upper case letters, using underscores as separators, as in this example:

```
public static final String COMPANY_NAME = "Mega awesome corp";
```

6.8.4 Static Methods in Java Library Classes

This may be a good time to reflect on the fact that the "main" method is marked as "static". Therefore, it is a method that belongs to the class that contains it. We have also seen the Math class being used to invoke methods directly, i.e.:

```
Math.random();
```

You should be able to see from this code that "random" is a static method; it is being invoked directly on the class rather than on an object. We never instantiate an object of the Math class because in fact all its methods are static (you can see this if you look at the Javadoc for the class). You could not create an object of the Math class even if you wanted to, because its constructor is marked as "private".

The String class also has several static methods, including "valueOf". This method takes a Java primitive type as a parameter and returns it as a String, i.e.

```
String aString = String.valueOf(value);
```

For example, it can convert a double to a String:

```
double realNumber = 3.1417;
String doubleString = String.valueOf(realNumber);
```

There are many different versions of "valueOf" because it is overloaded to work with all the primitive Java data types and is used by System.out.println when it displays primitive types:

```
System.out.println(3.1417);
// the double is implicitly converted to a String
// using String.valueOf
```

While we are on the subject of "System.out.println", it has an example of a public static field. "out" is actually a public static field of the System class (an object of the PrintStream class), and "println" is a method of that object.

From these few examples, you can see that static fields and methods are frequently used in Java.

Exercise 6.4

- Add a static method to your Course class that calculates the cost per head of a custom course that is charged at a flat rate, rather than per head
- Pass the flat rate and the number of participants to the method and return the cost per head
- Add a constant to your Course class that contains the name of the training company
- Display the value of the constant in your test code
- Update your test class to exercise your changes

6.9 Objects as Java Bean Components

In this final section, we will take a brief look at some of the simpler aspects of writing objects as components. The debate about the differences between objects and components can get very complicated, but the simplest definition of a component is that it is an object that can be "plugged-in" to an application such as a visual programming tool or a dynamic web page builder. For this to work, it must be easy for the application to "understand" the component. One simple way in which we can do this is to follow some standard naming patterns for our object methods. The rules for writing Java objects as components are described in the "JavaBeans" specification. The specification states that *"A Java Bean is a reusable software component that can be manipulated visually in a builder tool"*. Although the full specification is quite complex, it is useful to follow some of its more basic rules to make our classes more tool friendly.

The simple Die object from earlier in this chapter has a method that was named descriptively as "roll". Although this method name is expressive to the programmer, it does not follow a standard naming convention. This would make it difficult for a programming tool or other object environment to make assumptions about what the purpose of this method might be. One of the many aspects of a JavaBean is that it supports *properties*, and it is this aspect that we will explore here. Property related rules are:

- JavaBeans have properties that are defined by methods.
- A property is readable if it has a matching "get*Propertyname*" method.
- A property is writeable if it has a matching "set*Propertyname*" method.
- Readable Boolean properties can be defined by a method beginning with "is", rather than (or in addition to) a method beginning with "get".
- A property is not necessarily an attribute.

What do we mean by a property having a matching method? These relate to a standard way of writing method names. The name of a property is taken to be the name that follows "get" or "set" in the method name, where the first letter of the property is in lower case. For example, let us take the example of the Course class with its generated getters and setters. These follow the rules for JavaBean properties. The course class has readable and writeable properties called "name", "numberOfDays" and "pricePerPerson". An important point to make here is that the property name is determined entirely by the method names, not by the actual name of an internal field. If the field of the class was called "courseName" instead of "name" it would not make any difference to the name of the property. Returning to the Die class, the roll of the Die is not a JavaBean property (in terms of the specification) because the method does not begin with "get" or "set". To turn the Die into a basic JavaBean we need to rename "roll" to "getRoll". This should make it clear that a property is not a field; the Die class has no fields, but "roll" is a readable property (though not a writable one, since there is no "setRoll" method).

Note
You should be aware that some JavaBean environments (e.g. JavaServer Pages) require that a bean class has a zero arguments constructor, though this is not enforced by the specification. Further, although a Boolean property can be expressed by an "is…" method, there are some tools into which a bean may be put that do not use the "is" form of readable property and always use "get".

6.9.1 Reflection

What, then, is the purpose of following JavaBeans rules such as the property naming patterns that we have looked at? The reason is that it allows tools to "introspect" on JavaBean components and understand what certain methods are for. To do this, they use various forms of "reflection", which is the ability to get metadata (data about data) from a Java class. Java supports reflection with the "java. lang.reflect" package. We will look at one or two very simple aspects of reflection in order to demonstrate how JavaBean naming patterns can assist programming environments to find out about classes.

The first thing we can do is ask an object about its class. This is achieved using the "getClass" method, which returns an object of type java.lang.Class, e.g.

```
Class courseClass = javaCourse.getClass();
```

Note

You will get a warning from the compiler on this line. This is related to the use of generics, which we will cover in Chap. 12. In the meantime, you can safely ignore this warning.

Once we have access to the Class object, it has a range of methods that will tell us about the class. For example, we can use the "getName" method to tell us the fully qualified name of the class, or "getSimpleName" to get only the name of class, without the package name:

```
String fullClassName = courseClass.getName();
String simpleClassName = courseClass.getSimpleName();
```

We can get an array of all the methods that are declared in the class with "getDeclaredMethods", which returns an array of java.lang.reflect.Method objects.

```
Method[] methods = courseClass.getDeclaredMethods();
```

By calling "getName" on all the Method objects we can find out what all the methods are called:

```
for(int i = 0; i < methods.length; i++)
{
   System.out.println(methods[i].getName());
}
```

This example demonstrates some simple reflection on an object of the Course class (note the necessary import of the "Method" class from the "java.lang.reflect" package):

```
package com.foundjava.chapter6;

import java.lang.reflect.Method;

public class CourseReflection
{
  public static void main(String[] args)
  {
    Course myCourse = new Course("Agile Methods", 5, 20000.0);
    Class courseClass = myCourse.getClass();
    Method[] methods = courseClass.getDeclaredMethods();
    System.out.println(courseClass.getName() + " methods:");
    for (int i = 0; i < methods.length; i++)
    {
      System.out.println(methods[i].getName());
    }
  }
}
```

The output from this program is

```
com.foundjava.chapter6.Course methods:
getName
setName
getPricePerPerson
getNumberOfDays
setNumberOfDays
setPricePerPerson
getNumberOfCoursesCreated
```

The important point to note here is that a software tool can use these types of methods to find out about your class, and if you have followed JavaBean conventions such as property naming patterns then the tool knows about the properties of your objects. From the list of method names above, it would be able to infer that "numberOfDays", "pricePerPerson" and "name" are properties and it would know which ones were readable and which were writeable. One very useful application of JavaBeans with properties is that they can be used in JavaServer Pages (JSPs) to create dynamic content on web pages using special XML tags.

Exercise 6.5
Write a "Coin" class that encapsulates the code to simulate the throwing of a coin. The class should include a "getFace" method that returns either "heads" or "tails".

Exercise 6.6
The ancient Chinese "book of change" (the *I Ching*, pronounced "yee jing") describes a method of divination using 50 yarrow stalks. For those who do not have 50 yarrow stalks handy, 3 coins can be used instead. Write a class with a main method that simulates the flipping of 3 coins and displays the kind of hexagram line that they represent. This will be one of the following:

Three heads	Old Yang line	---- o ----
Three tails	Old Yin line	---- x ----
Two heads and a tail	Young Yang line	----------
Two tails and a head	Young Yin line	---- ----

Hold the Coin objects in an array.

Use appropriate Unicode characters to display the correct hexagram line as well as the name.

Exercise 6.7

A complete I Ching hexagram consists of six hexagram lines. Extend your answer to the previous exercise so that it displays a complete hexagram. Encapsulate your code inside a "Hexagram" class. This class should include a method to display a complete hexagram.

6.10   The "var" Keyword

The "var" keyword was added in Java 10. It is not the same as the use of "var" in loosely typed languages such as JavaScript or Python, where the type of the data or object referenced by a variable can change over time. Java remains a statically typed language, where the type of a variable or reference cannot be changed after declaration. In Java, "var" can only be used for local variable type inference, which means that we can declare local variables within a method without specifying their type. The actual type is inferred by the compiler from the data or object that the variable is referencing. For example, instead of creating a local variable like this:

```
String helloString = "Hello";
```

We could write

```
var helloString = "Hello";
```

"var" can only be applied to local variables, not fields or method signatures. To give a very simple, example of using "var" in a method, we might consider the following version of the "getRoll" method from the "Die" class:

```
public int getRoll()
{
   var randomNumberGenerator = new Random();
   var randomNumber = randomNumberGenerator.nextInt(6) + 1;
   return randomNumber;
}
```

Instead of "Random" and "int" being stated as the data types of the two local variables, they are both declared as "var". The compiler can infer that "randomNumberGenerator" is a Random object because of the call to the constructor.

Similarly, it can infer that "randomNumber" is an "int" because that is the return type of the "nextInt" method. A similar change can be made to the "main" method that uses a "Die" object

```
public static void main(String[] args)
{
  var die1 = new Die();
  var die2 = new Die();
  var diceTotal = die1.getRoll() + die2.getRoll();
  System.out.println("Total of 2 dice is :" + diceTotal);
}
```

So, what is the point of "var"? In essence, it is a readability mechanism. In some cases, having to refer to the type of an object when creating it can make code rather wordy and complex, and using "var" can make code more readable. It also acts as a cue to programmers to ensure that they name their variables clearly so that others reading the code do not lose any meaningful information.

One small thing to note is that although this section title refers to "var" as a keyword, it is more accurately a "reserved type name". This may seem like a subtle distinction, but it means that any legacy code that uses "var" as the name of a variable, method, or package will not be affected when upgrading to versions of Java that support "var".

Exercise 6.8
Look at the code you have written in the exercises for this chapter and see if there are local variables that could have their type declarations replaced with "var", for example, your hexagram code from Exercises 6.6 and 6.7.

6.11   Summary

This chapter opened with some discussion of object-oriented concepts such as information hiding and the encapsulation of state and behavior inside objects. This was followed by an illustration of how classes and their fields and methods are represented in the Unified Modeling Language (UML) . Subsequent code examples showed how new domain classes can be created in Java, along with their fields, methods and constructors, and how Eclipse provides automated support for some of these tasks. The overloading of the constructor method to provide ways of creating objects with different sets of arguments was also explained. Further discussion of encapsulation covered constructor chaining and the four visibility modifiers; "public", "private", "default" and "protected". At the end of the previous chapter, Javadoc code documentation was introduced. In this chapter, we saw that the Javadoc tool can be used to generate HTML documentation for our own classes, either from within Eclipse or from the command line. We also saw some of the special Javadoc tags that can be added to comment blocks to provide additional information in the generated Javadoc. The final part of the chapter explored more specific aspects of creating classes including static fields and methods, JavaBean components, reflection and the "var" keyword, which can be used with local variables to allow the compiler to infer their data types.

Objects Working Together: Association, Aggregation and Composition

7

Many objects can be seen as being made up of smaller objects. For example, a clock is made up of a number of components that together combine to make the whole object. The combination of objects may exist in many layers, with a larger component (such as the mechanism) being itself made up of a collection of smaller components. Figure 7.1 shows a mechanical clock as a combination of component parts.

Both *aggregation* and *composition* are terms that describe objects that are made up of other objects, but we can make some distinctions between these terms. Composition is simply a type of object relationship where the whole object and its component parts have a very close relationship such that all the objects are totally interdependent, for example, by having a *lifetime dependency*. This means that the lifetimes of the component parts are tied to the lifetime of the whole object. For example, the component parts of a mobile phone are usually discarded/recycled when the phone itself reaches the end of its useful life. Another way of thinking about composition is that the components are only accessible through the external interface of the composition, not independently, such as using the processor of a computer when the whole computer is being used. The processor would not be used in isolation. Where the components have no independent role outside a particular grouping, then we can describe this as a composition. In terms of the clock, we might regard the clock and its mechanical components as a composition, but the relationship between the clock and its battery as a looser aggregation relationship, since although the battery can be part of the clock it could also exist in another context. We might make a similar comparison using the example of a mobile phone. Subscriber Identity Module (SIM) or memory cards can be used in a phone but can also be taken out and used in other devices, so they are aggregated in the phone but are not part of a composition. Sometimes in designing object relationships it is useful to consider this distinction as it can affect the way we implement our classes.

© Springer Nature Switzerland AG 2020
D. Parsons, *Foundational Java*, Texts in Computer Science,
https://doi.org/10.1007/978-3-030-54518-5_7

Fig. 7.1 An object may be
made up of smaller
component objects

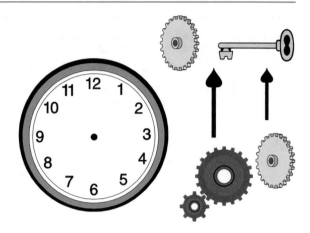

7.1 Aggregations as Collections

Composition relationships are very stable. In contrast, we often find that some aggregated objects are gathered together in much more dynamic and unstructured collections. Traffic jams, bus queues and jumble sales are examples of situations where objects are grouped together in rather transient and informal ways. Such collections generally appear in some kind of context; a road, a bus shelter, a church hall, which act as containers for the collections of objects. More specific examples of containers might be shopping trolleys, buses, vans, etc. In the world around us, objects are frequently in containers, perhaps at more than one level. For example, snacks may be put into small packets that are then put into large bags that are put into cardboard boxes that are then put into a container that is then put into the hold of a ship (Fig. 7.2)

The UML provides some different syntax for aggregation and composition so we can represent one or the other in design diagrams. Figure 7.3 shows the symbols for composition (a filled diamond) and aggregation (an empty diamond). In this design, we imply that a view is an aggregation of some shapes, but the shapes' lifetimes do not depend on the view, and they may be accessed by other objects directly. On the other hand, a shape is a composition of a series of points that together define the locations related to the shape (e.g. the corners of a polygon). Since these points only make sense in the context of a particular shape, their lifetimes linked to that of the shape, and they are only accessible through the shape object, not directly.

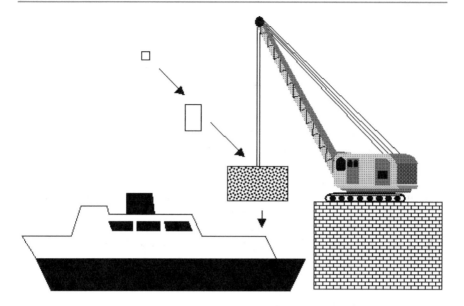

Fig. 7.2 Containers have other objects inside them, which may in turn contain other objects

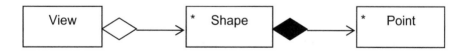

Fig. 7.3 Aggregation and composition symbols in the UML

7.2 Message Passing

In the real world, people and objects constantly interact. For example, we interact with clocks; we wind them up, set their alarms, change their batteries, reset their times and interact with them in many other ways. Parts of the clocks themselves also interact, for example, when an alarm is triggered by a particular time being reached by the clock. In object-oriented design, we call people who interact with objects "actors" and call the relationships between interacting objects "associations". We talk about objects "passing messages" to each other. Without these kinds of connections between objects, they serve no useful purpose, like a clock in the loft.

7.2.1   Object Association

Aggregation and composition are specific types of association. An association is simply a mechanism for objects of different classes (or even of the same class) to communicate with each other. Associations may be one-to-one (one object of a class is associated with one other object of a class), one-to-many (one object associates with many other objects of a class) or many to many (many objects of a class associate with many other objects of a class). Objects that work alone do not produce very useful systems. An object-oriented program consists of many objects collaborating to produce the required system behavior, as we saw with the example of the Course and CourseDelivery classes in the last chapter, when objects of these different classes were linked with one another through an association. In the preceding chapters we created some classes and tested them individually, but this is not enough to build an application that comprises multiple objects. In this chapter, we will see how a system can be made up of different objects that associate with one another.

7.2.2   Association Direction

Associations describe the relationships between objects of different classes (or indeed between different objects of the same class). These associations may be implemented either in one direction only or in both directions. A clock might, for example, associate with a calendar object. Messages might pass from the clock to the calendar every 24 h, to tell the calendar to change at midnight. Other messages might pass in the opposite direction, so that the calendar might tell the clock when to move an hour forward or back when the clocks change on a specific date (Fig. 7.4).

In the UML, an association that is not drawn with an arrowhead is assumed to be bidirectional (implemented in both directions). In Fig. 7.3, the associations have arrow heads showing the direction of the association; these are unidirectional associations (implemented in one direction only). Figure 7.5 shows a class diagram of

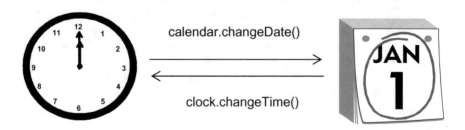

calendar.changeDate()

clock.changeTime()

Fig. 7.4   Messages might pass in both directions between a calendar and a clock

Fig. 7.5 Clock and Calendar have a bidirectional, one to one association

a Clock and a Diary class having a bidirectional association. Where no cardinality symbol is used (e.g. the "*" to mean "many") the association is assumed to be one-to-one; one Clock object associates with one Diary object.

7.2.3 Implementing Associations

So far, we have been talking about object-oriented concepts from a design perspective, but there comes a point where we must start talking specifically about how objects in software work. When we implement associations in Java code, this means that objects of one class will have fields referencing other objects. As a simple example, we will return to the Course class and its associations. So far, we have suggested that a Course may associate with many CourseDelivery objects. A CourseDelivery may associate with a single Location, where a CourseDelivery takes place (Fig. 7.6). Note that in this case we assume the associations are in one direction only. Unidirectional associations are easier to implement and maintain than bidirectional associations so are generally preferable from a coding perspective.

In terms of code, the Course would need to have a field that references many CourseDelivery objects. The best way to do this would be to use one of the Collection classes we cover later in this book, but in the meantime with the syntax we already know, we could implement this one-to-many association using an array. Note the naming convention; a field that references many objects is given a plural name, "deliveries" in this example:

```
public class Course
{
  private CourseDelivery[] deliveries;
  // can be created in the constructor
  ...
```

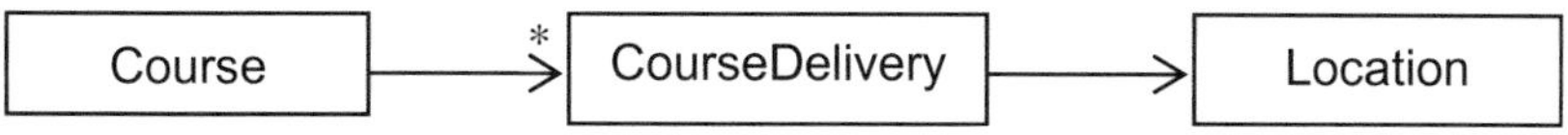

Fig. 7.6 Associations between Course, CourseDelivery and Location classes

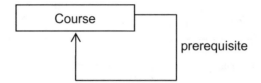

Fig. 7.7 An association between different objects of the Course class

The CourseDelivery class would have a field referencing a single Location object (this is a one-to-one association).

```
public class CourseDelivery
{
  private Location location;
// can be created in the constructor
```

Occasionally we need an association between objects of the same class. For example, a Course may have another Course as a prerequisite. In UML we would draw the association from the Course class back to itself (Fig. 7.7).

In terms of code, this simply means the Course class having a field referencing another Course:

```
public class Course
{
  private Course prerequisite;
```

7.3 Associating Objects: The Snakes and Ladders Game

In the following example we will see how several associations, including compositions, are implemented in a simulated game of Snakes and Ladders. It shows how various objects (game board, snakes, ladders, die, etc.) come together to produce a program. Snakes and Ladders (similar to the Chutes and Ladders game in the USA) is a traditional British game, derived from a much older Indian game, based on a board of 100 squares, some of which are connected by snakes or ladders (Fig. 7.8).

Players start on square 1, then throw a die to move counters in a zigzag fashion along each row of the board, moving up when they reach the end of a line. If they land on the head of a snake, then they must move down to its tail, and if they land at the foot of a ladder they can move to its head. The first player to land exactly on square 100 is the winner.

Note
These rules may be obvious to you but using this example with a multicultural class proved to me that it is not obvious to everyone!

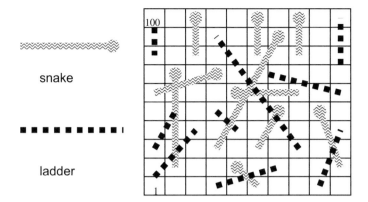

Fig. 7.8 A Snakes and Ladders board

The most important aspect of this example is that it is the first program we have seen that includes several types of object that we define ourselves. In previous examples we have seen programs that used various Java classes (String, Date) etc., or objects of our own classes, but so far we have not created objects of different classes of our own making and enabled them to communicate with one another. In Snakes and Ladders we will write six new classes and reuse the Die class from the previous chapter.

An example like this gives us the opportunity to consider some design decisions, in particular, deciding where responsibilities should lie. It is important in an object-oriented design to put responsibilities in the "best" class. Of course sometimes the "best" design is just a matter of opinion, there are many different ways to design a system, but one of the main guidelines for object-oriented design is to avoid having some objects that just contain data, and others that do all the process flow management. It is much better if data and processes are distributed through the classes in the place where they best fit. In the snakes and ladders game there are some objects that will need to be created, namely:

- GameBoard
- PlayerPiece
- BoardSquare
- Snake
- Ladder
- Die

And of course, there will also need to be an object to represent the game itself.

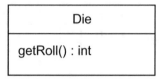

Fig. 7.9 The Die class as a UML diagram, specifying the return type of the "getRoll" method

Note
Some of the design decisions made in this example are not ideal, because we have not yet covered enough Java syntax to take full advantage of the coding options available.

The main design decision we must make is what responsibilities these objects should have. The obvious place to start is the Die class, since we already created this class in the last chapter. The job of a Die is to be rolled, a responsibility it already implements through the "getRoll" method (Fig. 7.9). This example of a class diagram also shows the type of the value returned from the method, in this case an int.

What about the PlayerPiece? We could keep track of which piece is on which square using the BoardSquare, or even the game itself, but the PlayerPiece needs some meaningful behavior if it is to have a useful role in the application, so we will give the PlayerPiece the responsibility of knowing which BoardSquare it currently occupies. Figure 7.10 shows the association between a PlayerPiece and a BoardSquare. The arrowhead on the association shows the direction of the association (i.e. a PlayerPiece has a reference to a BoardSquare object). To be able to have some way of differentiating separate PlayerPieces, they have a "color" field (this will have getters and setters, not shown here as they are not interesting behaviors). There are also getters and setters for the "currentPosition" field. These have been included in the diagram, to make it clear that there is also a "moveTo" method. Both "moveTo" and "setCurrentPosition" take a BoardSquare as a

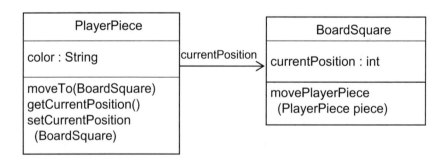

Fig. 7.10 The PlayerPiece class associated with its current BoardSquare

parameter, so what is the difference? This is just one way of designing the solution, but in this implementation the "setCurrentPosition" method is the first step in the process of moving the PlayerPiece, and the "moveTo" method is the optional next step. This is because moving a PlayerPiece can be a two-stage process; the initial move to the next square based on the throw of the die, and then the possible move up a ladder or down a snake.

PlayerPieces know which BoardSquare they are on, but BoardSquares also need to know where they are on the overall GameBoard. In our implementation we will use an array so the BoardSquare has a "currentPosition" field that contains an int, representing the index of the array that the BoardSquare occupies. It is also able to move a player piece to its own current position. The "movePlayerPiece" method takes a PlayerPiece as a parameter argument (Fig. 7.10). This is not a long-term association, just a transient relationship while the piece is moved.

How about the Snake and Ladder classes? These are quite interesting from a design perspective because they are very similar. In fact, they could be modeled as a single class that links two squares together; whether they take the player "up" or "down" on the board does not really make any difference to the implementation. However, from the perspective of trying to make the code readable and understandable, it may be better to stick with two separate classes, at least for now (Fig. 7.11).

The key aspect of the constructors of both classes is that the two BoardSquares that define the ends of the snake or ladder are passed to the constructor, so that as soon as a Snake or Ladder exists it knows where it fits on the board. Like the BoardSquare, the Snake and Ladder classes have a "movePlayerPiece" method. This is because, as previously described, a player's move may consist of two steps. First, they move to the next board square based on their throw of the die. Then they may need to be moved again, if they have landed on the head of a snake or the foot of a ladder.

What do we do about the relationship between Snakes, Ladders and BoardSquares? A BoardSquare needs to know if it contains the head of a snake, or the foot of a ladder (though it does not need to know if it has the tail of a snake or the head

Fig. 7.11 The Snake and Ladder classes

Snake
Snake(BoardSquare, BoardSquare) movePlayerPiece(PlayerPiece)

Ladder
Ladder(BoardSquare, BoardSquare) movePlayerPiece(PlayerPiece)

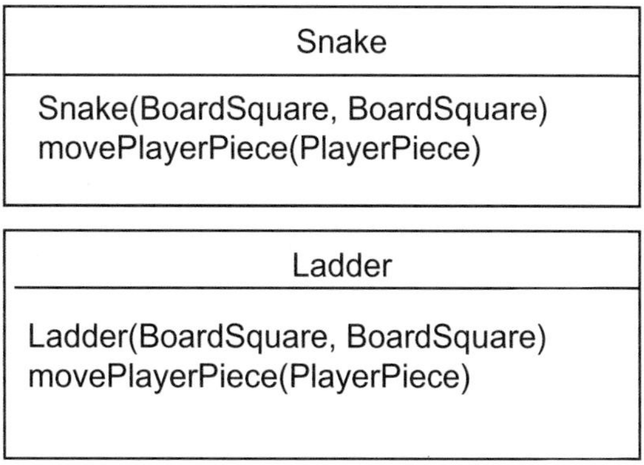

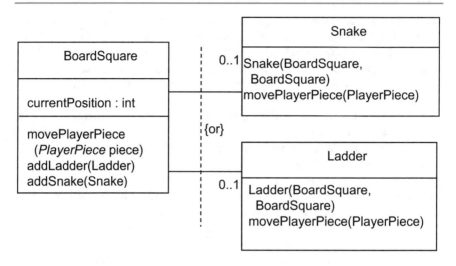

Fig. 7.12 The BoardSquare class and its optional association with either a Snake or a Ladder

of a ladder because these do not cause the PlayerPiece to move again). Therefore, we add methods to the BoardSquare class to add either a Snake or a Ladder (Fig. 7.12). This part of the design also shows some of the "multiplicity" of the associations, which indicate how many objects are involved in each association. The multiplicity "0.1" means that there can be either zero or one objects in the association. The "{or}" constraint, indicated by a dashed line across the two associations from square to snake and square to ladder, means that we cannot have both a snake and a ladder on any one square.

The next component to look at is the GameBoard class, which represents the overall Snakes and Ladders board, comprising 100 BoardSquares (Fig. 7.13). The GameBoard always starts the process of moving a PlayerPiece with its own "movePlayerPiece" method.

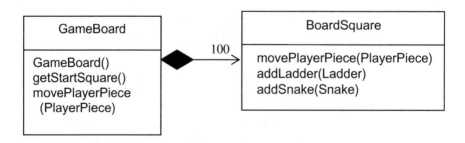

Fig. 7.13 The GameBoard class, a composition of 100 BoardSquares

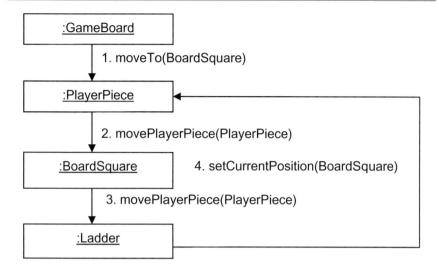

Fig. 7.14 UML collaboration diagram showing object interactions in the Snakes and Ladders game

All the diagrams we have been using so far represent static class relationships. However, Fig. 7.14 is a dynamic UML collaboration/communication diagram that indicates one possible sequence of message passing between objects. In these diagrams, which show objects rather than classes, an object is indicated by underlining the class name and preceding it with a colon. If the object has a specific name it can appear before the colon, but this can be omitted. This figure helps to explain how the various messages pass between the objects we have looked at so far when a PlayerPiece is moved and lands, in this example, on a BoardSquare containing the foot of a Ladder. First, the GameBoard tells the PlayerPiece to move itself to a BoardSquare. The BoardSquare then checks if it has a snake or a ladder. If it does (as in Fig. 7.14, where it has a ladder) it triggers that object to move the PlayerPiece to its final position for this move.

Finally, the SnakesAndLadders class acts as the program entry point, and creates the GameBoard and the PlayerPieces (Fig. 7.15). It has a "main" method that creates an instance of the class and triggers the "play" method. This handles the main game loop that iterates until the game is over.

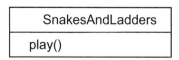

Fig. 7.15 The SnakesAndLadders class

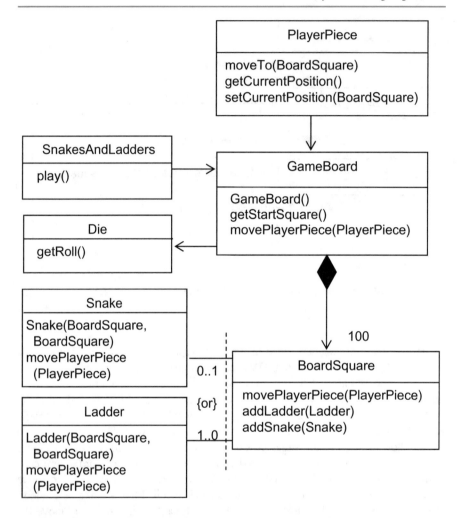

Fig. 7.16 UML class diagram showing the classes, methods and associations in the snakes and ladders program

Figure 7.16 shows the complete set of classes in the snakes and ladders game with their associations and public methods.

7.3.1 The Snakes and Ladders Game Source Code

In this section, we will run through the source code of the various classes in the Snakes and Ladders game. However, we will begin with a brief explanation of why most of these classes and methods are not marked as having "public" visibility.

7.3.1.1 Package Visibility

Classes that are not declared public have "package" visibility, so cannot be accessed from outside their package. This is appropriate where these classes do not have any role beyond the specific programming context in which they are being used. Consider the difference between the Die and Snake classes. A Die may be used in any number of game programs, so it was useful to make the class public so that other classes could easily reuse it across other packages. In contrast, the Snake class is totally tied to the game of Snakes and Ladders. It has no realistic chance of reuse outside this specific program so there is no need to make it a public class. In fact, none of the classes that are part of the snakes and ladders game are reusable in other contexts, so none need to be made public. The only public class is SnakesAndLadders so that it can be accessed and played from other places. If a class has package visibility, then it makes sense that its methods and constructors also have package visibility, unless they have "private" visibility.

Note

If you are working outside an IDE like Eclipse, you can put multiple non-public classes into the same source file, though there can be only one public class. The file name would match the name of the public class

7.3.1.2 The Snake and Ladder Classes

The Snake and Ladder objects need to be positioned on the board, so they can be referenced by the BoardSquares that they are placed on and reference the other BoardSquare that they point to. To set the position of a snake, there is a parameterized constructor that takes the head and tail positions as arguments:

```
Snake(BoardSquare head, BoardSquare tail) {
  setTail(tail);
  head.addSnake(this);
}
```

The reference to the tail of the snake is stored as a field, because the snake needs to be able to move a player piece to the square it ends at. However, there is no need to store a reference to the head, since this is kept by the BoardSquare (this is a bidirectional association). We set this reference by calling the BoardSquare's "addSnake" method, passing "this" snake as a parameter. This is a common way of passing references between objects. Similarly, the Ladder constructor stores the top of the ladder and passes itself back to the BoardSquare that contains its foot:

```
Ladder(BoardSquare top, BoardSquare foot) {
  setTop(top);
  foot.addLadder(this);
}
```

In both cases we omit the "public" prefix because the class itself is not public, so the constructor could not be called from outside its package anyway.

Apart from their constructors, the only other methods of Snake and Ladder are private getter and setter methods to manage the positions of the head/top or tail/foot. The lines of code that print to the console are only there in this example so that we can see what is going on when it runs—not something we would normally do in production code. This is the complete Snake class.

```
package com.foundjava.chapter7;

class Snake
{
  private BoardSquare tail;

  Snake(BoardSquare head, BoardSquare tail)
  {
    setTail(tail);
    head.addSnake(this);
  }

  private void setTail(BoardSquare tail)
  {
    this.tail = tail;
  }

  private BoardSquare getTail()
  {
    return tail;
  }

  void movePlayerPiece(PlayerPiece counter)
  {
    System.out.println("Down the snake to " +
      getTail().getPosition());
    counter.setCurrentPosition(getTail());
  }
}
```

The Ladder class is very similar

```
package com.foundjava.chapter7;

class Ladder
{
  private BoardSquare top;

  Ladder(BoardSquare top, BoardSquare foot)
  {
    setTop(top);
    foot.addLadder(this);
  }

  private void setTop(BoardSquare top)
  {
    this.top = top;
  }

  private BoardSquare getTop()
  {
    return top;
  }

  void movePlayerPiece(PlayerPiece counter)
  {
    System.out.println("Up the ladder to " +
    getTop().getPosition());
    counter.setCurrentPosition(getTop());
  }
}
```

7.3.1.3 The BoardSquare Class

The BoardSquare class might look rather odd with this design approach. This is because it is a class that needs to represent three different types of square:

1. A square with a snake's head
2. A square with a ladder's foot
3. A square with no snakes or ladders.

So that it can fulfill all three roles, each BoardSquare object contains references to both a Snake and a Ladder so that either can be placed on a particular square. There are also methods to add snakes or ladders and private methods to check if a snake or a ladder is present. The class also keeps track of the position of the BoardSquare in the array that represents the overall GameBoard. The main responsibility of an object of this class is to move a PlayerPiece to "this" BoardSquare, and possibly move it again along a Snake or a Ladder.

```
class BoardSquare
{
// we may use one or neither of these references
// for a particular square
  private Snake aSnake = null;
  private Ladder aLadder = null;
  private int position;

  BoardSquare(int position) {
    setPosition(position);
  }

  int getPosition() {
    return position;
  }

  private void setPosition(int position) {
    this.position = position;
  }

// we may want to add a snake head
  void addSnake(Snake s) {
    aSnake = s;
  }

// or add the foot of a ladder
  public void addLadder(Ladder l) {
    aLadder = l;
  }

// methods to find out if the square has a snake or a ladder
  private boolean hasSnake() {
    return null != aSnake;
  }

  private boolean hasLadder() {
    return null != aLadder;
  }

  public void movePlayerPiece(PlayerPiece counter) {
    counter.setCurrentPosition(this);
    if (hasSnake()) {
```

```
      aSnake.movePlayerPiece(counter);
    }
    if (hasLadder()) {
      aLadder.movePlayerPiece(counter);
    }
  }
}
```

You will notice that there is no error check here to ensure that a given square does not have both a snake and a ladder. This can be addressed by different design approaches that we will cover in the next chapter.

7.3.1.4   The GameBoard Class

The board has two major responsibilities:

1. To set up the squares that make up the board by creating them and adding snakes and ladders as appropriate. This is done according to the board layout shown in Table 7.1.
2. To start each move of a PlayerPiece by "rolling" the die and calling the "moveTo" method

Sometimes a method expects to be passed an object as a parameter. Where does this object come from? In many cases, the object will already have a reference in another part of a program, so its reference can simply be passed to the method. In other cases, the object will not necessarily need to exist anywhere else before it is needed by the method. The way that Snakes and Ladders are created here is to call "new" without a separate object reference, and the constructor implementation passes "this" snake or ladder to one of the BoardSquares passed as a constructor parameter. In this example the BoardSquare "squares[1]" will have a reference to the Ladder, and the Ladder will have a reference to BoardSquare "squares[38]":

```
new Ladder(squares[38], squares[1]);
```

This is the complete GameBoard class. Note how it begins by importing the Die class from another package:

Table 7.1   The positions of the snakes and ladders on the board

Ladders									
From:	1	4	9	21	28	36	51	71	80
To:	38	14	31	42	84	44	67	91	100
Snakes									
From:	16	47	49	56	62	64	87	93	95	98
To:	6	26	11	53	19	60	24	73	75	78

```
package com.foundjava.chapter7;
import com.foundjava.chapter6.Die;


class GameBoard
{
  private BoardSquare[] squares;
  private Die die;
// the array will be one square bigger than needed so that we
// can start from array element 1, ignoring element 0
  static final int MAX_SQUARES = 100;
  static final int START_SQUARE = 1;

// the constructor creates the squares and adds the
// snakes and ladders
  GameBoard()
  {
    die = new Die();
    squares = new BoardSquare[START_SQUARE + MAX_SQUARES];
    for (int i = START_SQUARE; i <= MAX_SQUARES; i++)
    {
// add the next Square object to the board
      squares[i] = new BoardSquare(i);
    }

// add the ladders
    new Ladder(squares[38], squares[1]);
    new Ladder(squares[14], squares[4]);
    new Ladder(squares[31], squares[9]);
    new Ladder(squares[42], squares[21]);
    new Ladder(squares[84], squares[28]);
    new Ladder(squares[44], squares[36]);
    new Ladder(squares[67], squares[51]);
    new Ladder(squares[91], squares[71]);
    new Ladder(squares[100], squares[80]);

// add the snakes
    new Snake(squares[16], squares[6]);
    new Snake(squares[47], squares[26]);
    new Snake(squares[49], squares[11]);
    new Snake(squares[56], squares[53]);
    new Snake(squares[62], squares[19]);
    new Snake(squares[64], squares[60]);
    new Snake(squares[87], squares[24]);
    new Snake(squares[93], squares[73]);
    new Snake(squares[95], squares[75]);
    new Snake(squares[98], squares[78]);
```

```
    }

  BoardSquare getStartSquare()
  {
    return squares[START_SQUARE];
  }
// this method adjusts the counter position
  void movePlayerPiece(PlayerPiece counter)
  {
    BoardSquare current = counter.getCurrentPosition();
    int nextPosition = current.getPosition() + die.roll();
    if(nextPosition > MAX_SQUARES)
    {
      System.out.println(
  "Sorry you need to land exactly on the last square to win!");
    }
    else
    {
      counter.moveTo(squares[nextPosition]);
    }
    System.out.println(counter.getColor() + " counter on " +
      counter.getCurrentPosition().getPosition());
  }
}
```

7.3.1.5   The Snakes and Ladders Class

This class simulates the playing of the game, and in this example is confined to creating a single PlayerPiece and moving it inside a "while" loop until it reaches square 100. This class and its methods are public, so objects of this class can be created and used from code in other packages.

```
public class SnakesAndLadders
{
// reference to the GameBoard
  private GameBoard board;
// the constructor creates the Board
  public SnakesAndLadders()
  {
    board = new GameBoard();
  }
// this method acts as a controller for playing the game
  public void play()
  {
    PlayerPiece counter = new PlayerPiece("Red");
    counter.setCurrentPosition(board.getStartSquare());
// iterate until we reach the end (square 100)
    while(counter.getCurrentPosition().getPosition()
```

```
        < GameBoard.MAX_SQUARES)
    {
          board.movePlayerPiece(counter);
    }
    System.out.println(counter.getColor() +
      " counter finished on " +
      counter.getCurrentPosition().getPosition());
  }
// 'main' creates a 'SnakesAndLadders' object and
// starts the game
  public static void main(String[] args)
  {
    SnakesAndLadders myGame = new SnakesAndLadders();
    myGame.play();
  }
}
```

Of course, every time we play the game the output will be different. Here is one example:

```
Up the ladder to 14
Red counter on 14
Red counter on 15
Down the snake to 6
Red counter on 6
Red counter on 11
Red counter on 17
Red counter on 20
Red counter on 24
Red counter on 30
Up the ladder to 44
Red counter on 44
Down the snake to 26
Red counter on 26
Red counter on 30
Red counter on 32
Red counter on 37
Red counter on 39
Red counter on 44
Red counter on 48
Up the ladder to 67
Red counter on 67
Up the ladder to 91
Red counter on 91
Red counter on 94
Red counter on 97
Sorry you need to land exactly on the last square to win!
Red counter on 97
Red counter on 100
Red counter finished on 100
```

7.3.2 When to Create Objects

Before leaving this example, we will briefly reflect on the difference between creating objects where they are declared as fields and creating them in a constructor. Take this part of the SnakesAndLadders class, where the GameBoard reference is declared as a field, but the object itself is created in the constructor.

```
// reference to the GameBoard
private GameBoard board;
// the constructor creates the Board
public SnakesAndLadders()
{
  board = new GameBoard();
}
```

We could have created the object where it was declared as a field, for example

```
// reference to the GameBoard
private GameBoard board = new GameBoard();
```

Given that both options are possible, why might we choose to only declare references as fields and create the objects in the constructor? There are two common reasons why we might do this:

1. When the object relationship is not a fixed composition but an association that might change over time. In this case the reference might not always need to point to the same object (or indeed any object). Separating the reference from the creation of the object gives us more flexibility.
2. When objects being created have parameterised constructors, and the parameter arguments are being passed down from the constructor of one object to the constructor of another. We might, for example, change the board class so that it could have different numbers of squares for different games, and pass this value to the board via the game constructor.

However, in some composition relationships it may well make sense to create the object when it is declared, rather than in the constructor.

Exercise 7.1
Add another PlayerPiece to the snakes and ladders game, and indicate which counter reaches the finish first.

7.4 Association, Aggregation or Composition?

In the snakes and ladders game, there are several associations between classes and an aggregation between Board and Square. This means that the Board object is made up of many BoardSquare objects. Given that the board and its squares are

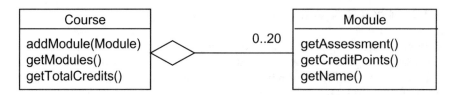

Fig. 7.17 Course is an aggregation of Module objects

tightly related, we might realistically regard this as a composition relation-ship. How, then, do we draw a distinction between the two? Although the lines between association, aggregation and composition may sometimes be blurred, we can say in general that the most important characteristic is ownership. In an association objects do not own each other, only communicate. In aggregation, one object may own other objects, but they may also have an independent lifetime and other associations. In composition, the whole owns its parts, and their lifetimes are probably identical. It is unlikely that the parts have any relationships with other objects outside the composition.

The remaining two examples in this chapter may help to demonstrate some of the differences between aggregation and composition. First, we look at the rela-tionship between a course of studies and the modules (subject areas) that it contains. For example, a training course in Java may contain modules in object orientation, exception handling and graphical user interfaces, among many others. Although a course is made up of modules, these modules may also appear in other courses and the modules in a course may be replaced by others. Therefore, we can regard this as an aggregation relationship (see Fig. 7.17). The second example mimics computer hardware components being composed of other pieces of hardware, where the larger component depends entirely on its parts and they have no separate existence. This is an example of composition (see the UML diagram in Fig. 7.22).

7.4.1 Aggregation Example

The classes in this example are the Course class, which we have introduced pre-viously, and the Module class. A Module represents a subject being taught as part of a larger course, so that a course on Java, for example, might have many modules relating to different aspects of the language. A module has three attributes:

1. The name of the module
2. A credit point rating for certification (e.g. 20 credit points for a full module or 10 credit points for a half module)
3. An assessment method (e.g. "practicum", "test", etc.).

The Module class in this example consists only of fields and their getters and setters. One would hope that more interesting behaviors would emerge in a more developed system.

```
package com.foundjava.chapter7;

public class Module
{
  private String name;
  private int creditPoints;
  private String assessment;

  public Module(String name, int points, String assess){
    setName(name);
    setCreditPoints(points);
    setAssessment(assess);
  }

  public void setName(String name){
    this.name = name;
  }

  public void setCreditPoints(int creditPoints){
    this.creditPoints = creditPoints;
  }

  public void setAssessment(String assessment){
    this.assessment = assessment;
  }

  public String getName(){
    return name;
  }

  public int getCreditPoints(){
    return creditPoints;
  }

  public String getAssessment(){
    return assessment;
  }
}
```

Course objects are aggregations of zero or more Modules. The UML diagram in Fig. 7.17 shows how the two classes relate. The maximum number of modules in a course is assumed to be 20.

The additional elements of the Course class for this example are an array of up to 20 Modules, and a public method to return this array. There is also an attribute with associated methods to keep track of the number of modules, which is important to help us add modules without going beyond the bounds of the array. To demonstrate a slightly more interesting aspect of the Course/Module relationship there is a "getTotalCredits" method that adds up the credits for all the modules in the course. Here are the parts of the Course class new to this example (familiar code from previous examples has been omitted).

```
public class Course
{
// an array of modules
  private Module[] modules = new Module[20];
  private int moduleCount = 0;

//some previously introduced code omitted here…

// 'addModule' adds a parameter module to the array.
  public void addModule(Module new_module)
  {
    if(moduleCount < modules.length)
    {
      modules[moduleCount] = new_module;
      moduleCount++;
    }
    else
    {
      System.out.println("Cannot add more modules");
    }
  }

  public int getTotalCredits()
  {
    int total = 0;
    for (int i = 0; i < getModuleCount(); i++) {
      total += getModules()[i].getCreditPoints();
    }
    return total;
  }


  public Module[] getModules() {
    return modules;
  }

  public int getModuleCount() {
    return moduleCount;
  }
```

Having assembled our aggregation, we can make objects of the Course class, add Module objects to them and see the result. The test class (ModuleRunner) does not do very much here, but we could continue to develop this system so that a collection of courses and related modules could be put into a catalogue, or scheduled into locations, providing various levels of aggregation.

```
public class ModuleRunner
{
  public static void main(String[] args) {
    Course myCourse = new Course("Software testing", 5, 2000);
    Module module1 = new Module
      ("Unit testing", 10, "Practicum");
    Module module2 = new Module
        ("Acceptance testing", 20, "Coursework");
    Module module3 = new Module("Boundary Values", 10, "none");
// add the modules to the course
    myCourse.addModule(module1);
    myCourse.addModule(module2);
    myCourse.addModule(module3);
// display the course details
    System.out.println(myCourse.getName()
      + " contains the following modules:");
    System.out.println
      ("Module name \t credit points \t assessment");
    for (int i = 0; i < myCourse.getModuleCount(); i++) {
      System.out.println(myCourse.getModules()[i].getName() +
      '\t' + myCourse.getModules()[i].getCreditPoints() +
      '\t' + myCourse.getModules()[i].getAssessment());
    }
    System.out.println("Total credits = " +
        myCourse.getTotalCredits());
  }
}
```

The output from running this class is

```
Software testing contains the following modules:
Module name          credit points        assessment
Unit testing         10                   Practicum
Acceptance testing   20                   Coursework
Boundary Values      10                   none
Total credits = 40
```

Exercise 7.2
Create a Prospectus class that is an aggregation of many courses. It should allow courses to be added and viewed. Write a test class that creates a Prospectus object and tests its methods.

7.5 Composition

The next example shows how object composition can be used to create objects from components that are tightly bound together. Real world objects are often clear examples of composition, because many objects are composed of smaller objects. Electronic devices are very much of this type and provide the context for this example.

7.5.1 Logic Gates

A logic gate is a fundamental component of digital electronics, and the behavior of some types of logic gate will be very familiar to anyone who has used a programming language. In Chap. 3 we looked at how Boolean operators can be used as part of the conditions used with selections ("if" statements) and iterations ("while" or "do…while" statements). These Boolean operators are shown in Table 7.2.

In electronics, these Boolean operators are implemented by components known as logic gates, which compare binary digits rather than conditions. For example, an AND gate has two or more inputs, each of which may have the value zero or one. It has a single output that will have the value one if, and only if, all the inputs are also one, otherwise the output will be zero (Fig. 7.18). To keep things simple our examples will assume that AND gates and OR gates have only two inputs.

An OR gate will again have two or more inputs and a single output, but in this case will output a one if any of the inputs have the value one. If all the inputs are zero, then the output will be zero (Fig. 7.19).

A NOT gate has a single input and a single output. All it does is convert an input of zero to an output of one, or an input of one to an output of zero (Fig. 7.20)

Operator	Meaning	Evaluates
&&	AND	Are both conditions true?
||	OR	Is either of the conditions true?
!	NOT	Is the condition false?

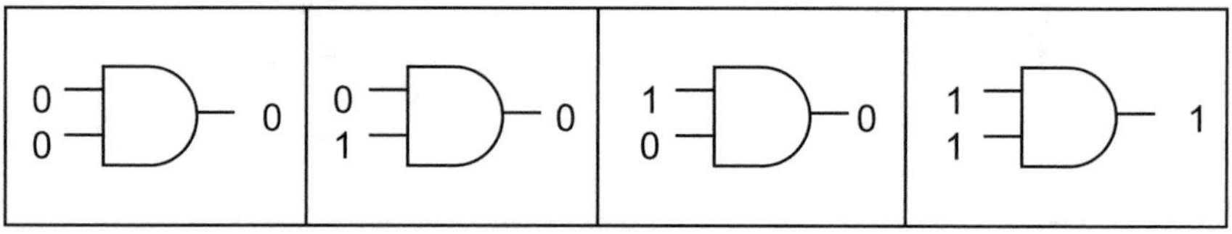

Table 7.2 Boolean operators and their meanings

Fig. 7.18 The possible inputs and outputs for AND gates

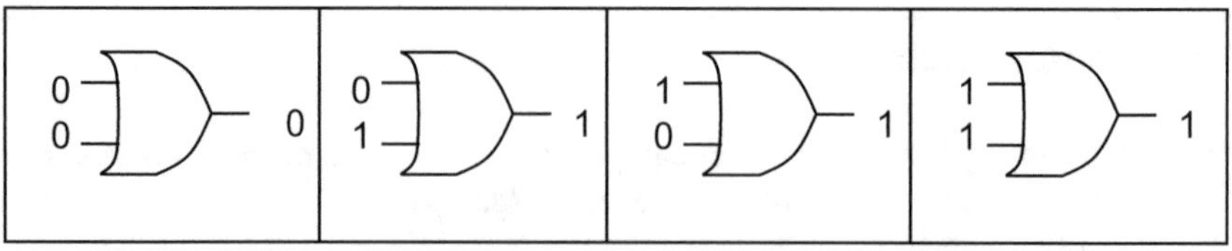

Fig. 7.19 The possible inputs and outputs for OR gates

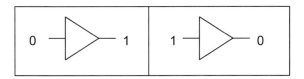

Fig. 7.20 The possible inputs and outputs for NOT gates

To model these three types of logic gate, we will create three classes. They are very simple, and indeed in this implementation they have no attributes and consist only of a single method. You might wonder why these methods are not marked as static, since the objects have no state. In fact, for these examples this would work fine, but later we will be using these classes to represent individual component objects so will not use a static method. These are the three classes, starting with the AndGate class. Note how the "return" statement is being used on both sides of the conditional statement. Remember that a return statement terminates execution of the method.

```
public class AndGate
{
  public int getOutput(int input1, int input2)
  {
    if(input1 == 1 && input2 == 1)
    {
      return 1;
    }
    else
    {
      return 0;
    }
  }
}
```

This is the definition of the OrGate class

```
public class OrGate
{
  public int getOutput(int input1, int input2)
  {
    if(input1 == 1 || input2 == 1)
    {
      return 1;
    }
    else
    {
      return 0;
    }
  }
}
```

Finally, the definition of the NotGate.

```
public class NotGate
{
  public int getOutput(int input1)
  {
    if(input1 == 1)
    {
      return 0;
    }
    else
    {
      return 1;
    }
  }
}
```

This test class shows how the gates respond to different combinations of input by displaying their output in a simple "truth table" format. Truth tables are often used to show the result of Boolean logic, and for numbers alone the order of the values is unimportant. For the gates with two inputs (AND gates and OR gates) a two-dimensional grid can be used to show the output for each pair of values, showing the physical as well as the logical combinations of inputs possible. For the single input NOT gate only one row is required. The code is a bit laborious, since it is mostly "println" statements. The tab stop characters ("\t") are written as Strings rather than chars (i.e. put in double quotes rather than single) to enable string concatenation in the output.

```
public class TruthTables
{
  public static void main(String[] args)
  {
    AndGate andGate = new AndGate();
    OrGate orGate = new OrGate();
    NotGate notGate = new NotGate();
// output the column headings for the AND gate truth table
    System.out.println("Truth table for AND gate");
    System.out.println("\t0\t1");
// output the truth table fir the AND gate
    System.out.println("0\t" + andGate.getOutput(0,0) + "\t" +
        andGate.getOutput(0,1));
    System.out.println("1\t" + andGate.getOutput(1,0) + "\t" +
        andGate.getOutput(1,1));
// output the column headings for the OR gate truth table
    System.out.println("Truth table for OR gate");
    System.out.println("\t0\t1");
// output the truth table for the OR gate
    System.out.println("0\t" + orGate.getOutput(0,0) + "\t" +
        orGate.getOutput(0,1));
    System.out.println("1\t" + orGate.getOutput(1,0) + "\t" +
        orGate.getOutput(1,1));
// output the column headings for the NOT gate truth table
    System.out.println("Truth table for NOT gate");
    System.out.println("\t0\t1");
// output the truth table for the NOT gate
    System.out.println("\t" + notGate.getOutput(0) + "\t" +
        notGate.getOutput(1));
  }
}
```

This is the output:

```
Truth table for AND gate
        0     1
0       0     0
1       0     1
Truth table for OR gate
        0     1
0       0     1
1       1     1
Truth table for NOT gate
        0     1
        1     0
```

On their own, gates have limited utility, but put them together into a larger composition and we can build a useful component. One very simple component is the half adder.

7.5.2   Half Adder Components

One of the fundamental operations of a computer is to perform arithmetic on binary numbers. It can do this by using collections of gates put together in particular ways. One component that we can build simply from gates is the "half adder", a component that is able to add two binary digits, producing a result and a carry. There are only four possible combinations of input bits to a half adder, and only three possible results (Fig. 7.21).

There are a number of ways of using gates of different types to build half adders, but a simple and useful example (which comes from *Illustrating Computers* by Day and Alcock) is one that uses the three types of gate we have looked at, namely the AND, OR and NOT gates. A half adder built from these components is shown in Fig. 7.22, along with a UML diagram of the classes. Because this is an example of the very strong form of aggregation known as composition, we use a filled diamond to indicate the relationship between the half adder and its component gates.

We can create a HalfAdder class in Java by making it a composition of objects of the various Gate classes. Returning to our previous discussion of whether we create

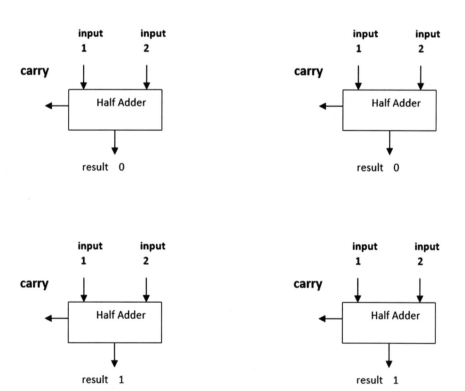

Fig. 7.21 The possible inputs to, and resulting outputs from, a half adder

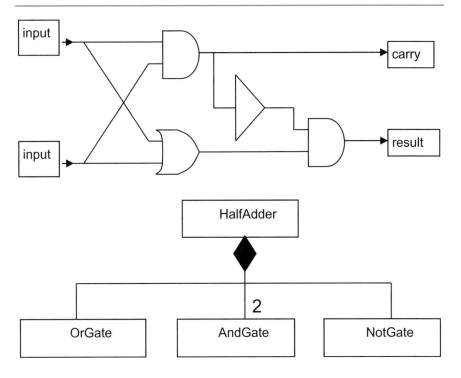

Fig. 7.22 A half adder composed of two AND gates, an OR gate and a NOT gate along with a UML class diagram showing the composition symbol

objects when they are declared or in the constructor, given that in a composition relationship the lifetime of the components and the composition is the same, it makes sense to create the gate objects when they are declared:

```
AndGate carryAndGate = new AndGate();
AndGate resultAndGate = new AndGate();
OrGate orGate = new OrGate();
NotGate notGate = new NotGate();
```

We also have two inputs and two outputs (represented by integers). Because the half adder requires that some outputs be used as inputs to other gates, the "setInput" method also declares some local variables to pass these values between gates. This is the complete class:

```
package com.foundjava.chapter7;

public class HalfAdder {
  AndGate carryAndGate = new AndGate();
  AndGate resultAndGate = new AndGate();
  OrGate orGate = new OrGate();
  NotGate notGate = new NotGate();
// inputs to the half adder
  private int input1;
  private int input2;
// outputs from the half adder
  private int result;
  private int carry;

// set the values of the input bits
  public void setInput(int in1, int in2) {
    input1 = in1;
    input2 = in2;
// get the carry value
    carry = carryAndGate.getOutput(input1, input2);
// get the result value
    result = resultAndGate.getOutput
        (orGate.getOutput(input1, input2),
          notGate.getOutput(carry));
  }

// return the result bit
  public int getResult() {
    return result;
  }

// return the carry bit
  public int getCarry() {
    return carry;
  }
}
```

Finally, we can test our HalfAdder class by making an object and sending data to the "setInput" method. This class tests the three possible combinations of input, 1 + 1, 1 + 0 and 0 + 0. Note that 1 + 0 means the same as 0 + 1 so will produce the same result.

```
package com.foundjava.chapter7;

public class HalfAdderTest
{
  public static void main(String[] args)
  {
// declare a half adder
    HalfAdder halfAdder = new HalfAdder();
// set the input to the half adder
    halfAdder.setInput(1, 0);
// display the resulting output from the half adder
    System.out.println("Input to the half adder is 1, 0");
    System.out.println("Result from half adder is "
      + halfAdder.getResult());
    System.out.println("Carry value from half adder is "
      + halfAdder.getCarry());
// set the input to the half adder
    halfAdder.setInput(0, 0);
// display the resulting output from the half adder
    System.out.println("Input to the half adder is 0, 0");
    System.out.println("Result from half adder is "
      + halfAdder.getResult());
    System.out.println("Carry value from half adder is "
      + halfAdder.getCarry());
// set the input to the half adder
    halfAdder.setInput(1, 1);
// display the resulting output from the half adder
    System.out.println("Input to the half adder is 1, 1");
    System.out.println("Result from half adder is "
      + halfAdder.getResult());
    System.out.println("Carry value from half adder is "
      + halfAdder.getCarry());
  }
}
```

Our test class produces the following results:

```
Input to the half adder is 1, 0
Result from half adder is 1
Carry value from half adder is 0
Input to the half adder is 0, 0
Result from half adder is 0
Carry value from half adder is 0
Input to the half adder is 1, 1
Result from half adder is 0
Carry value from half adder is 1
```

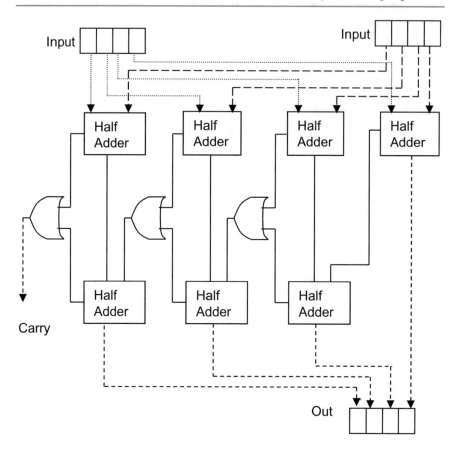

Fig. 7.23 A four-bit full adder composed of half adders and OR gates

Exercise 7.3
Using the existing HalfAdder and OrGate classes, write a FullAdder class that simulates the following diagram of a 4-bit full adder (Fig. 7.23, adapted from "*Illustrating Computers*" by Day and Alcock, 1982). Test the FullAdder by using it to add various combinations of four-bit numbers.

7.6 Summary

In this chapter, we have built on our knowledge of classes and objects to create larger programs based on different objects communicating with one another. We have seen different examples of the way that objects can work together.

- association: where independent objects talk to each other
- aggregation: where an object is made up of other objects that can vary
- composition: a very strong form of aggregation where the component objects are fixed.

We made some design decisions, based on what have done so far, that might not be optimal. For example, we created two classes (Snake and Ladder) that seemed to have much in common. Perhaps they could somehow be designed to share these common characteristics? In the next chapter we will look at inheritance and polymorphism, where classes can build upon existing classes to extend and refine their behaviors.

Inheritance, Polymorphism and Interfaces

8

From the classes and objects we have worked with so far, we recognize that identical objects belong to the same class, but what about objects that are similar rather than identical? How do we know, for example, that a particular object is a clock rather than any other type of object? We instinctively classify objects in the world to be of a type, by recognizing what is common between different but similar objects. A clock is anything that tells the time in some way, regardless of the technology or appearance of a particular clock. The class "clock" encompasses all we understand about the general concept of "clockness". A specific type of clock not only belongs to a specific class but also to higher level abstractions.

8.1 Abstraction

How abstract (general) is our concept of "clock"? In other words, how specific is our set of criteria for deciding what is or is not a clock? Is a dandelion clock really a clock? And does it have as much "clockness" as a wristwatch? How about a sundial? A candle clock? Stonehenge? These are not black and white questions, because there are different levels of detail that we use to classify things, from the very abstract (a clock tells the time) to the more closely defined (an examination clock appears to start accelerating half an hour before the end of an exam).

8.1.1 Inheritance

Because we can classify objects at different levels of detail, we can put these classes into a classification hierarchy, with the most abstract concepts at the top and the most detailed object descriptions at the bottom. At the highest point of such a hierarchy, we might put "object", our most abstract idea of what an object is.

© Springer Nature Switzerland AG 2020
D. Parsons, *Foundational Java*, Texts in Computer Science,
https://doi.org/10.1007/978-3-030-54518-5_8

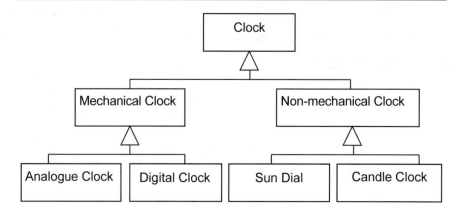

Fig. 8.1 A classification hierarchy showing how each type of clock is "a kind of" the class that it inherits from

The term inheritance is used to indicate that as we move down the hierarchy, each class inherits all the characteristics of the class above it, and then adds extra levels of detail, or class-specific behaviors. Every class is "a kind of" the class above it so that a digital clock is a kind of mechanical clock is a kind of timepiece. Figure 8.1 shows a classification hierarchy of some types of clock. We use the terms "subclass" and "superclass" to describe inheritance relationships. For example, "digital clock" is a subclass of (inherits from) "mechanical clock". "Mechanical clock" is therefore the superclass of "digital clock". Figure 8.1 uses the UML notation for inheritance, which is a solid line with a triangular arrowhead pointing from the subclass(es) to the superclass. Classes that are more than one level apart in the same hierarchy are known as "ancestors" and "descendants"; for example", in Fig. 8.1 Clock is an ancestor of Digital Clock, while Sun Dial is a descendent of Clock.

8.1.2 Polymorphism

One of the most important aspects of object-oriented programming is polymorphism, which means "many-shaped". Although there are several different types of polymorphism, the most fundamental is the ability of different objects to respond with different behavior to the same message. For example, an Analogue Clock object and a Digital Clock object would have different ways of displaying the time. The principle of polymorphism is that the same message (e.g. "showTime") could be sent to both objects and they would respond to it with different, class-specific behaviors. Figure 8.2 shows how these different types of clock respond to the same message.

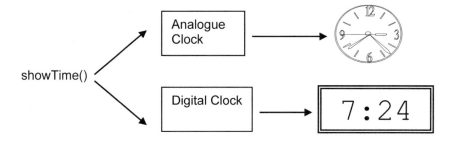

Fig. 8.2 Polymorphism allows different types of object to respond differently to the same message

8.1.3 The Relationship Between Inheritance and Polymorphism

As a language, Java always uses inheritance because all Java classes automatically inherit, either directly or indirectly, from the Object class. Figure 8.3 shows how all classes, whether standard Java classes or those we write ourselves, ultimately inherit from Object. The Object class has a number of methods, including "toString", which as we have seen from previous chapters returns a String

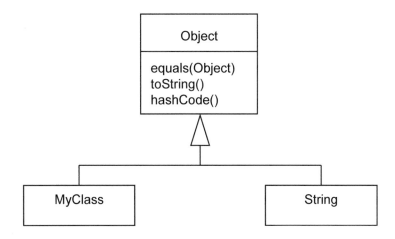

Fig. 8.3 A UML class diagram showing how all Java classes inherit from class Object

representation of the object, "equals", which compares two objects of the same class, and "hashCode" which, for reasons we will explain later, needs to be consistent with the "equals" method. All Java classes will inherit these methods, which they can either use "as is" (inheritance) or override with their own implementations (polymorphism).

The first example in this chapter, which we will use to explore some simple aspects of inheritance from the Object class, is the Location class, which we introduced previously in the context of the CourseDelivery class. A CourseDelivery takes place in a Location. This version of the class is very simple, and only contains three fields (an address (a String), a capacity (an int) and a cost per day (a double) and their getters and setters. Figure 8.4 shows a UML diagram of the Location class, including the data types of the three fields. The data types returned from the "get" methods are also shown. Like the UML syntax for field data types, the data type is separated from the method name by a colon, where there is no return type shown, this is because the methods have a "void" return type.

When we create classes in Eclipse, one of the elements of the "New Java Class" dialog, which we have ignored up until now, is the "Superclass" entry. Figure 8.5 shows how the superclass of Location will default to class java.lang.Object unless we supply the name of some other class to inherit from.

Here is the source code of our Location class with the default superclass of java. lang.Object, which is implicit so does not need to appear in the class declaration.

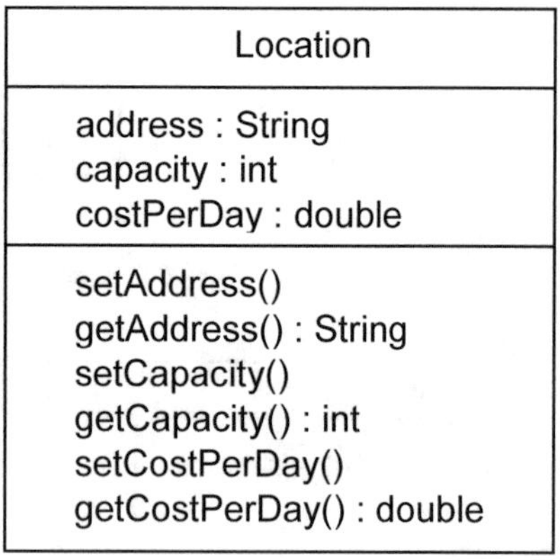

Fig. 8.4 The attributes and methods of the Location class

Location
address : String capacity : int costPerDay : double
setAddress() getAddress() : String setCapacity() getCapacity() : int setCostPerDay() getCostPerDay() : double

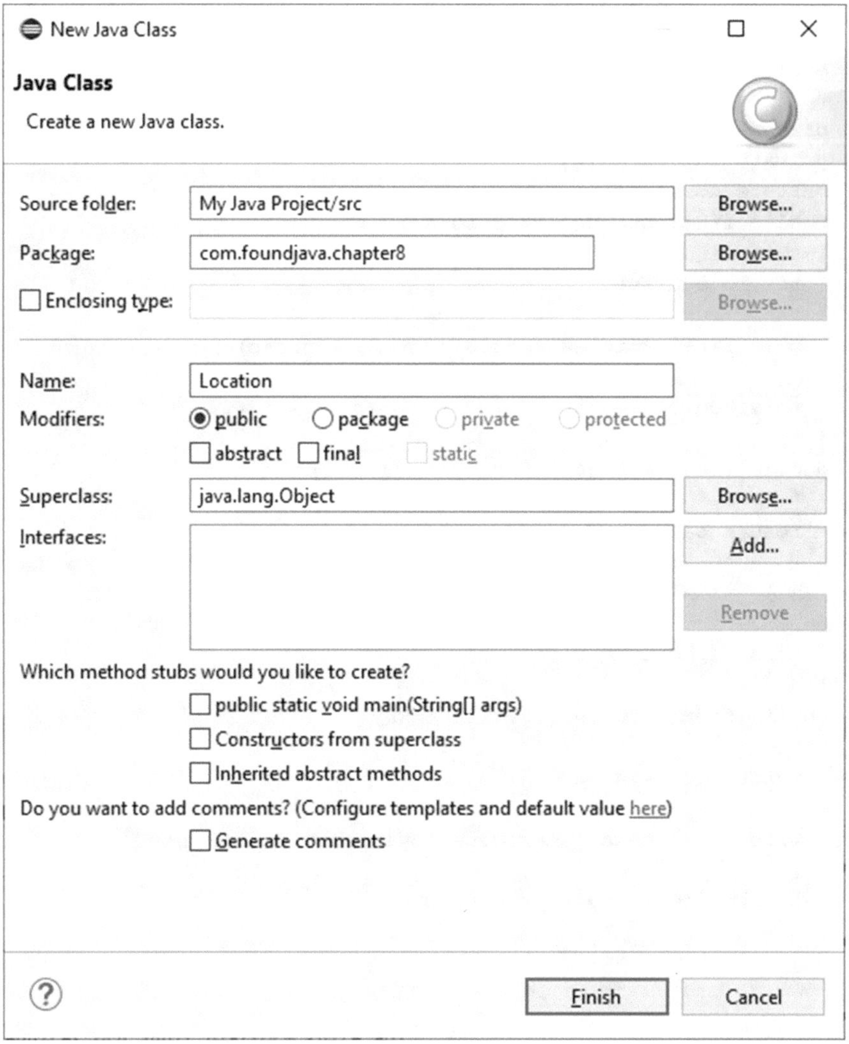

Fig. 8.5 The "New Java Class" dialog in Eclipse will default to using java.lang.Object as the superclass of any new classes you create

```java
package com.foundjava.chapter8;

public class Location
{
private String address;
private int capacity;
private double pricePerDay;
public final String getAddress()
{
  return address;
}
public final void setAddress(String address)
{
  this.address = address;
}
public final int getCapacity()
{
  return capacity;
}
public final void setCapacity(int capacity)
{
  this.capacity = capacity;
}
public final double getPricePerDay()
{
  return pricePerDay;
}
public final void setPricePerDay(double pricePerDay)
{
  this.pricePerDay = pricePerDay;
}
}
```

8.2   Inheriting from the Object Class

What does it mean when we say that all classes in Java ultimately inherit from Object? At a simple level, it means that all the methods of the Object class are automatically available to any classes that we create. In Java we specify that one class inherits from another by using the "extends" keyword. If you do not specify the class from which your own class inherits, it automatically defaults to extending Object. The declaration of the Location class could, in fact, have been written as

```
public class Location extends Object
{...
```

But this was not necessary as it is the default. However, if we want to inherit from classes other than Object then this must be explicitly stated, as we will see in later examples in this chapter.

Note

Java only supports single inheritance, which means that a Java class must directly inherit from only one other class.

Before looking at polymorphism, we will start with some basics of inheritance. We already know that objects have a default "toString" method. This is inherited from the Object class and returns the fully qualified class name of the object along with the hash code of its memory address. We have also seen in previous examples the effect of comparing two objects using the "==" operator. This returns "true" only if the two object references point to exactly the same object. The actual state of the objects is ignored. The default implementation of the "equals" method, also inherited from Object, does the same thing.

Here is a main method that demonstrates three Location objects inheriting the "toString" and "equals" methods from the Object class. Remember that "toString" is called implicitly whenever you put an object into a "System.out.println" statement. Two of the Location objects have the same state (all their fields are set to identical values), but by default, they will not be considered equal:

```
package com.foundjava.chapter8;

public class LocationTest
{
  public static void main(String[] args)
  {
    Location classroom1 = new Location();
    classroom1.setAddress("4th Floor, New Bank Building");
    classroom1.setCapacity(20);
    classroom1.setPricePerDay(300.0);

    Location classroom2 = new Location();
    classroom2.setAddress
      ("Seminar room 5, Central University Computing Lab");
    classroom2.setCapacity(40);
    classroom2.setPricePerDay(450.0);
```

```
Location classroom3 = new Location();
classroom3.setAddress
   ("Seminar room 5, Central University Computing Lab");
classroom3.setCapacity(40);
classroom3.setPricePerDay(450.0);
System.out.println("Classroom one: " + classroom1);
System.out.println("Classroom two: " + classroom2);
System.out.println("Classroom three: " + classroom3);

boolean isEqual = classroom2.equals(classroom3);
if(isEqual)
{
  System.out.println(classroom2 +
    " is equal to " + classroom3);
}
else
{
  System.out.println
    (classroom2 + " is not equal to " + classroom3);
}
  }
}
```

The output from this program is rather ugly but reinforces what we already know about objects; their default "toString" shows the object's name and package, and each object has a different hash code derived from its memory address. Also, if we compare two objects that have different memory addresses, they are not equal, even if they have the same state (the inequality message has been highlighted in bold text).

```
Classroom one: com.foundjava.chapter8.Location@81f9a3d0
Classroom two: com.foundjava.chapter8.Location@d573f6d7
Classroom three: com.foundjava.chapter8.Location@d573f6d7
com.foundjava.chapter8.Location@d573f6d7 is not equal to
com.foundjava.chapter8.Location@d573f6d7
```

8.2.1 Overriding the "toString" Method

Although the default version of "toString" is inherited from class Object by all other classes, we have already seen some Java classes implementing "toString" in a different way, for example the String and Date classes. These versions of "toString" are polymorphic; they override the default implementations with ones more suitable to those classes. We are also able to provide specialized versions of "toString" for our own classes by writing a method with the same signature (visibility, name, return type and parameter list) as the one in the Object class, namely:

```
public String toString()
```

From this signature, we can see that the "toString" method is public, returns a String and takes no parameters. Here, we provide our own version of the method for Location objects. It works by concatenating the simple class name (from the Class object), address, capacity and price, along with some suitable text labels, into a single String object, and then returning that String from the method:

```
public String toString()
{
   return this.getClass().getSimpleName() +  " " +
      getAddress() + " holds " + getCapacity() + " and costs " +
      getPricePerDay() + " per day";
}
```

A "toString" method can be written any way that you like, depending on how it is to be used. As well as providing a String that could be displayed in a user interface, it can also be helpful for logging and diagnostics as it enables us to represent any aspect of an object's state as a String using a method that is accessible on any object. Here is the output of the same test program after the "toString" method has been added to the Location class.

```
Classroom one: Location 4th Floor, New Bank Building holds 20
and costs 300.0 per day
Classroom two: Location Seminar room 5, Central University
Computing Lab holds 40 and costs 450.0 per day
Classroom three: Location Seminar room 5, Central University
Computing Lab holds 40 and costs 450.0 per day
Location Seminar room 5, Central University Computing Lab
holds 40 and costs 450.0 per day is not equal to Location
Seminar room 5, Central University Computing Lab holds 40 and
costs 4500.0 per day
```

8.2.2   Overriding the "equals" Method

Certainly, the output from our test code is more readable when it uses the polymorphic version of "toString", but what about the fact that the two Locations with
the same state are not equal? One option we have in Java is to override the "equals"
method so that we can compare object state instead of object addresses. As with
"toString", we can override the inherited implementation by writing our own version
of the method with the same signature. The signature of the "equals" method is:

```
public boolean equals(Object)
```

In our own implementation we must ensure that if the parameter object is null, or
the parameter object is not of the appropriate class to make a comparison, we return
"false". Otherwise, we are free to implement our definition of equality based on the
state of the objects. In this example, we start by returning "false" if the parameter is
null or not an object of the same class as the one hosting the method. If we get past
this test, we then compare the two objects, after casting the parameter Object to the
actual class type (note that casting object types use the same syntax as casting
primitive types). If they have the same address, capacity and price data then they are
considered equal, and we return "true", otherwise we return "false".

```
public boolean equals(Object object)
{
  if(object == null ||
     !(object.getClass().equals(this.getClass())))
  {
    return false;
  }
  Location other = (Location)object;
  if(getAddress() == other.getAddress() &&
     getCapacity() == other.getCapacity() &&
     getPricePerDay() == other.getPricePerDay())
  {
    return true;
  }
  else
  {
    return false;
  }
}
```

If we add this method to the Location class and run the test code again, then this
time classrooms 2 and 3 are shown to be equal (the equality message is highlighted
in bold print):

```
Classroom one: Location 4th Floor, New Bank Building holds 20
and costs 300.0 per day
Classroom two: Location Seminar room 5, Central University
Computing Lab holds 40 and costs 450.0 per day
Classroom three: Location Seminar room 5, Central University
Computing Lab holds 40 and costs 450.0 per day
Location Seminar room 5, Central University Computing Lab
holds 40 and costs 450.0 per day is equal to Location Seminar
room 5, Central University Computing Lab holds 40 and costs
450.0 per day
```

8.2.3 Overriding the "hashCode" Method

If we override the "equals" method, then we are also required to override the "hashCode" method. This is because "equals" and "hashCode" need to be consistent with each other. In their default implementations, both "equals" and "hashCode" relate to the memory address of the object. If we override "equals" to be based on the state of the object instead of its address, then "hashCode" should also be overridden to be based on the same state. Here is an implementation of the "hashCode" method for the Location class. The method must return an integer. In this method we reuse the "hashCode" of the String class (String already overrides the "hashCode" method) and then add the capacity and price (cast to an int) to return the hash code.

```
public int hashCode()
{
  return getAddress().hashCode() + getCapacity() +
    (int)getPricePerDay();
}
```

The reason for making the "hashCode" method use the same data as the "equals" method is that this is required when an object is indexed in a hash table, which is a data structure that stores objects using keys. The implementation of the object lookup uses both the "equals" and "hashCode" methods, so they need to be based on the same data.

To see the results of the polymorphic "hashCode" method, the following three lines can be added to the test code to display the hash codes:

```
System.out.println("Classroom one hashcode: " +
  classroom1.hashCode());
System.out.println("Classroom two hashcode: " +
  classroom2.hashCode());
System.out.println("Classroom three hashcode: " +
  classroom3.hashCode());
```

Here is the output. Note how the hash codes of classrooms two and three are identical.

```
Classroom one hashcode: -2114346032
Classroom two hashcode: -713820457
Classroom three hashcode: -713820457
```

Although our implementation is likely to generate unique hash codes for objects with a unique state, there is no guarantee that it will always do so. This is not a problem, as it is OK for objects to have the same hash code, even when they are stored in a hash table. There is, however, a danger in overriding equals and hash code in this way for objects that may change their state. The hash code will change if the object's fields are updated. For this reason, an object with this kind of "hashCode" method should not be modified while it is in a hash table.

8.2.4   Generating "hashCode" and "equals" Methods in Eclipse

Because it is so important that the "hashCode" and "equals" methods are updated together, Eclipse provides a built-in tool to do this. While editing the class, simply select "Source" → "Generate hashCode() and equals()..." and the implementation of both of these methods will be generated, based on the fields that you choose in the dialog. We will not include the generated code here, but if you try it out for yourself you will see that the generated implementation is considerably more detailed and complex than the rather basic implementations that have been shown in this chapter. However, how you wish to define the equality of your objects is up to you.

8.2.5   The @Override Annotation

Annotations in Java uses a set of "meta-tags" that relate to metadata (data about data). An annotation is preceded by the "@" symbol. One of the simplest annotations to use is "@Override" which we can put before any methods that are intended to override methods in a superclass. A big advantage of doing this is that if a method is annotated in this way but does not actually override a superclass method, the compiler will generate an error message. This ensures that we have correctly overridden the methods that we intend to. For example, we might make a mistake in the signature of the "toString: method, perhaps by using a lower case "s".

```
public String tostring()   // compiles
```

The problem here is that this is not a compiler error. The compiler simply treats this as being a different method from "toString", so it will not be polymorphic. If, however, we add the "@Override" annotation before the method, the compiler will tell us that we are not overriding any methods of the superclass:

```
@Override
public String tostring()    // will not compile
```

This is a very helpful aid to ensuring that our methods are as polymorphic as we expect them to be, so it is good practice to use the "@Override" annotation on all methods that override superclass methods.

Exercise 8.1
Add "toString", "equals" and "hashCode" methods to the Course class from the previous chapter. Remember that your implementations of "equals" and "hashcode" can be done in any way that you like but must be consistent with each other. Optionally, you can generate these methods using the Eclipse "Source" menu item. Write a class with a "main" method that creates a Course object and demonstrates these methods. Use the @Override annotation when writing these methods.

8.3 An Inheritance Hierarchy Using Abstraction

In this chapter, we have looked at how all Java classes, whether provided in a Java package or written by ourselves, inherit from (are subclasses of) Object. We can also inherit from our own classes to add extra functionality to an existing class and implement the polymorphic methods. In the next example, we will create a hierarchy of shapes. This is a very commonly used example of inheritance, and there are many different ways of creating such a hierarchy. In fact, Java itself provides something similar in the "java.awt.geom" package. However, the purpose of this example is not to attempt to produce a complete or even "correct" hierarchy of shapes, but simply to use the example to explore some important aspects of inheritance and polymorphism. The shape hierarchy used in this chapter is designed around generic concepts of shape, trying not to violate the Liskov substitution principle, which is a fairly complex concept but, simply put, says that an object of a subclass should be able to replace an object of a superclass without affecting any other part of the code. It is perhaps tempting to build a hierarchy of Java shapes around reusing code. Java's drawing methods for simple shapes (rather than lines and arcs) are based on rectangles, ovals, polygons and rounded rectangles. However, building a hierarchy based on simply trying to reuse these drawing methods through inheritance would put circles and ovals in the same part of the hierarchy, likewise squares and rectangles. This causes some interesting problems; for example, is Square a subclass of Rectangle? Or is Rectangle a subclass of Square? Certainly, making Square a subclass of Rectangle violates the Liskov substitution principle since a Square cannot have its side lengths independently changed, but we can hardly say that a Rectangle is a type of Square. This issue is not important of itself but serves to underline an important aspect of designing inheritance hierarchies, which is that they should not be designed around a desire to reuse code. Rather we should look for something that works well from the perspective of the overall design goals we have in our application, whatever they may be. The

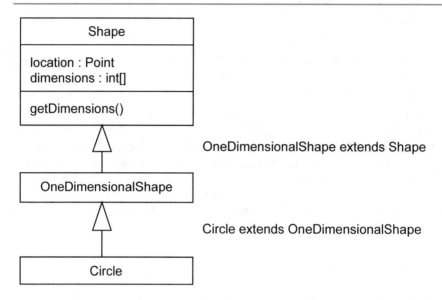

Fig. 8.6 Shape is the superclass of OneDimensionalShape, which in turn is the superclass of circle

approach used here (from many we could have chosen) is based on the dimensional properties of simple shapes, with a basic classification of shapes into those that have one dimension of measurement and those that have two.

Figure 8.6 shows a part (a vertical slice) of the inheritance hierarchy that we will use in this example. Since OneDimensionalShape is a subclass (specialization) of Shape, and Circle is a subclass of OneDimensionalShape, Circle will inherit all the fields and methods of OneDimensionalShape, which in turn inherits all of Shape's fields and methods, so Circle ultimately inherits from Shape too. Shape and OneDimensionalShape are both superclasses, or generalizations, of Circle.

Figure 8.6 only shows a few features of the classes, which we will develop in more detail throughout the following sections.

Previously, we have only been inheriting from class Object, so inheriting only the methods of that class. However, in this hierarchy, while Shape will be a subclass of Object, OneDimensionalShape inherits from Shape, and Circle inherits from OneDimensionalShape. For the purposes of this example, a OneDimensionalShape is one that can be represented using a single dimension, such as the radius of a circle or the side length of a square, whereas a TwoDimensionalShape would be one that would fit inside a rectangular bounding box with two dimensions (e.g. rectangles, ovals, rounded rectangles, etc.). In each level of the hierarchy, the class will explicitly extend the class from which it inherits:

```
public class className extends superclassName
{
// etc..
```

Shape has a "location" field (an instance of java.awt.Point) and a dimension field, which is an array of integers. These fields will be inherited by the subclasses, though depending on their visibility they may not be directly accessible in the subclasses. In other words, a "Circle" will have "location" field as part of its state but will not be able to access it directly if it is marked as "private". There are various ways of addressing this issue, which we will explore later.

8.3.1   Abstract Classes

All the classes that we have created in our previous examples have been concrete classes. This means that we can instantiate (create instances of) objects of these classes. An abstract class, on the other hand, is one that cannot be instantiated. Abstract classes occur in inheritance hierarchies, where they fulfill generalization roles that categorize certain types of object but do not represent the details required for an object that can be usefully created. In our shape hierarchy, both Shape and OneDimensionalShape are abstractions, rather than descriptions of concrete shapes. It makes no sense to have an instance of Shape, or OneDimensionalShape, though we would expect to be able to create instances of, for example, the Circle class. A class that extends an abstract class, and which is not abstract itself, is said to be a concrete implementation of the abstract class; Circle is a concrete implementation of the abstract OneDimensionalShape.

The "New Java Class" dialog in Eclipse includes an option to create an abstract class (Fig. 8.7). However, the only effect of this checkbox is to add the "abstract"

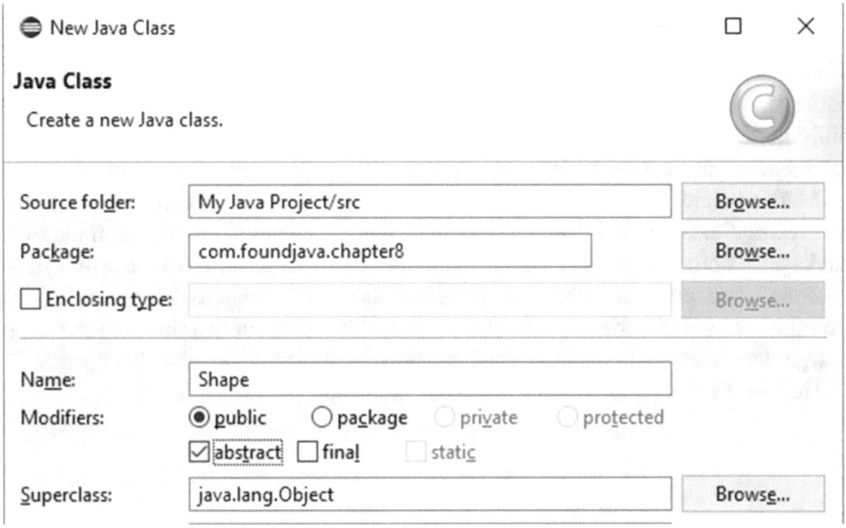

Fig. 8.7 Creating an abstract class in Eclipse (checking the "abstract" checkbox)

keyword to the class declaration, so this can easily be added or changed in the source file.

```
package com.foundjava.chapter8;

public abstract class Shape
{

}
```

8.3.2   Protected Visibility and Inheritance

As mentioned earlier, private fields (and methods) are inherited by subclasses but are not actually visible to them. This means that, for example, if the "location" field of the "Shape" class has private visibility, then any object of a subclass of Shape will have a location field, but the subclass methods will not be able to access it directly.

An alternative approach is to mark these fields as "protected". This makes them directly accessible to subclasses in any package and, also, to any other classes in the same package. For example, the "location" and "dimension" fields of "Shape" could be given protected visibility.

```
protected Point location;
protected int[] dimensions;
```

This type of visibility is specifically intended for use in inheritance hierarchies and allows subclasses to access fields and methods that have been inherited from a superclass. In fact, protected visibility is somewhat more open than package (default) visibility since a protected element is visible across its own package, as well as to subclasses in other packages. Given that all the code in this example is in one package, we could equally have used package visibility, but using protected visibility gives a better declaration of intent since it makes it clear that these elements are intended to be accessible to subclasses.

Marking fields as "protected" does, however, break encapsulation to some extent by making fields directly visible not only to subclasses but to all classes in the same package. Another approach, which maintains encapsulation, is to leave the fields "private" but provide public or protected accessor methods to them. In this example, we will demonstrate the use of protected fields but bear in mind that other design decisions about attribute (and method) visibility could have been made.

Here is the Shape class with protected fields and public methods.

```java
package com.foundjava.chapter8;

import java.awt.Point;

public abstract class Shape
{
  protected Point location;
  protected int[] dimensions;

  public Shape(Point location)
  {
    setLocation(location);
  }

  public int[] getDimensions()
  {
    return dimensions;
  }

  public void setDimensions(int[] dim)
  {
    this.dimensions = dim;
  }

  public Point getLocation()
  {
    return location;
  }

  public void setLocation(Point location)
  {
    this.location = location;
  }
}
```

8.3.3   Creating Subclasses

Creating a subclass in Java is simply a question of adding the "extends" keyword to the class declaration with the appropriate superclass name. The superclass can also be selected in Eclipse in the "New Java Class" dialog. You can either type the class name into the "Superclass" text field, or press the "Browse" button, which will search for class names that match what you type into the top of the dialog (Fig. 8.8). In this example, the OneDimensionalShape class is being created as a subclass of Shape. This again needs to be marked as "abstract".

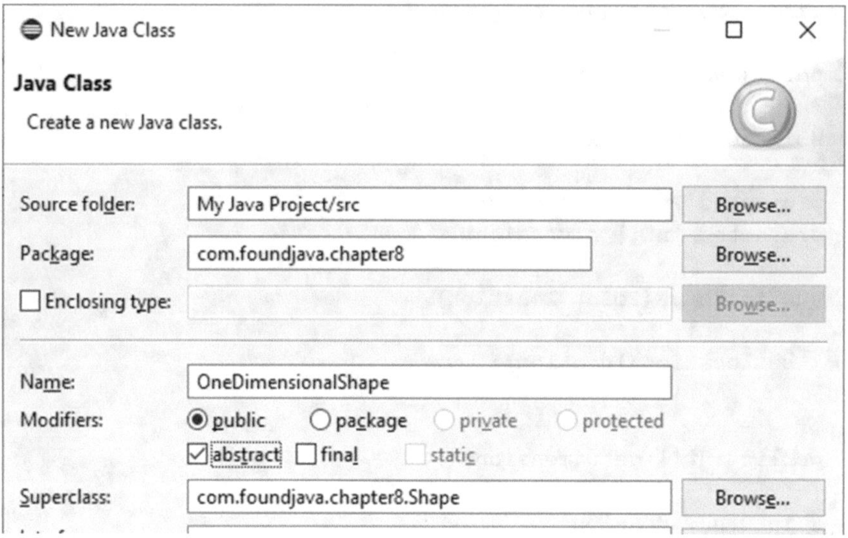

Fig. 8.8 Selecting a superclass in Eclipse

As before, the effect on the generated code of these dialog options is minimal, so the necessary keywords can be manually put into the source code if required. The class declaration of the OneDimensionalShape class should look like this, using both the "abstract" and "extends" keywords.

```
public abstract class OneDimensionalShape extends Shape
{

}
```

What methods, then, are appropriate to this abstract class? There are a couple of possibilities described here. One is that we might want any one-dimensional shape to be able to return its single dimension, which would be stored in the first element of the "dimensions" array. The following method would return this value.

```
public int getDimension()
{
  return dimensions[0];
}
```

More interestingly, there is a potential issue with the superclass version of "setDimensions", because it would allow an arbitrary array to be set. The following methods override this superclass version to ensure that only an array with a single value can be used to change the dimension of the shape. Note the use of the "super" keyword in this example. It explicitly calls the superclass version of the "setDimensions" method. This is essential to prevent the "setDimensions" method calling itself in a recursive loop. The distinction here between using "super" as opposed to the implicit "this" is therefore very important.

```
@Override
public void setDimensions(int[] dim)
{
  if (dim.length == 1) {
    super.setDimensions(dim);
  }
}
```

8.3.4   Calling Superclass Constructors

In previous examples we saw that we could chain constructors together within a single class, using "this(…)". A similar technique can be used in the constructors of an inheritance hierarchy. To call the constructor of a superclass, we can make a call to "super(…)". As a reminder, here is the constructor of the Shape class, which sets the location of the shape from the Point parameter argument.

```
public Shape(Point location)
{
  setLocation(location);
}
```

The OneDimensionalShape constructor also needs to set the position of the shape in its constructor, but we do not want to have the same code repeated here, so we make the call to the superclass constructor, to reuse the existing implementation. It is essential that the list of parameter arguments passed in the call to "super" matches one of the constructors that has been defined for the superclass.

```
public OneDimensionalShape(Point location, int dimension) {
  super(location);
// rest of constructor….
```

Note
If you do not call the superclass constructor explicitly there will be an implicit call to "super()," that is, a zero arguments constructor in the superclass. If this does not exist you will get compilation errors.

In the remainder of the constructor, we need to create the array and set the (single) dimension of the shape. Note that some internal encapsulation is used here. Rather than directly accessing the "dimensions" field, a temporary array is created, using the parameter value in an initializer list. This array is then passed to the "setDimensions" method. As we have discussed in previous examples, this type of internal encapsulation can help us to improve the robustness of our code by ensuring that any error checks we put into the "setDimensions" method are always called.

```java
public OneDimensionalShape(Point location, int dimension)
{
  super(location);
  int[] tempArray = {dimension};
  setDimensions(tempArray);
}
```

Here is the complete OneDimensionalShape class with the methods and constructor that we have previously discussed.

```java
package com.foundjava.chapter8;

import java.awt.Point;

public abstract class OneDimensionalShape extends Shape
{
  public OneDimensionalShape(Point location, int dimension)
  {
    super(location);
    int[] tempArray = {dimension};
    setDimensions(tempArray);
  }

  public int getDimension()
  {
    return dimensions[0];
  }

  @Override
  public void setDimensions(int[] dim)
  {
    if (dim.length == 1)
    {
      super.setDimensions(dim);
    }
  }
}
```

As we go further down the hierarchy to the concrete classes, the same process of constructors calling those in the superclass is repeated. For example, the Circle constructor calls its own superclass constructor in the OneDimensionalShape class. Here, two parameter arguments are passed to the superclass constructor, the location and the radius.

```
package com.foundjava.chapter8;

import java.awt.Point;

public class Circle extends OneDimensionalShape
{
  public Circle(Point location, int radius)
  {
    super(location, radius);
  }
}
```

Exercise 8.2
Given the classes discussed so far (Shape, OneDimensionalShape and Circle), write a class with a "main" method that creates an instance of the Circle class and uses its inherited methods, "setDimensions" and "getDimension".

8.3.5 Adding Further Subclasses

We will now turn our attention to the TwoDimensionalShape class, which has some differences from OneDimensionalShape. Again, the constructor creates a local array from the dimension parameters passed to it, but in this case, there are two dimensions, rather than one. As before, it then calls the superclass constructor. It contains utility methods for its own subclasses that are relevant to shapes in a rectangular bounding box. In this class, the first two elements of the "dimensions" array are available via "getHeight" and "getWidth" methods, again encapsulating the access to the underlying array. It has a different implementation of the "setDimensions" method, checking that the parameter array has two elements. Here is a complete class.

```java
package com.foundjava.chapter8;

import java.awt.Point;

public abstract class TwoDimensionalShape extends Shape
{
  public TwoDimensionalShape(Point location,
    int dimension1, int dimension2)
  {
    super(location);
    int[] tempArray = {dimension1, dimension2};
    setDimensions(tempArray);
  }

  public int getHeight()
  {
    return dimensions[0];
  }

  public int getWidth()
  {
    return dimensions[1];
  }

  @Override
  public void setDimensions(int[] dim)
  {
    if (dim.length == 2) {
      super.setDimensions(dim);
    }
  }
}
```

One of the concrete subclasses of TwoDimensionalShape is the Rectangle class. Like the Circle, it calls its own superclass constructor, in this case from the TwoDimensionalShape class. Here, three parameter arguments are passed to the superclass constructor, the location, the height and the width.

```java
package com.foundjava.chapter8;

import java.awt.Point;

public class Rectangle extends TwoDimensionalShape
{
  public Rectangle(Point location, int height, int width)
  {
    super(location, height, width);
  }
}
```

Exercise 8.3
Write a class with a "main" method that creates an instance of the Rectangle class and uses its inherited methods, "setDimensions", "getWidth" and "getHeight".

8.4   Dynamic Binding and Abstract Methods

Although in general terms, polymorphism is the use of the same method name in different classes, these classes are usually in the same inheritance hierarchy. This is because it enables us to implement a type of polymorphism known as *dynamic binding*. This is based on the ability of a superclass reference to point to an object of a subclass. We have seen in all our previous calls to an object constructor that the reference to an object has been the same type as the object itself. For example, to create a Circle object we would expect to use a reference of class Circle:

```
Circle myCircle = new Circle(new Point(0,0), 10);
```

However, a reference of a superclass can be used to reference an object of any subclass, so if our Circle class is a subclass of Shape, we can instead use a Shape reference to point to a Circle object.

```
Shape aShape = new Circle(new Point(0,0), 10);
```

This is a useful trick for supporting polymorphism; we can use superclass referencing as a way of invoking polymorphic methods on objects of subclasses. As we will see, this gives us flexibility when creating the control structures of programs that handle numbers of polymorphic objects.

The main restriction here is that we can only invoke a method on the object if that method appears in the public interface of the superclass. For example, if the Circle class has a "getArea" method that returns the area of the circle, then the Shape must also have a "getArea" method, or we cannot invoke the method on the reference, even though it is available on the object, for example, this method call on a Shape needs to be valid:

```
aShape.getArea();
```

In Fig. 8.9, we have two additional methods on the Circle class, "getArea" (which returns the area of the circle as a double) and "draw" (which uses a java.awt. Graphics object to draw on the screen) that apply to that class but have not been applied to the Shape class. To make it possible to invoke these polymorphic methods using a reference of type Shape, we need to add both methods to the Shape class.

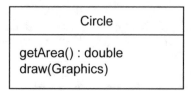

Fig. 8.9 The Circle class with "getArea" and "draw" methods added

An obvious problem here is that a Shape cannot calculate its area, or draw itself, so what implementation would we put into this class? In cases like this, where there is no meaningful implementation for the superclass method, we can use abstract methods. An abstract method, in addition to being labeled with the "abstract" keyword, has no method body; the signature simply ends with a semicolon:

```
public abstract double getArea();
public abstract void draw(Graphics g);
```

Note

From a design perspective, this mixing up of underlying object behavior and visual rendering is not a good separation of concerns. It is used in this example just make it easy to visually illustrate the outcomes of various code components.

A class that contains one or more abstract methods must itself be marked as "abstract", since without a full set of method implementations it cannot be instantiated. This also forces any subclasses to either implement the abstract methods, or they must also be marked as abstract.

Figure 8.10 shows a larger inheritance hierarchy of abstract and concrete shapes. In UML, an abstract class or method can be indicated by using italic text, as can be seen from the Shape class and its "getArea" and "draw" methods. The OneDimensionalShape and TwoDimensionalShape classes are also abstract and do not have to override the inherited "getArea" and "draw" methods. However, all the concrete classes at the bottom of the hierarchy must provide implementations of these methods.

Here is the complete implementation of the abstract Shape class. Note the abstract "getArea" and "draw" methods, added since the previous version of the class.

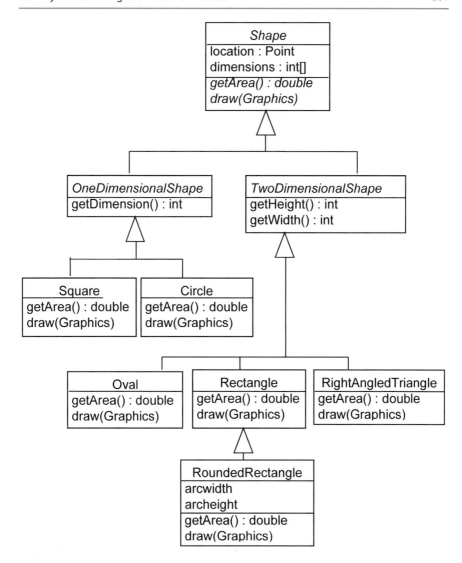

Fig. 8.10 The complete Shape hierarchy

```java
package com.foundjava.chapter8;

import java.awt.Graphics;
import java.awt.Point;

public abstract class Shape
{
  protected Point location;
  protected int[] dimensions;

  public Shape(Point location)
  {
    setLocation(location);
  }

  public int[] getDimensions() {
    return dimensions;
  }

  public void setDimensions(int[] dim) {
    this.dimensions = dim;
  }

  public Point getLocation() {
    return location;
  }

  public void setLocation(Point location) {
    this.location = location;
  }

  public abstract double getArea();

  public abstract void draw(Graphics g);
}
```

The other abstract classes remain unchanged. All the concrete classes will override both the "getArea" and "draw" methods. The following example is an updated version of the Circle class. The Math class is useful here in the "getArea" method, supplying both the value of PI, and the "pow" method which raises the first parameter value to the power of the second. The "draw" method draws a filled oval (there is a similar "drawOval" method that draws an unfilled oval). Note that this method is equally capable of drawing a circle, as well as an oval. The Graphics object passed as a parameter will be passed to the method from a graphical component.

```java
package com.foundjava.chapter8;

import java.awt.Graphics;
import java.awt.Point;

public class Circle extends OneDimensionalShape
{
  public Circle(Point location, int height)
  {
    super(location, height);
  }

@Override
  public double getArea()
  {
    return (Math.PI * (Math.pow(this.getDimension(), 2.0)));
  }

@Override
  public void draw(Graphics g)
  {
    g.fillOval(getLocation().x, getLocation().y,
    getDimension(), getDimension());
  }
}
```

Unlike the Circle, which is a subclass of OneDimensionalShape, the Oval class inherits from TwoDimensionalShape. Note how the implementation of its methods utilize the "getHeight" and "getWidth" methods from the superclass.

```java
package com.foundjava.chapter8;
import java.awt.Graphics;
import java.awt.Point;

public class Oval extends TwoDimensionalShape
{
  public Oval(Point location, int height, int width)
  {
    super(location, height, width);

  }

  @Override
  public double getArea()
  {
    return Math.PI * 0.25 * getHeight() * getWidth();
  }
  @Override
  public void draw(Graphics g)
  {
    g.fillOval(getLocation().x, getLocation().y,
      getHeight(), getWidth());
  }
}
```

The updated Rectangle, too, is a TwoDimensionalShape, so also uses the "getWidth" and "getHeight" inherited methods to calculate its area and draw itself.

```
package com.foundjava.chapter8;
import java.awt.Graphics;
import java.awt.Point;

public class Rectangle extends TwoDimensionalShape
{
  public Rectangle(Point location, int height, int width)
  {
    super(location, height, width);
  }

  @Override
  public double getArea()
  {
    return (this.getHeight() * this.getWidth());
  }

  @Override
  public void draw(Graphics g)
  {
    g.fillRect(getLocation().x, getLocation().y,
      getHeight(), getWidth());
  }
}
```

The RoundedRectangle class is a subclass of Rectangle (i.e. a concrete subclass of a concrete superclass) but adds a field to represent the corner radius that defines the size of the rounded corners.

```
package com.foundjava.chapter8;

import java.awt.Graphics;
import java.awt.Point;

public class RoundedRectangle extends Rectangle
{
  private int cornerRadius;

private int getCornerRadius()
{
  return cornerRadius;
}

private void setCornerRadius(int cornerRadius)
{
  this.cornerRadius = cornerRadius;
}
```

```java
  public RoundedRectangle(Point location, int width,
    int height, int cornerRadius)
  {
    super(location, height, width);
    setCornerRadius(cornerRadius);
  }

  @Override
  public double getArea()
  {
    double innerWidth = getHeight()-(getCornerRadius()*2);
    double innerHeight = getWidth()-(getCornerRadius()*2);
    return innerWidth * innerHeight + 2 * getCornerRadius()
       * (innerWidth + innerHeight) +
      (Math.PI * Math.pow(this.getCornerRadius(), 2.0));
  }

  @Override
  public void draw(Graphics g)
  {
    g.fillRoundRect
      (getLocation().x, getLocation().y, getHeight(),
       getWidth(), getCornerRadius(), getCornerRadius());
  }
}
```

The Square class is a subclass of OneDimensionalShape, so uses the inherited "getDimension" method to implement its own methods. It uses the same "fillRect" method on the Graphics class as the Rectangle to draw itself.

```java
package com.introjava.chapter8;
import java.awt.Graphics;
import java.awt.Point;
public class Square extends OneDimensionalShape
{
  public Square(Point location, int size)
  {
    super(location, size);
  }

  @Override
  public double getArea()
  {
    return Math.pow(getDimension(), 2);
  }

  @Override
  public void draw(Graphics g)
  {
    g.fillRect(getLocation().x, getLocation().y,
      getDimension(), getDimension());
  }
}
```

Finally, the RightAngledTriangle class is a TwoDimensionalShape, though it is quite possible that the two dimensions that are specified could be set to the same length. Calculating the area of a right-angled triangle is simple since it will be half the area of the bounding rectangle. There is no method on the Graphics class to specifically draw a triangle. Rather, there is a "fillPolygon" method that can be used to draw any closed polygon. This method takes as its parameters two integer arrays (the x-coordinates and the y-coordinates) and the number of points in the polygon. For a triangle, of course, there will be three sets of coordinates and the number of points will be three.

```
package com.foundjava.chapter8;
import java.awt.Graphics;
import java.awt.Point;

public class RightAngledTriangle extends TwoDimensionalShape
{
  public RightAngledTriangle(Point location, int dimension1,
    int dimension2)
  {
    super(location, dimension1, dimension2);
  }

  @Override
  public double getArea()
  {
    return (this.getDimensions()[0]*this.getDimensions()[1]/2);
  }

    @Override
    public void draw(Graphics g)
    {
      int xLocation = this.getLocation().x;
      int yLocation = this.getLocation().y;
      int[] xValues =
        {xLocation, xLocation, xLocation + getWidth() };
      int[] yValues = {yLocation, yLocation + getHeight(),
        yLocation + getHeight()};
      g.fillPolygon(xValues, yValues, 3);
    }
}
```

8.4.1   Using Polymorphic Methods

Having put this polymorphic hierarchy together, what does it enable us to do? The primary purpose of this type of programming is to enable us to write control structures at a level of abstraction that gives us flexibility about how we manipulate and interact with objects. The following example demonstrates the basic principles. It begins by creating an array of shapes. Each of the shapes being created is an instance of a concrete class but is accessed through a reference of the Shape class. Since this code example is only testing the "getArea" method of the classes, the Point parameter is not used and can be set to "null". After the creation of the array, there is a "for" loop that iterates through the array, invoking the "getArea" method on each of the objects. The key point here is that this code does not need to know anything about the actual classes of the objects that are being communicated with. Only the methods declared on the abstract class are required here. In this case, we are using both the polymorphism in our own hierarchy (the polymorphic "getArea" method) and polymorphism in the Java libraries (the "getClass" method of Object and the "getSimpleName" method of the Class class).

```
package com.foundjava.chapter8;

public class ShapeAreas
{
  public static void main(String[] args)
  {
    Shape[] shapes = {
            new Square(null, 250),
            new Rectangle(null, 25, 50),
            new Oval(null, 20,10),
            new Circle(null, 10),
            new RoundedRectangle(null, 25, 50, 10),
            new RightAngledTriangle(null, 100, 50),
          };

    for (int i = 0; i < shapes.length; i++)
    {
      Shape shape = shapes[i];
      System.out.println("The area of " +
       shape.getClass().getSimpleName() +
       " is " + shape.getArea());
    }
  }
}
```

This is the output from the program showing responses to the same method being invoked on objects of multiple subclasses:

```
The area of Square is 62500.0
The area of Rectangle is 1250.0
The area of Oval is 157.07963267948966
The area of Circle is 314.1592653589793
The area of RoundedRectangle is 1164.1592653589794
The area of RightAngledTriangle is 2500.0
```

To see the polymorphic effect of the "draw" methods, we will need to create a main method that is able to display a graphical window that shapes can be drawn on. We will cover UI programming in much more detail in later chapters but here is a class that displays some shapes in a graphical window. In this example, we see once again inheritance and polymorphism. We create a subclass of JFrame, which is the standard class for creating a graphical window in Java. This window has its title, size, close operation and visibility set in the "main" method. In the subclass, we override a polymorphic method called "paint". This method is automatically passed a Graphics object at runtime; we do not need to create a Graphics object anywhere in our code, it is created for us. In the "paint" method, we call the superclass version of the same method ("super.paint(g)"), which is not essential to make the program work but improves the redrawing behavior if the window is resized, then create the array of Shapes, this time giving them actual Point parameters to set their locations. Then a "for" loop iterates through the array, calling the various "draw" methods.

```
package com.foundjava.chapter8;

import java.awt.Graphics;
import java.awt.Point;

import javax.swing.JFrame;
public class DrawFrame extends JFrame
{
@Override
  public void paint(Graphics g)
  {
    super.paint(g);
    Shape[] shapes = {
      new Square(new Point(70,70), 70),
      new Rectangle(new Point(50,150), 25, 50),
      new Oval(new Point(100,220), 50,30),
      new Circle(new Point(175,100), 100),
      new RoundedRectangle(new Point(110,160), 40, 60, 20),
      new RightAngledTriangle(new Point(180, 210), 100, 50)
      };

    for (int i = 0; i < shapes.length; i++)
    {
      shapes[i].draw(g);
    }
  }

  public static void main(String[] args)
  {
    DrawFrame frame = new DrawFrame();
    frame.setTitle("Lots of shapes...");
    frame.setSize(400,400);
    frame.setDefaultCloseOperation(JFrame.EXIT_ON_CLOSE);
    frame.setVisible(true);
  }
}
```

The output will look like the window in Fig. 8.11: black shapes on a gray background.

Exercise 8.4

- Add an EquilateralTriangle class to an appropriate part of the existing shape hierarchy.
- Implement the "getArea" method. A web search will quickly enable you to find the formulae for calculating the area and altitude of an equilateral triangle.
- Implement the "draw" method. You can use the "fillPolygon" method to draw the triangle.
- Modify the DrawFrame and ShapeAreas classes so that they create at least one instance of your class.

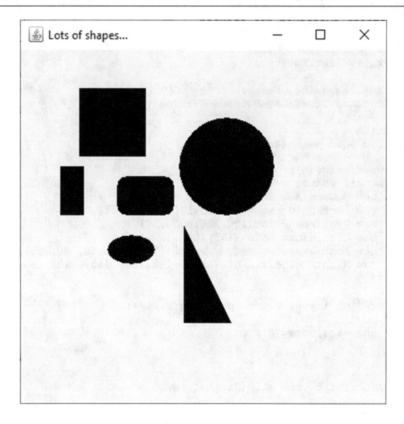

Fig. 8.11 Shapes drawn using the polymorphic "draw" method

8.5   Interfaces

An interface is like an abstract class with no state, in that it declares methods that have no implementation. It is, then, simply a list of method signatures (though there are some exceptions to this, as we will see later). There are some important differences, however, between classes and interfaces. Java does not support multiple inheritance, so a class can only ever extend one other class. With interfaces, however, we can choose to implement as many as we like in a single class. Implementing an interface means writing implementation code for each of the methods in the interface. Since classes can implement multiple interfaces, they can be used to address "cross cutting concerns" that would otherwise not fit neatly into an inheritance hierarchy. Different classes can implement interfaces polymorphically, as well as overriding superclass methods. You can have multiple references to the same object, each exposing a different set of methods, at the same time. Applying multiple interfaces in this way can give different perspectives on the same object, so an object of a single class may perform different roles in different parts of an application.

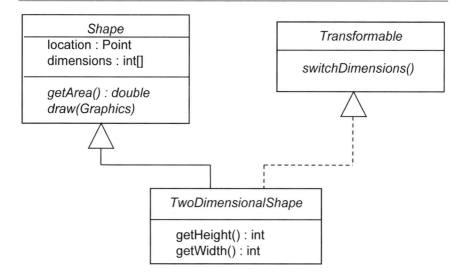

Fig. 8.12 TwoDimensionalShape implements the "Transformable" interface

In the UML, the implementation of an interface is shown with the same triangular arrowhead as inheritance but with a dashed rather than a solid line. In Fig. 8.12, the TwoDimensionalShape class is shown implementing an interface called "Transformable", with a method called "switchDimensions". Note how this implementation of an interface cuts across the inheritance hierarchy.

We use the keyword "interface" in place of "class" to declare an interface. The "abstract" keyword is not used, since an interface is automatically an abstraction. A new interface can be created in Java from the "File" menu or the pop-up menu by selecting "New" → "Interface". This will display the dialog box shown in Fig. 8.13, which has fewer options than the "New Java Class" dialog. However, it is possible for an interface to extend other interfaces, so this dialog includes an option to add any extended interfaces.

Here, we have created an interface called "Transformable" (which does not extend any other interfaces) and add a single method signature:

```
package com.foundjava.chapter8;

public interface Transformable
{
  public void switchDimensions();
}
```

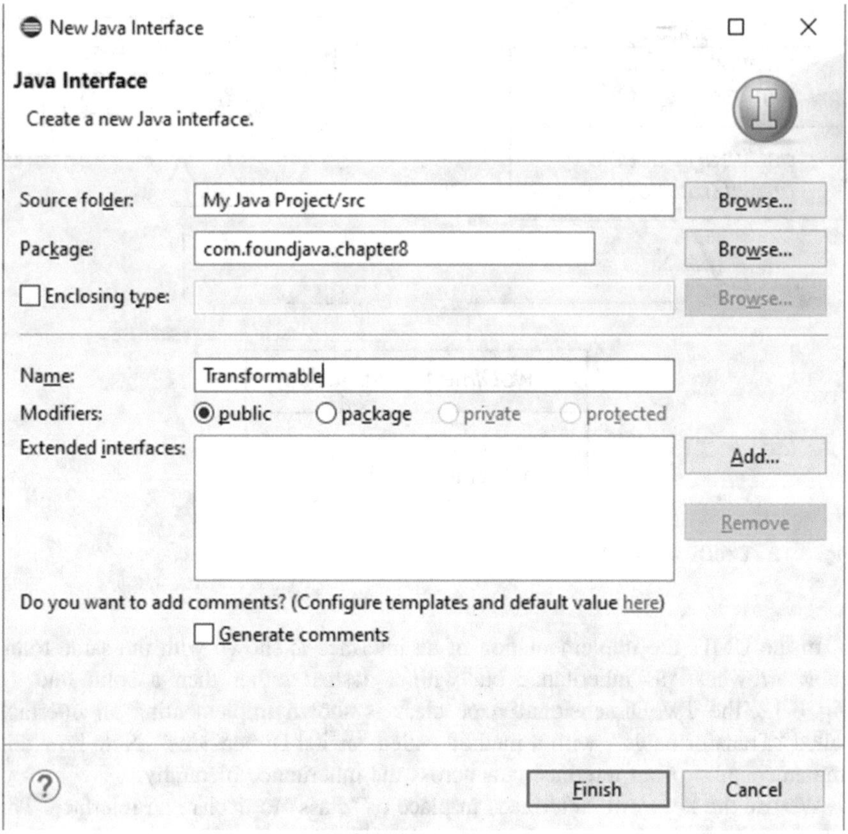

Fig. 8.13 Creating an interface in Eclipse

This interface declares a "switchDimensions" method which some (but not all) shapes can implement in some way to switch their dimensions. It should be reasonably obvious that it is only the TwoDimensionalShapes that can switch their dimensions. The interface leaves the implementation entirely up to implementing classes; all they need do is override the method signature with a concrete implementation of the method.

8.5.1 Naming Interfaces

There are some common conventions for naming interfaces. Because interfaces have no state and are only about method actions, using an action name (ending in "able") is often appropriate. That is how we have named the "Transformable" interface. Java itself includes several interfaces that follow this naming convention, including "Cloneable" (can be copied using a custom "clone" method) and "Serializable" (can be serialized across a stream, such as a file or a network connection). These types of "action" interfaces usually cut across hierarchies and only specify a small number of methods (sometimes only one).

In other cases, interfaces are used that have a one to one relationship with concrete classes in a specific implementation. With this type of interface, it typically contains a definition for all (or most) of the implementation class's public methods. There are several design reasons why it can be helpful to only expose an interface to client code but implement it with a concrete class that is not directly accessible. One example is database access, where a common set of interfaces is implemented by different sets of classes depending on which database platform you are connecting to, as we will see in Chap. 15 when we look at Java Database Connectivity (JDBC). In cases like this, there are two general approaches.

1. The interfaces are named using proper nouns, but the implementation classes end in "Impl", e.g. "Course" interface and "CourseImpl" class. This is the kind of approach taken when the interfaces are in the Java libraries and the concrete classes are implemented by third parties, such as external implementations of JDBC.
2. The interface name is prefixed interface with "I" and proper nouns are used for class names, for example, "ICourse" interface and "Course" class. This approach is one you are more likely to take in creating your own interfaces, as the "I" prefix makes it clear to other users of your code that this is an interface.

8.5.2 Implementing an Interface

We implement an interface with the "implements" keyword. The class must provide implementations for all the methods in the interface. This example is a simplistic transformation but serves to demonstrate the idea of an interface as a cross cutting concern.

```
public abstract class TwoDimensionalShape extends Shape
    implements Transformable
{
...

  public void switchDimensions()
  {
    int temp = dimensions[0];
    dimensions[0] = dimensions[1];
    dimensions[1] = temp;
  }
```

In a similar way to how a superclass reference can be used to reference an object of a subclass, an interface can be used to reference an object that implements that interface. Again, like a superclass, the reference can only be used to invoke methods that are available in the reference type. This means, for example, that if we create a RightAngledTriangle referenced by a Transformable interface reference, the single message we can send via that reference is "switchDimensions".

```
Transformable t = new RightAngledTriangle
    (new Point(180, 180), 100, 50);
t.switchDimensions();
```

However, we can also do some switching between references of different types, as long as they are compatible. For example, we can create an array of TwoDimensionalShapes.

```
TwoDimensionalShape[] shapes = {...etc.
```

Since TwoDimensionalShape implements Transformable, we can assign an array reference of Transformable to point to the same array.

```
Transformable[] transforms = shapes;
```

Now we can reference the same array using different types of reference—remember how the assignment of object references makes them point to the same objects? In this program, we create an array of shapes that are also referenced by the Transformable interface. In a "for" loop, we first draw the shapes in the current position using the array of Shape references, then transform the same objects using the array of Transformable references, then draw them again using the Shape references. To make the output a little clearer we set the color of the drawing to two shades of gray using a couple of static fields from the java.awt.Color class.

```
package com.foundjava.chapter8;

import java.awt.Color;
import java.awt.Graphics;
import java.awt.Point;

import javax.swing.JFrame;
public class TransformShapes extends JFrame
{
  public void paint(Graphics g)
  {
    super.paint(g);
    TwoDimensionalShape[] shapes =
    {
      new Rectangle(new Point(50, 150), 25, 50),
      new Oval(new Point(100, 220), 50, 30),
      new RoundedRectangle(new Point(110, 160), 40, 60, 20),
      new RightAngledTriangle(new Point(180, 210), 100, 50)
    };
    Transformable[] transforms = shapes;
    for (int i = 0; i < shapes.length; i++)
    {
      g.setColor(Color.GRAY);
      shapes[i].draw(g);
      transforms[i].switchDimensions();
      g.setColor(Color.DARKGRAY);
      shapes[i].draw(g);
    }
  }

  public static void main(String[] args)
  {
    TransformShapes frame = new TransformShapes();
    frame.setTitle("Shapes transformed");
    frame.setSize(400, 400);
    frame.setDefaultCloseOperation(JFrame.EXIT_ON_CLOSE);
    frame.setVisible(true);
  }
}
```

Figure 8.14 shows the output, with the four shapes transformed.

Exercise 8.5

- Create a "Rotatable" interface with a "rotate" method. Assume that this method rotates a shape 90° in a clockwise direction.
- Make any classes implement this interface that you think you can. You may need to rethink the way that the shapes currently store their locations and dimension information to get them to rotate in an appropriate manner.
- Having implemented one "rotate" method, add further methods to the interface to provide various types of rotation.

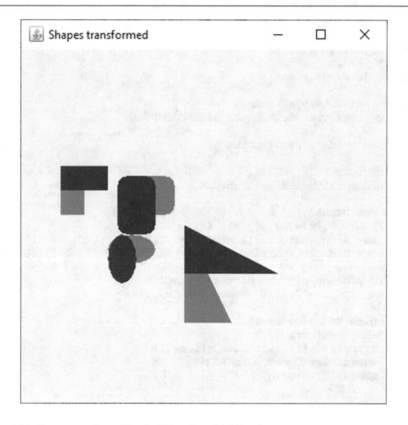

Fig. 8.14 Shapes transformed by the "Transformable" interface

Exercise 8.6

The "draw" method relates to graphical representations of shapes, but the Shape hierarchy might be used in contexts where graphical views are not required. This means that "draw" might be better specified by an interface, separate from the Shape hierarchy.

- Extract the "draw" method into an interface and remove it from the abstract classes.
- Make the concrete classes implement the "draw" method.
- Modify the DrawFrame class so that it draws the shapes using your interface.

Exercise 8.7

- Modify the Snakes and Ladders game so that both Snake and Ladder are subclasses of a superclass called Mover.

- Their common methods should be put into Mover. They should contain only their own constructors and a polymorphic 'showMessage' method that displays if the object is a snake or a ladder.
- Modify the BoardSquare class so that it has one reference to a Mover object rather than references to both a Snake and a Ladder.
- Use this reference to create the appropriate type of subclass object (Snake or Ladder) in the correct squares.
- Once the BoardSquare class has been modified, you can change the message passing mechanism described in Fig. 7.14 to one that uses the polymorphic methods of Mover to move the PlayerPiece to the correct square. Ensure that the whole game still works!

8.5.3   Further Aspects of Interfaces

In this chapter, we have defined interfaces as containing only one or more abstract method signatures. The implementation of these methods is done in any classes that implement the interface. One potential problem with this is that if a new method signature is added to an existing interface, then this will break any classes that already implement that interface since they will now be required to implement the new method. To overcome this problem, Java 8 introduced the ability to add default methods to an interface. This was not just for the benefit of developers writing Java code, it was also necessary for the developers of Java itself to be able to re-engineer parts of the JDK to incorporate lambda expressions into existing interfaces while making them backward compatible with existing code. A default method does not have to be implemented by classes that implement the interface, though they can optionally override the default implementation.

As an example of an interface with a default method, we will introduce another method to our existing Transformable interface called "resizeBy". A class implementing this method could allow an object to resize itself based on a scaling factor. The modified interface might look like this:

```
public interface Transformable
{
  public void switchDimensions();
  public void resizeBy(double scaleFactor);
}
```

The problem here, of course, is that any classes that currently implement the Transformable interface will be broken because they do not currently implement the "resizeBy" method. The solution to this negative impact on existing code is to make "resizeBy" a default method, with a default implementation:

```
public interface Transformable
{
   public void switchDimensions();
   default public void resizeBy(double scaleFactor)
   {
      System.err.println
         ("override this method to provide resizing behavior");
   }
}
```

In this example, there is no meaningful default behavior that can be provided, since in this context the interface cannot be aware of any object state that might relate to size. Any object that already implements the "Transformable" interface and calls this method will just generate a runtime error message. However, in other situations, a default method could include some meaningful code that does not require any object state in its implementation.

With the default implementation in place, any class implementing the interface can elect to override the default implementation of "resizeBy". For example, here is an implementation of "resizeBy" in "TwoDimensionalShape" that applies the scaling factor to both dimensions.

```
@Override
public void resizeBy(double scaleFactor)
{
   int height = getHeight();
   int width = getWidth();
   setDimensions(new int[] {height *= scaleFactor,
      width *= scaleFactor});
}
```

Of course, you may be thinking that this resizing behavior should be applied to all shapes, not just two-dimensional ones. That is a consequence of building an architecture by syntax example rather than good design principles. Feel free to improve the design as you see fit.

It is also possible for interfaces to have private methods. For example, we might choose to use some internal encapsulation in the default method of an interface. We have already covered the syntax for private methods so will not add a further example here.

Another feature of interfaces that were introduced in Java 8 was the option to include static methods. As we have seen in previous examples, a static method is one that can be executed directly by the class, rather than being invoked by an object. A static method on an interface can therefore be directly called using the interface. Static methods cannot access object state directly and must have a useful implementation or there is no point in having them. They also need to have a meaningful semantic relationship with the interface. The following example adds a static method to the Transformable Interface called "isTransformable". To reduce the amount of new syntax in this example, this is not the best possible implementation of this method but will suffice to demonstrate the principle of a static interface method.

The implementation of the "isTransformable" method relies on some reflection code, namely, the "getInterfaces" method of the Class class. This returns an array of all the interfaces implemented by the class, but only those directly implemented by it, not those implemented by superclasses. So, for this example to work, we will need to add "implements Transformable" to the signature of the Rectangle class. Note that because its superclass (TwoDimensionalShape) already implements this interface, Rectangle does not need to provide any implementation code.

```
public class Rectangle extends TwoDimensionalShape
   implements Transformable
```

The next example is an implementation of the "isTransformable" method of the "Transformable" interface. It is, of course, a static method. It takes a Shape as an argument since the method cannot know anything about object state unless an object is passed to it. "getClass().getInterfaces()" is called on it to get an array of interfaces implemented by the class, which (for simplicity's sake) we convert to a String using the static "toString" method of the Arrays class that can convert the content of an array to a single String (you will get a compiler warning on this line but we cannot fix that until we have introduced generics in a later chapter). Then we use the "contains" method of the String class to see if the name of the Transformable interface is in the array. If it is, we return "true", otherwise we return "false".

```
public static boolean isTransformable(Shape s)
{
   boolean isTransformable = false;
   String interfaces =
      Arrays.toString(s.getClass().getInterfaces());
   if(interfaces.contains("Transformable"))
   {
      isTransformable = true;
   }
   return isTransformable;
}
```

Here is a short test class that creates a Square and a Rectangle. Only the Rectangle directly implements the Transformable interface.

```
package com.foundjava.chapter8;

import java.awt.Point;

public class StaticInterfaceTest
{
  public static void main(String[] args)
  {
    OneDimensionalShape mySquare =
      new Square(new Point(100, 100), 10);
    TwoDimensionalShape myRectangle =
      new Rectangle(new Point(200, 200), 10, 8);
    System.out.println("Square is transformable: " +
      Transformable.isTransformable(mySquare));
    System.out.println("Rectangle is transformable: " +
      Transformable.isTransformable(myRectangle));   }
}
```

The output from running this code is as follows:

```
Square is transformable: false
Rectangle is transformable: true
```

8.6   Lambda Expressions

Another significant change to interfaces in Java 8 was the ability to use lambda expressions to implement any interface that has a single abstract method. A lambda expression is simply an anonymous function that does not have a name. Its main value is as a shorthand way of writing code that lets you write a function implementation in the same place you are going to use it. This is particularly useful if you are only going to use that function in one place, and the implementation is short. It avoids having to declare and write a separate method in a class somewhere else in the codebase.

To take a step back, and put Java lambda expressions in context, we should first note that Java does not support standalone functions. In an object-oriented language, functions always belong to a class or an object—they are class or object methods. Object methods are based around a set of state that relates to a specific object. However, there has been a move in recent years toward languages that support functional programming, such as Haskell, Scala, Erlang, Lisp and Clojure. The core requirement of a functional programming language is that it supports standalone functions, but Java has always been object-oriented and standalone functions have not been supported. In a functional language (at least at the simplest level) functions do not maintain any state, and if state data is passed around between functions then it is immutable (i.e. cannot be changed). Functions can also be passed around as references and used as the parameter arguments or return types of other functions (these are known as higher order functions).

Since both types of programming have their advantages (functional programming is particularly useful for concurrent systems) it made sense for Java to include at least some features of functional programming.

Let us suppose that Java did in fact support standalone functions. Since they would not maintain any internal state, we would expect them to receive any state that needed to be processed as parameter arguments, and for any results of the function to be returned. To give a very simple example, we could have a function that compared two numbers and returned the higher of these. The function might look something like this (this is not an anonymous function, but will help build toward Java lambda syntax):

```
double returnHigherValue(double val1, double val2)
{
  if(val1 > val2)
    return val1;
  else
    return val2;
}
```

To use the function, we would just need to call it directly:

```
double higherVal = returnHigherValue(3, 4);
```

However, since Java does not support such functions, a different mechanism that fitted within an object-oriented architecture was needed. This is where lambda expressions come in.

The lambda expressions introduced with Java 8 support (up to a point) functions that do not belong to classes. One of the reasons for introducing lambda expressions is to reduce code complexity. Often, Java requires us to create objects to host a single function, when it would be a lot simpler just to write the function on its own.

It is important to note that Java has not suddenly become a functional language. Rather, it supports some aspects of functional programming within the context of implementing certain types of interface.

8.6.1   Lambda Expression Syntax

There are a few variations in code style that can be used when writing lambda expressions, but at its simplest, the format of a lambda expression is

```
(function parameters) -> function definition
```

Note the arrow operator (a minus character followed by a greater than character) which indicates a lambda expression (we first saw this operator in Chap. 4 in the context of the switch expression). Lambda expressions in Java can only be used in the context of interfaces that have a single abstract method to be implemented (not including any private, default or static methods that the interface may also have). Since there is no ambiguity about which method is being implemented, the code for the expression can be quite simple.

Because a Java lambda expression requires an interface with a single abstract method, our example method would have to be part of an interface. For example:

```
public interface IValueCompare {
    double returnHigherValue(double val1, double val2);
}
```

Note the "I" prefix type of interface naming, since the "able" suffix we have been using does not really make sense with functions that do not get implemented by objects.

In the following code example, the method is implemented by the lambda expression, while the interface reference "compareImpl" gives us a reference through which we can call the function later.

```
IValueCompare compareImpl = (double val1, double val2) -> {
    if(val1 > val2)
        return val1;
    else
        return val2;
};
```

We can then invoke the lambda expression using the Interface reference "compareImpl".

```
System.out.println(compareImpl.returnHigherValue(3, 4));
```

The key thing to note is that we did not need to create a class to implement the interface; we only needed to provide the function implementation as a lambda expression.

One more thing we can note about our lambda expression is that (like "var") it can use type inference, where the compiler can infer the type of a data item from the context. The following version of the lambda expression is also perfectly fine—note how there is no need to provide the type (double) of the two arguments—this can be inferred from the signature in the interface.

```
IValueCompare compareImpl = (val1, val2) -> {
    if(val1 > val2)
        return val1;
    else
        return val2;
};
```

There are many other aspects to lambda expressions, some of which we will encounter in upcoming chapters.

Exercise 8.8

- Create an interface called IAverage with a method called "getMean" that takes an array of doubles as an argument and returns a double.
- Add a private method to the interface that takes an array of doubles as an argument and calculates and returns the mean average of the values in the array.
- Add a default method to the interface that calls the private method to calculate and return the mean average of an array of doubles.
- Create a class that implements the interface but does not provide an implementation of the "getMean" method.
- Create a class with a "main" method that creates an instance of your class that implements the interface and invokes the "getMean" method (the default method on the interface will be called).

Exercise 8.9
The previous exercise used default and private methods to implement the "getAverage" method of the IAverage interface. In this exercise, we will use a lambda expression to implement a method of the interface. This requires the interface to have a single abstract method.

- Add an abstract method called "getAverage" to the IAverage interface that takes an array of doubles as an argument and returns a double.
- Create a class with a "main" method and add code that implements the "getAverage" method of the interface using a lambda expression that calculates the mean average of an array of doubles.
- Add another lambda expression that implements the "getAverage" method so that it returns the median average of an array of doubles (assume the array is sorted into order).

8.7   Summary

In this chapter, we have seen how inheritance can be used to write closely related classes that have some fields and methods in common. In the code examples, a set of classes were organized into an inheritance hierarchy of super and subclasses that went beyond the default behavior of Java classes to inherit directly from class "Object". This use of inherence was built on to demonstrate how polymorphic methods can be written that allow objects of different classes to respond differently to the same method calls. Some examples were shown of classes providing polymorphic implementations of methods inherited from the "Object" class, such as "toString". The role of abstract classes and methods in inheritance hierarchies was demonstrated through the dynamic binding of a superclass reference to a subclass object. The "super" keyword was introduced in the context of calling the methods and constructors of a superclass, and the "@Override" annotation was used to ensure that methods correctly overrode those inherited from a superclass. The chapter also explained how Java interfaces can be used to provide common services across a range of implementing classes and concluded by exploring some of the enhancements to interfaces introduced with Java 8, including default methods, private methods and lambda expressions.

Exception Handling

9

Exceptions are an important aspect of Java programming because they enable us to deal efficiently, and in an object-oriented manner, with the unusual program flow, whether it is caused by technical issues or business processes. Prior to languages with built-in exception handling, such issues had to be dealt with by manually passing error codes around a program, without any encapsulation or standard ways of handling them.

Exceptions cover a range of issues from major programming errors like dividing an integer by zero, or trying to invoke methods on a null reference, to minor business process exceptions like a user entering an invalid area code in their address.

9.1 Java Exceptions

When an unusual condition arises in Java code, it can throw an exception. This means that it creates an object that represents that exception, encapsulates some information about it and gives the program a chance to do something about it. If nothing is done, the program will terminate. Since we do not want a program to terminate arbitrarily, we need to write code that is able to detect and handle any exceptions that may arise. In some cases, the compiler requires us to write code that can handle exceptions. In other cases, we need to anticipate the possibility ourselves. In addition, there are places where we may want to create exceptions explicitly, in situations where a business rule has been violated. Java provides syntax for handling all these possibilities.

© Springer Nature Switzerland AG 2020
D. Parsons, *Foundational Java*, Texts in Computer Science,
https://doi.org/10.1007/978-3-030-54518-5_9

9.1.1 The Exception Handling Hierarchy

The classes in Java that relate to exception handling appear in a hierarchy (Fig. 9.1). At the top of the hierarchy is the "Throwable" class, which represents all kinds of errors and exceptions that might occur in a Java program. A Throwable object can be created by the Java Virtual Machine at runtime or explicitly created using the "throw" keyword (see Table 9.1). There are two kinds of Throwable: Errors and Exceptions. Programmers need not concern themselves with instances of the Error class, since these represent runtime errors that applications cannot be expected to do anything about. One example of an Error subclass is VirualMachineError. This kind of error is not something that the average application is likely to be able to recover from. Application programmers should, however, be able to do something about instances of Exception and its subclasses. As the Javadoc for Exception says, "The class Exception and its subclasses are a form of Throwable that indicates conditions that a reasonable application might want to catch".

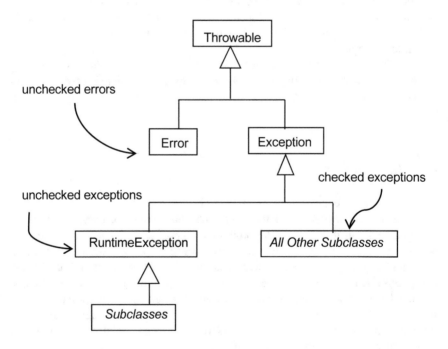

Fig. 9.1 The Java exception and error hierarchy

Table 9.1 Java exception handling keywords

Keyword	Usage
throws	Indicates that a method may throw an exception
try	Encloses a block of code that may throw an exception
catch	Follows "try"—encloses a block of code that is invoked if a specified exception is thrown
finally	Follows "try" or "catch"—encloses a block of code that executes regardless of whether any exceptions are thrown
throw	Allows the programmer to explicitly throw an exception

9.1.2 Checked and Unchecked Exceptions

There is another layer of the hierarchy beneath the Exception class that affects the way that we manage exceptions. One of the subclasses of Exception is RuntimeException. This class, and all its subclasses, represent exceptions that can be thrown during the normal operation of the Java Virtual Machine (as opposed to application errors). These are known as "unchecked" exceptions because we are not required by the compiler to handle any of these exceptions, though we might choose to do so to prevent them causing our programs to terminate. In contrast, the other exceptions that are direct subclasses of Exception are "checked" exceptions, which means that the compiler will ensure that we do something in our application code to handle them.

9.1.3 Exception Handling Keywords

The Java keywords that relate to exception handling are shown in Table 9.1. Note the distinction between "throws", which can appear on a method signature, and "throw", which is used to explicitly throw an exception in the body of a method.

9.2 Handling Checked Exceptions

Java will check, at compile-time, whether you are attempting to do something that might throw a checked exception, and if so, whether your program contains the code necessary to handle such an exception. Our first example uses the System class, which (in addition to having an "out" object field) has an "in" object field (an instance of a concrete subclass of the abstract InputStream class), with a zero arguments "read" method that reads the next byte of data from the input stream. It actually returns an int, but only one byte of the int is populated with data. This is adequate for reading a Unicode character from the keyboard in the range 0–255. The second line of the following "main" method casts the int to a char so that the character is displayed rather than the Unicode value. As it stands, this code will not compile. The compiler will signal the error "Unhandled exception type IOException" (IOException is in the java.io package).

```
package com.foundjava.chapter9;
public class ReadFromKeyboard
{
  public static void main(String[] args)
  {
    int myChar = System.in.read(); // will not compile
    System.out.println((char)myChar);
  }
}
```

The problem is with the InputStream's "read" method, which throws java.io. IOException, a checked exception. The exceptions that can be thrown by a method are stated in the method declaration, and the Javadoc for a class will tell you if any of its methods throw exceptions. If you check the Javadoc for the InputStream class, you will see that the signature of the "read" method is.

```
public abstract int read() throws IOException
```

If we just want the shortest route to get the code to compile, then the minimum response is to acknowledge that an exception may occur when using "System.in. read" by simply re-throwing the exception. This means adding another "throws" clause to the signature of the calling method, in this case, "main".

```
public static void main(String[] args)
    throws java.io.IOException
```

This allows the class to compile without dealing with any exception that might be thrown at runtime. If an exception does occur, the program will terminate. In the following version of the class, the code will compile because we have added "throws IOException" to the signature of the "main" method (the IOException class has also been imported).

```
package com.foundjava.chapter9;
import java.io.IOException;
public class ReadFromKeyboard
{
  public static void main(String[] args)
    throws java.io.IOException
  {
    int myChar = System.in.read();
    System.out.println((char)myChar);
  }
}
```

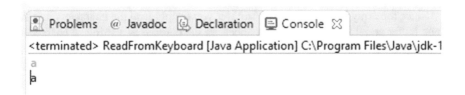

Fig. 9.2 Using the console for both input and output in eclipse

In Eclipse, when we run a program that uses "System.in.read", the output console is also used for input. You terminate the input by pressing the Enter key. Only the first character typed will be captured by the "read" method. Figure 9.2 shows the character "a" has been typed in and then echoed back to the same console.

9.2.1   Catching Exceptions: "try" and "catch"

Simply re-throwing a checked exception from the "main" method is not a particularly good way of dealing with it. The reason for having checked exceptions is that they may occur, so basically ignoring them will not lead to very robust applications. Therefore, instead of simply re-throwing an exception, we should do something to catch it ourselves. This has the benefit of allowing a program to continue running even if an exception has occurred. The syntax for doing this is based on the "try" and "catch" keywords:

```
try
{
   // do this
}
catch(anException e)
{
   // if it all went horribly wrong, do this
}
```

"anException" must either be one of the predefined exception classes that exist in Java or an object of an Exception subclass we have written ourselves (we will look at how to write and use custom Exception subclasses later in this chapter). It must also be an exception that could potentially be thrown by the code in the "try" block.

The next example uses a slightly different version of the "read" method that allows more than one character to be entered into an array of bytes. Again, it throws java.io.IOException.

```
public abstract int read(byte[] b) throws IOException
```

Since the array of bytes is not a String, if you simply read the characters into the byte buffer and display it, it will not appear in the console as a string of characters. Therefore, an intermediate step is required, where we create a String from the byte array. The String also needs to have any trailing spaces removed, which can be done with the "trim" method. This line of code does the conversion by using one of the many constructors available for the String class, and then trims the string:

```
inputString = new String(buffer).trim();
```

Note

If you want to be sure to remove any kind of leading or trailing whitespace that appears anywhere in the Unicode table then you can use the "strip" method instead of "trim".

In the following example, the "read" code is put into a "try" block, and any IOException that may be thrown is caught in the "catch" block. We must do something inside a "catch" block. If we catch an exception but do nothing, then all the information that was available in the original exception, to tell us what happened, is lost. The very least you should do in a "catch" block is display, or otherwise log, information about the exception. A simple way to do this is to call the "printStackTrace" method on the exception object that is generated when the exception is thrown. This is provided as a parameter to the "catch" block. Now that the Exception is being handled in the "try-catch" block, the "main" method no longer needs to have a "throws" clause. One thing to note about "try-catch" blocks is that because of scope we often need to declare variables outside of the "try" block to make them visible after the "catch", as in this example.

```
package com.foundjava.chapter9;
public class ReadBufferFromKeyboard
{
  public static void main(String[] args)
  {
    byte[] buffer = new byte[10];
    String inputString= null;
    try
    {
      System.in.read(buffer);
      inputString = new String(buffer).trim();
    }
    catch(java.io.IOException e)
    {
      e.printStackTrace();
    }
    System.out.println(inputString);
  }
}
```

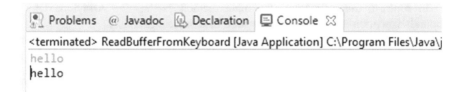

Fig. 9.3   Using the eclipse console for entering strings of characters

Now, if an IOException is thrown by the "read" method, instead of the program terminating, the code in the "catch" block will be executed. Figure 9.3 shows the input/output console when this program is run.

9.3   Handling Unchecked Exceptions

When you are using code that throws checked exceptions, the compiler gives you no choice but to do something about them. In addition, you can, if you choose to, handle unchecked exceptions as well. One example of an unchecked exception is the ArrayIndexOutOfBoundsException. For example, this piece of code will compile, but will throw an ArrayIndexOutOfBoundsException at runtime as soon as it attempts to access index 3 of the array:

```
package com.foundjava.chapter9;
public class ArrayIndexExample
{
  public static void main(String[] args)
  {
    int[] intArray = new int[3];
    for(int i = 0; i < 5; i++)
    {
      intArray[i] = i;
      System.out.println(intArray[i]);
    }
  }
}
```

The output will display something like the following message (the order of the standard and error output can become mixed up in Eclipse as they use different output streams):

```
Exception in thread "main" 0
1
2
java.lang.ArrayIndexOutOfBoundsException: 3
at
com.foundjava.chapter9.ArrayIndexExample.main(ArrayIndexExample
.java:10)
```

In contrast, this version of the main method catches the ArrayIndexOutOf BoundsException and allows the program to terminate normally.

```
package com.foundjava.chapter9;
public class ArrayIndexExample
{
  public static void main(String[] args)
  {
    int[] intArray = new int[3];
    for (int i = 0; i < 5; i++)
    {
      try
      {
        intArray[i] = i;
        System.out.println(intArray[i]);
      }
      catch (ArrayIndexOutOfBoundsException e)
      {
        e.printStackTrace();
      }
    }
  }
}
```

This time the output shows that the exception is thrown, but the loop carries on after the stack trace has been printed. We get two ArrayIndexOutOfBounds Exceptions occurring, but the program continues to the end of the loop.

```
0
1
2
java.lang.ArrayIndexOutOfBoundsException: 3
at
com.foundjava.chapter9.ArrayIndexExample.main(ArrayIndexExample
.java:11)
java.lang.ArrayIndexOutOfBoundsException: 4
at
com.foundjava.chapter9.ArrayIndexExample.main(ArrayIndexExample
.java:11)
```

9.3.1 Exiting

In most of the examples in this chapter, a "catch" block will be an opportunity to either ignore an exception and carry on or do something to fix the problem at runtime. In some cases, however, an exception occurs where there is no point in allowing the program to continue as it cannot reasonably recover. In cases like this, we can explicitly exit the program, using the "System.exit" method. This takes an integer parameter, where a non-zero value indicates an abnormal exit. Here, for example, we add a "System.exit" to a "catch" block and use the value "1" (an abnormal termination).

```
catch(Exception e)
{
  e.printStackTrace();
  System.exit(1);
}
```

9.4   Catching Multiple Exceptions

When writing code where many different exceptions may be thrown, it can get quite ugly and complex to have a whole series of separate "try-catch" blocks one after the other. A better approach is to have a single block of code that may potentially throw more than one type of exception. To handle this situation, a single "try" block can have more than one "catch" block following it. In the next example, we use "System.in.read" to attempt to read a number from the keyboard. Since the original keystrokes are read as an array of bytes, we need some way of converting these into a number. We have already seen how to convert a byte array into a trimmed String. Now we need a means of converting a String into a number.

As we know, Java has both objects and primitive types (int, double, etc.). To provide a bridge between them, Java provides a set of wrapper classes for all the built-in types allowing us to convert primitives to objects and vice versa. There are classes for all the types of numbers including Float, Integer, Double and Long. One advantage of these classes is that they provide static conversion methods to convert string representations of numbers into primitive values. For example, the "parseInt" method of the Integer class takes a String as a parameter and returns a value of the int data type. By this method, we can easily convert a String to an int, for example,

```
int anInt = Integer.parseInt("12345");
```

If the String passed as a parameter cannot be converted to an int, the method will throw a java.lang.NumberFormatException, though you do not have to put the method in a try block to get it to compile because this is an unchecked exception. However, it can be a useful exception to check for, so we will do so in this example. This is the complete class with a single "try" block followed by two "catch" blocks:

```
package com.foundjava.chapter9;
public class ReadIntegerFromKeyboard
{
  public static void main(String[] args)
  {
    byte[] buffer = new byte[10];
    int inputInt = 0;
    try
    {
      System.in.read(buffer);
      String inputString = new String(buffer).trim();
      inputInt = Integer.parseInt(inputString);
    }
    catch(java.io.IOException e)
    {
      e.printStackTrace();
    }
    catch(NumberFormatException e)
    {
      e.printStackTrace();
    }
    System.out.println(inputInt);
  }
}
```

Given any input that can be converted into an integer value, the program will run without throwing an exception, On the other hand, entering any non-numeric characters will cause the NumberFormatException to be thrown:

```
a
java.lang.NumberFormatException: For input string: "a"
at
java.lang.NumberFormatException.forInputString(Unknown Source)
at java.lang.Integer.parseInt(Unknown Source)
at java.lang.Integer.parseInt(Unknown Source)
0
at com.foundjava.chapter9.ReadBufferFromKeyboard.main
(ReadBufferFromKeyboard.java:13)
```

9.4.1   Ordering Multiple "catch" Blocks

As shown in the previous example, you can catch any number of exceptions at the end of a single "try" block, each in its own "catch" block. In the last example, the two exceptions were in different parts of the hierarchy so would not interfere with each other. However, if you have superclass and subclass exceptions following the same "try" block, then you must put the "catch" blocks in order from the bottom to the top of the hierarchy, for example,

```
try
{
...
}
catch(IOException e)
{
...
}
catch(Exception e)
{
...
}
```

The reason for this is that if you put an exception, which is further up the hierarchy, first, then that "catch" block will be the first one to be matched. In the example above, if the order of the "catch" blocks was reversed, since IOException is a subclass of Exception, if one is thrown then the Exception block will be matched first, and the IOException catch block will never be reached.

Exercise 9.1
In this section, we have looked at some aspects of handling basic keyboard input in Java. Given that this is not particularly simple, it is helpful to encapsulate the code that handles keyboard input inside a class. Building a reusable Keyboard class means that we do not have to write the same code repeatedly every time we want to get some data from the keyboard.

- Create a reusable Keyboard class that includes methods to read a single character, a String or an integer from the keyboard.
- Include the required exception handling.
- Add a method to input a floating-point number, using the "parseDouble" method of the Double class to implement the method.
- Test your Keyboard class in a "main" method.

9.5 Throwing an Exception with "throw"

In the examples, we have seen so far, we have been using Java exceptions that may be thrown by the Java virtual machine. Sometimes, however, we need to take responsibility for throwing exceptions ourselves. This is what the "throw" keyword is for, it enables us to choose situations in which we wish to create and throw exception objects, usually in response to some business rule that has been violated.

Back in Chap. 6, we looked at the role of "setter" methods in guarding an object's fields from being set to inappropriate values. One example was the number of days of the duration of a Course; there would be a sensible range of durations beyond which we would not want the number of days to be set. Certainly, we would not want negative values, and since the Java "int" type is unsigned, we would get no protection from that just by using the data type. In this example, we will add some conditional code to the "setNumberOfDays" method that will explicitly throw an exception if the parameter value supplied to it is less than 1 or more than 10 (of course we could apply any rule for a value range that we wanted to).

What kind of exception should we throw? Java has many exception classes that cater for various types of exception, but the one that would be most appropriate here would be the IllegalArgumentException. In previous examples, exceptions have been automatically thrown, but in this case, we must both create and explicitly throw the exception ourselves since the Java Virtual Machine cannot judge if a parameter violates a business rule. In the body the method, we can use an "if" statement containing a "throw" to create the exception, if required. The "throw" keyword is followed by an IllegalArgumentException object, created using the constructor that takes a String as a parameter. This parameter is intended to be used for an error message. In the following revised version of the "setNumberOfDays" method, an IllegalArgumentException is thrown if the "numberOfDays" parameter is out of range. Note the addition of the Javadoc "@throws" annotation in the comment block. IllegalArgumentException is an unchecked exception so client code will not be forced by the compiler to be aware that it may be thrown. Therefore, the addition of a Javadoc comment is helpful to potential users of the method.

```
/**
 * @param numberOfDays
 * @throws IllegalArgumentException
 */
public void setNumberOfDays(int numberOfDays)
      throws IllegalArgumentException
{
  if (numberOfDays < 1 || numberOfDays > 10)
  {
    throw new IllegalArgumentException(numberOfDays +
      " is outside the valid range of 1 - 10");
  }
  else
  {
    this.numberOfDays = numberOfDays;
  }
}
```

The final piece of the jigsaw is in the client code that creates a Course and calls the "setNumberOfDays" method. In this code, we attempt to set the number of days to "12" to deliberately trigger the exception:

```
package com.foundjava.chapter9;
public class CreateCourse
{
  public static void main(String[] args)
  {
    try
    {
      Course c = new Course();
      c.setNumberOfDays(12);
    }
    catch(IllegalArgumentException e)
    {
      e.printStackTrace();
    }
  }
}
```

The output from running this program is

```
java.lang.IllegalArgumentException:  12  is  outside  the  valid
range of 1 - 10
at
com.foundjava.chapter9.Course.setNumberOfDays(Course.java:89)
at
com.foundjava.chapter9.CreateCourse.main(CreateCourse.java:10)
```

You can see that the error message parameter to the exception constructor is printed as part of the stack trace.

One problem now is that the constructor calls the "set" method, but someone creating a Course object will not know that an IllegalArgumentException may be thrown. We can address this by adding the necessary "throws" clause to the constructor.

```
public Course(String name, int days, double price)
    throws IllegalArgumentException
```

Again, we can add a "@throws" to the Javadoc comment. This simply makes it clear to users of the class that the parameterized constructor may possibly throw this exception.

9.5.1 Delegating Responsibility

Being able to explicitly throw exceptions, as we did in the previous example, is a very useful way of ensuring the logic of our programs because it means that if something goes wrong in an application that is not a Java system error then we can still use the built-in exception handling mechanism to signal the error to that part of the code that must handle the problem.

The examples used so far in this chapter simply ignore any exceptions being thrown, printing the stack trace and carrying on. However, in real systems, we would expect to do something about them. For example, if a piece of code was attempting to set an illegal value for a Course constructor, it should be made aware of this so that the error could be corrected. In many cases, information about the exception would need to be propagated all the way back to the user interface, so that the user could correct the error.

We saw in our very first example that a method can delegate the responsibility for an exception by simply re-throwing it on the signature of the enclosing method. We know, for example, that the "read" methods of System.in throw IOException. If we use this method inside another method, we could simply add the "throws IOException" clause to the enclosing method

```
public char readChar() throws IOException
{
    return (char)System.in.read();
}
```

Any code that calls the readChar method must now handle the IOException.

To ensure that an exception is received by all parts of the system that need to be aware of it, we can both handle an exception and then re-throw it. This enables us to, for example, log the exception at the point where it occurs, but also notify the calling code of the exception. Here, we catch an IOException and then re-throw it.

```
public char readChar() throws IOException
{
    try
    {
        return (char)System.in.read();
    }
    catch (IOException e)
    {
        e.printStackTrace();
        throw e;
    }
}
```

You could also create and throw a different exception within the catch block. For example, you might have a catch block that catches an unchecked exception but creates and throws a checked exception. We will look at an example of this at the end of the next section.

Exercise 9.2

- Modify the "setName" method from the Course class so that it throws a NullPointerException if the parameter passed to it is null.
- Write a "main" method to test your exception handling.
- The "throws" keyword on a method signature may be followed by more than one exception type, in a comma-separated list. For example:

```
public char readCharFromKeyboard()
  throws IOException, Exception
{
    ...
}
```

Modify the signature of the parameterized constructor of the Course class so that it throws both IllegalArgumentException and NullPointerException.

- Modify your "main" method, so it can catch both types of exceptions. Use different constructors in separate "try...catch" blocks.

9.6 Writing and Using Custom Exceptions

So far, we have only looked at handling types of exception that are already provided by the Java libraries, but we can also write our own custom exceptions that are specific to our own applications. For example, we might want to validate processes that our programs perform, and throw exceptions that are unique to those processes, rather than using generic Java exceptions. Another issue is that some Java exceptions are unchecked, meaning that the compiler will not insist that they are handled. We might prefer to throw a checked exception, which means they must be subclasses of Exception.

To take a simple example, let us assume that we want to create a BankAccount class, to which various types of transaction may be posted. We might apply a business rule that an account cannot be debited more than it currently holds. In addition, we might want this to be a checked exception, so that client code is required to be able to handle the exception, meaning that an unchecked exception like IllegalArgumentException will not suffice.

To manage this requirement, we will use inheritance to write a custom exception class. You can create your own checked exception class by subclassing java.lang. Exception.

```
public class TransactionException extends Exception
{
      . . .
}
```

Writing a custom exception is very simple. All we have to do is to write a subclass of java.lang.Exception. The Exception class has four constructors with various combinations of parameters. If you create a subclass of Exception but do not override any of these, the only one that will be available will be the default (zero arguments) constructor. Therefore, we often choose to override some or all of the other constructors. Eclipse gives some assistance with overriding constructors. In Fig. 9.4, the "New Java Class" dialog is being used to create a new class as a

Fig. 9.4 Checking the "Constructors from Superclass" button when creating a subclass of exception

subclass of Exception. If the "Constructors from superclass" checkbox is checked, then stubs of all the inherited constructors will be added to the newly created class.

If we create the TransactionException with all its inherited constructors, all four will be added to the class. Note that not only are the stubs generated but the necessary calls to "super" are also added. The constructors that take a "Throwable" as a parameter enable a series of exceptions of different types to be chained. This means that we can create one exception object as a result of some other type being thrown and add the previous one as a parameter to this one. The whole chain of exceptions will appear in the stack trace.

```
package com.foundjava.chapter9;
public class TransactionException extends Exception
{
  public TransactionException() {
    // TODO Auto-generated constructor stub
  }
  public TransactionException(String message) {
    super(message);
    // TODO Auto-generated constructor stub
  }
  public TransactionException(Throwable cause) {
    super(cause);
    // TODO Auto-generated constructor stub
  }
  public TransactionException(String message, Throwable cause)
  {
    super(message, cause);
    // TODO Auto-generated constructor stub
  }
}
```

Custom exceptions can have a more interesting set of methods than just constructors. For example, we can populate the exception object with other data about the context of the exception, but in many cases, this is not necessary.

9.6.1   Throwing a Custom Exception

Throwing a custom exception is just like throwing one from a Java exception class. You create an instance of the exception and use the "throw" keyword. In this example, the "debit" method throws a TransactionException. In the body of the method, if the attempted debit is greater than the available balance, the exception is thrown.

```
public void debit(double amount) throws TransactionException
{
  if(this.getBalance() < amount)
  {
    throw new TransactionException("insufficient funds");
  }
  // if OK then carry on
}
```

9.6.2   "finally" Blocks

In the examples of "try" blocks, we have seen so far in this chapter, "try" has always been followed by a "catch" block. There is also the option of using a "finally" block, which can either follow the last catch block or even replace it. The "finally" block is optional, but when present, its code is always executed, regardless of whether or not an exception is thrown in the "try" block. The exception to this is if a catch block has called "System.exit", in which case the "finally" block will not be executed. The sequence of blocks is:

```
try
{
    // some code that we try to execute
}
catch (Exception ex)
{
    // some code that will only be executed
    // if the exception is thrown
}
finally
{
    // some code that will always be executed,
    // whatever happens in the 'try' and 'catch' blocks
}
```

Alternatively, we can omit the catch block(s) altogether and simply have a "try" and a "finally"

```
try
{
    // some code that we try to execute
}
finally
{
    // some code that will always be executed,
    // whatever happens in the 'try' block
}
```

"finally" blocks are generally used when it is necessary to clean up some resources regardless of whether or not our code was successful. For example, we may have opened a connection to a file or a database in the "try" block. Whether or not everything works, we should still try to close these connections. In some cases, this can get complex if the code in the "finally" block also requires some exception handling, so a "finally" block may itself contain "try" blocks. In the end, if exceptions continue to be thrown, we may not be able to do what we are attempting to do in the "finally" block.

9.6.3 "try-with-resources"

In cases such as those outlined above, where resources have been opened and need to be closed regardless of whether an exception has been thrown, there is the "try-with-resources" statement. We do not actually write "try-with-resources", in fact, it is just a "try" block, but "try" is followed by code that opens some kind of resources such as a file or a database connection, in the following format.

```
try(code to open resource here)
{
//…
}
// No requirement for "catch" or "finally" –
// these are optional
```

The resource that is opened in the "try-with-resources" statement can be any object that object that implements java.lang.AutoCloseable. "try-with-resources" will automatically try to close the resource if an exception is thrown without the need for either a "catch" block or a "finally" block, though these can also be added for other exception handling code. We will see some code examples of the "try-with-resources" statement in later chapters where Java code connects to external resources.

Exercise 9.3

- Create a BankAccount class with a "balance" field and associated "getters" and "setters".
- Implement the "debit" method to either debit the balance or throw a TransactionException.
- Write a "main" method to test your debit method. In a "try" block, set the original balance of the account, then make a few debits until the exception is thrown.
- Add a "finally" block after your "try-catch" block that simply displays a message on the console, demonstrating that the "finally" block will be executed even if an exception has been thrown.

9.6.4   Re-Throwing Custom Exceptions

In the previous section, we suggested the possibility of re-throwing a different exception in a "catch" block, perhaps replacing an unchecked exception with a checked exception. In this example, the CourseManager class has an "addCourse" method that attempts to create a Course object from its parameter arguments and add the course to an array. There are three possible exceptions that could be thrown by this code, two from the constructor itself, and one from the array. In this code, each "catch" block throws an instance of a custom exception called CourseConstructorException, which is a checked exception (a subclass of Exception). In each case, the constructor used is the one that takes as its arguments a String (an error message) and the original exception object.

```
package com.foundjava.chapter9;
public class CourseManager
{
  private Course[] courses = new Course[10];
  private int courseCount = 0;
  public void addCourse(String name, int days, double cost)
      throws CourseConstructorException
  {
    try
    {
      courses[courseCount] = new Course(name, days, cost);
      courseCount++;
    }
    catch(IllegalArgumentException e)
    {
      e.printStackTrace();
      throw new CourseConstructorException
        ("Duration must be 1-10 days", e);
    }
    catch(NullPointerException e)
    {

      e.printStackTrace();
      throw new CourseConstructorException
        ("Course name cannot be null", e);
    }
    catch(ArrayIndexOutOfBoundsException e)
    {
      e.printStackTrace();
      throw new CourseConstructorException
          ("Cannot add any more courses", e);
    }
  }
}
```

In the following "main" method, there are three separate "try" blocks containing calls to the "addCourse" method. Each one deliberately causes one of the three underlying exceptions to be thrown, but in each case, the received exception will be a CourseConstructorException.

```
public static void main(String[] args)
{
  CourseManager courseManager = new CourseManager();
  // try with a null course name
  try
  {
    courseManager.addCourse(null, 3, 1000.0);
  }
  catch (CourseConstructorException e)
  {
    e.printStackTrace();
  }
  // try with zero days
  try
  {
    courseManager.addCourse("Java", 0, 1000.0);


  }
  catch (CourseConstructorException e)
  {
    e.printStackTrace();
  }
  // try to add more than 10 courses
  try
  {
    for(int i = 0; i < 11; i++)
    {
      courseManager.addCourse("A course", 3, 1000.0);
    }
  }
  catch (CourseConstructorException e)
  {
    e.printStackTrace();
  }
}
```

The various stack traces that are generated by this "main" method display both the CourseConstructorException and the underlying exception that was originally thrown. This is the exception trace from attempting to create a course with a null course name. The underlying NullPointerException triggers a CourseConstructorException.

```
java.lang.NullPointerException: Course name is null
at com.foundjava.chapter9.Course.setName(Course.java:72)
at com.foundjava.chapter9.Course.<init>(Course.java:42)
at com.foundjava.chapter9.CourseManager.addCourse
(CourseManager.java:12)
at com.foundjava.chapter9.CourseManager.main
(CourseManager.java:38)
com.foundjava.chapter9.CourseConstructorException: Course name
cannot be null
at com.foundjava.chapter9.CourseManager.addCourse
(CourseManager.java:23)
at
com.foundjava.chapter9.CourseManager.main(CourseManager.java:38
)
Caused by: java.lang.NullPointerException: Course name is null
at com.foundjava.chapter9.Course.setName(Course.java:72)
at com.foundjava.chapter9.Course.<init>(Course.java:42)
at
com.foundjava.chapter9.CourseManager.addCourse(CourseManager.ja
va:12)
... 1 more
```

This is the stack trace produced when attempting to create a course with zero as the number of days. This time it is an IllegalArgumentException that triggers the CourseConstructorException.

```
java.lang.IllegalArgumentException:  0  is  outside  the  valid
range of 1 - 10
at
com.foundjava.chapter9.Course.setNumberOfDays(Course.java:93)
at com.foundjava.chapter9.Course.<init>(Course.java:43)
at com.foundjava.chapter9.CourseManager.addCourse
(CourseManager.java:12)
at com.foundjava.chapter9.CourseManager.main
(CourseManager.java:47)
com.foundjava.chapter9.CourseConstructorException:
Duration must be 1-10 days
at com.foundjava.chapter9.CourseManager.addCourse
(CourseManager.java:18)
at com.foundjava.chapter9.CourseManager.main
(CourseManager.java:47)
Caused by: java.lang.IllegalArgumentException: 0 is outside the
valid range of 1 - 10
at
com.foundjava.chapter9.Course.setNumberOfDays(Course.java:93)
at com.foundjava.chapter9.Course.<init>(Course.java:43)
at com.foundjava.chapter9.CourseManager.addCourse
(CourseManager.java:12)
       ... 1 more
```

Finally, this is the exception trace displayed when we try to add too many courses to the array, where the CourseConstructorException is triggered by an ArrayIndexOutOfBoundsException.

```
java.lang.ArrayIndexOutOfBoundsException: 10
at com.foundjava.chapter9.CourseManager.addCourse
(CourseManager.java:12)
at com.foundjava.chapter9.CourseManager.main
(CourseManager.java:58)
com.foundjava.chapter9.CourseConstructorException:   Cannot   add
any more courses
at com.foundjava.chapter9.CourseManager.addCourse
(CourseManager.java:28)
at com.foundjava.chapter9.CourseManager.main
(CourseManager.java:58)
Caused by: java.lang.ArrayIndexOutOfBoundsException: 10
at com.foundjava.chapter9.CourseManager.addCourse
(CourseManager.java:12)
        ... 1 more
```

Exercise 9.4

- In Chap. 7, we created a Module class. A Course holds a reference to an array of Module objects. Potentially, this could lead to an ArrayIndexOutOfBounds Exception. Add some exception handling code to the Course class so that attempting to add too many modules to a course will not cause the program to crash.
- Write a test "main" method to test out your exception handling code.

Exercise 9.5

- Create an Exception class called "ModuleException" as a subclass of Exception.
- Integrate this into your answer to Exercise 9.4 so that the ArrayIndexOutOf BoundsException gets re-thrown as a ModuleException.

9.7   Optional: An Alternative to "null"

Back in the 1990s, when Design Patterns were very fashionable, Bobby Woolf published the "Null Object" pattern. The basic concept behind this pattern was that sometimes when one object is collaborating with another; it does not always require that collaborator to do anything. For example, we might have a collection of Customer objects and are searching for a specific middle name. If we query one of those customers for the middle name and the customer does not have one, we simply ignore it and move on to the next Customer. In typical Java code, we might do this by checking to see if a reference to an object (in this case a String containing the middle name) is "null". However, it would be better if the code could treat a collaborator that does nothing the same way it treats one that provides some behavior. Dealing with the NullPointerExceptions that may occur in a system that has many layers of objects can lead to complex coding. For example, let us suppose that we are checking the names of employees in a department. There might be some code that looks like this:

```
String nextMiddleName = getDepartment(dept).getEmployees().
next().getMiddleNames().getFirst();
```

The problem is that the first middle name of an employee may be null, so a NullPointerException will propagate up through the layers of objects. Using the java.util.Optional class makes the code simpler because it removes the need for the conditional statement that checks for a null reference. While not exactly an implementation of the Null Object pattern, the Optional class, introduced with Java 8, provides similar features.

Note
The Optional class is a "value-based" class, meaning that the equality of two Optional objects is based only on their state, not on their object identity.

Here is the beginning of a simple Employee class, which just contains name-related fields. The key aspect to note here is that "MiddleName" is an "Optional" object. This code uses generics, which we will cover in more detail in Chap. 12, but in this case, "Optional <String>" means that this Optional object is of type String.

```
package com.foundjava.chapter9;
import java.util.Optional;
public class Employee
{
    private String givenName;
    private Optional<String> middleName;
    private String familyName;
```

The getters and setters for the other fields are like those we have seen before, so here we just show the ones related to the "middleName" field:

```
public String getMiddleName()
{
    return middleName.orElse(" ");
}
public void setMiddleName(String middleName)
{
    this.middleName = Optional.ofNullable(middleName);
}
```

The "getMiddleName" method uses the "orElse" method of the Optional object to set up an alternate value if the value of "middleName" is "null". In this case, it returns a String containing a space. The "setMiddleName" method sets the value of the Optional to be "ofNullable". This method allows the value of the Optional to be "null". This short test code shows the Optional in action. Although one of the employees has a middle name that is set to "null", no NullPointerExceptions is thrown due to the Optional being used:

```java
package com.foundjava.chapter9;
public class DepartmentRunner
{
  public static void main(String[] args)
  {
    Department dept = new Department();
    dept.addEmployee(new Employee("Martin","Luther","King"));
    dept.addEmployee(new Employee("Malcolm",null,"X"));
    for(Employee el : dept.getEmployees())
    {
      char midInitial = el.getMiddleName().charAt(0);
      System.out.println(midInitial);
    }
  }
}
```

Here is the output from running the code. Note that no exception is thrown. The middle name for the second employee has been replaced by a space by the Optional object, so all we see is the "L", which is the first letter of the first employee's middle name.

9.8 Summary

This chapter has explored various aspects of exception handling in Java, including the keywords; "throws", "try", "catch", "finally" and "throw". In order to understand how to use these keywords in our code, we have seen how the exception hierarchy divides exception types into checked exceptions, which are checked by the compiler and require code to handle them, and unchecked exceptions, where the compiler does not enforce exception handling code (though it may still be very useful to include this). We saw that although the Java runtime includes many exception types, that we will also find it useful to create our own subclasses of Exception to represent custom exceptions, these customized to domain-specific business rules that we may need to enforce in an application. Exceptions provide us with a robust and flexible method for dealing with these issues. We concluded the chapter with a brief example of using the Optional class, which can limit the likelihood of NullPointerExceptions being thrown by an application.

Unit Testing with JUnit

10

Testing has always been an important part of software development, but in recent years, it has become more of a programmer activity, particularly with the growth in popularity of agile methods. Programmers are expected to be able to write and run unit tests against their code. A unit test is designed to test a single unit of code, for example, a single class, or part of a class.

A test is binary; it either passes or it fails. This means we must know what our criteria for "pass" and "fail" are before we can write a test. A test should also be automated as much as possible; it should require no human interaction in order to run, should assess its own results, and notify the programmer only when it fails. This is not to say that there is no need for manual testing; this is still very important. However, the more testing we can automate, the more we can focus our manual testing efforts on those aspects of the system that really require the human imagination of exploratory testing.

Unit testing focuses on the smallest components of object-oriented code, where individual class behavior is exposed through methods, testing both the class interface (black box testing) and its implementation (white box testing). This distinguishes it from, for example, acceptance or integration testing, where the tests cover larger parts of a system and may involve many components and architectural layers. Unit testing provides clarity of purpose during detailed design, early defect elimination (i.e.. before integration) and helps us to "embrace change" when specifications evolve.

Unit testing encourages early agreement on the format or values of arguments. For example, how would you define an investment instrument for a financial system? An international standard such as an International Securities Identification Number (ISIN), or an internal company naming system? Equally importantly, under what conditions are exceptions thrown? And what kinds of exceptions are thrown

© Springer Nature Switzerland AG 2020
D. Parsons, *Foundational Java*, Texts in Computer Science,
https://doi.org/10.1007/978-3-030-54518-5_10

by different methods? Unit testing also relates to Bertrand Meyer's "Design by Contract" where pre-conditions must be met by the caller and post-conditions must be guaranteed by methods since unit tests need to set up specific pre-conditions and test that post-conditions meet expectations. Unit testing ensures that such issues are addressed early in the design process.

By adopting an automated unit testing framework, such as JUnit, to support your unit tests, you can build tests quickly and easily and run them repeatedly as regression tests to ensure that changes to the code have not broken parts of the software that were written previously. Test frameworks enable refactoring (changing the design of code without changing its behavior). They can also provide valuable project health metrics and an indication of code stability.

Unit testing can support the agile practice of test-driven development, where the first tests are written before the unit under test. This provides further support for thinking of testing as a component of the design. Writing the tests upfront gives more focus on pre-conditions, post-conditions and the format and values of arguments.

The general process is to alternate between coding and testing, rather than doing all the code and then writing all the tests (or, indeed, writing all the tests and then writing all the code). We develop unit tests in parallel with the classes being tested, even writing the first test before the class if using a test-driven approach, which helps to clarify the requirements of the class prior to its development. Unit tests should be under version control in parallel with what they test. A class should not be integrated with other code until it has passed all its unit tests, and the unit tests should be integrated with an automated build process and used as regression tests.

10.1   The JUnit Test Framework

JUnit is a publicly available Java unit testing framework written by Kent Beck (otherwise well known for being the originator of eXtreme Programming) and Erich Gamma (perhaps best known for being an author of the "Gang of Four" Design Patterns book). The open source software and documentation can be downloaded from http://www.junit.org. There are many additional tools and extensions for JUnit, for example, for testing web components. As its popularity has grown, there have been other similar unit testing frameworks created for other languages, which together have become known as the xUnit family of test frameworks.

10.1.1   Using JUnit with Eclipse

JUnit has a simple API that (since version 4) uses annotations to enable you to plug the framework classes into your own test code. Since JUnit 5, there have been three different subprojects that comprise the overall framework: JUnit Platform, JUnit Jupiter and JUnit Vintage. For the developer writing unit tests, JUnit Jupiter is the most important of these. Junit 5 requires Java 8 or later to run. Many "jar" files need to be available on the "modulepath" in order for us to use the framework. To simplify this, JUnit is provided as an Eclipse library but is not automatically added to the modulepath of a project. To add JUnit to a project, select its properties (select "Properties" from the "Project" menu option) and select the "Java Build Path", "Libraries" tab. Press the "Add Library…" button and then choose "JUnit" (Fig. 10.1). Click the "Next" button, and on the next dialog (Fig. 10.2) select

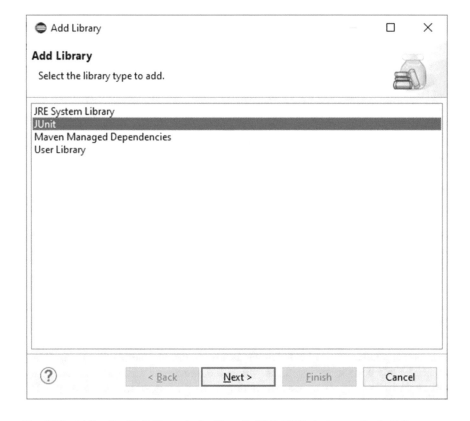

Fig. 10.1 Adding the JUnit library in the "Java Build Path" Project properties in Eclipse

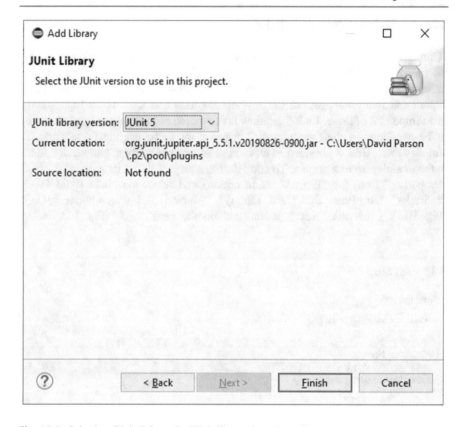

Fig. 10.2   Selecting JUnit 5 from the JUnit library drop-down list

"JUnit 5" from the drop-down list (the older versions, 3 and 4, are also available) then click "Finish". You should see that the JUnit 5 library has been added to the project's modulepath (Fig. 10.3).

10.2   Test Cases and Units Under Test

A class that contains unit tests is known as a *test case*. In order to start using JUnit, we need some code to be tested, known as the *unit under test*. In this chapter, we will begin by writing some tests for a simple class intended to represent ISO 216 documents. ISO 216 is the international standard that defines the "A" and "B" series of paper sizes, including A3 and A4. A class like this might be used, for example, as part of an application that sends data in document format to a printer. The

Fig. 10.3 JUnit 5 added to the Java Build Path in the Project Properties dialog

example here has very few methods but does have a couple of constructors, including one that will set the width and height of the paper from the name of the format, passed as a String argument to the constructor. Since all measurements in ISO 216 are in whole millimeters, we can use the "int" data type to represent the height and width of the document. Only two of the many "A" and "B" paper sizes are included here, A4 (210 mm $\times$ 297 mm) and A3 (297 mm $\times$ 420 mm).

```java
package com.foundjava.chapter10;

public class ISO216Document
{
  private int width;
  private int height;

  public ISO216Document(int width, int height) {
    setWidth(width);
    setHeight(height);
  }

  public ISO216Document(String size)
  {
    if(size.equals("A4"))
    {
      setWidth(210);
      setHeight(297);
    }
```

```
  if(size.equals("A3"))
  {
    setWidth(297);
    setHeight(420);

  }
}

public int getWidth() {
  return width;
}

public void setWidth(int width) {
  this.width = width;
}

public int getHeight() {
  return height;
}

public void setHeight(int height) {
  this.height = height;
}
}
```

10.2.1   Creating a JUnit Test Case

At its simplest, to write a JUnit test case, we write a class that imports the org.junit.
jupiter.api.Test class, along with at least one method of the "Assertions" class and
has at least one method with a @Test annotation. The tests are self-contained and
executed in the same way, by JUnit test runners. Eclipse has a built-in test runner
that is easy to use. In this section, we will go through the basic steps to create and
run a simple test case class with a single test method.

You can add a new "JUnit Test Case" to an Eclipse project by selecting
"New" → "JUnit Test Case" from the "File" → "New" menu item. This will show
the "New JUnit Test case" dialog (Fig. 10.4). In this example, we are creating a test
case called "ISO216DocumentTestCase". To use JUnit 5, make sure that "New
JUnit Jupiter test" is selected.

Fig. 10.4 Creating a JUnit test case with the "New JUnit Test Case" dialog

With the default settings, the "New JUnit Test Case" dialog will generate a class with the most important imports and a method with a default "fail" response..

```
package com.foundjava.chapter10;

import static org.junit.jupiter.api.Assertions.*;

import org.junit.jupiter.api.Test;

class ISO216DocumentTestCase {

    @Test
    void test() {
        fail("Not yet implemented");
    }

}
```

If you want to generate a stub that is targeted toward a specific class to be tested, the "New JUnit Test Case" dialog includes an option to choose the "Class under test" (Fig. 10.4). This option allows you to browse for the class to be tested and, on the following dialog (the "Next" button will be enabled if you choose a class under test), you can select the methods to be tested. Figure 10.5 shows the two constructors being selected. You can choose as many of the available methods as you like.

The following code would be generated from the dialog selection in Fig. 10.5.

```
package com.foundjava.chapter10;

import static org.junit.jupiter.api.Assertions.*;
import org.junit.jupiter.api.Test;

class test {

  @Test
  void testISO216DocumentIntInt() {
      fail("Not yet implemented");
  }

  @Test
  void testISO216DocumentString() {
      fail("Not yet implemented");
  }

}
```

The following section explains the various features of the code. The call to the "fail" method should be removed when you write the body of the test method as it deliberately makes the test fail until you have implemented it (we discuss the "fail" method later in this chapter). You should bear in mind that setting up only one test for a method is not enough, so you would need to manually add other test methods to the test case to get adequate test coverage.

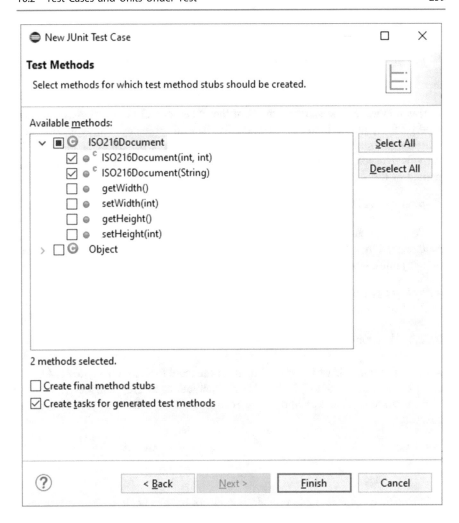

Fig. 10.5   Selecting methods to test when creating a new JUnit test case

10.2.2   Required Imports

As the generated class stub demonstrates, a JUnit test case needs to import classes from the JUnit Jupiter framework. Many of the classes we use directly are in the "org.junit.jupiter.api" package. First, we import the static methods of the org.junit. jupiter.api.Assertions class. The main job of a test is to make assertions which compare the expected result from a piece of code with what we get. The methods that make these assertions in JUnit are specified as static methods of the org.junit. jupiter.api.Assertions class. Because the methods are all static, they need to be invoked on the class, rather than on an object. To enable us to do this without constantly having to refer to the Assert class, we can use a static import, which is a little different from the imports we are familiar with from previous chapters. Note the use of the "static" keyword and the wildcard that appears *after* the class name

```
import static org.junit.jupiter.api.Assertions.*;
```

This imports all the static methods of the Assertions class. You can, of course, import the required methods individually instead of using the wildcard, and Eclipse's "organize imports" option will replace the wildcard with the specific methods that you use. For example, this line imports only the static "assertEquals" method of the Assertions class.

```
import static org.junit.jupiter.api.Assertions.assertEquals;
```

We also need to import any annotation classes needed (each annotation is implemented by a class). The essential annotation is "@Test", so we need to import the org.junit.jupiter.api.Test class.

```
import org.junit.jupiter.api.Test;
```

10.2.3   Writing Test Methods

We must provide at least one test method for the class for it to run any tests. All test methods must be preceded by a "@Test" annotation, or they will be ignored by JUnit at runtime. A test method must return "void" and take no parameters, for example,

```
@Test
public void myTestMethod()
{ ...
```

The method name is not important. It does not have to begin with "test" (though it used to, in earlier versions of JUnit).

We also need to ensure that each test method has at least one *assertion* in it since simply running code is not enough to test it. We must compare the actual results of the test with what we expect them to be. Assertions compare two values to see if they are the same. If they are not, failure is signaled to the test framework. There are several overloaded "assert..." methods in the Assertions class that we can use to test code. In this example, we use the "assertEquals" method to compare two integer values, in this case representing the expected and actual values returned from the "getWidth" method of an ISO216Document object.

```
package com.foundjava.chapter10;

import static org.junit.jupiter.api.Assertions.assertEquals;
import org.junit.jupiter.api.Test;

public class ISO216DocumentTestCase
{
  @Test
  public void testA4Width()
  {
    ISO216Document doc = new ISO216Document("A4");
    assertEquals(210, doc.getWidth());
  }
}
```

The "assertEquals" method compares the expected result (the first parameter argument) with the actual result (the second argument). If they are not equal, it flags an error to the test framework at runtime. The method is overloaded to work with all data types.

10.2.4   The Eclipse Test Runner

A JUnit test case is run using a test runner. Eclipse has its own graphical test runner that can be run with any JUnit test case class. All you need do is right click on the test class and select "Run As..." → "JUnit Test" to invoke the graphical test runner, which appears as a tab or can be detached as a floating window. Figure 10.6 shows the graphical test runner after running the ISO216DocumentTestCase. When a test is run using a graphical test runner, the number of test methods executed is displayed along with a red or green progress bar (depending on the success of the tests).

Let us try adding another test method that will deliberately break the code. Writing tests to break the current implementation is a standard approach in test-driven development. Each time we break the code with a test it gives us the opportunity to make the code itself more robust. Here, we add a "testA4Height" test method, but pass "a4" as the parameter argument.

```
@Test
public void testA4Height()
{
  ISO216Document doc = new ISO216Document("a4");
  assertEquals(297, doc.getHeight());
}
```

Since the current constructor only recognizes "A4" as a valid string, it fails to set the value of the height field for the document, so it defaults to zero.

Fig. 10.6 A successful test indicated in the Eclipse JUnit test runner

This is a good example of the need to agree on the formats and values of arguments to methods, which this type of testing process brings to the fore so we can make these design decisions early before they turn into bugs later in the development process.

When the modified test case is run, a list of all test failures will appear in the main window of the test runner. Selecting a failure in the upper pane will display the full error message in the lower pane (Fig. 10.7). In this test run, because of the failed second test, a red bar appears in the test runner window. It also shows that the "testA4Width" method passed the test, but all tests must pass for the bar to be green.

Fig. 10.7 Test failures indicated in the Eclipse JUnit test runner

Now we need to fix the current error in the unit under test, so that it can cope with lower case letters. The String method "equalsIgnoreCase" will enable us to accept Strings where the letter can be in either upper or lower case:

```
public ISO216Document(String size)
{
  if(size.equalsIgnoreCase("A4"))
  {
    setWidth(210);
    setHeight(297);
  }
  if(size.equalsIgnoreCase("A3"))
  {
    setWidth(297);
    setHeight(420);
  }
}
```

This might not be the complete (or only) solution to the issue of different String formats being passed to the constructor but makes the code pass the current set of tests, which is the important thing. If we want to expose other weaknesses in the implementation, for example, not having a sensible default paper size, we need to write other tests to break the code, fix the code again, and keep going until we have run out of ideas about how to break the code. Once we have made this fix, if we run the test case again then the tests will pass, and the bar will be green (Fig. 10.8).

Exercise 10.1

• Add "testA3Width" and "testA3Height" methods to the ISO216Docu-mentTestCase class.
• Run the tests and ensure that they pass.
• Modify the ISO216Document class so that the size of the paper is set to A4 by default.
• Write a test method to check that if the constructor is passed an empty string, that the height and width of the paper are correctly set to the default.
• Make sure that your updated class passes all the tests.

10.3   Types of Assertions

In the example test methods we have seen so far, we have been using the "assertEquals" method. This method is overloaded both by parameter types and by the number of parameters. For primitives, there are two "assertEquals" methods for each primitive type, one with two parameters (the values being compared) and another with an additional message parameter.

Fig. 10.8 The Eclipse JUnit test runner after all tests in a test case have been passed

The version we have been using takes two integer parameters, the expected value and the actual value. The other version of the method takes three parameters; the two values being compared, and an additional String message parameter, that is,

```
// 2 parameters
assertEquals(int expectedValue, int actualValue)
// 3 parameters
assertEquals(int expectedValue, int actualValue,
   String message)
```

The version of the method that has the "message" parameter simply uses this String as part of the output if the assertion fails. There are many similar overloaded methods for testing other data types.

10.3.1   Asserting Floating-Point Equality

For floating-point values (float or double), there is a "delta" argument (the allowable margin of error). Since floating-point arithmetic on floats or doubles can lead to small errors, we must take this into account when writing tests. The delta argument appears after the two floating-point values in the argument list. If there is a message String, it appears as the last argument.

```
assertEquals(double expectedValue, double actualValue,
    double delta)
```

or

```
assertEquals(double expectedValue, double actualValue,
    double delta, String message)
```

For example, if we wanted to test the "getArea" method of the Rectangle class from Chap. 8, we would need to supply a delta value.

```
@Test
public void testRectangleArea()
{
   Rectangle r = new Rectangle(null, 12, 14);
   assertEquals(168.0, r.getArea(), 0.001);
}
```

The delta value can be zero if the test requires 100% accuracy.

10.3.2   Object Equality

As well as testing primitive values, the "assertEquals" method can also compare objects (using the "equals" method).

```
assertEquals(Object expected, Object actual)
```

The "assertSame" methods check if two references point to the same object. This may have a different meaning than using "assertEquals" if the "equals" method has been overridden for the class of objects being tested.

```
assertSame(Object expected, Object actual)
```

For example, we might want to check if two references point to the same object.

```
assertSame(policy, policyCopy);
```

Whereas in other circumstances, we might want to see if two objects of the same class have the same state (assuming "equals" has been overridden to enable this).

```
assertEquals(policy1, policy2);
```

10.3.3 Other Assertions

As well as "assertEquals" and "assertSame", which both check for equality, there are several other types of assertion. This section introduces some of these but there are others. You are recommended to read the JUnit documentation for full details of the available assertions.

Assertions with Boolean conditions check if a condition is true or false. These assertions are made with the "assertTrue" or "assertFalse" methods, which again are overloaded to allow an optional message parameter, in addition to the required Boolean condition. Since any conditional statement can be checked with this kind of assertion, these give great flexibility over what we want to test.

Back in Chap. 4, there was some code written to test if the simulated roll of a die was within the range 1–6, but that code did not use any objects or a test framework. This version of the test uses the "assertTrue" method to check that the "getRoll" method of the Die class from Chap. 6 does indeed generate a number between 1 and 6.

```
package com.foundjava.chapter10;

import static org.junit.jupiter.api.Assertions.assertTrue;
import org.junit.jupiter.api.Test;
import com.foundjava.chapter6.Die;

public class DieTestCase
{
  @Test
  public void testDie()
  {
    Die die = new Die();
    int dieValue = die.getRoll();
    assertTrue(dieValue >= 1 && dieValue <= 6);
  }
}
```

Object references can be checked to see whether or not they are "null", using the "assertNull" and "assertNotNull" methods:

```
assertNull(Object obj)
assertNull(String message, Object obj)
assertNotNull(Object obj)
assertNotNull(String message, Object obj)
```

It may be useful to use these assertions when an object has another object as its field. We may want to ensure that a field is pointing to "null", or an aggregated object, depending on its expected state. In this example, we use the Location class from Chap. 8. Since it has a zero arguments constructor, we expect the String "address" field to be "null" when an object is first created. However, if the "setAddress" method is called this field should no longer be "null". The test methods in the following test case check that these assumptions are correct.

```
package com.foundjava.chapter10;

import static org.junit.jupiter.api.Assertions.*;
import org.junit.jupiter.api.Test;

import com.foundjava.chapter8.Location;

public class LocationTestCase
{
  @Test
  public void testLocationAddressNull()
  {
    Location location = new Location();
    assertNull(location.getAddress());
  }

  @Test
  public void testLocationAddressNotNull()
  {
    Location location = new Location();
    location.setAddress("The Old Fire Station");
    assertNotNull(location.getAddress());
  }
}
```

Note
Even when using an Optional object as a field, tests for "null" may be necessary since Optional objects can be configured to allow null values to be returned.

Exercise 10.2
In the sample exercise code available for this book, you will find a RectangularArea class to test. Create a JUnit test case for this class and add test methods as appropriate to the class, for example,

- `testArea`
- `testPerimeter`
- `testOrientation`
- `testIsSquare`
- etc.

In the spirit of test-driven development, this testing requires a "white box" approach. You need to know about the implementing code, not just the external interface of the methods from a "black box" perspective.

10.4 Exceptions and Timeouts

Not all testing is about expecting code to produce the correct results. Sometimes we expect code to throw an exception. Testing that expected exceptions do occur is just as important as testing code where we do not expect any exceptions. JUnit provides an "assertThrows" method that allows us to specify an expected exception based on code expressed in an executable lambda expression.

```
Assertions.assertThrows(Exception, executable);
```

The test will fail either if no exception is thrown or a different exception type is thrown. The constructor of our Course class can throw a couple of exceptions. One of these is the IlegalArgumentException that will be thrown if the number of days is outside the range 1–10. In this test method we pass zero as the number of days and expect the IllegalArgumentException to be thrown.

```
@Test
void testExpectedException()
{
  Assertions.assertThrows
    (IllegalArgumentException.class, () -> {
       new Course("Java",0,1000.0);
  });
}
```

As long as the expected exception actually gets thrown, the test will pass.

Another Assertion that includes an executable lambda expression is "AssertTimeout", which causes a test to fail if it takes longer than a specified time in milliseconds to complete. This is useful for testing non-functional requirements related to performance, as well as preventing a whole set of other tests in the same regression test suite from being stalled by waiting for one particular response. The following example test (which does not do anything useful, just executes an empty loop many times) will fail if it does not complete in less than a millisecond.

```
class TimeoutTest
{
    @Test
    void testTimeout() {
    assertTimeout(Duration.ofMillis(1), () -> {
      for(int i = 0; i < 1000000000; i++)
      {}
    });
  }
}
```

10.5   Forcing Failures

Most of the time, test failures are triggered by the JUnit framework. Occasionally, however, we may want to trigger a test failure ourselves, based on some failure of a business rule or unexpected exception. This can be done with the "fail" method, which, like assertions, comes in several versions, including one with a message and 'Throwable" arguments:

```
fail(String message, Throwable cause)
```

These methods are particularly useful when you want to force failures in "catch" blocks inside test methods; for example, we might put a "try-catch" block around our test code and be ready to catch any arbitrary and unexpected exception that might occur.

```
try
{
  // some code…
}
catch(Exception e)
{
  // force a failure for JUnit to pick up
  fail("exception thrown", e);
}
```

The reason for doing this is that if we let unexpected exceptions happen in test code, the whole test will terminate and no other test methods will be executed. If we catch the exception and trigger the "fail" method, the other test methods in the test case will continue to run (though of course the test runner will signal the test failure). This is a somewhat contrived example since we know that attempting to access module index 100 will throw an exception.

```
@Test
public void generalExceptionTest()
{
  try
  {
    Module module = course.getModules()[100];
  }
  catch(Exception e)
  {
    fail(e.getMessage(), e);
  }
}
```

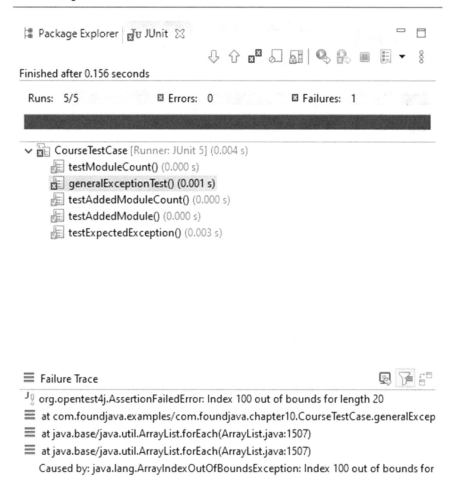

Fig. 10.9 Test runner output showing the triggering of a "fail" method from a catch block, enabling subsequent tests to be executed

Figure 10.9 shows that the triggering of "fail" from the "generalExceptionTest" method causes that test to fail but allows the remaining test methods in the test case to be executed.

10.6   Arranging a Test with @BeforeEach and @AfterEach Methods

In addition to its test methods, a test class may also include "BeforeEach" and "AfterEach" methods. These methods are useful for creating a test fixture, initializing data and freeing up resources respectively.

@BeforeEach methods initialize data for a test

```
@BeforeEach
public void setUp() throws Exception
{...
```

@AfterEach is for freeing up resources after a test

```
@AfterEach
public void tearDown() throws Exception
{...
```

Note that these methods are executed before and after each test method, not before and after the whole set of tests in the test case, because individual tests should not interfere with each other. For example, if the "BeforeEach" method initializes test data it must do so before every test method, not just before the first.

10.6.1   The 3A Pattern

Tests have a common pattern, described by Bill Wake as "Arrange-Act-Assert" (often shortened to "3A")

1. Arrange—create some objects
2. Act—stimulate them
3. Assert—check the results

The first step (arrange) is often the same from test to test. It is generally a good idea to restrict your test methods to having a single assertion for each test. This ensures that each test method is only testing one aspect of the unit under test, so that when a test fails it is easy to isolate the assertion that has failed. If a method contains several assertions and the first one fails, the others will not get tested until the first assertion succeeds. A consequence of this is that we may want to set up an object in a repeatable way and then run many tests against that same object state. If we do this in every single test method, then we get lots of code duplication, with the potential for errors that this will introduce. Here, for example, is a test method that might be used with the Course class. Most of the method is taken up with setting up the object to test.

```
@Test
public void testModuleCount()
{
  Course course = new Course ("Java", 3, 1000.00);
  Module module1 = new Module
    ("Exception Handling", 10, "Test");
  Module module2 = new Module("Swing UI", 15, "Assignment");
  Module module3 = new Module
    ("UI Design", 10, "Presentation");
  Module module4 = new Module
    ("Unit Testing", 10, "Unit Test");
  course.addModule(module1);
  course.addModule(module2);
  course.addModule(module3);
  course.addModule(module4);
  assertEquals(4, course.getModuleCount());
}
```

This object might be useful for running many different tests against, but we do not want all this set up code in every test method. This is where a "BeforeEach" method is useful. We only need to write the setup code once, instead of in every single test.

When you create a JUnit test case in Eclipse, the "New JUnit Test Case" dialog has several checkbox options (Fig. 10.10). In this dialog, "setUp" will generate the stub of a "@BeforeEach" method, and "tearDown" will generate the stub for an "@AfterEach" method.

Note
The names "setUp" and "tearDown" are names of the equivalent methods used in earlier versions of the JUnit framework.

The stub of the "setUp" method will be generated like this. The name of the method is not important, only the annotation.

```
@BeforeEach
public void setUp() throws Exception
{
}
```

We can put the setup code into this method, and then the test method only needs to contain the assertion. We must, however, make sure that the object being tested is available throughout the class, so a reference to it needs to be declared as a field of the test case. In this way, the "BeforeEach" method and the Test methods can all access the same field that references the Course object.

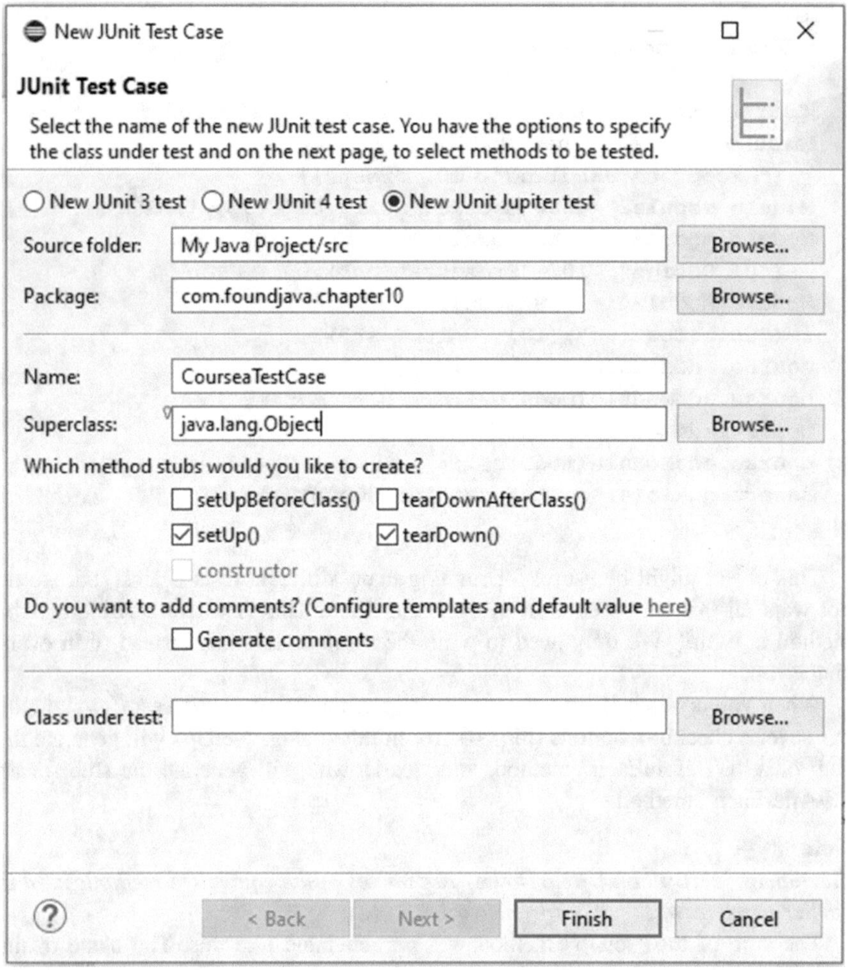

Fig. 10.10 Generating a "BeforeEach" method using the Eclipse "New JUnit Test Case" dialog

```
public class CourseTestCase
{
  private Course course;
```

In the "BeforeEach" method, we use the "course" field to reference the Course object to be tested.

```
@BeforeEach
public void setUp() throws Exception
{
  course = new Course ("Java", 3, 1000.00);
  Module module1 = new Module
    ("Exception Handling", 10, "Test");
  Module module2 = new Module("Swing UI", 15, "Assignment");
  Module module3 = new Module
    ("UI Design", 10, "Presentation");
  Module module4 = new Module
    ("Unit Testing", 10, "Unit Test");
  course.addModule(module1);
  course.addModule(module2);
  course.addModule(module3);
  course.addModule(module4);
}
```

The test methods will also use the "course" field to access the test object. We can also add methods that change the state of the object and run tests against it. Since the "BeforeEach" method gets executed before each test, the Course and its Modules will be recreated for every test, so there is no danger of separate tests interfering with each other. Here, three separate test methods are executed against the Course object. Two of these modify their own versions of the object but will not impact on the objects created for other tests.

```
@Test
public void testModuleCount()
{
  assertEquals(4, course.getModuleCount());
}


@Test
public void testAddedModuleCount()
{

  Module module = new Module
    ("Collections", 10, "Assignment");
  course.addModule(module);
  assertEquals(5, course.getModuleCount());
}


@Test
public void testAddedModule()
{
  Module module = new Module
    ("Collections", 10, "Assignment");
  course.addModule(module);
  Module module5 = course.getModules()[4];
  assertEquals(module, module5);
}
```

10.6.2   @BeforeAll and @AfterAll Methods

Whereas "BeforeEach" and "AfterEach" methods are executed before and after each individual test method, it is also possible to execute some code once, before or after all the test methods in a single test case, using the "@BeforeAll" and "@AfterAll" annotations. "@BeforeAll" methods initialize data for a set of tests:

```
@BeforeAll
public static void setUpBeforeClass() throws Exception {…
```

@AfterAll is for freeing up resources after a set of tests:

```
@AfterAll
public static void tearDownAfterClass() throws Exception {…
```

Unlike "BeforeEach" and "AfterEach", the methods that use these annotations must be static (though there are some advanced settings in JUnit that can override this). Care is required when using these annotations since it is essential to make sure that each test is isolated from other tests. If a resource is created in "BeforeAll" and modified by a test, then that could affect all subsequent tests. However, there are some good reasons why you may want some setup code to execute once before a series of tests. For example, we may want to open a connection to an external resource such as a test database. It would be very inefficient to open and close a database connection for every single test method, so opening the connection before all the tests and then closing it at the end would be better. In other cases, we may want to initialize a large and complex object for testing but only read data from it in a series of tests. Since this would not change the object's state, we could create it once (using a static field) and then execute a whole series of test methods that interact with the object without changing it. To guarantee that we do not change the object, we could create an interface for the class that exposes only the methods that do not change the object and use that interface in the test code.

Exercise 10.3

- Due to a change in requirements, the ISO216Document now needs to cope with the U.S. "Letter" size. Rather inconveniently this measures 8½ by 11 in. (215.9 mm × 279.4 mm) and is not part of ISO216.
- Write a test case for a suitably renamed class that can create an instance in letter size and maintain its measurements in floating-point millimeter values as well as inches.
- Add all the methods to the test case that you think are needed to test "Letter" sized documents.
- Once you have written the test case, rewrite the class to pass all the tests.

10.7 Writing a Test Suite

One of the important aspects of automated unit testing is the ability to rerun tests every time a new code is integrated, to ensure that nothing has been broken in the existing code by recent changes. This process is known as "regression testing". One way of helping to create regression tests is by building test suites. A test suite comprises one or more tests, grouping them so that they can be run together. You can create a test suite using the "@RunWith" and "@SelectClasses" (and/or "@SelectPackages") annotations. The current classes to create a test suite rely on some JUnit 4 code that support the "@RunWith" annotation from the "vintage" module. (By the time you read this, a full Junit 5 runner may be available). The "SelectClasses" annotation specifies which test cases to add to the suite. A single test class just appears inside parentheses, for example:

```
@SelectClasses(CircleTestCase.class)
```

If more than one class is to be tested, which is more likely for a test suite, the comma-separated list of classes is surrounded by braces:

```
@SelectClasses({CircleTestCase.class,
        RectangleTestCase.class})
```

Selecting packages takes a similar form, for example:

```
@SelectPackages("com.foundjava.chapter10")
```

This example class, "ShapeSuite", runs two other test classes, RectangleTest and CircleTest.

```
package com.foundjava.chapter10;

import org.junit.platform.runner.JUnitPlatform;
import org.junit.platform.suite.api.SelectClasses;
import org.junit.platform.suite.api.SuiteDisplayName;
import org.junit.runner.RunWith;

@RunWith(JUnitPlatform.class)
@SuiteDisplayName("Shape Suite")
@SelectClasses({CircleTestCase.class,
  RectangleTestCase.class})
public class ShapeSuite {
}
```

You can add as many test classes to a suite as you like, including other test suite classes, allowing you to build up a large set of regression tests over time that can be run from a single test suite.

Exercise 10.4
Write a test suite that runs all the test case classes that you have created for the previous exercises.

10.8 Summary

This chapter introduced the concept of unit testing which, as part of an overall test strategy, not only helps to improve code quality but can also help to drive the design of code. The examples in this chapter used the JUnit 5 test framework, which makes it easy to create and run unit tests that make assertions against code (in units under test) to ensure that it behaves as expected. Several different types of assertion were demonstrated in code examples, including those that deal with exception handling, timeouts and forced failures. We saw how JUnit is included as an Eclipse library that can be added to the build path of a project and how test cases can easily be created and run using the integrated graphical test runner. The chapter explained how individual test cases are created, along with the required annotations to run tests and to set up code for testing. It also introduced the creation of test suites that enable multiple test cases to be run together. Some related issues such as test-driven development, "3A" and regression testing were also discussed.

Exploring the Java Libraries

11

In this chapter, we will take a brief look at some of the commonly used classes in the Java libraries. The examples covered here are intended to be just a small sample of the possible set of classes that you might want to use. The main purpose of the chapter is to encourage you to reuse existing classes as much as possible in your programming, not to "reinvent the wheel". One of the key things that object-oriented programming offers is the ability to reuse existing classes. Reuse has two major advantages. First, you save your own time by not having to implement the code. Second, code in standard libraries has already been extensively tested so there is no need to test it yourself. If you find yourself needing to perform a particular process or create a particular type of object then you may find that a suitable implementation already exists in Java, particularly if the process or class could be considered to be a general-purpose one rather than being domain specific. The most important thing is to become used to using the Javadoc as a frequent resource, checking to see what classes are in the library that you might be able to reuse before writing any new code.

This chapter only covers a small number of packages in the standard Java runtime environment. There are, of course, many more packages and classes not covered here, not to mention huge numbers of other libraries available, either commercially or through open source projects, that you can use in your own code. In fact, the art of Java programming is in assembling components from other sources in a useful and robust way, rather than writing code from scratch.

11.1 Frequently Used Classes in the "java.lang" Package

We will begin this chapter with a brief overview of some of the classes in the "java. lang" package, almost all of which we have already used to some extent in previous chapters.

© Springer Nature Switzerland AG 2020
D. Parsons, *Foundational Java*, Texts in Computer Science,
https://doi.org/10.1007/978-3-030-54518-5_11

- java.lang.Object
- java.lang.Math
- java.lang.System
- java.lang.Class
- Wrapper classes—java.lang.Integer, etc.

11.1.1   The java.lang.Object Class

We saw in Chap. 8 that Object is at the root of the Java class hierarchy, so acts as a superclass for all other classes. This means that every class inherits the methods that are defined in the Object class. The Object class defines the default behavior for all objects through methods we have used in previous chapters:

```
equals(java.lang.Object)  // returns a boolean
getClass()    // returns a Class object
toString()    // returns a String representation of the object
hashCode()    // returns an integer for indexing hash tables
```

Object also provides the "wait", "notify" and "notifyAll" methods that relate to multithreading. These methods will be covered in Chap. 16. The only other methods on the Object class are "finalize" and "clone".

```
protected void finalize() throws Throwable
protected Object clone() throws CloneNotSupportedException
```

11.1.1.1   The "finalize" Method
The "finalize" method gets called on an object if it is garbage collected. Since there is no guarantee that a given object will ever be garbage collected during the runtime of a program, there is similarly no guarantee that this method will ever be called. Its role is to provide an opportunity for an object to release any resources that it may be holding before it is disposed of. For example, it might be used to ensure that a file that the object has opened is closed before the object is garbage collected.

Both the "finalize" and "clone" methods have "protected" visibility on the Object class, so are not automatically available as public methods of subclasses. It is unlikely that you would want "finalize" as a public method. However, it is possible that you might want to make the "clone" method public.

11.1.1.2   The "clone" Method
"clone" makes a copy of the current object. By default, it only makes a *shallow copy*, which means that any object or array referenced in the copied object will

point to the same objects like the ones being copied. In that sense, the "clone" method is, by default, equivalent to using the assignment operator, that is,

```
Object object2 = object1;
```

by default, is equal to

```
Object object2 = object2.clone();
```

This is like the "equals" method, which by default has the same behavior as the equality operator. As we saw in Chap. 5, the problem with copying references is that changes made to an object using one reference will also affect the other reference, because they point to the same object. Like "equals", however, "clone" can be overridden to give a different behavior. We generally override "clone" in order to provide a *deep copy* of an object. Making a deep copy means that changing any reference fields of the copy will not affect the reference fields of the original object, and vice versa. Like overriding "equals", we must provide an implementation that overrides the superclass version. The basic implementation should always return "super.clone".

```
@Override
public Object clone() throws CloneNotSupportedException
{
   return super.clone();
}
```

In addition, the class being cloned must also implement the "Cloneable" interface. Otherwise, the CloneNotSupportedException will be thrown.

```
public class CloneExample implements Cloneable
{...
```

Thus far, we have made the class Cloneable, but calling the "clone" method will only make a shallow copy of an object. To make a deep copy, any reference fields to objects or arrays should be manually copied, and the clone should be made to refer to these copies rather than the originally referenced objects. Here, for example, a class has a field which is an array of integers. In the "clone" method, we begin by calling "super.clone" to get the cloned object. We then manually copy all the values in the clone's array (for this example, we assume this is accessible via a method of this class called "getArray") into a new array. Then the clone is made to reference the new array, containing copied data. Since arrays automatically support the Cloneable interface they keep this example reasonably simple.

```
@Override
public Object clone() throws CloneNotSupportedException
{
  CloneExample clone = (CloneExample)super.clone();
  int[] clonedArray = getArray();
  int[] copiedArray = new int[clonedArray.length];
  for(int i = 0; i < clonedArray.length; i++)
  {
    copiedArray[i] = clonedArray[i];
  }
  clone.setArray(copiedArray);
  return clone;
}
```

Now, if an object of the class is cloned, the clone will have an entirely separate array field to the original object.

Note

You must be careful when making deep copies if they chain too many objects together. You may find that the copies can be very large.

Exercise 11.1

- Override the "clone" method for the Course class so that it makes a deep copy of its array of Modules.
- Write a JUnit test case that shows that your clone method is, in fact, making a deep copy (this will involve cloning a course, changing the modules of the original course and testing that the clone remains unchanged).

11.1.2   The java.lang.Math Class

All the methods in the Math class are static methods. These methods allow a user to construct and evaluate mathematical expressions. To provide the maximum range of values and flexibility when dealing with different data types, they are either overloaded to cope with all relevant parameter (primitive) types or assume that any parameters and return types are of type double. Any other numeric data types that get used by these methods are simply promoted to type double. Table 11.1 shows some examples that work with doubles.

Table 11.1 Some example methods of the Math class

Method	Usage	Example
`doubleMath.pow(doublex,doubley)`	Returns the value of x raised to the power of y	$\mathrm{Math.pow}(2,3)//=8$
`doubleMath.ceil(doublex)`	Returns the smallest integer greater than or equal to x	$\mathrm{Math.ceil}(5.2)//=6$
`doubleMath.sqrt(doublex))`	Returns the square root of x	$\mathrm{Math.sqrt}(9)//=3$

Table 11.2 The (approximate) values for Math.E and Math.PI as specified in the Javadoc

java.lang.Math		
`publicstaticfinaldouble`	E	2.718281828459045
`publicstaticfinaldouble`	PI	3.141592653589793

Table 11.2 shows how the values of E and PI are specified in the java.lang.Math class. Both values are, of course, approximations, limited to 15 decimal places. The Math class includes two public constants, "E" and "PI"

```
public static final double E;
// the base of the natural logarithms.

public static final double PI;
// the ratio of the circumference of a circle
// to its diameter.
```

Exercise 11.2

Use the "Math.pow" and "Math.sqrt" methods to calculate the hypotenuse (longest side) of a right-angled triangle.

According to Pythagoras, the square of the hypotenuse is equal to the sum of the squares of the other two sides. Your code needs to:

- Calculate the squares of the two shorter sides.
- Add these squares together.
- Find the square root of this value; this will be the length of the longest side.

Use a "test first" approach. Begin by writing a JUnit test case that expects a correct answer, for example, the hypotenuse of a right-angled triangle with side lengths of 12 and 5 is 13. Once you have written the tests, write the unit under test.

11.1.3   The java.lang.System Class

Like the Math class, all the methods in the System class are static methods. These methods provide platform-independent access to underlying system functions. The System class also has the static fields "in", "out" and "err" to represent standard input, standard output, and standard error output respectively. We have used "System.out" and "System.in" in previous examples. "System.err" is often used to separate normal output from error output. The following short program deliberately throws an ArithmeticException by dividing an integer by zero. The "try" block uses "System.out" while the "catch" block uses "System.err". Note that the "printStackTrace" method can take a PrintStream object (the class that both "System.out" and "System.err" belong to) as a parameter. Here, we explicitly use "System.err", though this is in fact the default choice for stack traces.

```java
package com.foundjava.chapter11;

public class DivideByZero
{
  public static void main(String[] args)
  {
    try
    {
      System.out.println("About to do some arithmetic");
      int x = 1;
      int y = x/0;
    }
    catch(ArithmeticException e)
    {
      System.err.println("Oh dear...");
      e.printStackTrace(System.err);
    }
  }
}
```

When the program is run in Eclipse, you should see that the standard output is in black text, but the error output is in red text. The order of the messages may also vary as the output is being sent through different streams.

```
About to do some arithmetic
Oh dear...
java.lang.ArithmeticException: / by zero
at com.foundjava.chapter11.DivideByZero.main
(DivideByZero.java:11)
```

The idea of having separate streams for standard and error output is that they could potentially be directed to separate places. You might, for example, choose to write error output to one log file and standard output to another. The system class includes the methods "setOut" and "setErr" to do this; you can pass these methods a different PrintStream object than the one they use by default.

Note
While you can use standard and error outputs for logging, it is now preferable to use the dedicated logging system introduced within Java 1.4 (see the java.util. logging package), or use a third-party logging system. This will provide a much broader and more configurable set of logging services than just writing to PrintStreams.

11.1.4 Wrapper Classes

As we know, Java has both objects and primitive types (int, double, etc.). To provide a bridge between them, Java provides a set of wrapper classes for all the built-in types allowing us to convert primitives to objects and vice versa. There are matching classes for all the primitive types: Byte, Short, Character, Integer, Long, Float, Double and Boolean. In most cases, the name of the wrapper is the same as the name of the primitive (albeit with the class names in Pascal case) except for Integer (wraps "int") and Character (wraps "char"). These classes allow Java to construct an object whose state reflects the value of a given primitive data type. They also serve to wrap the value in an object that allows methods to be added to its representation. These methods are not the same for all wrappers but are appropriate to the types of data that they encapsulate. For example, the Boolean class includes static final fields for TRUE and FALSE than can be used to represent Boolean objects in their two possible states.

```
Boolean aBoolean = Boolean.TRUE;
aBoolean.equals(new Boolean(true)); // true
```

The character class has many methods that allow us to find out about the character being contained. For example, the "isDigit" method returns "true" if the character is a numeric digit.

```
Character aCharacter = new Character('c');
aCharacter.isDigit(); // false
```

As we saw in Chap. 9, when we used the Integer class to convert characters entered at the keyboard into numbers, wrapper classes for numeric values have static "parse…" methods that convert Strings to numbers; for example, the Integer class has a "parseInt" method

```
int year = Integer.parseInt("1066");
```

As well as providing various useful utility methods, the wrappers provide an important tool in using the Collections framework, which we look at in the next chapter. Whereas arrays can contain either object references or primitives, Java collection classes such as ArrayList can only hold objects. If you want to store a primitive data type in a collection, the primitive values must be put into wrapper objects before being added, as in this example, which uses the "valueOf" method of the Integer class:

```
int myInt = 25;      // cannot be added to a Java collection
Integer myInteger = Integer.valueOf(myInt);
// myInteger can be added to a collection
```

While this can be done automatically using a technique called "autoboxing", it is important to understand that the wrapper classes are always used to put primitives into a collection, whether we do it explicitly or not.

All the wrapper classes have overloaded "valueOf" methods that allow objects to be created from either primitive values of the appropriate type or Strings, apart from the Character class, which only has a "valueOf" method that takes a "char" as an argument.

11.2 Classes in the "java.util" Package

The classes we have looked at so far have been from the java.lang package. The java.util package, which contains generic utility classes, also contains many commonly used classes including the Collection classes that we will look at in the next chapter. There are a few other classes in java.util that may be of interest, including the Locale and Currency classes, which we introduce in the following sections.

11.2.1 Factory Methods

In the code examples that follow, there are several examples of *factory methods*. A factory method is a common design pattern for creating objects without calling a constructor. Factory methods are static, and similar in syntax to the static methods that we have seen in earlier examples in that they are called on a class rather than on an object. However, they have the specific role of returning a newly created object. This is often done where the class has more information about the type of object that we want to create than we have ourselves. Factory methods often return an object of a subclass of the one that implements the method. A good example of this is where the configuration of a newly created object can vary depending on the international "locale" in which the object is being created. The Locale and Currency classes described in the following sections can use the default locale for the current system and create objects appropriate to that locale.

11.2.2   The Locale Class

Many elements of data vary according to their international locale. Characteristics that vary around the world include language (and the character sets that support a given language), datelines and time zones, and the formatting of numbers and currencies. This means that some operations in a program are "locale-sensitive". The role of the Locale class is to enable information to be tailored for the user, based on their region, to support the internationalization of applications.

There a several different ways of creating a Locale object, but the simplest is to use the "forLanguageTag" factory method. The possible set of language tags is defined in the IETF BCP 47 standard. The language tag for United States English, for example, is "en-US", used here with the "forLanguageTag" method to create a Locale for that region.

```
Locale USLocale = Locale.forLanguageTag("en-US");
```

For some Locales, the Locale class provides several constants that can be used instead of having to create a Locale object. For convenience, there are constants based on both country and language. For example, Locale.FRANCE is the constant for the country of France while Locale.FRENCH is the constant for the French language (which of course is also used in countries other than France). We will see an example of Locales in use in the next section.

11.2.3   The Currency Class

The Currency class represents information about international currencies. Creating a Currency object is done through the "getInstance" factory method, which requires a Locale object as an argument. For example, we can create a Locale object and pass this to the "getInstance" method:

```
Locale USLocale = Locale.forLanguageTag("en-US");
Currency USCurrency = Currency.getInstance(usLocale);
```

Alternatively, we can use one of the Locale constants, for example:

```
Currency UKCurrency = Currency.getInstance(Locale.UK);
```

The information available from a Currency object includes the ISO 4217 currency code (a text string the represents a currency), the ISO 4217 currency number, the currency symbol and the number of fraction digits. These values are accessible through various methods on the Currency class, for example:

```
System.out.println(UKCurrency.getNumericCode());
System.out.println(UKCurrency.getDisplayName());
System.out.println(UKCurrency.getSymbol());
System.out.println(UKCurrency.getCurrencyCode());
```

The output from these methods in a UK Locale is as follows.

```
826
British Pound
£
GBP
```

Exercise 11.3
Create a "Money" class that can represent an amount of money in a specific currency. Use the services of the Currency class to help implement your Money class. Add overloaded static "getInstance" factory methods to your class, one that takes one argument (and amount of money) and defaults to the current locale and another that that takes a Locale object as a second argument.

Add a "toString" method to your Money class that returns the amount of money using the currency symbol at the front and the currency code at the end, for example:

```
$250USD
```

Write a "main" method that creates Money objects from different locales and displays their amounts.

11.3   NumberFormat Classes in the "java.text" Package

The NumberFormat classes in the "java.text" package provide a tool for formatting numbers as Strings and converting Strings to numbers. These classes include "format" methods that make it easy to customize number formatting. The same classes have "parse" methods to convert Strings to objects or primitive types (Fig. 11.1).

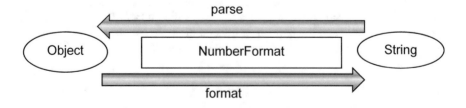

Fig. 11.1 NumberFormat classes in the java.text package parse Strings into Number objects and format Number objects into Strings

11.3.1   Formatting Numbers

Factory methods of the NumberFormat class such as "getNumberInstance" are used to create formatting objects.

```
NumberFormat numFormat = NumberFormat.getNumberInstance();
```

The NumberFormat object will default to the current locale if no argument is passed to the "getNumberInstance" method, or a locale can be provided as an argument. It will have some default behaviors when formatting numbers (or numeric variables) passed as arguments to the "format" method.

For example, it will have a default number of decimal places that it displays, and will round the result:

```
String s1 = numFormat.format(1234.56789); // s1 = "1,234.568"
```

Another default behavior is to remove any trailing zeros from the number after the decimal point, for example:

```
String s2 = numFormat.format(1234.00); // s2 = "1,234"
```

These behaviors can, however, be configured in various ways. For example, we can specify how many digits we want to appear after the decimal point, using the "setMaximumFractionDigits" method:

```
numFormat.setMaximumFractionDigits(2);
s1 = numFormat.format(1234.56789); // s1 = "1,234.57"
```

Note
The format methods of the NumberFormat class need to be passed something that can be formatted as a number. If the argument cannot be formatted then a java. lang.IllegalArgumentException will be thrown at runtime.

11.3.2   Formatting Currencies

A special instance of the NumberFormat class can be created to enable the formatting of values that represent a currency.

```
NumberFormat localFormat =
  NumberFormat.getCurrencyInstance();
```

The factory method "getCurrencyInstance", when used without any arguments, uses the current locale to determine the type of currency and the format of the output. Here, for example, we format a double into a currency String (the output here assumes a dollar locale).

```
double value = 1234.5;
System.out.println(localFormat.format(value));// "$1,234.50"
```

If you want to format currencies from specific locales, these can be passed as an argument to the "getCurrencyInstance" factory method. Here, we create an instance in the "GERMANY" locale, so the value is formatted in Euros by passing a constant from the Locale class as the argument:

```
NumberFormat euroFormat =
   NumberFormat.getCurrencyInstance(Locale.GERMANY);
System.out.println(euroFormat.format(1234.0));
// "1.234,00 €"
```

In this example, the "JAPAN" locale is used, so the value is formatted in Yen.

```
NumberFormat yenFormat =
   NumberFormat.getCurrencyInstance(Locale.JAPAN);
System.out.println(yenFormat.format(1234.0)); // "¥1,234.00"
```

Of course, this use of locales is purely about the format of currencies, not their actual values; they do nothing to convert between currencies. In addition, the output from a "format" method is a String, not a Currency object, so does not contain any further information about the currencies being formatted. It is also possible that your computer may not support all the necessary character sets to show the currencies for all available locales.

11.3.3 Parsing Numbers

The "parse" methods of the NumberFormat class can parse Strings that contain the representations of numbers, and return instances of the Number class, which is the superclass of the number wrapper classes such as Integer and Double. The Number class has various methods to return primitive numbers; "byteValue", "doubleValue", "intValue", etc. Since the original number may not exactly match the type returned by the method, some element of truncation or rounding is possible. The "parse" method throws the checked exception "java.text.ParseException", so the code needs to handle this. Here, we parse a String representing a floating-point number. The "doubleValue" is the complete floating-point number as a double, but the "intValue" is truncated to return an int.

```
NumberFormat numParser = NumberFormat.getNumberInstance();
try
{
  Number num = numParser.parse("1234.5");
  System.out.println(num.doubleValue());    // 1234.5
  System.out.println(num.intValue());       // 1234
}
catch (ParseException e)
{
  e.printStackTrace();
}
```

11.3.4 Parsing Currencies

Strings representing currency values can also be parsed into Number objects, which can then be used to return primitive values. In this example, we parse a String in the currency format of the UK locale into a Number and then return the "doubleValue". A ParseException will be thrown if the currency String is formatted for the wrong locale.

```
NumberFormat parseCurrency =
  NumberFormat.getCurrencyInstance(Locale.UK);
try
{
  // must be a parseable string in the currency
  // of the current Locale
  var currencyValue =
    parseCurrency.parse("£5,432.10").doubleValue();
  System.out.println(currencyValue);       // 5432.1
}
catch (ParseException e)
{
  e.printStackTrace();
}
```

Exercise 11.4
Add a method to the BankAccount class (the one you created in Exercise 9.3) to return a formatted balance. Use a currency instance of the NumberFormat class.

Exercise 11.5
Update your Money class so the "toString" method uses a currency instance of the NumberFormat class to format the amount. Append the currency code to the end.

Exercise 11.6
In your BankAccount class, replace the double field that represents the balance of the account with a java.math.BigDecimal. Use the Javadoc to find out how to use

this class in your code so that the methods still work. Write a JUnit test case for your BankAccount class.

11.4   Dates and Times in the "java.time" Package

In Chap. 5 we introduced the java.util.date class. Although this class has not been deprecated, since Java 8 there has been a newer package called "java.time" that contains a new set of date and time-related classes that overcome some of the issues with the earlier date and time representations in Java. The classes in this package are thread safe, with more consistent APIs that follow a functional programming style. The classes in the package make extensive use of factory methods, creating immutable objects with methods that frequently return modified copies of themselves so method calls can be chained together. In the next few sections, we provide a very brief introduction to the basic features of the LocalDate, LocalTime and LocalDateTime classes. There is much more to these classes than the methods outlined here, so refer to the Javadoc if you need to find out more about using dates and times in Java.

11.4.1   The LocalDate Class

The main Date class is LocalDate, which returns the current date in the local time zone. A LocalDate does not contain any time-related data but does contain date-related fields such as "day-of-year", "day-of-week" and "week-of-year". Here, a LocalDate is created using the "now" factory method.

```
LocalDate today = LocalDate.now();
System.out.println(today);
```

By default, "toString" returns the date in YYY-MM-DD format, for example:

```
2020-04-01
```

A LocalDate is immutable and is a value-based class, meaning that LocalDate objects should be compared using the "equals" method, not the "==" operator. Although the object is immutable, various methods can be called to create modified copies of the date, for example, "minusDays".

```
LocalDate yesterday = LocalDate.now().minusDays(1);
```

Dates can also be created for a specific date by passing year, month and day arguments to the "of" method. The month can either be passed as an integer in the range 1–12 or one of the enums (enumerated types) defined in the Month class that uses the names of the months rather than their numbers. Enumerated types are basically sets of related constants. This example uses an enum for the month:

```
LocalDate dateOfBirth = LocalDate.of(2012, Month.JANUARY, 1);
```

Again, further methods can be called to create modified copies of the immutable date

```
LocalDate twentyFirst = dateOfBirth.plusYears(21);
```

11.4.2   The LocalTime Class

The LocalTime class represents a time with no date information. Like the Local-Date class, it has a "now" method that creates an object representing the time of its creation. and an "of" method that allows its time to be set using arguments, for example:

```
LocalTime time = LocalTime.now();
LocalTime specifiedTime = LocalTime.of(12,15);
```

The "of" method used above specifies the hours and minutes, but there are other versions that take different numbers of arguments. This is the output from the example LocalTime objects (note how the current time includes the seconds and nanoseconds):

```
20:10:37.441414200
12:15
```

11.4.3   The LocalDateTime Class

Having covered in brief the key aspects of the LocalDate and LocalTime classes, we finally look at the LocalDateTime class which, unsurprisingly, combines both a date and a time. The syntax is similar to that we have already seen, for example:

```
LocalDateTime dateTimeNow = LocalDateTime.now();
LocalDateTime pastDateTime =
      LocalDateTime.of(1970, 1, 1, 0, 0);
```

The output should also come as no surprise:

```
2020-04-02T20:19:06.498307
1970-01-01T00:00
```

11.4.4   Formatting Dates and Times

Back in Chap. 5 we used the java.util.Formatter class to format java.util.Date objects using format Strings. Formatting dates and times in the "java.time" package is much easier using the classes in the "java.time.format" package. The DateTimeFormatter class provides many formatting options for both dates and times. One of the simplest of these is the "ofLocalizedDate" method, which creates a DateTimeFormatter object that deals only with the date (not the time) and can be passed one of the FormatStyle constants of SHORT, MEDIUM, LONG or FULL to specify the output format

```
DateTimeFormatter formatter =
  DateTimeFormatter.ofLocalizedDate(FormatStyle.SHORT);
```

Passing a DateTimeFormatter object to the "format" method of the date returns a String containing the formatted date:

```
String dateText = date.format(formatter);
```

When printed out it has this format:

```
31/03/20
```

If you don't like this short format, you can choose one of the other built-in formats defined by constants (MEDIUM, LONG and FULL). For example, this will create a formatter using the FULL format style:

```
DateTimeFormatter formatter =
    DateTimeFormatter.ofLocalizedDate(FormatStyle.FULL);
```

Displaying the same date in FULL format will look like this:

```
Thursday, 1 January 1970
```

To display elements of the time, rather than the date, use the "ofLocalizedTime" factory method. Note that in this example only the SHORT and MEDIUM formats will work because the LONG and FULL formats require more detail than is included in a LocalTime.

```
LocalTime time = LocalTime.now();
DateTimeFormatter timeFormatter =
  DateTimeFormatter.ofLocalizedTime(FormatStyle.MEDIUM);
String timeText = time.format(timeFormatter);
System.out.println(timeText);
```

The output from this code, showing the time in the MEDIUM format, looks something like this:

```
11:04:05 pm
```

For the longer formats that include time zone information, a ZonedDateTime object needs to be used, since this is the only class that handles time zones.

```
ZonedDateTime zonedTime = ZonedDateTime.now();
DateTimeFormatter zonedTimeFormatter =
   DateTimeFormatter.ofLocalizedDateTime(FormatStyle.FULL);
String zonedTimeText = zonedTime.format(zonedTimeFormatter);
System.out.println(zonedTimeText);
```

This is the output from the full format of the ZonedDateTime:

```
Thursday, 2 April 2020 at 8:31:25 pm New Zealand Daylight
Time
```

In addition to the four standard formats, the DateTimeFormatter has an "ofPattern" method that allows you to specify exactly how you want the date and/or time to appear using special characters. In this example, we apply a pattern so that the date appears in the order day, month, year, separated by forward slashes (case *is* significant here).

```
LocalDate date = LocalDate.of(1970,1,1);
DateTimeFormatter customDateFormat =
   DateTimeFormatter.ofPattern("dd/MM/yy");
String dateText = date.format(customDateFormat);
System.out.println(dateText);
```

This pattern leads to the date being formatted as the following String:

```
01/01/70
```

The pattern string parameter determines the way that the date is formatted, according to the table of patterns shown in Table 11.3. You cannot use any letters other than these, but you are free to use any punctuation symbols.

As well as the characters themselves being important, the number of them also affects how that element of the date is formatted. In general, if the number of pattern letters is four or more, the full form is used; otherwise, a short or abbreviated form is used (if available). Here is a slightly different version of our last example (the change in punctuation does not affect the date values, but the number of characters does):

```
DateTimeFormatter customDateFormat =
   DateTimeFormatter.ofPattern("dd-MMMM-yyyy");
```

This is the String that is returned. Using three "M" characters displays an abbreviated month name.

Table 11.3 Date and time patterns as they appear in the Javadoc

Letter	Date or Time Component	Presentation	Examples
G	era	text	AD; Anno Domini; A
u	year	year	2004; 04
y	year-of-era	year	2004; 04
D	day-of-year	number	189
M/L	month-of-year	number/text	7; 07; Jul; July; J
d	day-of-month	number	10
g	modified-Julian-day	number	2451334
Q/q	quarter-of-year	number/text	3; 03; Q3; 3rd quarter
Y	week-based-year	year	1996; 96
w	week-of-week-based-year	number	27
W	week-of-month	number	4
E	day-of-week	text	Tue; Tuesday; T
e/c	localized day-of-week	number/text	2; 02; Tue; Tuesday; T
F	day-of-week-in-month	number	3
a	am-pm-of-day	text	PM
h	clock-hour-of-am-pm (1–12)	number	12
K	hour-of-am-pm (0–11)	number	0
k	clock-hour-of-day (1–24)	number	24
H	hour-of-day (0–23)	number	0
m	minute-of-hour	number	30
s	second-of-minute	number	55
S	fraction-of-second	fraction	978
A	milli-of-day	number	1234
n	nano-of-second	number	987654321
N	nano-of-day	number	1234000000
V	time-zone ID	zone-id	America/Los_Angeles; Z; −08:30
v	generic time-zone name	zone-name	Pacific Time; PT
z	time-zone name	zone-name	Pacific Standard Time; PST
O	localized zone-offset	offset-O	GMT + 8; GMT + 08:00; UTC-08:00
X	zone-offset 'Z' for zero	offset-X	Z; −08; −0830; −08:30; −083015; −08:30:15
x	zone-offset	offset-x	+0000; −08; −0830; −08:30; −083015; −08:30:15
Z	zone-offset	offset-Z	+0000; −0800; −08:00
p	pad next	pad modifier	1
'	escape for text	delimiter	
''	single quote	literal	'
[	optional section start		
]	optional section end		

(continued)

Table 11.3 (continued)

Letter	Date or Time Component	Presentation	Examples
#	reserved for future use		
{	reserved for future use		
}	reserved for future use		

```
01-Jan-1970
```

Using four "M" characters for the month would lead to the following output, with the full month name:

```
01-January-1970
```

Here is a final example, which also includes the full day name.

```
DateTimeFormatter customDateFormat =
  DateTimeFormatter.ofPattern("EEEE dd MMMM, yyyy");
```

The resulting string would be

```
Thursday 01 January, 1970
```

11.4.5 Parsing Dates

The LocalDate's "parse" method can be used to convert Strings to Dates. In this case, the String pattern used in the "ofPattern" method of the DateTimeFormatter determines the way that dates are parsed (passed as an argument to the "parse" method). The data passed as the String argument must be in the expected format for the parse to succeed, so where possible, the simpler the better. However, the number of characters is not important when parsing, only when formatting. In this case, only one character for each element of the date is needed when specifying the pattern string.

```
DateTimeFormatter dateFormat =
  DateTimeFormatter.ofPattern("M/d/y");
LocalDate parsedDate = LocalDate.parse
  ("10/22/2012", dateFormat);
System.out.println(parsedDate);
```

The output from this example is the standard "toString" output from the LocalDate object.

```
2012-10-22
```

Exercise 11.7

- Use a LocalDate and the "of" method to create and set a specific date.
- Format the Date using a consistent separation character (e.g. "/").
- Use the "split" method of the String class to split the formatted date into separate values and display them.

The "split" method can be used to split a String using a separator String. It returns an array of Strings, for example, in this example a space is used as the separator String:

```
String st = new String("this is a test");
String[] split = st.split(" ");
```

11.5 Summary

This chapter covered a small sample of classes from some of the packages in the Java libraries. We began with some coverage of the Object class, and the "clone" method, before looking at some other classes in the "java.lang" package (Math, System and the wrapper classes). This was followed by coverage of two classes from the "java.util" package (Locale and Currency). Next, we looked at classes from the "java.text" package that help us to format and parse numbers and currencies. The final package covered in this chapter was "java.time", which provides classes for representing dates and times, as well as the "java.time.format" package which contains classes for formatting that data from these objects.

Hopefully, these examples will encourage you to reuse existing library classes as much as possible and become familiar with using the Javadoc to explore the classes and methods that may save you from unnecessarily writing new code, so you can concentrate on the code that really does need to be written.

The Collections Framework and Generics

12

In this chapter, we will look at some classes from the Java Collections Framework that can be used to contain collections of other objects. This framework makes extensive use of both inheritance and interfaces to provide both reuse and consistency across many different types of collection. The components of the framework include familiar data structures such as arrays, lists, maps and queues, as well as related algorithmic operations such as searching and sorting. The collections framework starts from the idea that every type of container is either a Collection or a Map. Both Collection and Map are interfaces that provide a common set of method signatures that all implementing classes should support. A Collection is something that contains elements, whereas a Map defines a mapping between keys and objects.

12.1 Objects that Contain Objects

A collection is an object that exists purely to hold a dynamic or unmodifiable collection of other objects. Unlike a composition relationship, the objects in a dynamic collection are not fixed; they can be added and removed at will. In previous chapters, we have used arrays as simple data structures that can contain objects, but arrays provide no services beyond indexed access, and cannot be dynamically resized. The Collections framework provides a more robust and powerful object-oriented approach to implementing object collections. The Collections API is a unified framework for both representing and manipulating collections, independent of their implementation. Different underlying data structures may vary in the ways that they hold and index the objects they contain but implement consistent interfaces, comprising a standard set of methods for accessing and maintaining collections. For example, all collection classes have an "add" method for adding new elements. In addition to having several public methods themselves, collections are also *iterable*; they can return an "Iterator" object that

© Springer Nature Switzerland AG 2020   299
D. Parsons, *Foundational Java*, Texts in Computer Science,
https://doi.org/10.1007/978-3-030-54518-5_12

can scan over the contents of a collection one object at a time. Iterators provide a simple mechanism for looking through any type of collection, whether or not that particular collection provides methods for doing so directly. The Deque (pronounced "deck", and short for "double ended queue") class, for example, does not itself allow all of its elements to be accessed directly because it is a data structure that normally allows access only to the objects at either end of the queue. By using an Iterator, however, we can view the contents of a Deque without having to add methods to its public interface that would not normally be appropriate for queue objects.

Of course, not all data structures are the same, either conceptually (e.g. a queue, a set and a list have different semantics) or in their implementations (e.g. not all collections are indexed). Therefore, in addition to the generic set of methods, each collection class has its own unique features.

12.1.1   Associations and Collections

Collections have an important role in implementing associations between objects. "One to many" or "many to many" relationships are best implemented with collections (rather than arrays). For example, the UML class diagram in Fig. 12.1 shows four classes from a banking domain. An account can have many transactions A (joint) account can have many customers, a customer can have many accounts. All of these "many" relationships need to be implemented so that an object can maintain relationships with many objects of another class, and in most cases, a collection or a map would be the most appropriate way of doing this. For example, a BankAccount might maintain a Collection of Transaction objects posted to it, while a Bank might hold a Map of BankAccounts, using the account numbers as keys. Of course in a business domain example like this, the underlying long term relationships between these objects would be represented in a data store, but for programming processes like generating reports, statements, etc., these relationships have to be modeled in runtime objects, which is where classes from the collections framework are important.

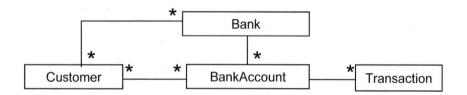

Fig. 12.1 Associations in a banking domain that should be implemented with collections

12.2   The Core Collection Interfaces

The Collections framework is built on a set of interfaces that provide a consistent approach to the classes that implement their methods. Figure 12.2 shows the core interfaces in the Collections framework. One aspect of UML notation used here is the "interface" *stereotype* keyword. Stereotype keywords are enclosed in "guillemets" (pronounced "gee-may") which look like double-pointed brackets. Using this notation makes it clear that these are interfaces, not classes.

   The Iterable interface, which all other collection interfaces extend, represents a group of objects that can be iterated over. The interface declares the "iterator" method, which returns an Iterator object that can access each element of a collection in turn. It also allows the use of a special "for" loop, which provides a more encapsulated way of using an Iterator.

   The "Collection" interface is the root interface of the Collection hierarchy in terms of the collection objects themselves. It represents a group of objects that can be added to. In addition to classes being able to implement multiple interfaces, interfaces themselves can extend other interfaces. Interfaces such as Queue, Set and List further extend the Collection interface. A Queue can represent both FIFO

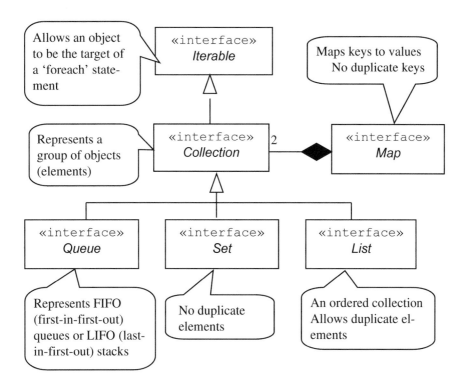

Fig. 12.2   The core interfaces in the Collections framework

(first-in-first-out) queues and LIFO (last-in-first-out) stacks, depending on how it is used. A List is simply an ordered sequence of elements, whereas a Set is also a sequence of elements but one that does not contain any duplicates.

Another core interface in the framework is the Map, representing objects that map keys to values. In a map, each key must be unique and map to at most one value. Although a Map is not a subtype of Collection, it relates closely to the rest of the framework, because the keys and values in a map are themselves collections (a Map is a composition of two collections). Not shown in 12.2 are SortedSet (which extends Set) and SortedMap (which extends Map).

Note
All the interfaces and classes in the Collections framework are in the java.util package, with the exception of the Iterable interface, which is in java.lang.

12.2.1   Partial Implementations of the Core Interfaces

The core interfaces in Fig. 12.2 are partially implemented in a group of abstract classes (Fig. 12.3). These make the core interfaces easier to implement. The concrete classes in the Collections framework inherit from these abstract classes.

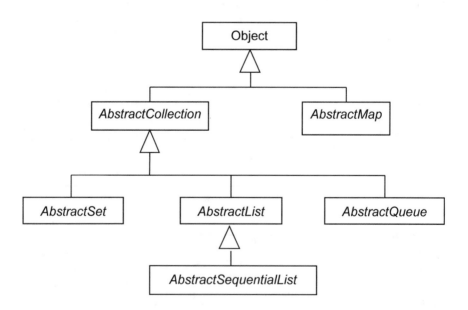

Fig. 12.3 Abstract classes in the Collections framework

12.2.2   Concrete Implementations of the Core Interfaces

Table 12.1 shows the main general-purpose classes that implement the core interfaces. Their names are based on combining the implementation of the data structure
(first) with the interface being implemented (second), where the interfaces are Set,
List, Deque and Map, and the implementations are HashTable, Array, Tree, LinkedList and HashTable + LinkedList. For example, the TreeSet is a balanced tree
implementation of the Set interface, and the ArrayList is a resizable array implementation of the List interface. Note that the LinkedList class implements both the
List and Deque interfaces. There are several other classes in the framework, but
they are more specialized.

In previous examples, we have used arrays to hold collections of objects. The
nearest Collection type to an array is an ArrayList. In some ways, an ArrayList is
very similar to an array, in that it contains an ordered collection of objects that can
be accessed using a zero-based index. However, an ArrayList is much more
powerful than an array. An ArrayList will dynamically resize itself if it is already
full when an attempt is made to add an object to it. An array, in contrast, will simply
throw an ArrayIndexOutOfBounds exception. The ArrayList class also encapsulates many useful methods and characteristics that are not available with simple
arrays, which have no methods and only a single "length" field. The other collection
classes provide a range of data structures that can cater for most application needs.
We might still use arrays occasionally, usually for reasons of efficiency, but in most
cases, we should use collections rather than arrays.

12.2.3   Legacy Classes

The Vector, HashTable and Stack classes were originally in JDK 1.0. They have
been superseded by the ArrayList, HashMap and ArrayDeque classes respectively,
but have been retrospectively included in the Collections framework by being
retrofitted with methods that are consistent with the framework, though for backward compatibility their old methods remain. Their continued existence is partly to
support legacy applications but also because they are still required in Java ME

Table 12.1 General purpose classes in the Collections framework, with names based on a
combination of interface and implementation

Interfaces	Implementations				
	HashTable	Resizeable Array	BalancedTree	LinkedList	HashTable + LinkedList
Set	HashSet		TreeSet		LinkedHashSet
List		ArrayList		LinkedList	
Deque		ArrayDeque		LinkedList	
Map	HashMap		TreeMap		LinkedHashMap

(Micro Edition) programming where there is no collections framework. Unlike the newer collection framework classes, they are synchronized (single-threaded).

12.3   Typesafe Collections with Generics

In the early versions of the Collections framework, collection classes could only contain Object references. This meant that collections were not typesafe. Collection constructors were not able to specify the types of objects that they were intended to contain. Here is a constructor call that creates an untyped LinkedList:

```
LinkedList list = new LinkedList();
```

This linked list could have any type of object added to it without any kind of type checking. Here we add a String:

```
List.add("A String");
```

Retrieving an object from an untyped collection means having to cast it to its appropriate type. For example, if we wanted to remove the first String object from the list (using the "getFirst" method, which is specific to LinkedList collections) it would need to be cast from Object to String.

```
String s = (String)myCollection.getFirst();
```

Knowing that the collection contains Strings is something that, as a programmer, you would have to infer from other parts of the code. The compiler can offer no assistance, and without compile-time type checking, there is a possibility of run time ClassCastExceptions being thrown if we attempt to cast to the wrong type. To overcome this problem, Java has included *generics* in the Collections framework since Java 5, making collections typesafe. Classes support generics where they allow a type variable to be included in their declarations. This type of variable is used to specify the type of object that the collections will store. The type stored in the collection is declared inside angle brackets after the collection type when declaring a reference. This also applies to the constructor call. For example, to declare a generic reference for an ArrayList of Integers we would include the type to be stored in the collection after the collection reference.

```
LinkedList<Integer> list = null;
```

The constructor call also includes the type to be stored, between the constructor name and the parentheses:

```
list = new LinkedList<Integer>();
```

Note

You cannot type a collection using a primitive type. Only reference types can be stored. Values of primitive types need to be put into objects of a suitable wrapper class before they can be added to a collection.

A typesafe list removes the need for casting. If we use generics so that the collection is typed to contain, for example, String objects, then the compiler can infer that the "getFirst" method returns a String, not an Object and no casting is required.

```
LinkedList<String> stringList = new LinkedList<String>();
stringList.add("A String");
String s2 = stringList.getFirst();
```

If you look at the Javadoc for the "getFirst" method, you will see that the signature is declared like this:

```
public E getFirst()
```

The "E" represents the element type that the LinkedList contains (where generics are used for classes outside the collections framework the normal convention is to use "T" to represent the type in the Javadoc).

Although the collections framework still allows untyped collections to be created, this is for backward compatibility and is not recommended for new code. The compiler will give you a warning if you try to create collection objects without using generics.

12.4   A Concrete Collection Class: The ArrayList

ArrayLists are extensible collections of arbitrary objects that allow you to add, access, search and remove elements. An ArrayList's capacity grows incrementally. Because they are built using different underlying implementations, ArrayLists and LinkedLists have some different methods. For example, with a LinkedList we can remove the first or last objects in the collection, whereas with an ArrayList you can only remove items by using their index in the collection. As well as small differences in how the two types of list can be used, a LinkedList can work slightly more efficiently if you change the contents of the collection frequently.

If an ArrayList is created using the zero arguments constructor, then the initial capacity defaults to 10.

```
ArrayList<String> monthNames = new ArrayList<String>();
```

However, setting the initial capacity using a parameterized constructor can improve efficiency if it avoids unnecessary resizing of the collection:

```
ArrayList<String> monthNames = new ArrayList<String>(12);
```

12.4.1 Adding and Retrieving Objects

One of the methods of the Collection interface is "add", which means that all collections (including ArrayList) will have an "add" method available. Here, we create an ArrayList of Strings, and add some Strings to it:

```
ArrayList<String> monthNames = new ArrayList<String>();
monthNames.add("January");
monthNames.add("February");
```

To retrieve an object from a collection, there is no common "get" method in the Collection interface. This is because different types of collection have different ways of allowing access to the elements, depending on their underlying data structures. Since the ArrayList represents an ordered collection, it implements the "List" interface. This interface supports a "get" method that can take an integer parameter to act as an index into the collection. These indexes are zero-based, very much like the indexes used with a basic Java array. Access to ArrayLists, however, is only through their methods; they cannot be accessed using the square bracket syntax used with arrays.

This line of code uses the "get" method with an array index of zero, so for our example ArrayList it would print out "January":

```
System.out.println(monthNames.get(0));
```

Contrast this "get" method with, for example, the methods of the PriorityQueue class, which implements the Queue interface and has no "get" methods, providing instead a "peek" (or "remove") method to access the object at the head of the queue.

The following code fragment demonstrates some of the other methods of the ArrayList class. Like the other classes in the framework, some methods are common to all collections (such as the "remove" method that takes an object as a parameter) but others are specific to implementations of the List interface, such as the "add", "get" and "remove" methods that are able to use index values (only List types support indexed access to elements).

```
System.out.println(monthNames.contains("March"));  // false
System.out.println(monthNames.indexOf("February"));  // 1
System.out.println(monthNames.get(0));    // "January"
```

Unlike an array, an ArrayList will dynamically resize as you add elements, and you can also insert elements at a specified index. However, you need to ensure that element insertion is done in a valid position. You cannot insert an element using an index value that is beyond the current bounds of the ArrayList. In the following example, the comments show what would be in the ArrayList after each operation, using the standard "toString" format of an ArrayList object.

```
monthNames.add("April");  // ["January", "February", "April"]
monthNames.add(2, "March");
// ["January", "February", "March", "April"]
monthNames.remove(0);  // ["February", "March", "April"]
monthNames.remove("March"); // ["February", "April"]
```

12.4.2   Wrapping and Autoboxing

Only objects (i.e. anything descended from class Object) can be added to collections. To add values of primitive types to a collection they need to be wrapped in the appropriate wrapper object (e.g. Integer, Double, etc.) before being added to the Collection, for example by using Integer.valueOf to wrap an int:

```
ArrayList<Integer> monthDays = new ArrayList<Integer>();
monthDays.add(Integer.valueOf(31);
```

However, "autoboxing" (and unboxing) means we do not need to explicitly refer to the wrapper classes. Primitives can be added directly to a collection (the wrapper is still being used but is implicit).

```
ArrayList<Integer> monthDays = new ArrayList<Integer>();
// autobox
monthDays.add(28);
// no casting to matching wrapper required on retrieval
int januaryNumber = numberList.get(0);
```

Autoboxing makes it look like collections can contain primitives, but it is important to understand that they are always wrapped in objects, even if that does not have to be done manually in our own code. The collection will always have its type declared using the appropriate wrapper class.

12.4.3   Iterators

Iterators provide an easy way to sequence through the objects in any collection. All collections have an "iterator" factory method to return an implementation of Iterator able to work with that type of collection. It is a factory method because the collection knows what type of iterator implementation to return to us. We do not need to know about the concrete class being used, only the methods of the interface. The Iterator interface only has two guaranteed methods:

```
boolean hasNext()
// Returns true if the iteration has more elements.
E next()
// Returns the next element in the iteration
```

We can use a "while" loop to iterate over the collection and return each object in turn using these two methods. There is also a "remove" method that removes the last element returned by the iterator from the collection. However, this is an optional operation so is not supported by every type of iterator. While the framework attempts to provide consistent encapsulated operations for different types of collection, not every implementation can support every operation. In such cases, methods are considered optional. A collection method may throw a java.lang. UnsupportedOperationException if an unsupported optional operation is called. The "remove" method is one that throws this exception (it is an unchecked exception, so the compiler does not require it to be caught).

When we use the "iterator" method, we need to use generics to specify the type of object being returned by the iterator, for example,

```
Iterator<String> iter = monthNames.iterator();
```

If the iterator is typed, then when we return the "next" object from the iterator, it will not need casting.

```
while(iter.hasNext())
{
   String monthName = iter.next();
   System.out.println(monthName);
}
```

Once an iterator has reached the last element in a collection, it cannot be reset. To iterate over the collection again, a new iterator object must be retrieved from the collection.

12.4.3.1 ListIterator

Any class that implements the List interface is also able to return a ListIterator, using the "listIterator" factory method. A ListIterator takes advantage of the underlying implementation of List collections to provide a few methods in addition to the basic methods on the Iterator interface. Among other things, we can traverse a List in both directions, as the ListIterator has a "previous" method as well as a "next" method. There are also methods to return the index value of the next or previous item to be returned by the iterator.

12.4.3.2 Enhanced "for" Loop

As an alternative to directly using an Iterator object, Java provides an enhanced "for" loop that makes iteration through a collection easier, if the only thing you want to do is iterate over the collection (as opposed to using the optional methods of Iterator or ListIterator). This is available for any class that implements the Iterable interface (which includes all the collections in the framework). Instead of creating an Iterator object, we can directly loop through the collection, with the next element returned into a local reference variable each time the loop iterates. In this example, "monthNames" is the name of the collection, and "aString" is the local variable name.

```
for(String aString : monthNames)
{
  System.out.println(aString);
}
```

12.4.3.3   Lambda Expressions

There is yet another way to iterate through a collection, and that is by using a lambda expression. The Iterable interface has a default "forEach" method that performs a given action on each object in the collection. You may recall that a Java lambda expression must implement the single abstract method of an interface. In this case, the interface is java.util.function.Consumer, which has an abstract "accept" method. The "forEach" method takes a Consumer as an argument, so it is the "accept" method that the lambda expression is (anonymously) implementing. The code is simple enough:

```
monthNames.forEach(monthName -> {
  System.out.println(monthName);
});
```

If you think this looks slightly different from the lambda expression that we introduced in Chap. 8, you are right. First, we are not creating a reference to the lambda expression for later execution, so there is no specific reference to the interface being implemented. We are just embedding the lambda expression as the argument to the "forEach" method. The other is that since there is only one argument ("monthName") it does not need to appear in parentheses (though adding parentheses would also be fine).

12.4.4   An ArrayList of Module Objects

In the next example, we will refactor the Course and Module classes from Chap. 9 so that the association between a course and its modules is implemented using an ArrayList rather than an array. This will make the code more robust (no need to worry about going beyond the bounds of an array) and enable us to use methods and iterators on the collection that are not available with arrays. The array field in the course will be replaced by an ArrayList.

```
private ArrayList<Module> modules = new ArrayList<Module>();
```

This leads to some other changes in various methods of the class. The "addModule" method no longer needs to be concerned with throwing an exception, and we no longer need a manual counter. We just add a module to the ArrayList, and it will automatically resize if it needs to.

```
public void addModule(Module newModule)
{
  modules.add(newModule);
}
```

The "getTotalCredits" method simply iterates through the collection, in this example using the special "for" loop.

```
public int getTotalCredits()
{
  int total = 0;
  for (Module m : modules)
  {
    total += m.getCreditPoints();
  }
  return total;
}
```

The "getModules" method no longer returns an array but an ArrayList of Modules.

```
public ArrayList<Module> getModules()
{
  return modules;
}
```

Finally, the "getModuleCount" method no longer needs to rely on the manual counter, but simply returns the current size of the ArrayList.

```
public int getModuleCount()
{
  return modules.size();
}
```

Overall, the code using the ArrayList is both simpler and more robust than the equivalent code using an array.

Turning our attention to the unit tests from Chap. 10, the test for going beyond the bounds of the array is no longer required. There is one other change to the tests. The "testAddedModule" method needs to be modified so that it uses the "get" method of the ArrayList rather than using an index value (in square brackets) on the array.

```
public void testAddedModule()
{
  Module module = new Module
    ("Collections", 10, "Assignment");
  course.addModule(module);
  Module module5 = course.getModules().get(4);
  assertEquals(module, module5);
}
```

This test contains an example of an "antipattern" (i.e. a common pattern that you should not necessarily follow). This antipattern has various names, including the "Law of Demeter", "don't talk to strangers" and "train wreck". It is the following line that exhibits this behavior:

```
Module module5 = course.getModules().get(4);
```

What we are doing is accessing the ArrayList via the Course and then accessing a method of the ArrayList directly. This kind of code can be regarded as a bad practice, as it breaks encapsulation. An alternative design strategy is to encapsulate access to the ArrayList by adding, for example, a "getModule" method to the Course class.

```
public Module getModule(int index)
{
  return modules.get(index);
}
```

Now the test can be written without breaking encapsulation:

```
@Test
public void testAddedModule()
{
  Module module = new Module
    ("Collections", 10, "Assignment");
  course.addModule(module);
  Module module5 = course.getModule(4);
  assertEquals(module, module5);
}
```

Note
The idea that chaining together a series of method calls is bad design practice is only true if it breaks the encapsulation of state data within objects. If coding using a functional programming style, the chaining together of method calls is an expected pattern. In functional programming, methods do not maintain state, and any representation of state is immutable, so there is no breaking of encapsulation.

Exercise 12.1
Create a Bank class that contains a collection of BankAccount objects, using a LinkedHashSet. Add methods to the Bank class to add BankAccounts to the bank and display the balances of all the accounts currently in the bank.

12.4.5   Unmodifiable Collections

One of the features of functional programming is that it works with immutable (cannot be changed) data. Rather than working with a data set that might change in the middle of a process, it will create an immutable copy of that data set. Java syntax uses the term "unmodifiable" rather than "immutable" because even though it is possible to create an unmodifiable collection, it is not possible to guarantee that any of the items within that collection cannot be modified elsewhere in the code. However, as the Javadoc states, "if an unmodifiable collection contains all immutable elements, it can be considered effectively immutable".

This can be very helpful in complex programming environments where different parts of the system might be accessing the same data. To adopt this type of coding, Java 9 and 10 both introduced some new ways to create unmodifiable collections. It could still be done with earlier versions of Java but with more complex coding. Here, for example, is the code to create an unmodifiable copy of a List, using the static "List.copyOf" method. In this example we create and populate a List, then make an unmodifiable copy. Attempting to add another object to the unmodifiable copy will throw an UnsupportedOperationException.

```
List<String> colors = new ArrayList<String>();
colors.add("Red");
colors.add("Blue");
colors.add("Green");
List<String> immutableColors = List.copyOf(colors);
// adding to the List
colors.add(0, "black");
// trying to add to the unmodifiable List
// throws an UnsupportedOperationException
immutableColors.add(0, "Black");
```

There are several methods like this that support the simple creation of unmodifiable collections. We will not cover any more of them here as they are something of a specialist requirement but check the Javadoc for options if you have the need to work with unmodifiable collections.

12.5   Maps

A Map allows a stored object to be accessed by using another object as a key. A Map therefore consists of a set of "key" objects, each associated with a single "value" object. The types of both the keys and the values need to be specified. In this example, a HashMap (one of the implementations of the Map interface) uses Strings for both the keys and the values to represent a simple phone book. Both of these types, separated by commas, need to be specified in the angle brackets.

```
HashMap<String, String> phonebook =
    new HashMap<String, String>();
```

Although in this example the keys and values are both the same type, they could also be of different types.

When you add elements, using the "put" method, you must supply both a key and a value of the correct types.

```
phonebook.put("Faith", "555-123456");
phonebook.put("Hope", "555-232323");
phonebook.put("Charity", "555-343456");
```

Inserting an object with a key that is equal to an existing key replaces the existing object.

```
phonebook.put("Hope", "555-999999");
```

Values are accessed by their keys.

```
System.out.println(phonebook.get("Hope")); // "555-999999"
```

They can also be removed using their keys.

```
phonebook.remove("Faith");
```

There are several other Map methods, including the following examples, which allow you to check the current contents and state of the Map.

```
System.out.println(phonebook.isEmpty()); // false
System.out.println(phonebook.size()); // 3
System.out.println(phonebook.containsKey("Faith")); // false
System.out.println(phonebook.containsValue("555-343456"));
// true
```

The HashMap also includes an overloaded "toString" method that displays the current contents of the Map

```
System.out.println(phonebook); // uses "toString"
```

Note
The order in which items appear in a Map is based on the hashcode, so appears arbitrary. Hashcodes are not data keys and cannot be used as such.

12.5.1 Map Views

Map implementations provide views of their contents from three perspectives. From Fig. 12.4, we can see that a Map is made up of Collections. The keys are a Set (because they must be unique), whereas the values are a Collection (duplicates are allowed). In addition, we can get a view of each key-value pair in the Map, returned

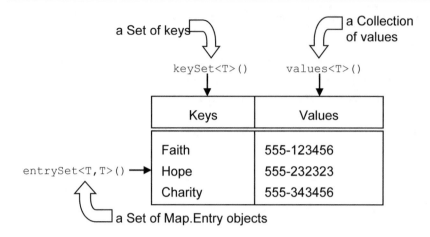

Fig. 12.4 The three views of a Map

as a set of Map.Entry objects. It is important to remember that these Collections are just views of the Map, not separate collections, and should not be used beyond short-term iterations. Other access to the Map should be directly through its methods.

In this example, we use an Iterator to scan the keys and retrieve their associated values using the get method. The set of keys is returned from the "keySet" method:

```
Set<String> names = phonebook.keySet();
```

We can then iterate over this set, and use each key to get its associated value from the Map.

```
for (String name : names)
{
  System.out.println(name + "\'s number is " +
    phonebook.get(name));
}
```

If we only wanted a collection of the values we could instead use the "values" method to return a Collection, for example,

```
Collection<String> phoneNumbers = phonebook.values();
```

Again, we could iterate over this collection to get access to the values. The following code shows how we can get a Set of Map.Entry objects from the "entrySet" method, allowing us to iterate over all the key-value pairs in the Map.

```
Set<Map.Entry<String, String> entrySet =
    phonebook.entrySet();
for (Map.Entry<String, String> row : entrySet)
{
  System.out.println(row);
}
```

12.5.2 Using a TreeMap

The next example uses a TreeMap (which implements the SortedMap interface) to implement a simple appointment diary, using dates as the keys and names (strings) as the values. Unlike a HashMap, a TreeMap provides a sorted order of keys. In the appointment diary, it may be useful to have the dates of appointments sorted into order. The keys in this example will be LocalDateTime objects.

Unlike Array-based structures there is no concept of an initial size when using an underlying tree-based implementation, which contrasts with the HashMap implementation of the Map interface, which provides a default initial capacity (of 16). In this example, a TreeMap is included as a private attribute of the Diary class (called "appointmentSlots") using the zero arguments constructor. The Map is typed to have LocalDateTime objects as keys and Strings as values:

```
private TreeMap<LocalDateTime, String> appointmentSlots =
new TreeMap<LocalDateTime, String>();
```

Entries are made into this Map via the "makeAppointment" method, which puts the key and its associated value into the Map (where "key" in this case is a LocalDateTime object and "value" is a String). The "showAppointments" method uses the "keySet" method of the Map to get the set of keys, then iterates through these keys to access the values. To format the output, individual fields are returned from the LocalDateTime by using "getter" methods.

This is the complete class (including a "main" method):

```java
package com.foundjava.chapter12;
import java.util.Set;
import java.util.TreeMap;
import java.time.LocalDateTime;

public class Diary
{
  private TreeMap<LocalDateTime, String> appointmentSlots =
    new TreeMap<LocalDateTime, String>();

  public void makeAppointment(String name, int year,
    int month, int day, int hour, int minute)
{

  LocalDateTime key = LocalDateTime.of

    (year, month, day, hour, minute);

  appointmentSlots.put(key, name);

}

public void showAppointments()
{
  String currentName;
    Set<LocalDateTime> appointments =
      appointmentSlots.keySet();
    for(LocalDateTime dateTime : appointments)
  {
      currentName = appointmentSlots.get(dateTime);
      System.out.println(currentName +
      " has an appointment on " + dateTime.getDayOfMonth()
      + " " + dateTime.getMonth()+ " "
      + dateTime.getYear()
        + " at " + dateTime.getHour() + ":"
      + dateTime.getMinute());

  }
  }
  public static void main(String[] args)
  {
  // create a Diary object
    Diary diary = new Diary();
  // add three appointments to the diary
    diary.makeAppointment("Great King of Terror",
      1999, 7, 1, 10, 30);
    diary.makeAppointment("Santa Claus",
      2020, 12, 24, 23, 59);
    diary.makeAppointment("Neville Chamberlain",
```

```
        1938, 9, 28, 12, 0);
    // display the appointments in the diary
        diary.showAppointments();
    }
}
```

The output from Appointments shows that the sequence of entries in Map is sorted in date order.

```
Neville Chamberlain has an appointment on 28 SEPTEMBER 1938 at 12:0
Great King of Terror has an appointment on 1 JULY 1999 at 10:30
Santa Claus has an appointment on 24 DECEMBER 2020 at 23:59
```

Exercise 12.2
Add several String objects to an ArrayList. Iterate over the ArrayList and get each element in turn, putting it into a HashMap, indexed by an integer counter. Write the HashMap to standard output to view its contents (it has a "toString" method for this).

Exercise 12.3
Add a method to the Diary class called "removeAppointment" that, given a date, will remove any appointment on that date. This can be implemented using the "containsKey" (that returns a boolean value) and "remove" (that removes an element) methods of TreeMap that both take an object of the appropriate key class as an argument. Add a "findAppointment" method to the class. This can also use "ContainsKey".

Exercise 12.4
Write a JUnit test for the Diary class. Include a test for your "removeAppointment" method.

12.6 Utility Classes

The utility classes provide various methods that act on objects of collection classes and arrays, generally using static methods. The Collections class has static methods for manipulating collections: searching, sorting, rotating, etc. Similarly, the Arrays class has static methods for manipulating arrays. Some of the methods of these utility classes, such as those for binary searching, sorting and finding minimum and maximum values, must be able to apply an order relation to the objects that they are manipulating. There are two ways of applying order relations; either implementing the Comparable interface on the objects to be sorted or creating an external Comparator object.

Applications often need to search or sort objects. For example, most card games require some concept of card order (i.e. which card can be played next, or scores higher). The next example is based on some aspects of a card game, which will include both shuffling and sorting playing cards. In this section, we will see how to apply both the Comparable and Comparator interfaces to the sorting process.

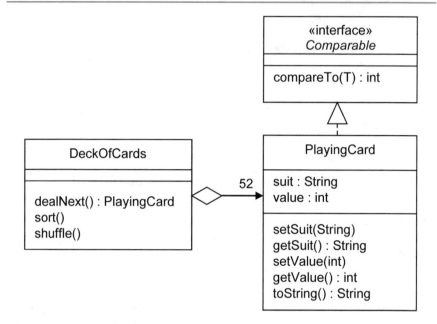

Fig. 12.5 The classes in the DeckOfCards example

Figure 12.5 shows the classes we are going to use in this example. The classes represent objects used in card games; PlayingCard and DeckOfCards. The PlayingCard class has two fields, "suit" and "value", and their associated getters and setters. It also implements the "Comparable" interface, and overrides "toString". The DeckOfCards is an aggregation of 52 PlayingCard objects. It includes methods to deal, sort and shuffle the cards.

12.6.1   Comparing Objects with the Comparable Interface

In Fig. 12.5, the PlayingCard class implements the Comparable interface, so the class declaration includes this implementation (Comparable is in the java.lang package so no import statement is required). Since the interface uses generics, the type that is being compared must be specified. In this case, we are comparing PlayingCards:

```
public class PlayingCard implements Comparable<PlayingCard>
{...
```

This interface declares only one method (with "T" being the generic type of the object):

```
public int compareTo(T object);
```

It is up to the implementing class to provide code for this method that compares the receiving object with the parameter object to put them in order. If "this" object (the one the "compareTo" method is applied to) is of a lower order than the parameter then the method should return a negative integer. If they are the same it should return zero. If it is of a higher order then it should return a positive integer. For our example, we will order playing cards by their face value, ignoring the card's suit. All the method does is subtract the face value of the parameter object from "this" object and return the difference, which may be positive, negative or zero.

```
public int compareTo(PlayingCard card)
{
    return this.getValue() - card.getValue();
}
```

Objects that implement the Comparable interface (and indeed, objects that are used by Comparators) should override "equals" in a way that is consistent with the implementation of the comparison method. This avoids potentially inconsistent behaviors if these objects are stored in SortedSets or SortedMaps. Therefore, we should override the "equals" method of PlayingCard to compare the card values.

```
@Override
public boolean equals(Object object)
{
    if(object == null
        || !(object.getClass().equals(this.getClass())))
    {
        return false;
    }
    PlayingCard other = (PlayingCard)object;
    if(getValue() == other.getValue())
    {
        return true;
    }
    else
    {
        return false;
    }
}
```

Here is the complete PlayingCard class (note the "toString" method which uses a "switch" statement to convert the value of the card into a String, naming the aces and picture cards where necessary). The constructor requires the card's suit and value to be passed as parameters.

```
package com.foundjava.chapter12;
public class PlayingCard implements Comparable<PlayingCard>
{
  private String suit;
  private int value;
  public PlayingCard(String suit, int value)
  {
    setSuit(suit);
    setValue(value);
  }
  private void setSuit(String suit)
  {
    this.suit = suit;
  }
  private void setValue(int value)
  {
    this.value = value;
  }
  public String getSuit()
  {
    return suit;
  }
  public int getValue()
  {
    return value;
  }
  @Override
  public String toString()
  {
    String cardName;
    switch (value) {
      case 1:
        cardName = "Ace";
        break;
      case 11:
        cardName = "Jack";
        break;
      case 12:
        cardName = "Queen";
        break;
      case 13:
        cardName = "King";
        break;
```

```
      default:
        cardName = String.valueOf(getValue());
    }
    return cardName + " of " + suit;
  }
  @Override
  public int compareTo(PlayingCard card)
  {
    return this.getValue() - card.getValue();
  }
  @Override
  public boolean equals(Object object)
  {
    if(object == null ||
      !(object.getClass().equals(this.getClass()))))
    {
      return false;
    }
    PlayingCard other = (PlayingCard)object;
    if(getValue() == other.getValue())
    {
      return true;
    }
    else
    {
      return false;
    }
  }
}
```

The following example demonstrates some of the methods of the PlayingCard class, including the "toString" method

```
package com.foundjava.chapter12;
public class ComparingCards
{
  public static void main(String[] args)
  {
    PlayingCard card1 = new PlayingCard("Hearts", 1);
    PlayingCard card2 = new PlayingCard("Diamonds", 13);
    int compare = card1.compareTo(card2);
    if(compare > 0)
    {
      System.out.println(card1 + " scores more than " +
        card2);
    }
    else
    {
      if(compare < 0)
      {
        System.out.println(card1 + " scores less than " +
          card2);
      }
      else
      {
        System.out.println(card1 + " scores the same as " +
          card2);
      }
    }
  }
}
```

The output from this example would be

```
Ace of Hearts scores less than King of Diamonds
```

Changing the values of the cards provided to the constructors would give different outputs.

This JUnit test case provides tests for the three possible outcomes of the "compareTo" method when used with PlayingCards. Note how the method (and the test) only concerns itself with the face value of the card, not the suit. The Jack of Hearts and the Jack of Diamonds are equal when compared.

```
package com.foundjava.chapter12;
import static org.junit.Assert.*;
import org.junit.Test;
public class PlayingCardTestCase
{
  @Test
  public void testLessThan()
  {
  PlayingCard card1 = new PlayingCard("Hearts", 1);
  PlayingCard card2 = new PlayingCard("Diamonds", 13);
  int compare = card1.compareTo(card2);
  assertTrue(compare < 0);
}
@Test
public void testGreaterThan()
{
  PlayingCard card1 = new PlayingCard("Hearts", 12);
  PlayingCard card2 = new PlayingCard("Diamonds", 4);
  int compare = card1.compareTo(card2);
  assertTrue(compare > 0);
}
@Test
public void testSame()
{
  PlayingCard card1 = new PlayingCard("Hearts", 11);
  PlayingCard card2 = new PlayingCard("Diamonds", 11);
  int compare = card1.compareTo(card2);
  assertTrue(compare == 0);
}
}
```

Now that we can create PlayingCard objects, we need to be able to put them into a deck. In this example, we will use a LinkedList as the collection that implements the aggregation in the DeckOfCards. The value of using a LinkedList here is that we can "deal" from it (i.e. we can remove the object at the beginning of the list).

```
private LinkedList<PlayingCard> deck =
    new LinkedList<PlayingCard>();
```

It will be useful to have a private getter method for this collection that we can use inside the class:

```
private LinkedList<PlayingCard> getDeck()
{
  return deck;
}
```

The "dealNext" method returns the card at the top of the pack, using the "removeFirst" method of the LinkedList.

```
public PlayingCard dealNext()
{
  return deck.removeFirst();
}
```

In the constructor, 52 cards are added to the deck, using the "add" method of the Collection interface. We need to provide the suit name to the constructors of the cards, so in this example, we use a static final array field of the class with the suit names hardcoded into it.

```
public static final String[] SUITS =
  {"Hearts","Diamonds","Spades","Clubs"};
```

A couple of other constants are also useful here, to represent the number of cards in a suit (13), and the number of suits in the deck (4). Using these constants will avoid magic numbers (numeric literals) appearing in the code.

```
public static final int SUIT_SIZE = 13;
public static final int NUMBER_OF_SUITS = 4;
```

There is a nested loop in the constructor to create the PlayingCards and add them to the deck; the outer loop counts through the 4 suits, and the inner loop counts through the 13 cards in each suit. When we add a new PlayingCard to the deck, the "suitIndex" value, which is counting from 0 to 12, needs to have 1 added to it to get card numbers in the range 1–13.

```
public DeckOfCards()
{
  for(int suitCount = 0; suitCount < NUMBER_OF_SUITS;
     suitCount++)
  {
    for(int suitIndex = 0; suitIndex < SUIT_SIZE;
      suitIndex++)
    {
      deck.add(new PlayingCard(SUITS[suitCount], suitIndex
        + 1));
    }
  }
}
```

12.6.2   The Collections Class

The Collections class is a set of static methods that perform operations on collections. In our DeckOfCards we will use methods of the Collections class to sort and shuffle the deck. The Collections class has many useful methods including searching, reversing and providing read-only copies of collections. Most of these methods work at the interface level. The signature of the "shuffle" method for example is

```
static void shuffle(List list);
```

meaning that it can handle anything that implements the List interface (i.e. any ordered Collection). The "shuffle" method randomly reorders the objects in the collection, so we can use this inside our DeckOfCards class to shuffle the cards.

```
public void shuffle()
{
  Collections.shuffle(getDeck());
}
```

Here is the complete DeckOfCards class, which we can deal from and shuffle.

```
public class DeckOfCards
{
  public static final int SUIT_SIZE = 13;
  public static final int NUMBER_OF_SUITS = 4;
  public static final String[] SUITS =
    { "Hearts", "Diamonds", "Spades", "Clubs" };
  private LinkedList<PlayingCard> deck =
    new LinkedList<PlayingCard>();
  private LinkedList<PlayingCard> getDeck()
  {
    return deck;
  }
  public DeckOfCards()
  {
    for(int suitCount = 0;
      suitCount < NUMBER_OF_SUITS; suitCount++)
    {
      for(int suitIndex = 0;
        suitIndex < SUIT_SIZE; suitIndex++)
      {
        deck.add(new PlayingCard(SUITS[suitCount],
          suitIndex + 1));
      }
    }
  }
  public PlayingCard dealNext()
  {
    return getDeck().removeFirst();
  }
  public void shuffle()
  {
    Collections.shuffle(getDeck());
  }
}
```

In this very simple program, we simulate a card game where two players are each dealt three cards. The winner is the player with the highest total card score. Since the constructor creates the deck of cards in suit and number order, we must shuffle the deck before dealing with any cards.

```
package com.foundjava.chapter12;
import java.util.ArrayList;
public class SimpleCardGame
{
  public static void main(String[] args)
  {
    DeckOfCards deck = new DeckOfCards();
    deck.shuffle();
    PlayingCard card = null;
    ArrayList<PlayingCard> player1Hand =
      new ArrayList<PlayingCard>();
    ArrayList<PlayingCard> player2Hand =
      new ArrayList<PlayingCard>();
    int player1Score = 0;
    int player2Score = 0;
    for(int i = 0; i < 3; i++)
    {
      card = deck.dealNext();
      player1Hand.add(card);
      player1Score += card.getValue();
      card = deck.dealNext();
      player2Hand.add(card);
      player2Score += card.getValue();
    }
    System.out.println("Player 1 hand " + player1Hand);
    System.out.println("Player 2 hand " + player2Hand);
    System.out.println("Player 1 scored " + player1Score +
        " Player 2 scored " + player2Score);
  }
}
```

Here is some sample output from running the game.

```
Player 1 hand [King of Clubs, 2 of Hearts, 10 of Hearts]
Player 2 hand [9 of Diamonds, King of Hearts, 10 of Diamonds]
Player 1 scored 25 Player 2 scored 32
```

The "sort" method of the Collections class can be used to sort the DeckOfCards into order.

```
Collections.sort(List);
```

The problem here is that this version of the "sort" method will use the PlayingCard's implementation of the "compareTo" method to sort the objects into order. Since our implementation of "compareTo" does not take suits into account, the deck will not sort into the traditional order, where cards are sorted first by suit and then by number.

To provide an alternative sorting implementation, you can pass a Comparator as the second parameter and it will use this to handle the sort order.

```
Collections.sort(List, Comparator);
```

In the next section, we will create a suitable Comparator object for sorting the deck.

12.6.3   Creating a Comparator

The Comparator interface represents an order relation being applied to two parameter objects. This interface can be implemented to order elements regardless of whether or not they implement Comparable. This is useful where we want to sort objects of classes that we have not written ourselves, and therefore cannot add additional interfaces to. It can also be useful to provide alternative ways of sorting the same types of objects. You can only implement the Comparable interface in one way for a given class but can create as many different Comparators as you like. The Comparator interface requires that you provide an implementation of the "compare" method.

```
int compare(T o1, T o2)
```

In addition, it declares the "equals" method.

```
boolean equals(Object obj)
```

Because all Objects have an "equals" method inherited from Object, the compiler will not require this to be overridden. The Javadoc states that:

> it is *always* safe *not* to override Object.equals(Object). However, overriding this method may, in some cases, improve performance by allowing programs to determine that two distinct comparators impose the same order.

In the following Comparator implementation, PlayingCards are ordered by both number and suit (in alphabetical order). Since the suit in this case is stored as a String, we can use the existing "compareTo" method of the String class to sort the suits. Comparing the card value, if the cards are in the same suit, is done by using the existing Comparable interface implementation. If PlayingCard did not implement Comparable, we could manually apply an order relation.

```
package com.foundjava.chapter12;
import java.util.Comparator;
public class CardComparator
    implements Comparator<PlayingCard>
{
  public int compare(PlayingCard card1, PlayingCard card2)
  {
    int suitComparison =
        card1.getSuit().compareTo(card2.getSuit());
    if(suitComparison != 0)
    {
      return suitComparison;
    }
    return card1.compareTo(card2);
  }
}
```

Here is a sort method added to the DeckOfCards class that uses the "sort" method of the Collections class and the CardComparator.

```
public void sort()
{
  Collections.sort(deck, new CardComparator());
}
```

This "main" method shows the effect of first shuffling the deck and then sorting it.

```
public static void main(String[] args)
{
  DeckOfCards cardDeck = new DeckOfCards();
  cardDeck.shuffle();
  Iterator<PlayingCard> iter = cardDeck.getDeck().iterator();
  while (iter.hasNext())
  {
    System.out.println(iter.next());
  }
  cardDeck.sort();
  iter = cardDeck.getDeck().iterator();
  while (iter.hasNext())
  {
    System.out.println(iter.next());
  }
}
```

The output from this test program is rather long, so this sample has been truncated:

```
5 of Diamonds
King of Diamonds
4 of Spades
King of Spades
10 of Spades
9 of Spades
//etc..

Ace of Clubs
2 of Clubs
3 of Clubs
4 of Clubs
5 of Clubs
6 of Clubs
7 of Clubs
//etc..
```

From this point on, we have a deck of cards that we could use in any number of card games, though we might need to have further specialized Comparators for different games where the semantics of card order are different (e.g. "aces high").

Exercise 12.5
Not all card decks use the "French Suit" of diamonds, clubs, spades and hearts. Other possible suits include:

- Latin suit: swords, chalices, coins and clubs
- Brisca (Spanish) suit: gold, swords, cups and clubs
- Germanic suit: bells, acorns, leaves and hearts.

Add a parameterized constructor to the DeckOfCards class so that an integer argument can be provided to select the deck type (using static final fields). Write a JUnit test for your deck to confirm that the suit is correctly set.

Exercise 12.6
Table 12.2 shows how a class that implements the Deque interface can act as a Stack, with methods that match the usual stack operations of "push" (add an element to the top of the stack), pop (remove the element from the top of the stack) and "peek" (see the element at the top of the stack without removing it).

There are some card games where there are common pools of cards. Players can draw a card from the top of the main pool, which is facedown, and discard cards by adding them back to the top of another pool, which is faceup. However, players can

Table 12.2 Methods of the Deque interface and their equivalent generic stack operations	Generic Stack Operations	Equivalent Deque Method
	Push	addFirst(e)
	Pop	removeFirst()
	Peek	peekFirst()

also choose to draw the top card from the faceup pool, so this pool acts like a stack. Create a "CardPool" class that uses a Collection that implements the Deque interface. Provide appropriate methods for PlayingCards to be both drawn from the top of the pool and be returned to the top of the pool. Because this pool is faceup, players should also be able to check to the card at the top of the pool before choosing whether not to draw the card.

To test your class, write JUnit test methods for pushing cards onto the pool, popping cards from the pool and peeking at the top card.

Exercise 12.7

Create a "Hand" class that represents a set of cards held in a player's hand. Use this Hand class to write the beginnings of a game of 21 (also known as Pontoon). The game will have a dealer and one player. The dealer and the player are both dealt with three cards. The one with the highest score (calculated by adding the card values together) wins, unless the total is over 21, in which case the hand is "bust". All picture cards count as 10. The dealer wins all draws.

12.7 Generics and Inheritance

The collections we have look at so far have been typed to a single class. This can cause problems when we want to write generic utility methods that act on collections of objects in inheritance hierarchies. The following class contains a static utility method that iterates through a collection of Objects and prints them on the console.

```
public class GenericPrinter
{
  public static void printElements
    (Collection<Object> myCollection)
    {
      for (Object myObject : myCollection)
      {
        System.out.println(myObject);
      }
    }
}
```

The problem with a method like this is that it cannot be used to iterate over subclasses of the collection's declared type. In this example, only a collection of type Object can be passed to the "printElements" method. If we try to pass a collection that is typed to something other than Object, for example, a collection of Strings, this will lead to a compiler error.

```
ArrayList<String> monthNames = new ArrayList<String>();
monthNames.add("January");
monthNames.add("February");
GenericPrinter.printElements(monthNames); // compiler error
```

Although String is a subclass of Object, we cannot print a collection of Strings using this method. The resulting compiler error states that:

The method printElements(Collection < Object >) in the type GenericPrinter is not applicable for the arguments (ArrayList < String >)

To create a more generic method that can process objects of subclasses, we can specify the type of the collection using the "?" wildcard. This makes the collection passed to the method of an unknown type, meaning that any type of collection can be processed by the method.

```
public static void printAnyElements
    (Collection<?> myCollection)
{
  for(Object myObject : myCollection)
  {
    System.out.println(myObject);
  }
}
```

This method can print any type of collection.

```
GenericPrinter.printAnyElements(monthNames); // will compile
```

Note
You cannot add any objects to a collection created using this wildcard. It is only appropriate for utility methods that handle existing collections like the one in the example.

12.7.1 Specifying Bounds

In the previous example, we began with a method that could handle classes of type object, then used a wildcard to allow the method to work with any type. Sometimes, however, we want methods that handle a specific class and its subtypes, in order to call methods specific to that class hierarchy. For example, we might want to write a method that can work with any Shape object (assuming the Shape class we created in Chap. 8, which has a "getArea" method). The following code will display the area of any Shape in a collection of Shapes.

```
public static void displayShapeProperties
    (Collection<Shape> shapes)
{
  for(Shape s : shapes)
  {
    System.out.println("The area of " + s +
      " is " + s.getArea());
  }
}
```

This works fine in terms of using a polymorphic reference of type Shape to reference subclass objects. Unfortunately, it would not handle a collection typed to a subclass, like Square. The following ArrayList, for example, could not be passed to the "displayShapeProperties" method.

```
ArrayList<Square> squares = new ArrayList<Square>();
squares.add(new Square(null, 250));
GenericPrinter.displayShapeProperties(squares);
// will not compile
```

We can overcome this restriction by using a *bounded wildcard*. Bounded wildcards let us specify that collections typed to a subclass are compatible with this method. In this example, we can specify that any collection containing subclasses of Shape can be passed to the method.

```
public static void displayAnyShapeProperties
    (Collection<? extends Shape> shapes)
{
  for (Shape s : shapes) {
    System.out.println("The area of " + s +
      " is " + s.getArea());
  }
}
```

Now, "Shape" is the upper bound of the wildcard. We could pass a collection of type Square to this method, or TwoDimensionalShape, or indeed any other subclass of Shape.

```
GenericPrinter.displayAnyShapeProperties(squares);
// will compile
```

Exercise 12.8
Create a class with a method that will take a collection of any subtype of Number as a parameter and print out its contents on the console. Test your methods using:

(a) A collection of Integers
(b) A collection of Doubles.

12.8   Collection Streams

The Java Stream API was added to Java 8 and supports a functional programming approach to handling Collections (or other sequences of objects) in Java using lambda expressions. The classes and interfaces in the Stream API are in the "java. util.stream" package. Any Collection can return an implementation of the Stream interface using the "stream" method of the given collection. Here is an example of obtaining a Stream from an ArrayList of PlayingCard objects. First, we assume there is a list of PlayingCards called "hand":

```
List<PlayingCard> hand = new ArrayList<PlayingCard>();
```

From this we can create a Stream of PlayingCard references using the "stream" factory method.

```
Stream<PlayingCard> cardStream = hand.stream();
```

The reason for creating this Stream is so that we can apply one or more operations to the content of the ArrayList to create a resulting value or Collection. Stream operations do not manipulate the content of the original Collection so can be chained together in a functional programming style. These operations together make up a *stream pipeline,* consisting of the original data source (a Collection in the following examples), zero or more intermediate operations that transform the stream into another stream and a terminal operation that produces the result. A stream pipeline can be thought of as acting like a query on the stream source. Here is a very simple example that just applies the "count" method to count the number of items in the stream.

```
long cardCount = cardStream.count();
```

Note that once the terminal operation has been performed, the stream is closed. This means that in the example above, the "cardCount" reference could not be used for any more stream operations unless assigned to a new stream.

One way in which streams can be used on a Collection is to create another Collection that contains a subset of the original objects. In the following line of code, a stream is created from an ArrayList of PlayingCard objects. Note that in this example, to make the code more concise and to ensure that we get a new stream that has not already been closed; we call the "stream" method as part of the pipeline instead of declaring a separate variable. The terminal operation will return a List ("selectedList"). However, before that happens there is an intermediate operation ("filter") that applies a predicate to each element (referred to by the local variable name "card" in these examples) to determine if it should be included. The predicate is implemented by a lambda expression, which in this example selects only those cards in the "Hearts" suit. Then the "collect" method creates the List to be returned using the static "toList" method of the java.util.stream.Collectors class (putting each operation in the pipeline on a separate line is not necessary but aids readability).

```
List<PlayingCard> selectedSuit = hand.stream()
    .filter(card -> card.getSuit().contentEquals("Hearts"))
    .collect(Collectors.toList());
```

Here is a complete example class that processes a "hand" of 10 random playing cards to produce a List of those in the "Hearts" suit:

```
package com.foundjava.chapter12;
import java.util.ArrayList;
import java.util.List;
import java.util.stream.Collectors;
import java.util.stream.Stream;

public class HandOfCardsStream
{
  public static void main(String[] args)
  {
    DeckOfCards cardDeck = new DeckOfCards();
    cardDeck.shuffle();
    List<PlayingCard> hand = new ArrayList<PlayingCard>();
    for(int i = 0; i < 10; i++)
    {
      hand.add(cardDeck.dealNext());
    }
    System.out.println("Hand of cards dealt \n" + hand);
    List<PlayingCard> selectedSuit = hand.stream()
      .filter(card -> card.getSuit().contentEquals("Hearts"))
      .collect(Collectors.toList());
    System.out.println("Filtered hand (hearts only)\n" +
      selectedSuit);
  }
}
```

The output of course will vary from run to run depending on the cards randomly "dealt", but here is one example.

```
Hand of cards dealt

[Queen of Clubs, 6 of Hearts, 10 of Hearts, 9 of
Spades, Ace of Hearts, 9 of Hearts, Ace of Clubs,
King of Diamonds, 2 of Spades, 4 of Spades]
Filtered hand (hearts only)
[6 of Hearts, 10 of Hearts, Ace of Hearts, 9 of Hearts]
```

In all the following examples, we assume that the same code has been used to create the "hand" of ten cards, to which each of the Stream examples is being applied.

In the previous example, a Stream was used to create a collection that contained a subset of the original elements using the "filter" method. The "map" method, in contrast, applies a function to each of the elements in the stream to create a new Collection or Map containing the converted data. In this example, we use "map" to convert the names of each card in the hand to upper case, creating a List of Strings.

```
List<String> upperCaseSuits = hand.stream()
    .map(card -> card.getSuit().toUpperCase()).
    .collect(Collectors.toList());
```

Here is an example output from this code (will vary from run to run).

```
Upper case suits: [CLUBS, HEARTS, SPADES, SPADES, SPADES,
SPADES, HEARTS, SPADES, CLUBS, DIAMONDS]
```

As we saw with the "count" method earlier in this section, not all Stream operations result in a Collection. For example, we can use the "max" or "min" methods with Comparators to return the object in the stream with the highest or lowest value. In this example, we use "max" to find the PlayingCard with the maximum value. The "get" method returns the resulting PlayingCard. Note the use of the double colon "method reference" operator, which can be used as a shorthand in lambda expressions. In this example, "PlayingCard::getValue" is used instead of the more explicit but less concise "card -> card.getValue()". In both cases the "getValue" method is applied to each of the PlayingCards in the collection:

```
PlayingCard highest = selectedSuit.stream()
    .max(Comparator.comparing(PlayingCard::getValue))
    .get();
```

In this slightly different example, we use the "min" method after applying a filter that selects only those cards in the "Spades" suit, returning the one with the lowest value (note that this code will throw an exception if there are no Spades in the randomly generated hand of cards).

```
PlayingCard high = hand.stream()
    .filter(card -> card.getSuit().equals("Spades"))
    .min(Comparator.comparing(PlayingCard::getValue))
    .get();
```

In this example, the "summingInt' method of the Collectors class is used with the "collect" method to add all the card values together.

```
int cardSum = hand.stream()
    .collect(Collectors.summingInt(PlayingCard::getValue));
```

For the final example in this section, we will refer back to Sect. 12.4, where we went through four different ways of iterating through a Collection: an Iterator, a ListIterator, an enhanced "for" loop and a lambda expression. There is yet another option, which is to use a stream and the "forEach" method, which iterates through the elements of the stream. This is of course very similar to the lambda expression in Sect. 12.4 but applying "forEach" to the stream instead of the Collection.

```
hand.stream()
    .forEach(System.out::println);
```

The examples in this section have shown some of the possibilities of using Streams, but there are many other aspects to the API not covered here that provide different ways of processing data from Collections or other sequences of objects.

Exercise 12.9
Create an ArrayList of Integers and apply the following Stream methods to it:

- Use "max" to return the highest value.
- Use "min" to return the lowest value.
- Apply the "forEach" method to print out each Integer in the stream.
- Apply a filter to return a List containing only those Integers above a certain value.
- Make sure there are some duplicate values in your original ArrayList, then apply the "distinct" method to create a List that contains only the distinct values.

Exercise 12.10

All the processing of Integer objects in Exercise 12.9 can be done using a Stream, but there are further numeric processes that can be performed on an IntStream, which provides a stream of primitive ints.

- Create an IntStream using the static "of" method which take a comma-separated list of ints as its argument.
- Apply the "sum" method to the IntStream, which returns an int.
- Create another IntStream and apply the "average" method, which returns an OptionalDouble object.

12.9   Summary

In this chapter, we have looked at some aspects of the Collections Framework and used it to manage collections of objects. We began by outlining some of the main interfaces in the framework, including Iterable, Collection and Map, and saw how these can be used to implement object associations. We looked at the general-purpose classes in the Collections framework that link together high-level interfaces and specific types of implementation such as the ArrayList, which implements the List interface with an underlying array implementation, and Tree-Map, which implements the SortedMap interface using a tree-based implementation. The use of generics to create typesafe collections was explained, along with ways of applying generic types within inheritance hierarchies. The chapter also described how interfaces are used by the framework to provide common services across a range of implementing classes, and how some of these vary due to the features of the different implementations used. Code examples illustrated the differences between Collections and Maps, the various ways in which Iterators can be used to scan the contents of collections, and how unmodifiable collections can be created. Utilities such as the Collections class and the Comparator interface were demonstrated, illustrated with examples of methods such as "sort" and "shuffle" that can be applied to Collection objects. Some of the interfaces, classes and methods from the Streams API were explored, with various examples applied to an ArrayList of domain objects.

Input and Output Streams

13

A stream is an ordered sequence of bytes flowing from a source to a destination. The implementation of Streams in Java aims to encapsulate any kind of serial input or output into a library of classes that provide a consistent set of abstractions (interfaces and abstract classes), regardless of the source or the sink (destination) of the data. The lower level details specific to those types of source or destination are handled by the stream, and do not have to be handled by the programmer. For example, the differences between writing to a file and writing to the screen console are handled by the implementations of the relevant classes. A program may write and read data to and from files, the console, the keyboard, networks or other programs, all using similar methods, implemented by stream library classes that encapsulate the low-level differences between the various types of data transfer, providing higher level abstractions for the programmer to use (Fig. 13.1).

13.1 Java Stream Classes

The stream classes have been developed in different stages over the lifetime of Java, and there are stream classes in both the "java.io" and "java.nio" packages. The original streams in JDK 1.0 only handled basic input and output of bytes and Java primitives, so JDK 1.1 added readers and writers to handle character I/O. These classes are in the java.io package. Although these classes are adequate for many applications they are not particularly scalable for enterprise-level applications, so from JDK 1.4, there has been an evolving set of classes in the NIO (New Input/Output) library (the "java.nio" package) designed to provide more scalable stream implementations. This is an ongoing process and there have been further NIO_2 (NIO enhancements) classes in subsequent releases. In this chapter, we will cover the basics of stream handling in the "java.io" package and provide a brief introduction to "java.nio".

© Springer Nature Switzerland AG 2020   339
D. Parsons, *Foundational Java*, Texts in Computer Science,
https://doi.org/10.1007/978-3-030-54518-5_13

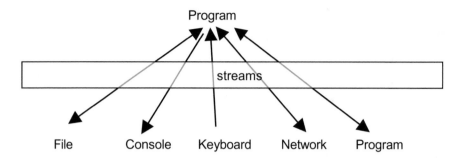

Fig. 13.1 Streams provide high-level abstractions that minimize the differences between different types of data transfer

13.1.1   Different Types of Stream

There are many different types of stream in the libraries, but there is a general categorization we can make in terms of the types of data that certain streams are designed to handle. The four types of data are bytes, primitives, characters and objects, and there are separate families of stream classes that are used to handle these types (Table 13.1). This is something of an oversimplification of the stream libraries but captures some key concepts.

The lowest level streams are byte streams that operate on bytes and byte arrays. These are implemented by the InputStream and OutputStream classes and their subclasses.

Filter streams use lower level byte streams as part of their implementation, so to create a filter stream we also need to create an associated input or output stream. Some filter streams operate on primitive data types (ints, doubles, etc.). These are implemented by classes that extend DataInput and DataOutput.

Character streams contain 16-bit Unicode characters and operate on characters, character arrays and Strings. These are implemented by the Reader and Writer classes and their subclasses

Object streams read and write objects. These are represented by the ObjectInputStream and ObjectOutputStream classes. These are concrete classes that extend InputStream and OutputStream and also implement several interfaces.

Table 13.1   Types of stream and the data types that they handle

Stream type	Data types	Related classes
Byte streams	Bytes (and arrays of bytes)	InputStream/OutputStream
Filter streams	Java primitives	DataInput/DataOutput
Character streams	Characters and Strings	Reader/Writer
Object streams	Objects	ObjectInputStream/ObjectOutputStream

Although streams can be used over many different types of serial connection, most of the examples in this chapter use file streams, because these can easily be used to demonstrate both input and output.

13.2 Byte Streams

Byte streams are represented by an inheritance hierarchy that has the abstract InputStream and OutputStream classes at the top. These abstract classes have some behavior implemented by concrete subclasses. Figure 13.2 shows some of the main methods of the InputStream and OutputStream classes.

OutputStreams write raw bytes to their destination. The "write" method takes either an array of bytes or an int as a parameter. In the latter case, although the parameter is typed as an int, only the lower order byte of the int is written to the output stream; the other three are ignored. The "flush" method ensures that any buffered output data is written to its destination (closing the stream will also cause it to flush). When using an InputStream, there is a "read" method that returns an int (again only the lower order byte is actually used) and other "read" methods that return the data into byte arrays passed as parameters. These methods that read arrays also return an int, containing either the number of bytes read or −1 if there are no more bytes on the input stream. The "available" method estimates how many bytes will be available for the next "read" operation on the stream.

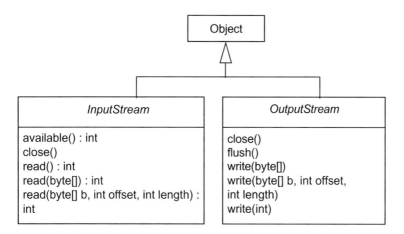

Fig. 13.2 The main methods of the InputStream and OutputStream abstract classes

13.2.1 Streaming Bytes to and from Files

FileOutputStream is a concrete subclass of OutputStream and can be used to write bytes to files. The constructor shown here creates the file regardless of whether a file of that name already exists (but will not create folders).

```
OutputStream outfile = new FileOutputStream("hello.txt");
```

Alternatively, we can append an existing file by passing "true" as a second parameter argument.

```
OutputStream outfile =
    new FileOutputStream("hello.txt", true);
```

Although the "write" methods only work at the byte level, they can be used to write ASCII characters to the output stream since these only require one byte to represent the character, for example,

```
outfile.write('a'); // ASCII chars can be bytes
```

However, we would not normally use FileOutputStreams for character data. They are only for use when we want to write byte-level data to file, such as image data. Even then, there are higher level streams that would probably be better options. As we will see later, the main reason for needing to know about low-level streams is that they support the functionality of higher level streams. Given this, the following example should be taken as a basic outline of syntax rather than good practice for writing characters to files. It does, however, cover some core aspects for handling output streams that apply to any type of stream:

1. Many operations on streams throw java.io.IOException, so this must be handled.
2. File operations throw java.io.FileNotFoundException so this also needs to be handled. Since this is a subclass of IOException, it must be handled first if there is more than one "catch" block.
3. Streams should always be closed when you have finished using them. The best what to do this is to use the "try-with-resources" construct, which ensures that the resources are closed if an exception occurs. This requires the code that opens the stream to be added to the "try".
4. If an output stream is neither flushed nor closed, there is no guarantee that any data will be written.

Here is the full class that writes some individual characters (as bytes) to a file:

```java
package com.foundjava.chapter13;

import java.io.FileNotFoundException;
import java.io.FileOutputStream;
import java.io.IOException;
import java.io.OutputStream;

public class FileOutputExample
{
  public static void main(String[] args)
  {
    try(OutputStream outfile =
      new FileOutputStream("hello.txt"))
    {
      outfile.write('h');
      outfile.write('e');
      outfile.write('l');
      outfile.write('l');
      outfile.write('o');
      outfile.flush();
      System.out.println("Data written to file");
    }
    catch (FileNotFoundException e)
    {
      e.printStackTrace();
    }
    catch(IOException e)
    {
      e.printStackTrace();
    }
  }
}
```

If you run this example, which does not include a file path, the file will be created in the default folder, which in Eclipse will be the project folder. If you right click on the project to get the pop-up menu and then select "Refresh", you should see the created text file's name appear in the Package Explorer window. If you double click on the file, Eclipse will open it in an editor window.

Having created the file using a FileOutputStream we can read the data back into a program using a FileInputStream. FileInputStream is a concrete subclass of InputStream and can be used to read bytes from files. One of the constructors takes the name of a file as a parameter.

```java
InputStream infile = new FileInputStream("hello.txt");
```

Since the "available" method returns the number of bytes left in the stream, we can use this method to control a "while" loop that reads bytes (using the "read" method that reads one byte at a time) from the input stream.

```
while(infile.available() > 0)
{
// read returns the next byte in the file
  int byteValue = infile.read();
// do something with the byte
```

Alternatively, we could read the stream data directly into a byte array.

```
byte[] buffer = new byte[100];
int bytesRead = infile.read(buffer);
// do something with the byte array
```

Here is a complete program to read from an input file stream. This example uses a "while" loop but could equally read directly into a byte array. It casts each returned int into a char in order to print it to the console.

```
package com.foundjava.chapter13;

import java.io.FileInputStream;
import java.io.FileNotFoundException;
import java.io.InputStream;
import java.io.IOException;

public class FileInputExample
{
  public static void main(String[] args)
  {
    try(InputStream infile =
      new FileInputStream("hello.txt"))
    {
      int readByte = 0;
      while(infile.available() > 0)
      {
        readByte = infile.read();
        System.out.print((char)readByte);
      }
    }
```

```
   catch (FileNotFoundException e)
   {
     e.printStackTrace();
   }
   catch(IOException e)
   {
     e.printStackTrace();
   }
  }
}
```

13.3 Filter Streams

The basic idea of a filter stream is that it wraps around the basic functionality of another, lower level, stream and can then transform the data and/or provide additional functionality (Fig. 13.3).

One useful example of a filter stream is one that wraps a byte stream to work with Java primitive data types. The concrete classes that do this are DataInput-Stream and DataOutputStream. Because these classes require the services of lower level byte streams, their constructors require these other streams to be passed as parameters. In the following example, a FileOutputStream object (a byte stream) is created and then passed to the constructor of a DataOutputStream object. The filter stream will use the services of the byte stream to help implement its methods.

```
OutputStream fileOut = new FileOutputStream("data.dat");
DataOutputStream dataOut = new DataOutputStream(fileOut);
```

We can make this rather more concise (and easy to use in a "try-with-resources" construct) by wrapping the first constructor inside the other and using "var" rather than "DataOutputStream":

```
var dataOut = new DataOutputStream
   (new FileOutputStream("data.dat"))
```

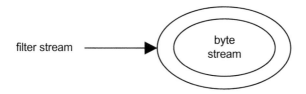

Fig. 13.3 Filter streams wrap lower level byte streams

The concrete DataInputStream and DataOutputStream classes inherit from FilterStream classes but also implement the DataInput and Data Output interfaces respectively (Fig. 13.4). These interfaces define the read or write methods for Java primitives that the classes implement (Fig. 13.4 shows a subset of these).

The DataOutputStream class has methods to write different types of Java primitive to the stream. For example, we might want to write the fields from a Course object to a file. Leaving aside the module data, a course includes its name (a String), the number of days duration (an integer) and the price (a double). The following example shows how we would write these data types to a DataOutputStream. The "writeUTF" method writes a String to the stream, the "writeInt" method writes an integer and "writeDouble" writes a double. There are similar methods for writing all the Java primitive types.

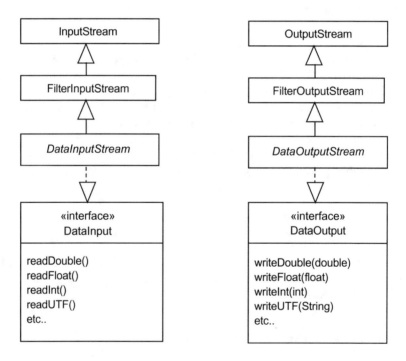

Fig. 13.4 DataInputStream and DataOutputStream inherit from filter streams and implement interfaces that declare their read and write methods for Java primitives

```
package com.foundjava.chapter13;
import java.io.DataOutputStream;
import java.io.FileNotFoundException;
import java.io.FileOutputStream;
import java.io.IOException;

public class DataOutputExample
{
  public static void main(String[] args)
  {
    try(var dataOut = new DataOutputStream
       (new FileOutputStream("data.dat")))
    {
      dataOut.writeUTF("Intro to Java");
      dataOut.writeInt(3);
      dataOut.writeDouble(1000.0);
      System.out.println("Data written to file");
    }
    catch (FileNotFoundException e)
    {
      e.printStackTrace();
    }
    catch(IOException e)
    {
      e.printStackTrace();
    }
  }
}
```

If you open the "data.dat" file in an editor window after running this code, you should be able to see that it is mostly non-human-readable bytes, with the exception of the String, which will appear as readable characters.

In a similar vein, a DataInputStream would need to wrap an InputStream object and has appropriate "read" methods for all the Java primitive types. The following code fragment would be able to read data back from the file created by the code in the previous example. The important thing here is that the data must be read back in exactly the right order because the different data types use different byte-level representations. Therefore, to read from a DataInputStream you must know the exact data types and sequences that you are trying to read from the stream.

```java
package com.foundjava.chapter13;

import java.io.DataInputStream;
import java.io.FileInputStream;
import java.io.FileNotFoundException;
import java.io.IOException;

public class DataInputExample
{
  public static void main(String[] args)
  {
    try(var dataIn = new DataInputStream
      (new FileInputStream("data.dat")))
    {
      String name = dataIn.readUTF();
      int numberOfDays = dataIn.readInt();
      double price = dataIn.readDouble();
      System.out.println(name + ", " + numberOfDays +
        " days, $" + price);
    }
    catch(FileNotFoundException e)
    {
      e.printStackTrace();
    }
    catch(IOException e)
    {
      e.printStackTrace();
    }
  }
}
```

If the data is successfully read, the console output should appear like this:

```
Intro to Java, 3 days, $1000.0
```

The stream library also includes a RandomAccessFile class, which combines the functionality of both DataInputStreams and DataOutputStreams in a single file handling object. As well as implementing the methods of both the DataInput and DataOutput interfaces, it provides methods for managing a file pointer which can be set to read or write at any position in the file. Where primitive types need to be regularly both written and read, using a single RandomAccessFile would be a better approach than separate input and output file objects.

Table 13.2 Transaction data for Exercise 13.1	Account number	Amount	Transaction type	Date
	1009876	145.50	DR	2020-12-03
	1876253	1267.00	CR	2020-11-30
	1192873	45.30	CR	2021-02-15

Exercise 13.1

Table 13.2 shows some data about financial transactions.

Create a class with a "main" method that writes this data to a file. Assume that the account number is to be written as an integer and the transaction amount as a double. The transaction type could be written as a String or two separate characters. Use a LocalDate to represent the date in the program. Since there is no method on a DataOutputStream to write a LocalDate, write the date as a String to the file.

When you have successfully written the data to a file, create another class with a "main" method that can read the data from the file and display it, suitably formatted, on the console. Use a DateTimeFormatter to parse the date String back into a LocalDate object.

13.4 Readers and Writers

Readers and Writers are in a separate hierarchy from the stream classes that we have looked at so far. They have a similar set of methods but handle characters and Strings, not bytes or primitives (Fig. 13.5). Reader and Writer are both abstract classes with some behavior implemented by subclasses. These are the preferred streams to use when reading and writing character data.

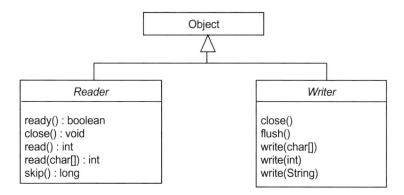

Fig. 13.5 The Reader and Writer classes, and some of their methods

13.4.1 Buffered Readers and Writers

For efficiency, we generally use the BufferedReader and BufferedWriter classes for character data. These are concrete subclasses of the abstract Reader and Writer classes. In addition, there are other concrete subclasses that the buffered readers and writers use as part of their implementation. For example, the BufferedWriter constructor requires a Writer object to be passed as a parameter argument. The type of Writer used will depend on the type of stream that we want to write to. For example, to write data to a file, we would use a FileWriter object. In this code fragment, a BufferedWriter wraps a FileWriter. The "write" method can be used to write Unicode characters or Strings to the output stream. The "newLine" method provides a platform-independent way of writing a new line character.

```
package com.foundjava.chapter13;

import java.io.BufferedWriter;
import java.io.FileNotFoundException;
import java.io.FileWriter;
import java.io.IOException;

public class BufferedWriterExample
{
  public static void main(String[] args)
  {
    try(var writer = new BufferedWriter
      (new FileWriter("characterfile.txt")))
    {
      writer.write("I am the first line of the file");
      writer.newLine();
      writer.write("I am the second line of the file");
      writer.newLine();
      writer.flush();
    }
    catch (FileNotFoundException e)
    {
      e.printStackTrace();
    }
    catch (IOException e)
    {
      e.printStackTrace();
    }
  }
}
```

BufferedReaders provide efficient reading of characters, arrays and lines from character streams. The constructor expects a Reader object (such as a FileReader) as a constructor parameter. The "read" method can read a single Unicode character from the input stream, while the "readLine" method can read lines of text into Strings, as shown in this code example:

```java
package com.foundjava.chapter13;

import java.io.BufferedReader;
import java.io.FileReader;
import java.io.FileNotFoundException;
import java.io.IOException;

public class BufferedReaderExample
{
  public static void main(String[] args)
  {
    String textLine = null;
    try(var textReader = new BufferedReader
      (new FileReader("characterfile.txt")))
    {
      while (textReader.ready())
      {
        textLine = textReader.readLine();
        System.out.println(textLine);
      }
    }
    catch (FileNotFoundException e)
    {
      e.printStackTrace();
    }
    catch (IOException e)
    {
      e.printStackTrace();
    }
  }
}
```

13.5   PrintStreams and PrintWriters

We have seen System.out and System.err being used for output to the console in previous chapters. These objects are instances of the PrintStream class, which is a subclass of FilterOutputStream and has overloaded methods to print any type of Java primitive or object to an output stream. Both System.out and System.err normally print to the console but we can use PrintStreams with other output streams too. The PrintWriter class is very similar to the PrintStream, in fact, it has the same methods, but is a subclass of Writer. Unlike a PrintStream it can use the services of a Writer object; one of its constructors can take a Writer object as a parameter. A PrintWriter should be used in preference to a PrintStream when the output is writing characters rather than bytes. For example, if we want to write text to a file, then a PrintWriter would be the obvious choice. Using a PrintWriter to write to the output stream is just like using System.out to write to the console:

```java
public class PrintWriterExample
{
  public static void main(String[] args)
  {
    try(var printOut = new PrintWriter
      (new FileWriter("story.txt")))
    {
      printOut.println("My Story");
      printOut.print("Chapter ");
      printOut.println(1);
      printOut.print("One upon a Time, in fact " +
        LocalDate.now() + "\nThe End");
      printOut.close();
    }
    catch (IOException e)
    {
      e.printStackTrace();
    }
  }
}
```

13.6   The File Class

The File class can be used to represent files in the operating system, and also provides some methods to interact with the file system; for example, the File class can be used to delete files, rename files, make directories and list the files in a directory. The File constructor takes a file name as a parameter, either including the path and file name together or with the path and filename as separate parameters.

```
File f1 = new File("/temp/temp.txt");
// path and filename as one parameter
```

or

```
File f1 = new File("/temp","temp.txt");
// path and filename as separate parameters
```

Once a File object has been created it can be passed to the constructor of a file stream object.

```
FileInputStream infile = new FileInputStream(f1);
```

To work across different platforms, your file paths cannot include platform-specific separators between folder names (e.g. the "\" separator is used in Windows but the "." and "/" separators are used in other operating systems). You can build platform-independent folder paths using the static "separator" field of the File class.

```
String sep = File.separator;
File file = new File(sep + "data" + sep + "hello.txt");
FileInputStream infile = new FileInputStream(file);
```

We will see the File class being used in subsequent examples.

Note
Java 7 added new features including the java.nio.Path interface and the java.nio. Files class that provide many additional features for file handling and are compatible with the java.io.File class. However, for the basic usage in this chapter, the java.io.File class is adequate on its own.

13.7   Streaming Objects

Object streams provide a means for streaming objects as single units of data. This can be useful in sending copies of objects from one virtual machine to another and can also be used to store objects in files. Streaming objects to files is not a very flexible way of maintaining object persistence beyond the run of a program. We would normally use a database for that, as explained in Chap. 15. However, it can be useful for short term storage of objects.

In order for an object to be written to a stream, it must implement the java.io. Serializable interface. This is a "marker" interface, in that classes do not actually have to implement any methods in order to use it. If a class implements the Serializable interface, then Java allows it to be streamed. If we make a class Serializable, then we can save objects of that class in a file or send them between different virtual machines.

You can read and write any Serializable objects using ObjectInputStreams and ObjectOutputStreams. As with previous examples, their constructors wrap lower level stream objects. For example, an ObjectOutputStream wraps an OutputStream. It has a "writeObject" method to stream an object. The following code fragment writes a LocalDate object to a file (the LocalDate class implements the Serializable interface).

```
public class WriteObject
{
  public static void main(String args[])
  {
    try(var objectOut = new ObjectOutputStream
      (new FileOutputStream(new File("date.dat")))))
    {
      objectOut.writeObject(LocalDate.now());
    }
    catch (IOException e)
    {
      e.printStackTrace();
    }
  }
}
```

Similarly, the ObjectInputStream wraps an InputStream, and has a "readObject" method. Since this returns an Object, the result must be cast to the actual type. As well as the usual exception handling related to files, when reading objects we also have to catch java.lang.ClassNotFoundException, which is thrown if the Java class loader does not know about the class of an object that it is trying to load.

```
public class ReadObject
{
  public static void main(String args[])
  {
    try(var objectIn= new ObjectInputStream
      (new FileInputStream(new File("date.dat"))))
    {
      LocalDate fileDate = (LocalDate)objectIn.readObject();
      System.out.println(fileDate);
    }
    catch (ClassNotFoundException e)
    {
      e.printStackTrace();
    }
    catch (IOException e)
    {
      e.printStackTrace();
    }
  }
}
```

Note

An alternative to implementing Serializable is to implement the Externalizable interface. This requires you to write custom stream handling code inside your objects so in most cases it is much easier just to implement Serializable.

13.7.1 The "instanceof" Operator

In the code that reads an object from a file, it would be helpful if we could find out what type of object was being read before attempting to cast it. The same issue arises if we have a method that accepts an Object as an argument—how do we handle the situation where the type of the object is not be the one we expected? The "instanceof" operator, also known as the "type comparison operator", enables us to check the type of an object. In the following modified version of the code that reads an object from a file in the previous example, the "instanceof" operator is used to check if the object is a DateTime before casting it.

```java
public static void main(String args[])
{
  try(var objectIn = new ObjectInputStream
    (new FileInputStream(new File("myobjects.dat"))))
  {
    Object o = objectIn.readObject();
    if(o instanceof LocalDate)
    {
      LocalDate fileDate = (LocalDate)o;
      System.out.println(fileDate);
    }
    else
    {
      System.out.println("Object read from file was a " +
        o.getClass().getName());
    }
  }
  catch (ClassNotFoundException e)
  {
    e.printStackTrace();
  }
  catch (IOException e)
  {
    e.printStackTrace();
  }
}
```

13.7.2   Serializing Course Objects

In the next example, we will use object serialization to save a Course object (and its Modules) to file and retrieve it again. The only change required to the existing classes is to implement the java.io.Serializable interface. This must be done for both the Course and Module classes:

```java
public class Course implements Serializable
{
// etc.
```

```java
public class Module implements Serializable
{
// etc.
```

For this example, a polymorphic version of "toString" has also been added, to make things more readable in the example code that retrieves Courses from the file:

```
@Override
public String toString()
{
  StringBuilder moduleNames = new StringBuilder();
  for(Module module : getModules())
  {
    moduleNames.append(module.getName() + ", ");
  }
  return getName() + " is a " + getNumberOfDays() +
    " day course costing " + getPrice() +
    " and contains the modules " + moduleNames;
}
```

The next step is to write some code that will serialize Course objects to a stream. For this example, we will again use a file stream, saving objects to disk and retrieving them again.

The objects will be taken from a Collection (an ArrayList) using an iterator, and written out one at a time using the "writeObject" method:

```
for(Course course : courses)
{
  objectsOut.writeObject(course);
}
```

To read in multiple objects, we need a loop that checks the "available" method to see if there are any bytes available for reading. We must check the underlying file stream, not the object stream. In the loop, we read objects from the object stream using the "readObject" method. Since this returns type Object, we need to cast to class Course before adding the object to the Collection.

```
while(fileStream.available() > 0)
{
  courses.add((Course)objectsIn.readObject());
}
```

Here is a complete class with static methods that can be used to read and write collections of Course objects to and from file.

```
package com.foundjava.chapter13;

import java.io.File;
import java.io.FileInputStream;
import java.io.FileOutputStream;
import java.io.IOException;
import java.io.ObjectInputStream;
import java.io.ObjectOutputStream;
import java.util.ArrayList;
import java.util.Collection;

public class CourseFileHandler
{
  public static void saveCourses
    (File file, Collection<Course> courses)
  {
    try(var objectsOut = new ObjectOutputStream
      (new FileOutputStream(file)))
    {
      for(Course course : courses)
      {
        objectsOut.writeObject(course);
      }
    }
    catch(IOException e)
    {
      System.out.println(e);
    }
  }

  public static Collection<Course> load(File file)
  {
    Collection<Course> courses = new ArrayList<Course>();
    try(var fileStream = new FileInputStream(file))
    {
      var objectsIn = new ObjectInputStream(fileStream);
      while(fileStream.available() > 0)
      {
        courses.add((Course)objectsIn.readObject());
      }
    }
```

```
      catch(IOException e)
      {
         System.out.println(e);
      }
      catch(ClassNotFoundException e)
      {
         System.out.println(e);
      }
      return courses;
   }
}
```

The CourseFileHandler can be used to write collections of Courses to file.

```
Collection<Course> courses = new ArrayList<Course>();
courses.add(course);
//etc.
File file = new File("myobjects.dat");
CourseFileHandler.saveCourses(file, courses);
```

Similarly, a collection of Courses can be read.

```
File infile = new File("myobjects.dat");
Collection<Course> courses =
   CourseFileHandler.load(infile);
```

Exercise 13.2
Create a Transaction class that has the fields defined in Table 13.2, along with their getters and setters. Make the class implement the Serializable interface, and override "toString" to provide a readable String representation of a Transaction. Write a JUnit test that writes a Transaction object to a file and then reads it back again, testing that the state of the object has been correctly restored from the file. Can you write a JUnit test for the "toString" method?

13.8 The New IO Library

The new input-output (NIO) libraries in the java.nio package provide classes that support multiplexed, non-blocking input and output. The NIO classes can blend many different streams (channels) together into one, and each of these channels may stream data at rates independent of the others. The main types of classes in the library are Buffers, Channels, Selectors and Charsets (see Table 13.3). Selectors are beyond the scope of this chapter, but we will provide a brief introduction to Buffers, Charsets and Channels.

Table 13.3 The main types in the NIO class library

Class Types	Characteristics
Buffers	Containers for data. Concrete subclasses for different data types
Charsets (and their associated decoders and encoders)	Translate between bytes and Unicode characters
Channels	Represent connections to entities capable of performing I/O operations
Selectors and selection keys	Together with selectable channels define a multiplexed, non-blocking I/O facility

13.8.1   Buffer Classes

There are various Buffer classes that extend the abstract class java.nio.Buffer. These classes are tailored to contain specific Java primitive data types, namely, ByteBuffer, CharBuffer, DoubleBuffer, FloatBuffer, IntBuffer, LongBuffer and ShortBuffer. Regardless of the data types that these buffers contain, they have some common methods; "put" methods are used to put data into a buffer, and "get" methods are used to get data out of a buffer. Because these methods are tailored to the data types that they handle, they are not defined in the Buffer superclass but in the various subclasses of Buffer.

There are several invariants associated with buffers that it is important to understand before using buffers in code. These relate to the mark, position, limit and capacity values. None of these values can be negative.

```
0 <= mark <= position <= limit <= capacity
```

A buffer's *capacity* is the number of elements it contains. This never changes. The *limit* can be less than the capacity and stores the index of the first element that should not be accessed. This is useful for example when we have put data into the buffer. When getting that data out, we only want to read back data up to the limit, not from the entire buffer. The *position* is the index of the next element to be read or written and is never greater than its limit. When a buffer is created, its position will be zero.

We read and write data between the current buffer position and the limit. This range can be the whole of the available buffer but may also be limited to part of it, if the position is greater than zero and/or the limit is less than the capacity.

The "mark" is used with the "reset" method. It does not have to be used, but when its value has been set, calling the "reset" method will move the current position to the mark.

There are some common methods of buffers that relate to these invariants:

```
clear()
```

- Clears the buffer ready for a new sequence of operations that will put data into the buffer.
- Sets the limit to the capacity and the position to zero.

```
flip()
```

- Makes the buffer ready for a new sequence of operations that will get data from the buffer.
- Sets the limit to the current position and the position to zero.

```
rewind()
```

- Makes a buffer ready for rereading the data that it already contains.
- The limit is unchanged, but the position is set to zero.

13.8.1.1 ByteBuffers

We can read and write data using ByteBuffers, an abstract subclass of Buffer that has factory methods to create concrete ByteBuffer objects. These must be allocated before use; the "allocate" factory method takes the capacity of the buffer (in bytes) as a parameter.

```
ByteBuffer buffer = ByteBuffer.allocate(1024);
```

The "allocate" method returns a *non-direct* ByteBuffer. A ByteBuffer may alternatively be *direct*, if we create it using the "allocateDirect" factory method.

```
ByteBuffer buffer = ByteBuffer.allocateDirect(1024);
```

Given a direct buffer, the Java virtual machine will try to perform native I/O operations directly. Given a non-direct byte buffer, there will be an intermediate buffer used before (or after) each invocation of I/O operations. It is possible to gain some performance improvement, in some cases, when using direct buffers.

The "put" and "get" methods of ByteBuffer only work with bytes and byte arrays. However, values of different primitive types can be added to or retrieved from a ByteBuffer using type-specific "put" and "get" methods: "putInt", "getInt", "putChar", "getChar", etc.

```
buffer.putInt(1);
```

As you add data to the buffer, the current position will move to the end of the data that has been added. Therefore, the buffer needs to be flipped between reading and writing, so that the position can be reset to the beginning of the buffer.

```
buffer.flip();
```

Then we can get values from the buffer, using the appropriate "get" methods, for example,

```
int myInt = buffer.getInt();
```

13.8.2 File Channels

Once a buffer contains data it can be written to a channel. "Channel" is an interface implemented by several different concrete channel classes, one of which is the FileChannel (java.nio.channels.FileChannel). These channels are safe for use with multiple threads. They are created from a standard stream object (the necessary "getChannel" methods have been added to the older java.io stream classes). Here, a FileChannel is retrieved from a FileOutputStream.

```
FileOutputStream fileout =
    new FileOutputStream("myintfile.dat");
FileChannel fc = fileout.getChannel();
```

Data can then be written to the channel from the ByteBuffer

```
fc.write(buffer);
```

Here is a complete program that writes some integer data to a file channel.

```
package com.foundjava.chapter13;

import java.io.File;
import java.io.FileOutputStream;
import java.io.IOException;
import java.nio.ByteBuffer;
import java.nio.channels.FileChannel;
```

```
public class FileChannelWriteInt
{
  public static void main(String[] args)
  {
    ByteBuffer buffer = ByteBuffer.allocate(1024);
    buffer.putInt(1);
    buffer.putInt(2);
    buffer.putInt(3);
    buffer.flip();
    try(var fileout = new FileOutputStream
      (new File ("myintfile.dat")))
    {
      FileChannel fc = fileout.getChannel();
      fc.write(buffer);
      fc.close();
    }
    catch (IOException e)
    {
      e.printStackTrace();
    }
  }
}
```

13.8.2.1   Reading from a Channel

When reading data from a channel, we need to read into an allocated buffer. Once the data has been read in, we again need to flip the buffer before attempting to access the data, to ensure that the position is set to the beginning of the buffer. There are "get" methods for different data types, but to read back from the file created in the previous example we will need to read integers, using the "getInt" method. The "hasRemaining" method can be used to determine if there is still unread data in the buffer.

```
public class FileChannelReadInt
{
  public static void main(String[] args)
  {
    ByteBuffer buffer = ByteBuffer.allocate(1024);
    try(var filein = new FileInputStream
      (new File ("myintfile.dat")))
```

```
  {
    FileChannel fc = filein.getChannel();
    fc.read(buffer);
    buffer.flip();
    while(buffer.hasRemaining())
    {
      System.out.println(buffer.getInt());
    }
    fc.close();
  }
  catch(IOException e)
  {
    e.printStackTrace();
  }
  }
}
```

13.8.3   View Buffers

ByteBuffers have methods that can put and get different primitive types of data within the same buffer. However, we often handle data in a buffer that has a consistent type. In this situation, we can create a view buffer for that type. For example, if we are writing or reading integers, we can create an integer view buffer (an IntBuffer) from the ByteBuffer and use methods tailored to deal with integers. The ByteBuffer class has the following factory methods, each of which can return a view buffer for a specific primitive type: "asCharBuffer", "asDoubleBuffer", "asIntBuffer", "asLongBuffer" and "asShortBuffer". For example, to create a view buffer for integers, we can call the "asIntBuffer" method on a ByteBuffer.

```
ByteBuffer buffer = ByteBuffer.allocate(1024);
IntBuffer intBuf = buffer.asIntBuffer();
```

The "put" and "get" methods of this IntBuffer work with integers rather than bytes.

```
intBuf.put(50);
intBuf.put(25);
intBuf.flip();
int num1 = intBuf.get();
```

13.8.4 Charsets and String Data

The previous NIO classes we have looked at work at the ByteBuffer level, with views specific to Java primitive types. In contrast, Charsets and CharBuffers let us work with Strings. A java.nio.charset.Charset is created for a specific character encoding and has factory methods to create encoders and decoders for moving character data between CharBuffers and ByteBuffers. In this example, a Charset is created using "utf-8" encoding using the "forName" factory method, which returns a Charset object appropriate for that encoding. This is then used to create an encoder, using the "newEncoder" factory method, which can put character data into a ByteBuffer using the chosen character encoding. The "encode" method throws a CharacterEncoding exception that needs to be handled. It takes as its parameter a CharBuffer, which can be created from a String using the static "wrap" method, which converts Strings or arrays of characters into CharBuffers.

```
Charset charset = Charset.forName("utf-8");
CharsetEncoder encoder = charset.newEncoder();
ByteBuffer buffer = null;
try
{
  buffer = encoder.encode
    (CharBuffer.wrap("a string\nanother string"));
}
catch (CharacterCodingException e)
{
  e.printStackTrace();
}
```

Once a CharBuffer has been encoded into a ByteBuffer, the ByteBuffer can be written to a channel, as we have seen in previous examples. To read Strings back from a channel, we must first read the data from the channel into a ByteBuffer, then flip the ByteBuffer to prepare it for decoding into a CharBuffer. The "toString" method of CharBuffer will return a String.

```
Charset charset = Charset.forName("utf-8");
CharsetDecoder decoder = charset.newDecoder();
ByteBuffer buffer = ByteBuffer.allocate(1024);
try(var filein = new FileInputStream
    (new File("myencodedfile.txt")))
```

```
{
  FileChannel fc = filein.getChannel();
  fc.read(buffer);
  buffer.flip();
  CharBuffer cbuf = decoder.decode(buffer);
  String s = cbuf.toString();
  System.out.println(s);
  fc.close();
}
```

Exercise 13.3
- Create a StringFileHandler class.
- Add a static method to write a String to a given file using appropriate classes from the java.nio package and its sub-packages.
- Add another static method to read a String from a given file.
- Test your StringFileHandler class methods.

13.9 Summary

In this chapter, we have looked at a range of different types of input and output stream, handling the input and output of bytes, primitives, Strings and objects. The examples in this chapter focused on file handling because this makes it easy to demonstrate both input and output, but the chapter also explained how there are other sources and sinks of data, for example, keyboard input and console output. Code examples showed how lower level stream classes support the implementation of higher level filter steams by being passed to their constructors. Reader and Writer streams that handle text-based data were contrasted with the stream classes that handle primitive data types. Methods of the File class that allow Java code to interact with the file system were demonstrated, along with streams that can handle the input and output of objects that implement the Serializable Interface. As well as some of the main classes in the java.io package, the chapter covered the basics of the Buffers, Charsets and Channels in the java.nio package.

Automatic Building and Testing with Ant

14

Ant ("Another Neat Tool") is a Java-based build tool which uses a combination of Java and XML to create platform-independent build and deploy scripts. Being written in Java, it has the advantage over some other build tools of working on any platform. It is open source and is available free from the Apache Software Foundation (http://ant.apache.org/). It uses an XML build file (called "build.xml" by default) containing *targets* and *tasks*. Ant is used in many Java projects and can be invoked directly from many other tools, including Eclipse. The Apache Ant project has spawned subprojects such as Ivy (a dependency manager). There are other similar tools around, such as Maven and Gradle but Ant is ideal for relatively simple builds.

So far, we have been manually compiling and running our programs and unit tests within Eclipse, but this is not a very efficient way of building and testing code. It is also not very helpful if we want to run our build and test processes outside of Eclipse. In addition, there are a number of other tasks that we will need to do in relation to our Java code such as packaging it into Java Archive (JAR files) and deploying it so that it can be run in its intended deployment environment. Ant provides a simple way of automating these processes.

Although Ant is easy to run from the command line, in this chapter, we will focus on using it within Eclipse since the Ant plugin is already integrated into the IDE.

14.1 Using Ant in Eclipse

Because Ant is a standard component of Eclipse, no external configuration is needed to use it. To create a new Ant build script, select "New" → "File" from a project's pop-up or "File" menu. Make sure the file you are creating is in the "src" folder of your project. Name the file "build.xml". Eclipse will recognize this file name as being an Ant build file and will add an ant icon next to the file in the

© Springer Nature Switzerland AG 2020
D. Parsons, *Foundational Java*, Texts in Computer Science,
https://doi.org/10.1007/978-3-030-54518-5_14

Fig. 14.1 Ant build files
(with an ant icon) in the
Eclipse package explorer

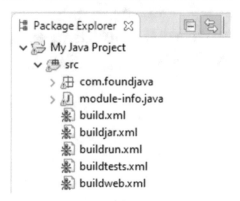

package explorer window. In fact, Eclipse will recognize any XML file that begins
with the word "build" (e.g. "buildjar.xml"), and includes a valid "project" root
element, as an Ant build file (though you may have to close it and then reopen it
with the Ant editor to trigger this behavior). Figure 14.1 shows the various Ant files
we will create in this and subsequent chapters listed in the Package Explorer with
the ant icon.

Note
*Eclipse can also build a new project from an existing Ant "build.xml" file
(Fig. 14.2), as long as the file contains a "javac" task, which is the Ant task that
runs the Java compiler.*

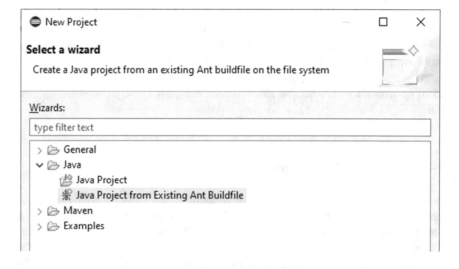

Fig. 14.2 Eclipse can build a new project from an existing Ant "build.xml" file

14.2   The Ant Build File—"build.xml"

An Ant build file can specify a series of tasks to be performed such as:

- Removing and recreating output folders to ensure a clean build
- Compiling Java source code
- Creating Java Archive (JAR) files or other deployment formats
- Copying files to distribution locations
- Running Java applications
- Running JUnit tests

In order to be able to write an Ant build file that can perform these kinds of actions, we need to understand *properties*, *tasks* and *targets*, and how an Ant build file is structured.

The "build.xml" file basically consists of a project which compromises a set of *tasks* that perform operations such as compiling code, building jar files or copying files to deployment folders. Tasks are put into named *targets* that can be invoked using their names. The build file can also specify *properties*; aliases for named resources such as files and directories that we can refer to repeatedly within the file.

The root element of the file is the "project" element, which includes an attribute to specify the name of the project. This attribute is optional in most cases but is required if the build file is used to create a new Eclipse project (Fig. 14.2). The "project" element must include the "default" attribute which specifies the default target, the one that is executed if Ant is invoked without a named target. In the following example, it is a target called "compile". We may also choose to define the base directory ("basedir") of the files used in this build, from where any file paths will be assumed to start. Here, the base directory is set to the current folder (using "."), though this is in fact the default. The body of the "project" element is empty here, apart from an XML comment (between the "<!--" and "-->" characters).

```
<project name="Ant Project" default="compile" basedir=".">
  <!--
    build file properties and targets in here
    there must be a target with the default name
  -->
</project>
```

14.2.1   Ant Properties

The "project" element can include any number of "property" elements that give local names to various components such as file and directory names used in the build file. These are empty elements that have "name" and "value" attributes.

For example, we might define a property named "build" with the value of the folder path where we will put the compiled byte code ("C:\javasource" in this example).

```
<property name="build" value="C:\javasource"/>
```

Properties need to be declared before they are needed, so they are usually listed at the top of the build file. Once a property has been declared, it can be referred to inside an Ant build file using this syntax.

```
${propertyname}
```

For example, to refer to the value of our "build" property, we only need to use its name.

```
${build}
```

The point of doing this, of course, is to ensure that each piece of information (such as the name of the "build" folder) only needs to appear in the build file once. After that, the property name can be used instead. This means that changes (e.g. to the name of a folder) only need to be made in one place in the build file.

14.2.2 Tasks and Targets

Built-in tasks can be used in every Ant build file. There is a huge range of tasks available in Ant, but the ones we will focus on in this chapter will be those that relate to the file system (e.g. creating folders), some JDK tools (such as the Java compiler) and running JUnit test cases.

Some of the tasks that we will be looking at in this chapter are listed in Table 14.1.

A target contains one or more tasks. For example, one target might include a single task to compile Java files to class files, while another target might include multiple tasks, perhaps to create a folder, create a Java Archive (JAR) file and

Table 14.1 Some Ant tasks and their purposes

Ant task	Purpose
mkdir	Creates directories
delete	Removes files or directories
copy	Copies files or directories
javac	Invokes the java compiler
java	Runs compiled. class files on the Java Virtual Machine
jar	Creates Java Archive (JAR) files
junitlauncher	Runs JUnit tests

deploy that JAR to the newly created folder. An Ant task is defined as an XML element in the build file. Tasks may have attributes and/or additional nested elements, depending on the complexity of the task. The "mkdir" task, for example, is very simple, since it only has a single attribute; the name of the directory to be created. Since there are no nested elements, it is written as an empty element (no closing tag).

```
<mkdir dir="directory_name" />
```

The "javac" task, which compiles Java source code, has two attributes to specify the source and destination directories.

```
<javac srcdir="source_dir" destdir="destination_dir"/>
```

As we will see later, the "javac" element may appear in different forms and may have nested elements inside it.

It is possible to write a build file that contains tasks that are not inside targets, but this makes it impossible to do anything other than have these tasks all execute in order whenever the build file is run. Tasks alone cannot be grouped or managed individually. In addition, the Ant build file requires at least one target, since one must be specified in the "default" attribute of the project element. Generally, then, all tasks should appear inside targets.

A target element must have a "name" attribute and may also have an optional "description" attribute. You can name your targets anything you like. The following example Ant target, which has been called "prepare", contains the "mkdir" task to create a directory (note also the use of the previously defined "build" property name).

```
<target name="prepare" description="create a build folder">
  <mkdir dir = "${build}" />
</target>
```

This target, called "compile", uses the "javac" task to compile Java files. Again, property names are being used. Including the "includeantruntime" attribute, which defines whether the Ant runtime is to be included in the classpath when compiling, is necessary to avoid a warning message when the build file is run. The Ant documentation suggests that it is usually best to set this to "false", so the compilation is not dependent on the environment in which it is run.

```
<target name="compile" description=
"compile source code">
  <javac srcdir="${src}" destdir="${build}"
    includeantruntime="false"/>
</target>
```

Here is an example Ant build file ("build.xml"), drawing together some of the property and target examples we have already introduced, along with some additional entries. It begins by creating two properties to refer to the "source" and "build" folders to be used by the project (these are intended to be outside of the Eclipse project folder). The first target ("prepare"), creates the "source" and "build" folders, then copies a Java source file ("Die.java") from the appropriate Eclipse source folder (which includes the subfolders for the package that the class belongs to) into the external source folder being used by the build.

The second target ("compile") compiles all the code in the source folder and puts the generated byte code into the build folder.

```
<project name="Ant Project" default="prepare" basedir=".">
    <property name="build" value="c:\AntProject\javabuild"/>
    <property name="source" value="c:\AntProject\javasource" />

    <target name="prepare"
        description="create folders and copy source code">
        <mkdir dir="${build}"/>
        <mkdir dir="${source}"/>
        <copy todir="${source}"
            file="com\foundjava\chapter6\Die.java"/>
    </target>

    <target name="compile"
        description="compile all source code">
        <javac srcdir="${source}" destdir="${build}"
        includeantruntime="false"/>
    </target>

</project>
```

14.3 Running an Ant Build File in Eclipse

When an Ant build file is open in the Eclipse tab, the "outline" pane will show the various properties, targets and tasks that are in the file, and indicate the default target (Fig. 14.3). The project and its targets can be expanded or collapsed to modify the view. In Fig. 14.3, the target nodes have been expanded to show the tasks. The icons on the bar at the top of the pane also allow you to toggle the visibility of different parts of the build file.

Outline
Ant Project
build
source
prepare [default]
mkdir ${build}
mkdir ${source}
copy
compile
javac

Fig. 14.3 The "Outline" pane showing an Ant build file with its targets and tasks, including the default target

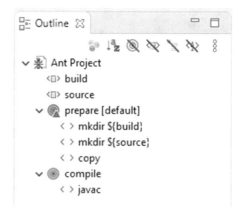

When an Ant build file is run by right clicking on the file, either from the Outline pane or the Package Explorer, and choosing the "Run As" → "Ant Build" option, the default target ("prepare") will be run.

The output from the build script will appear in the console (Fig. 14.4). Note that, by default, tasks will only be run if they need to, therefore directories will only be created if they do not already exist.

In the Outline pane, any task can be run as an Ant Build. To run a non-default target in the build file, you can right click on that specific target in the Outline and select "Run As" → "Ant Build" for that target. Figure 14.5 shows the "compile" target being chosen (note that the "compile" target will not run correctly unless the "prepare" target has been run already).

Exercise 14.1

- Create an Ant build file in Eclipse to copy the source code of the MyJavaProgram class from Chap. 2 to a folder outside of Eclipse and compile it so that the byte code is written to another folder.

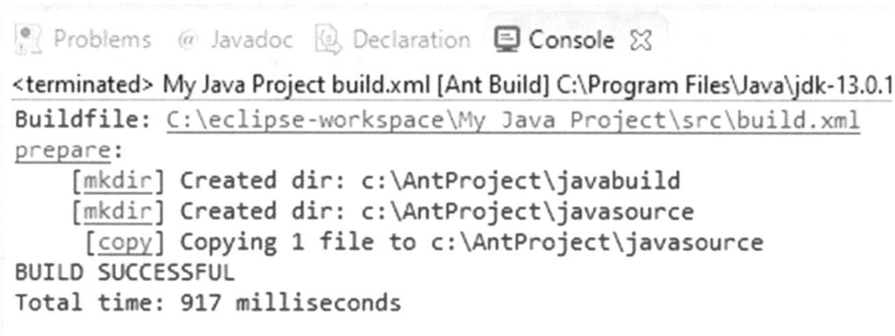

Problems
Javadoc
Declaration
Console
<terminated> My Java Project build.xml [Ant Build] C:\Program Files\Java\jdk-13.0.1
Buildfile: C:\eclipse-workspace\My Java Project\src\build.xml
prepare:
[mkdir] Created dir: c:\AntProject\javabuild
[mkdir] Created dir: c:\AntProject\javasource
[copy] Copying 1 file to c:\AntProject\javasource
BUILD SUCCESSFUL
Total time: 917 milliseconds

Fig. 14.4 Output from running an Ant build script in the Eclipse console

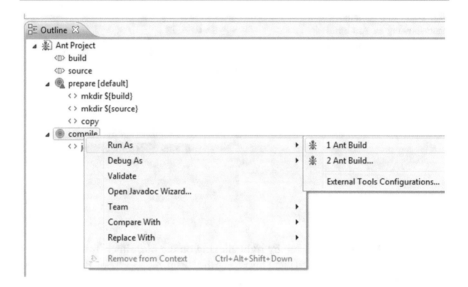

Fig. 14.5 The pop-up menu in the Outline window that allows you to select individual targets to be executed

- Run the Ant build and check that the compiled byte code is in the expected folder.
- Run the compiled code from the command line.

14.4 Packaging Code with the Ant "jar" Task

When code is built for deployment, it is often packaged into one or more Java Archive (JAR) files to enable easy deployment. To prepare multiple files to be added to a JAR file, they need to be copied to the appropriate folder. Ant provides a nested "fileset" element inside the "copy" element to make it possible to copy all the files in a folder. In this example, all the files in the "com.foundjava.chapter8" folder are copied to the source folder so they can be added to the JAR.

```
<copy todir="${source}">
  <fileset dir="com\foundjava\chapter8"/>
</copy>
```

To build a JAR file in Ant, there is a "jar" task, which has the name of the output file ("destfile") as a required attribute. This is expressed in this example using a property name for the output folder (this example assumes that a property called "dist" has been created to refer to a distribution folder). In addition, the base directory (the location of the code to be put into the JAR) is specified here.

```
<property name="dist" value="c:\AntProject\javadist" />

<target name="package">
  <jar destfile="${dist}/mycode.jar" basedir="${build}" />
</target>
```

The "jar" task outlined above creates a JAR file in the "dist" folder from all the compiled code in the "build" folder but does not specify the main class. This is appropriate for JAR files that act as libraries of classes to be used by an application. In other cases, however, we will want to create a JAR file that can be run directly, using a specific class as the program entry point. When using the "jar" task, a runnable JAR can be created by including the nested "manifest" element to set the "Main-Class" entry, for example:

```
<target name="package">
  <jar destfile="${dist}/mycode.jar" basedir="${build}">
    <manifest>
      <attribute name="Main-Class"
          value="com.foundjava.chapter8.DrawFrame" />
    </manifest>
  </jar>
</target>
```

14.4.1 Target Dependencies

Often one target will depend on another being executed first. We can specify these dependencies with the "depends" attribute of the "target" element. For example in our build file, we might want to ensure that the code is compiled before the "jar" file is created (the "package" target depends on the "compile" target), and in turn that directories are prepared before the source code is compiled (the "compile" target depends on the "prepare" target; see Fig. 14.6).

We can implement this chain of dependencies by making one target depend on another; for example, the "compile" target needs to depend on the "prepare" target.

```
<target name="compile" depends="prepare"
    description="compile all source code">
  <javac srcdir="${source}" destdir="${build}"
    includeantruntime="false"/>
</target>
```

If a target depends on another target, then Ant will execute the other target first. This means that if we run the "compile" target then the "prepare" target will always be run first (if it needs to). This also means that it would be safe to change the build file's default target to "compile" since there would be no danger of attempting the "compile" target without the directories first being prepared.

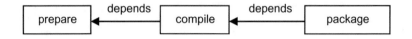

Fig. 14.6 Targets that are dependent on each other in an Ant build

Similarly, if the "package" target depends on "compile", then we can call the "package" target and both the "prepare" and "compile" targets will be executed first.

Here is the complete build file ("buildjar.xml") with its required dependencies, as shown in Fig. 14.6. Note that to ensure a clean build it deletes the various folders and recreates them before putting anything in them.

```xml
<project name="Ant Project" default="package" basedir=".">
  <property name="build" value="c:\AntProject\javabuild" />
  <property name="source" value="c:\AntProject\javasource" />
  <property name="dist" value="c:\AntProject\javadist" />

  <target name="prepare"
      description="create output folders for the build">
    <delete dir="${build}" />
    <delete dir="${source}" />
    <delete dir="${dist}" />
    <mkdir dir="${build}" />
    <mkdir dir="${source}" />
    <mkdir dir="${dist}" />
    <copy todir="${source}">
     <fileset dir="com\foundjava\chapter8"/>
    </copy>
  </target>

  <target name="compile" depends="prepare"
      description="compile all source code">
    <javac srcdir="${source}" destdir="${build}"
      includeantruntime="false"/>
  </target>

  <target name="package" depends="compile">
    <jar destfile="${dist}/mycode.jar" basedir="${build}">
      <manifest>
        <attribute name="Main-Class"
          value="com.foundjava.chapter8.DrawFrame" />
      </manifest>
    </jar>
  </target>

</project>
```

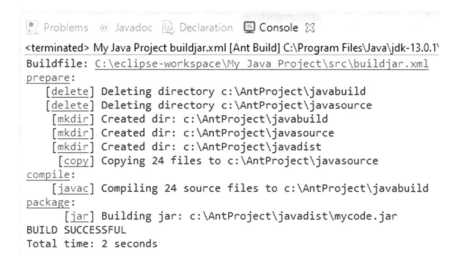

Fig. 14.7 Targets and tasks being executed in order, based on target dependencies

Calling Ant using the "package" target will generate console output that shows every target and the tasks invoked (Fig. 14.7).

After the build file has been run, if you look at the contents of the MANIFEST. MF file in the generated JAR, you should see something like the following, including the "Main-Class" entry.

```
Manifest-Version: 1.0
Ant-Version: Apache Ant 1.10.7
Created-By: 13.0.1+9 (Oracle Corporation)
Main-Class: com.foundjava.chapter8.DrawFrame
```

In the next section, we will see how you can run this JAR file using Ant, but a JAR file with the main class can be run directly from the command line using the "java" command with the-"jar" option in the folder where the JAR has been deployed to, for example:

```
C:\AntProject\javadist>java -jar mycode.jar
```

Ensure that the PATH has been set to the "bin" folder of your Java installation prior to running the "java" command.

14.5   Running Code, Forking and Classpaths

Although Ant is primarily used as a build tool, it can also be used to run code. The
"java" task can be used to run any class with a "main" method but requires some
configuration. Running code requires a suitable classpath to be set, so in the build
file, the "java" task includes a "classpath" element that can include "pathelement"
entries to add resources to the classpath. In addition, the "fork" attribute (if set to
"true") allows the Java runtime to be launched in a separate VM to the one running
the Ant tasks.

```
<target name="run" depends="compile">
  <java classname="com.foundjava.chapter8.DrawFrame"
      fork="true">
    <classpath>
      <pathelement location="${build}" />
    </classpath>
  </java>
</target>
```

The "java" task can also be used to run a JAR file, as long as that JAR file has a
main class defined in its manifest.

```
<target name="runjar" depends="package">
  <java jar="${dist}/mycode.jar" fork="true" />
</target>
```

Exercise 14.2

- Modify your Ant build file from Exercise 14.1 by adding a target to run the class
- Add another target to package the compiled class into a JAR file
- Add a further target to run the JAR file
- Add the required dependencies between targets
- Run the build file and check that all the steps complete successfully
- Run your JAR file from the command line.

14.6   Running Tests

As well as building and running code, we can use Ant to run JUnit tests. Ant has a
special "junitlauncher" task that can be used to run selected test classes. At the time
of writing, the lack of classes to support test suites in JUnit 5 without using some
classes from JUnit 4 means that in this section we will only look at running
individual test classes.

In this example, the source code that will be compiled will be based on the "com.foundjava.chapter10" package, which includes the JUnit test case examples. However, since these have dependencies on classes from other packages, all these need to be included in the source files/filesets to ensure successful compilation.

Note that after all the files have been copied across, the "ShapeSuite.java" file is deleted from the "source" folder, since this relies on JUnit 4 classes that will not be included in the classpath for this example. Leaving this file in the source folder would cause a compilation failure when the "compile" task is run.

```
<target name="prepare" description="create an output folder
   for the build">
   <delete dir="${build}" />
   <delete dir="${source}" />
   <delete dir="${dist}" />
   <mkdir dir="${build}" />
   <mkdir dir="${source}" />
   <mkdir dir="${dist}" />
   <copy todir="${source}"
      file="com\foundjava\chapter6\Die.java"/>
   <copy todir="${source}">
      <fileset dir="com\foundjava\chapter8" />
      <fileset dir="com\foundjava\chapter9" />
      <fileset dir="com\foundjava\chapter10" />
   </copy>
   <delete file="${source}\ShapeSuite.java"/>
</target>
```

14.6.1   Setting the Classpath with a "path" Element

In previous build file examples, the classpath for the "java" task was set using a nested "classpath" element that explicitly specified a classpath for that task. Sometimes the same classpath can be used by multiple tasks in the same build file, in which case it can be helpful to specify a reusable classpath using the "path" element. "path" may contain multiple "pathelements", each one referring to a different path or file. This is very useful when using Ant to run JUnit tests since quite a few JAR files need to be on the classpath.

This example, which sets the name of the path to "project.classpath", includes all the required JAR files from JUnit 5 along with "build" folder. The JUnit 5 JAR files can be downloaded from the junit.org website. However, you also need to download two additional JAR files from other websites: the "apiguardian-api" JAR and the "opentest4j" JAR. Without all these JAR files on the classpath your test will not compile and run (of course your version numbers may be slightly different). For this example, all the required JAR files have been put into a single folder to make the path simple.

```
<path id="project.classpath">
  <pathelement path="c:\junit5\junit-jupiter-api-5.5.2.jar" />
  <pathelement
    path="c:\junit5\junit-platform-launcher-1.6.0.jar" />
  <pathelement
    path="c:\junit5\junit-platform-commons-1.6.0.jar" />
  <pathelement
    path="c:\junit5\junit-platform-engine-1.6.0.jar" />
  <pathelement
    path="c:\junit5\junit-jupiter-engine-5.5.2.jar" />
  <pathelement path="c:\junit5\apiguardian-api-1.0.0.jar" />
  <pathelement path="c:\junit5\opentest4j-1.2.0.jar" />
  <pathelement path="${build}" />
</path>
```

The "id" of the path provides a unique identifier within the build file that can be used by other tasks. Here, a "javac" task includes a reference to the classpath, using the nested "classpath" element, where the "refid" attribute refers to the previously defined "project.classpath".

```
<target name="compile" depends="prepare"
    description="compile all source code">
  <javac srcdir="${source}" destdir="${build}"
    includeantruntime="false">
    <classpath refid="project.classpath" />
  </javac>
</target>
```

Note that if "javac" includes a "classpath" it is no longer an empty element but has the "classpath" element nested inside it.

14.6.2   Running Tests with the "junitlaucher" and "test" Elements

The "junitlauncher" task element has many attributes that can be used to configure the test process. Most have default values, making it easy to get a "junitlauncher" task up and running with minimal configuration. Nested inside the "junitlauncher" element, "test" elements can be used to run individual test classes. The only required attribute for the "test" element is "name" (the name of the JUnit test class). In addition, since all the JUnit and associated JAR files will need to be on the classpath, along with the build folder, the "project.classpath" is included in the "classpath" element. The following "junit" target example also shows two other possible attributes for the "junitlauncher" element: "printsummary", which by default is "off", and if turned on shows a summary of the tests that have been run, and "haltonfailure" which if set to "true" will halt the tests if a failure occurs.

```
<target name="junit" depends="compile"
    description="run JUnit 5 tests">
  <junitlauncher printsummary="true" haltonfailure="true">
    <classpath refid="project.classpath"/>
    <test name="com.foundjava.chapter10.RectangleTestCase"/>
    <test name="com.foundjava.chapter10.CircleTestCase"/>
  </junitlauncher>
</target>
```

Figure 14.8 shows the "junit" target being run successfully (no failure messages from the test).

Exercise 14.3

- Design the tasks and targets for an Ant build file to build the Die class and the DieTestCase class from Chap. 10.
- Include a target that will run your JUnit test.
- Add one of your own test cases from the exercises into the build.

14.7 Installing and Configuring Ant Outside Eclipse

In this chapter, we have used the Ant plugin that is integrated into Eclipse. However, you can use Ant as a standalone tool to build and deploy applications by downloading a zip archive from the Apache Ant project website, and unzipping it into a suitable directory (e.g. c:\ant).

Ant requires that you set up two environment variables, "JAVA_HOME" and "ANT_HOME". "JAVA_HOME" must be set to the root folder of your Java SDK installation, while "ANT_HOME" should be set the root folder of your Ant installation. You must also add "ANT_HOME\bin" to your system path so you can invoke Ant from the command line. Once Ant has been installed and assuming the environment has been set up properly, it can be run from the command line simply by typing "ant". By default, it looks for an Ant build file (written in XML) called "build.xml" in the current folder, though other files and/or folder names can be specified.

If you want to run JUnit tests with an external installation of Ant, you can add all the required JAR files to the "lib" folder of your Ant installation.

```
□ Console ⊠
<terminated> My Java Project buildtests.xml [Ant Build] C:\Program Files\Java\jdk-13.0.1\bin\javaw.exe
Buildfile: C:\eclipse-workspace\My Java Project\src\buildtests.xml
prepare:
     [delete] Deleting directory c:\AntProject\javabuild
     [delete] Deleting directory c:\AntProject\javasource
     [delete] Deleting directory c:\AntProject\javadist
      [mkdir] Created dir: c:\AntProject\javabuild
      [mkdir] Created dir: c:\AntProject\javasource
      [mkdir] Created dir: c:\AntProject\javadist
       [copy] Copying 1 file to c:\AntProject\javasource
       [copy] Copying 49 files to c:\AntProject\javasource
     [delete] Deleting: c:\AntProject\javasource\ShapeSuite.java
compile:
      [javac] Compiling 49 source files to c:\AntProject\javabuild
junit:
[junitlauncher] Test run finished after 194 ms
[junitlauncher] [         2 containers found      ]
[junitlauncher] [         0 containers skipped    ]
[junitlauncher] [         2 containers started    ]
[junitlauncher] [         0 containers aborted    ]
[junitlauncher] [         2 containers successful ]
[junitlauncher] [         0 containers failed     ]
[junitlauncher] [         1 tests found           ]
[junitlauncher] [         0 tests skipped         ]
[junitlauncher] [         1 tests started         ]
[junitlauncher] [         0 tests aborted         ]
[junitlauncher] [         1 tests successful      ]
[junitlauncher] [         0 tests failed          ]
[junitlauncher] Test run finished after 105 ms
[junitlauncher] [         2 containers found      ]
[junitlauncher] [         0 containers skipped    ]
[junitlauncher] [         2 containers started    ]
[junitlauncher] [         0 containers aborted    ]
[junitlauncher] [         2 containers successful ]
[junitlauncher] [         0 containers failed     ]
[junitlauncher] [         1 tests found           ]
[junitlauncher] [         0 tests skipped         ]
[junitlauncher] [         1 tests started         ]
[junitlauncher] [         0 tests aborted         ]
[junitlauncher] [         1 tests successful      ]
[junitlauncher] [         0 tests failed          ]
BUILD SUCCESSFUL
Total time: 3 seconds
```

Fig. 14.8 A JUnit test being run by an Ant script (in the "junit" target)

14.8 Summary

In this chapter, we have introduced Ant ("Another Neat Tool"), a build tool that can
be used to automate the build and deploy process, as well as running and testing
code. We began by seeing how an Ant build file (by default called "build.xml") can
be created to copy source code out of Eclipse and build it independently of the IDE,

while still being able to run the build scripts themselves from within Eclipse. Various aspects of an Ant build file were introduced, including properties, tasks and targets. Several Ant targets were demonstrated in different build files, including creating and deleting files and directories, compiling Java, creating Java Archive (JAR) files and running code. Target dependencies, which allow multiple targets to be run in a specific sequence, were also described. We have seen that Ant can be used to run JUnit 5 tests by including a set of required JAR files on the classpath and demonstrated some of the options within the "junitlancher" task, which runs JUnit 5 test cases. Finally, we saw how Ant can be run from the command prompt outside Eclipse

Java and the Database (JDBC)   15

The data in Java programs does not last beyond a single run of a program. Most applications require some more persistent storage of state than this, and in most cases, we will use a database. While streaming data to and from a sequential file can be useful in some contexts, it does not allow the querying, performance, availability and accessibility of database storage. Therefore, we need to know how to get data in and out of a database so we can use it in our applications. There are several different types of databases available, including hierarchical, object oriented, XML and, increasingly in the era of big data, NoSQL databases. However, the most popular commercial databases are currently relational. The focus of this chapter is on how to bridge between the table schemas of a relational database and Java code using JDBC (Java Database Connectivity).

The job of JDBC is to enable a Java application to connect to a relational database, and execute Structured Query Language (SQL) statements, in order to store and retrieve the state of any objects that need to be persistent outside of the runtime of the application. The advantage of using the services of a relational database is that we can store our object data reliably and efficiently using data storage tools that are well developed and widely used. The disadvantage is that using a relational database with an object-oriented program requires some object-relational mapping, where we must convert our data between object-oriented and relational structures. Object-relational mapping is a very large topic, so the coverage in this chapter is very introductory.

15.1 An Example Database

In this chapter we will be working with a simple database that will represent two entities from previous programming examples, "course", and "module". Each course may have multiple modules, while to keep things simple, each module

© Springer Nature Switzerland AG 2020   385
D. Parsons, *Foundational Java*, Texts in Computer Science,
https://doi.org/10.1007/978-3-030-54518-5_15

belongs to only one course. Figure 15.1 shows the two tables with their column names and foreign key relationship.

15.2   Using MySQL

This chapter assumes that you have a basic understanding of relational databases and SQL However even if you have experience with relational databases, you may not be familiar with the particular commands used with the MySQL database management system, so before moving onto Java code, we will cover some of the basics of using MySQL.

MySQL Community Edition is a popular open source database system. It is a fully featured Relational Database Management System (RDBMS), with various tools to help with configuration and management. If you are running Windows, MySQL can be run as a Windows service so does not necessarily have to be manually started.

Note

This section refers to MySQL Community Edition installed under Windows, but there are versions of MySQL for several different operating systems. Oracle owns and sells the commercial versions of MySQL. At the time of writing the current version was version 8.

When MySQL is installed it includes the command line client as one of the options you can launch, among other tools. When you start the command line client, it will ask you for the password which would be configured when MySQL was installed. If you log in successfully you will see a "mysql" prompt after the copyright notices (Fig. 15.2).

Note

When you want to exit the command line client, simply type "exit" or "quit" at the "mysql" prompt.

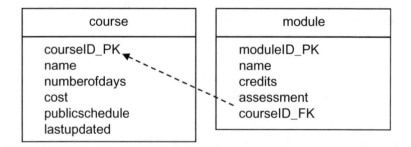

Fig. 15.1 The columns in the two database tables and their foreign key relationship

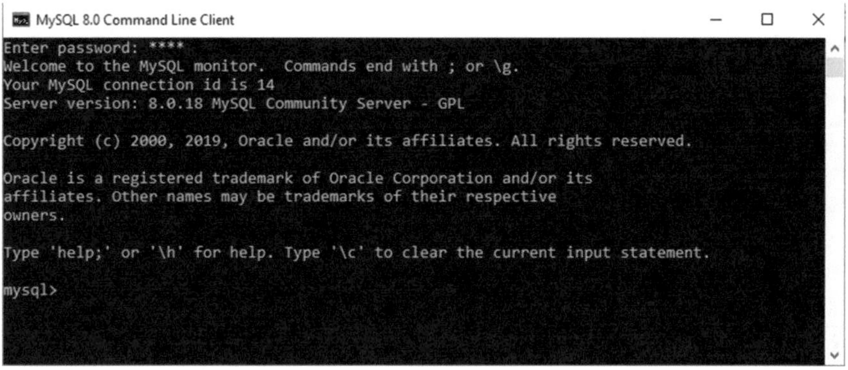

Fig. 15.2 The MySQL command line client

15.2.1 Creating a New Database

To create a new MySQL database, use the "create database" command, that is,

```
create database databasename;
```

For example, to create a new database called "courses", we would enter the following command (note the semicolon required at the end of the command).

```
create database courses;
```

When using the command line client, all commands need to be terminated by a semicolon. If you type a line that does not end in a semicolon and press the "Enter" key, MySQL will keep giving you a prompt, waiting for either more lines of the command or a semicolon to be entered. This facility means that you can enter a single command over a series of lines, and the command will only be executed when you add the semicolon at the end.

The "show databases" command will list all the databases that have been created.

```
show databases;
```

If you have created the "courses" database you should see it added to list of databases that come as part of the MySQL installation.

```
+--------------------+
| Database           |
+--------------------+
| courses            |
| information_schema |
| mysql              |
| performance_schema |
| sakila             |
| sys                |
| world              |
+--------------------+
```

We can connect to any available database with "use *databasename*". To connect to the "courses" database, we would enter the following command:

```
use courses;
```

This should result in the "Database changed" message coming back from MySQL. At this point, however, the database has no schema, so there is not much to connect to. The next step is to set up the schemas of the tables in the database using SQL. SQL is the standard language for accessing relational databases and allows you to:

- Create tables (CREATE statements)
- Insert data rows into tables (INSERT statements)
- Update (change) data in tables (UPDATE statements)
- Retrieve data from tables according to various criteria, that is, to execute queries (SELECT statements)
- Remove rows from tables (DELETE statements)
- Perform other operations connected with data and table management, such as dropping tables from the database (DROP statements).

SQL is reasonably standard across different relational databases but there are some areas where they vary, so SQL written for MySQL may not work for other databases without some modifications and vice versa.

15.2.2   Generating Primary Keys

When using artificial (non-data) keys as primary keys in the database, we need some way of generating unique key values. There are various strategies for this, but a simple approach is to let the database generate primary keys for us. In MySQL this is very simple; we just add "AUTO_INCREMENT" to the configuration of the primary keys, for example,

```
CREATE TABLE course (
  courseID_PK INTEGER NOT NULL PRIMARY KEY AUTO_INCREMENT
etc…
```

This does not prevent us from providing a primary key value if we want to, but if we do not then MySQL will generate a new integer key every time a new record is inserted.

Note
Different databases have different ways of generating keys, so the AUTO_-INCREMENT syntax used with MySQL will not be portable to other databases. An alternative approach is to manage key generation with our own database independent implementation.

15.2.3   Using a DDL Script

Entering SQL to set up and populate tables manually can be a tedious and error-prone process. A much better option is to write all the SQL statements into a Data Definition Language (DDL) file that can be executed in one go by MySQL. A DDL file simply combines a series of SQL statements together.

Here is a DDL file to create the two tables from Fig. 15.1. All the tables have artificial primary keys that are auto incremented. The foreign key from modules to courses is not specified as a formal constraint, to keep the example as simple as possible.

```
USE courses;
DROP TABLE course;
CREATE TABLE course (
 courseID_PK INTEGER NOT NULL PRIMARY KEY AUTO_INCREMENT,
 name VARCHAR(35),
 numberofdays INTEGER,
 costperperson FLOAT,
 publicschedule BOOLEAN,
 lastupdated DATE
);

INSERT INTO course (name, numberofdays, costperperson, pub-
licschedule, lastupdated) VALUES
('Introduction to Java',3,1000.00,true,'2020-08-11');
INSERT INTO course (name, numberofdays, costperperson, pub-
licschedule, lastupdated) VALUES
('Agile Programming Techniques',2,650.00,false,'2020-12-01');
```

```
DROP TABLE module;
CREATE TABLE module (
moduleID_PK INTEGER NOT NULL PRIMARY KEY AUTO_INCREMENT,
name VARCHAR(35),
credits INTEGER,

assessment VARCHAR(20),
courseID_FK INTEGER
);


INSERT INTO module (name, credits, assessment, courseID_FK)
VALUES ('Basic Concepts', 10, 'Test', 1);
INSERT INTO module (name, credits, assessment, courseID_FK)
VALUES ('Object Orientation', 15, 'Assignment', 1);
INSERT INTO module (name, credits, assessment, courseID_FK)
VALUES ('Collections', 10, 'Presentation', 1);
INSERT INTO module (name, credits, assessment, courseID_FK)
VALUES ('Unit Testing', 10, 'Unit Test', 1);
INSERT INTO module (name, credits, assessment, courseID_FK)
VALUES ('Exception Handling', 10, 'Test', 1);
INSERT INTO module (name, credits, assessment, courseID_FK)
VALUES ('Swing UI', 15, 'Assignment', 1);
INSERT INTO module (name, credits, assessment, courseID_FK)
VALUES ('Streams', 10, 'Presentation', 1);
INSERT INTO module (name, credits, assessment, courseID_FK)
VALUES ('JDBC', 10, 'Test', 1);
INSERT INTO module (name, credits, assessment, courseID_FK)
VALUES ('Refactoring', 10, 'Test', 2);
INSERT INTO module (name, credits, assessment, courseID_FK)
VALUES ('Test Driven Development', 15, 'Assignment', 2);
INSERT INTO module (name, credits, assessment, courseID_FK)
VALUES ('Continuous Integration', 10, 'Presentation', 2);
INSERT INTO module (name, credits, assessment, courseID_FK)
VALUES ('Automated Acceptance Testing', 10, 'Unit Test', 2);
```

To execute a DDL file in MySQL you use the "source" command, followed by the path and filename. You have to be careful here, because the separator character between subfolders in the path must be a forward slash, not a backslash. In this example, we assume that the DDL file is called "courses.ddl" and resides in a folder called "ddlfiles" on C: drive.

```
source C:/ddlfiles/courses.ddl;
```

15.2.4 Viewing Table Schema

In MySQL, the "show tables" command lists all the tables in the database to which you are connected. In our case there are two tables.

```
+-------------------+
| Tables_in_courses |
+-------------------+
| course            |
| module            |
+-------------------+
```

To see the schema of a table, we can use the "describe" command, which shows the schema of the named table:

```
describe course;
```

This is the table schema that MySQL will display.

```
+--------------+-------------+------+-----+---------+-------------+
| Field        | Type        | Null | Key | Default | Extra       |
+--------------+-------------+------+-----+---------+-------------+
| courseID_PK  | int(11)     | NO   | PRI | NULL    |auto_increment
| name         | varchar(35) | YES  |     | NULL    |
| numberofdays | int(11)     | YES  |     | NULL    |
| costperperson| float       | YES  |     | NULL    |
| publicschedule| tinyint(1) | YES  |     | NULL    |
| lastupdated  | date        | YES  |     | NULL    |
+--------------+-------------+------+-----+---------+-------------+
```

15.2.5 Creating an Authorized MySQL User

When we connect to a MySQL database from a Java program, the connection code will only be able to access the database if MySQL has been configured with an anonymous user (no username and password required). Since this will not necessarily always be the case, and indeed since having an anonymous user for the database would clearly be a security risk in any real-world system, we will make sure that we can connect from our Java code to MySQL by creating a user with the necessary access privileges to the database. To do this we need to log onto MySQL as the root user and grant access privileges to a user identified by a username and a password.

The first step is to create the user, with their name, the database URL and their password. In this example, the username is "javaclient" and the password is "foundjava". Because in these examples MySQL is running on the local machine, the URL will be "localhost".

```
create user 'javaclient'@'localhost' identified by
   'foundjava';
```

Once a user has been added, they can be granted various privileges on selected databases. The following "grant" command provides a general set of privileges, including creating, updating and deleting records, across all tables in the "courses" database.

```
grant all privileges on courses.* to 'javaclient';
```

It will then be possible to connect to the "courses" database from Java programs with the username "javaclient" and the password "foundjava".

Table 15.1 summarizes the MySQL commands we have introduced in this section when using the MySQL Command Line Client.

Table 15.1 MySQL commands

MySQL Command	Meaning
create database dbname	Create a new database
use dbname	Connect to an existing database
show databases	Show the names of all databases
show tables	Show the names of all tables in the current database
exit / quit	Both exit from MySQL
source path/filename	Execute a SQL script file
describe tablename	Show the schema of a table
create user 'username'@'url' identified by 'password';	Create a new user with the given username and password
grant privilege type on dbname.tablename to 'username'	Grant privileges to resources to this user

15.3   Java Database Access with JDBC

Having set up a database to work with, the next step is to see how we can access
data stored in a relational database from Java code so that it can be used to provide
persistent and sharable data.

Java Database Connectivity (JDBC) is based on the concepts previously
demonstrated by Open Database Connectivity (ODBC), a Microsoft technology
based on a standard approach known as the *Call Level Interface* (CLI) defined by
the SQL Access group in the early 1990s. The basic idea of ODBC was that any
application could interact with any relational database that used SQL if they were
both ODBC compliant, meaning that they could both use an intermediate ODBC
layer to communicate. The intermediate level consists of a core library, that the
application uses, and a supporting database driver, that links the standard library to
specific databases (Fig. 15.3).

JDBC takes a very similar approach, with the difference being that the core
library is written in Java, and the driver layer consists of a JDBC driver rather than
an ODBC driver.

15.3.1   JDBC Drivers

The JDBC API, which is similar to the core library in ODBC, is a "thin" API which
lets us use SQL commands within our Java objects. JDBC specifies mostly interfaces, with only a few classes. This is because much of the implementation is done
at the JDBC driver level. The implementing classes for different JDBC drivers are
supplied by different vendors. These vendors may be database suppliers (such as
Oracle, Microsoft and IBM), application server vendors, third party suppliers or
open source projects. The main job of the JDBC driver is to enable communication
between a Java program and a database, and to convert between Java types (such as
"String") and SQL types (such as "VARCHAR").

There are four different types of JDBC driver with different characteristics.
Sometimes there is no choice about which driver you can use with a given database,

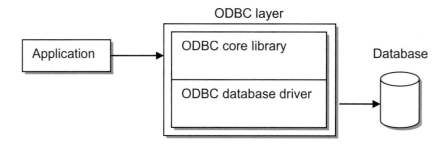

Fig. 15.3 The architecture of ODBC, upon which JDBC is based

but common databases often have many possible drivers available. Which driver you use will depend on various factors such as which types are available for your database, how much you are willing to pay for one and how well a specific driver performs in practice. Not all drivers provide the same support, and there are different versions of JDBC (at the time of writing the most recent version is 4.3) which may not all be supported by a specific driver. The four types of drivers are shown in Fig. 15.4. Type 1 drivers are only appropriate if you are already using an ODBC connection and want to reuse it from a Java application. Otherwise they are not a good choice because the multiple levels of translation from JDBC to ODBC to the database are inefficient. Type 3 drivers are used to connect from a database client to a remote server. From that point on the server itself will need another type of driver to connect to the database. In most cases we will be choosing between a type 2 driver and a type 4 driver. Since a type 4 driver has no levels of translation between Java and another API, we would expect a type 4 driver to be the best option. However, this may not be the case in practice so in a real project it is best to test all the available drivers and see which one is best at meeting requirements such as performance, features and cost.

The driver we will be using in these examples is the type 4 MySQL Connector/J driver, which can be freely downloaded as an archive from the MySQL website. This archive needs to be unzipped into a suitable location on your computer. Inside

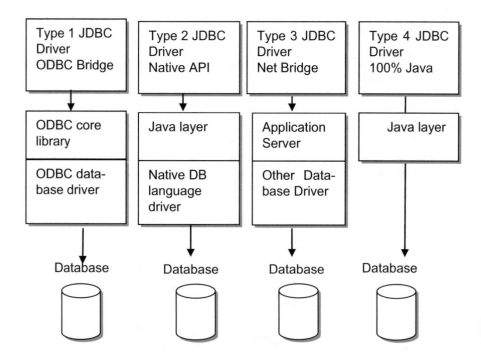

Fig. 15.4 The four types of JDBC driver

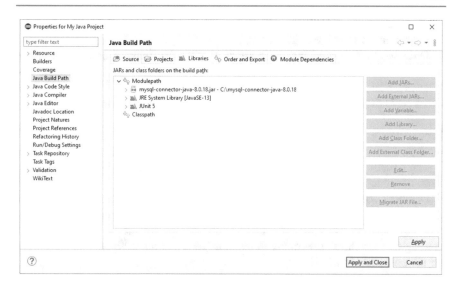

Fig. 15.5   Adding the MySQL Java connector JAR file to an Eclipse project

the main folder of the unzipped archive there will be a JAR file containing the driver called "mysql-connector-java-8.0.18-bin.jar" (or something similar depending on the version).

To use the driver in Eclipse, the JAR file that contains it must be available on the classpath/modulepath. This can be done by selecting "Properties" from the Project menu, then selecting the "Java Build Path", "Libraries" tab (Fig. 15.5). This is the same dialog that we previously used to add JUnit to the modulepath. However, in this case the JDBC driver is not an internal library but an external JAR. Press the "Add External JARs…" button and browse to the location of the JAR file containing the MySQL driver. Once it has been selected, it should appear in the "Libraries" list. Then click "OK".

If you want to run database access code from the command line, outside of Eclipse, you will need to set the classpath on the command line, for example,

```
set classpath=%CLASSPATH%;path/databaselibrary.jar;.
```

15.3.2   Making a Two-Tier Connection

The tiers in a two-tier connection are a Java program and a database, connected via a JDBC Driver. The first step for a Java program using JDBC is to use the JDBC driver to make a connection to the database. The connection can then be used to send SQL commands to the database, using the methods of Java classes and interfaces from the JDBC libraries. For two-tier connections, all these classes and interfaces are in the "java.sql" package.

Once we have loaded the database driver, we can make a connection to the database. To do this we need to know the database URL and the username and password that will authenticate our program to the database. MySQL database URLs have the following format:

```
jdbc:mysql://hostname:portnumber/databasename
```

The default port is usually 3306, and if we are connecting to a database on the same machine then the host can be "localhost".

Database connections are made using the static "getConnection" method of the DriverManager class (from the "java.sql" package). This method returns a Connection object. In this code fragment we connect to a database called "courses" running on "localhost" (assuming the default port) and the username and password we set up earlier in MySQL.

```
Connection connection = DriverManager.getConnection
  ("jdbc:mysql://localhost/courses","javaclient","introjava");
```

The exception handling for code that connects to a resource such as a database can use the "try-with-resources" construct, which ensures that the resources are closed if an exception occurs. This requires the code that makes the connection to the database to be added to the "try":

```
try(Connection connection = DriverManager.getConnection
  ("jdbc:mysql://localhost/courses","javaclient", "foundjava"))
```

Note
The com.mysql.cj.jdbc.Driver is the type 4 driver supplied with the MySQL Connector/J download that the DriverManager will use in these examples. However, there are other drivers from various sources that can be used with MySQL.

15.4   SQL Exceptions

Most of the methods in the "java.sql" classes and interfaces can throw "java.sql. SQLException". Since this is a checked exception, we must use "try...catch" blocks around our database access code or it will not compile, for example,

```
try(Connection... )
{
  // JDBC code
}
catch(SQLException e)
{
  //...handle exception
}
```

15.5 Executing SQL Queries and Updates Using JDBC

Once we have successfully connected to the database, we can create "Statement" objects, using the "createStatement" method of the connection, for example,

```
Statement statement = connection.createStatement();
```

At this point we are now ready to start executing SQL commands such as SELECT, INSERT, UPDATE and DELETE against the database, wrapped in Java code.

We can read data from the database by using the "executeQuery" method of the statement. This is passed a SQL query as an argument and returns a ResultSet object that contains the result of the query. Here, for example, we execute a single SELECT statement to retrieve all the rows from the "course" table.

```
ResultSet results = statement.executeQuery
  ("SELECT * FROM course");
```

We can get the data from a ResultSet by iterating over it with a "while" loop. Each iteration gives us the next row from the database query.

```
while(results.next())
{
  // process the next row returned by the query
}
```

15.5.1 Processing ResultSets

One of the jobs of a JDBC driver is to translate between SQL and Java types. It is important to understand these translations when mapping between Java classes and relational table schemas. Table 15.2 shows the standard mappings between SQL types and Java types, and the methods of the ResultSet interface that are used to retrieve these values. These ResultSet methods retrieve Java data from the results of

SQL queries. A can be seen in Table 15.2, they each begin with "get", followed by a data type, for example, "getString", which is used to retrieve data from character columns such as VARCHAR, and "getInt", which is used where the column is of type INTEGER.

The parameter passed to the "get…" methods of the ResultSet may be either the column number or the column name. Here, for example, we use the column number to retrieve the second column from the result of the query against the "course" table, which is the "name" column (of type VARCHAR). Unlike, for example, array indexes, result set index numbers start at one rather than zero.

```
String courseName = results.getString(2);
```

However, it is not good practice to access columns by number, since this may be unreliable if the database schema is changed. It is much better to retrieve data by column name. We would therefore use the name "name" instead of the number "2":

Table 15.2 The standard mapping from SQL types to Java types and ResultSet methods

SQL Type	Java Type	ResultSet Method
CHAR	String	getString
VARCHAR	String	getString
LONGVARCHAR	String	getString
NUMERIC	java.math.BigDecimal	getBigDecimal
DECIMAL	java.math.BigDecimal	getBigDecimal
BIT	boolean	getBoolean
TINYINT	byte	getByte
SMALLINT	short	getShort
INTEGER	int	getInt
BIGINT	long	getLong
REAL	float	getFloat
FLOAT	double	getDouble
DOUBLE	double	getDouble
BINARY	byte[]	getBytes
VARBINARY	byte[]	getBytes
LONGVARBINARY	byte[]	getBytes
DATE	java.sql.Date	getDate
TIME	java.sql.Time	getTime
TIMESTAMP	java.sql.Timestamp	getTimeStamp

```
String courseName = results.getString("name");
```

The Java data types returned by the "get" methods are generally straightforward, but when you retrieve a Date from the ResultSet using the "getDate" method, you should note that it returns a java.sql.Date, not a java.util.Date.

Note
Although the "try-with-resources" construct closes the connections to resources automatically, it should be noted if you want to close ResultSets, Statements or Connections manually they should be closed in the reverse order that they were opened; ResultSet first, then Statement, then Connection.

```
results.close();
statement.close();
connection.close();
```

closure of these resources will otherwise be automatic, but explicit closure can free database resources more quickly.

Here is a complete Java program that makes a connection to the "courses" database using the MySQL JDBC driver, executes a SELECT query on the "course" table and then prints the contents of the result set to standard output. Note that in this example there is no explicit closing of connections, since these will be closed by the "try-with-resources" construct.

```
package com.foundjava.chapter15;

import java.sql.Connection;
import java.sql.DriverManager;
import java.sql.ResultSet;
import java.sql.SQLException;
import java.sql.Statement;

public class ResultSetExample
{
  public static void main(String[] args)
  {
// make a connection to the database
    try(Connection connection = DriverManager.getConnection
  ("jdbc:mysql://localhost/courses","javaclient", "foundjava"))
    {
      Statement statement = connection.createStatement();
// execute a query
      ResultSet results = statement.executeQuery
         ("SELECT * FROM course");
// declare variables to receive the data from the ResultSet
      int id = 0;
      String name = null;
```

```
        int numberOfDays = 0;
        double costPerPerson = 0;
        boolean publicSchedule = false;
        java.sql.Date lastUpdated = null;
        System.out.println("id\tName\tDuration\tCost\t" +
            "On public schedule\tLast Updated");
// process the ResultSet
        while (results.next())
        {
            id = results.getInt("courseID_PK");
            name = results.getString("name");
            numberOfDays = results.getInt("numberofdays");
            costPerPerson = results.getDouble("costperperson");
            publicSchedule = results.getBoolean("publicschedule");
            lastUpdated = results.getDate("lastupdated");
            System.out.println(id + "\t" + name + "\t" +
                numberOfDays + "\t" + costPerPerson + "\t" +
                publicSchedule + "\t" + lastUpdated);
        }
    }
    catch (SQLException e)
    {
        e.printStackTrace();
    }
    }
}
```

This is the output from the program. Note that the rather clumsy use of tab characters will not guarantee a good column layout, since this depends on the length of the data in the "name" field.

```
id   Name        Duration     Cost    On public schedule      Last Updated
1    Introduction to Java     3         1000.0 true     2020-08-11
2    Agile Programming Techniques  2  650.0  false  2020-12-01
```

Exercise 15.1
For the exercises in this chapter you will need the JAR file containing the MySQL database driver on the classpath/modulepath (the "Java Build Path" in Eclipse).

- Create the "courses" database in MySQL and populate it using the "courses.ddl" file.
- Write a Java class with a "main" method that connects to your "courses" database.

- Execute a query to read all the rows in the "module" table into a ResultSet.
- Iterate through the ResultSet and write a selection of the data to standard output.

Exercise 15.2

- Write a Java class with a "main" method that connects to your "courses" database.
- Execute a query to read all the rows in the "course" table where the cost is less than 1,000 into a ResultSet.
- Iterate through the ResultSet and write the data to standard output.

15.5.2 Updating Records

Updates, which change the data by inserting, modifying or deleting records, are supported by the "executeUpdate" method of the "Statement" interface. Since updates are not queries, they do not return a result set. They do, however, return an integer value that indicates the number of rows affected by the update. Here, for example, is an update that inserts a new record into the "course" table and returns the number of rows updated into a variable. We assume in the following examples that "rowsUpdated" has already been declared as an "int" variable:

```
rowsUpdated = statement.executeUpdate
("INSERT INTO course (name, numberofdays, cost, publicschedule,
    lastupdated) VALUES
    ('Python for Snake Charmers',4,1500.00,true,'2012-12-11')");
```

Here are examples of updating and deleting, again using the "executeUpdate" method:

```
rowsUpdated = statement.executeUpdate
    ("UPDATE course SET publicschedule=true
        WHERE courseID_PK=2");

rowsUpdated = statement.executeUpdate
    ("DELETE FROM course WHERE name='Introduction to Java'");
```

Exercise 15.3

- Write a Java class with a "main" method that connects to your "courses" database.
- Execute an update that adds a new course to the database with one new module. Ensure that the foreign key from the module to the course is set correctly.

15.6   Using Prepared Statements

Prepared statements are useful where similar SQL commands are to be executed with different data. For example, it will be a common update to change the state of the "lastupdated" field whenever a course has been modified. By using a prepared statement, we can reuse the same piece of code to update different records. The SQL string used as the parameter to the "prepareStatement" method (of the "Connection" interface) has one or more placeholders where data can be provided. These are indicated by question marks, for example,

```
PreparedStatement prepstatement = connection.prepareStatement
   ("UPDATE course SET lastupdated = ? WHERE courseID_PK = ?");
```

To use a prepared statement, each placeholder is populated using "set" methods based on the data type of the column. These are very similar to the "get" methods used with a result set. Because PreparedStatements use variables, we need to know which Java data types to use for these "set" methods. Table 15.3 shows the mappings from Java types to SQL types, and the associated "set" methods of the PreparedStatement interface.

Table 15.3 The standard mapping from Java types to SQL types

Java Type	PreparedStatement Method	SQL Type
String	setString(int, String)	VARCHAR or LONGVARCHAR
java.math.BigDecimal	setBigDecimal(int, BigDecimal)	NUMERIC
boolean	setBoolean(int, boolean)	BIT
byte	setByte(ine, byte)	TINYINT
short	setShort(int, short)	SMALLINT
int	setInt(int, int)	INTEGER
long	setLong(int, long)	BIGINT
float	setFloat(int, float)	REAL
double	setDouble(int. double)	DOUBLE
byte[]	setBytes(int, byte[])	VARBINARY or LONGVARBINARY
java.sql.Date	setDate(int, Date)	DATE
java.sql.Time	setTime(int, Time)	TIME
java.sql.Timestamp	setTimeStamp(int, TimeStamp)	TIMESTAMP

The first parameter to the "set" methods is always the integer index number of the relevant placeholder, and the second parameter is the value being set. The mapping for Strings will normally be VARCHAR but will use LONGVARCHAR instead if a VARCHAR is not large enough. The situation is similar for byte arrays, which can map to two different binary types depending on the required size.

The placeholders are numbered from left to right, starting at "1". The following example executes an update using a PreparedStatement, setting the "lastupdated" column to the current date, based on selecting a given primary key. Since there are two placeholders required for this example, the first will be numbered "1" and the second will be numbered "2". Here we set the values of the two placeholders, then execute the update. Because one of the values we are setting is a date, a java.sql. Date object is required. To create an object of this class using the current date, this example uses a LocalDate passed to the Date's constructor.

```
LocalDate localDate = LocalDate.of(2021, 4, 25);
java.sql.Date sqlDate = java.sql.Date.valueOf(localDate);
prepstatement.setDate(1, sqlDate);
prepstatement.setInt(2, 2);
prepstatement.executeUpdate();
```

Because a prepared statement has already been configured with an SQL statement, we do not need to pass any parameters to the "executeUpdate" method.

The point of doing this is that the same prepared statement can be used multiple times, for example (assuming a much larger database than we currently have!).

```
LocalDate localDate = LocalDate.of(2022, 3, 5);
java.sql.Date sqlDate = java.sql.Date.valueOf(localDate);
prepstatement.setDate(1, sqlDate);
prepstatement.setInt(2, 254);
prepstatement.executeUpdate();
```

This reuse not only makes our Java code more elegant, it actually makes it much more efficient, because the underlying SQL code that a prepared statement uses only needs to be generated once, rather than each time as it would be for individual Statement objects.

Exercise 15.4
The PreparedStatement interface has an "executeQuery" method for executing SELECT statements. Modify your code to use a PreparedStatement to query individual courses based on their name.

15.7   Summary

In this chapter we saw how to create and populate a database using the MySQL Relational Database Management System (RDBMS). We also saw how a JDBC driver enables Java code to connect to and interact with a relational database using a standard API. Examples covered the execution of queries to create a ResultSet, and the execution of updates. We also saw how PreparedStatements can be set up that can be efficiently reused for common types of interaction with the database.

The level of interaction between Java and the database described in this chapter is at the very simple level of moving data in and out of the database. It does not really address the much broader issue of object-relational mapping. Readers interested in further detail of how objects can be made persistent in a relational database should explore the Java Persistence API, which can be used with both SQL and NoSQL databases.

Multithreading

16

One of the increasingly important features of Java, as multiprocessor computers have become commonplace, is that it allows us to write programs with multiple threads. Many programming languages run with a single thread of control, meaning that the program can do only one thing at a time. A multithreaded language allows programs to do more than one thing at the same time, to perform multiple tasks concurrently. Even on a single processor, programs can appear to perform different tasks simultaneously by swapping between them at high speed. As a traditional mainframe computer can have many terminals connected to it at the same time, a single Java program can have many threads running at once. All Java programs have a main user thread, but other child threads can be spawned from it. These can be either *user threads*, like the thread that runs a "main" method, or *daemon threads* running in the underlying virtual machine. There must be at least one user thread running for the program to continue. When you create your own threads, they are usually user threads, but can also be set to be daemon threads. You might do this to ensure that these threads do not keep running after other user threads have stopped.

Each thread is a separate computation unit but is not a separate process. Rather, thread-based multitasking allows parts of the same program to run concurrently and share data and code with other threads in the same program. Threads are said to be *lightweight*, whereas processes are *heavyweight*.

In this chapter we will look at threads, first creating and running a single thread of control and then looking at how programs can be multithreaded to perform more than one task simultaneously. Multithreaded programs can be written using either inheritance (inheriting from class Thread) or by implementing the Runnable interface. Java provides intrinsic support for synchronizing the activities of multiple threads together through methods of the Object class, which all other objects inherit.

© Springer Nature Switzerland AG 2020
D. Parsons, *Foundational Java*, Texts in Computer Science,
https://doi.org/10.1007/978-3-030-54518-5_16

16.1   Creating and Running a Thread

The first example is a class that uses a single thread of control. Running a program with a single thread object does not look very different to a program that uses the normal user thread, but this example introduces some important syntax. In the program, a thread describes the journey of a tortoise. One way to use threads in a Java program is to create a class that inherits from the Thread class and can therefore use its inherited methods. In this case, class Tortoise inherits from (extends) Thread.

```
public class Tortoise extends Thread
```

Its constructor sets the name of the thread by calling a parameterized superclass constructor (this name can be returned using the "getName" method). If we used the zero arguments constructor instead, the default name of the thread would be similar to "Thread-0".

```
public Tortoise(String name)
{
    super(name);
}
```

The Tortoise must override the "run" method of Thread, which defines what happens when a thread is running (the inherited version of "run" does nothing). In this case, not a lot happens, except that the tortoise slowly travels 10 steps.

```
@Override
public void run()
{
    int sleepTime;
    for (int i = 0; i < 10; i++)
    {
        // further code here
    }
    System.out.println(getName() + " has finished!");
}
```

The journey is slowed using the static Thread method "sleep" that puts the thread to sleep for the specified number of milliseconds. "sleep" has a checked exception, java.lang.InterruptedException, that must be handled. This exception can be explicitly triggered by the "interrupt" method of the Thread class (a thread can interrupt itself).

```
sleepTime = (int)(Math.random() * 1000);
try
{
  Thread.sleep(sleepTime);
}
catch (InterruptedException e)
{
  System.out.println("Interrupted");
}
```

When the "run" method finishes, the thread dies (hopefully the tortoise lives on of course). Here is the complete class.

```
package com.foundjava.chapter16;

public class Tortoise extends Thread
{
// set the name of the thread in the constructor
  public Tortoise(String name)
  {
    super(name);
  }

// override the 'run' method to provide the behavior of
// the thread
  @Override
  public void run()
  {
// local variable to store a random waiting time
    int sleepTime;
// loop ten times (the tortoise travels ten meters)
    for (int i = 0; i < 10; i++)
    {
// use 'getName' to display the name of the thread
      System.out.println(getName() + " has gone " +
        i + " meters");
// generate a random delay
      sleepTime = (int) (Math.random() * 1000);
```

```
// 'sleep' for the specified time
   try
   {
      Thread.sleep(sleepTime);
   }
   catch (InterruptedException e)
   {
      System.out.println("Interrupted");
   }
   }
   System.out.println(getName() + " has finished!");
}
```

The following "main" method creates a new instance of the Thread subclass (Tortoise) and sets it off using the "start" method of Thread. "start" indirectly calls the Thread's "run" method.

```
public static void main(String[] args)
{
   // create a 'Tortoise' object
   Tortoise racingTortoise = new Tortoise("Tortoise");
   // use its 'start' method to make its thread run
   racingTortoise.start();
}
```

Running this class produces (rather slowly!) the following output:

```
Tortoise has gone 0 metres
Tortoise has gone 1 metres
Tortoise has gone 2 metres
Tortoise has gone 3 metres
Tortoise has gone 4 metres
Tortoise has gone 5 metres
Tortoise has gone 6 metres
Tortoise has gone 7 metres
Tortoise has gone 8 metres
Tortoise has gone 9 metres
Tortoise has finished!
```

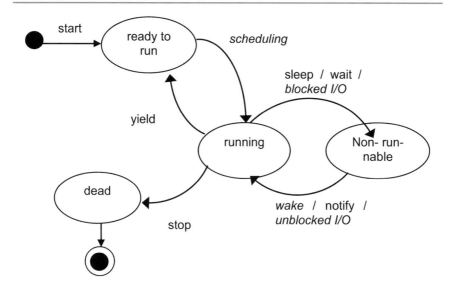

Fig. 16.1   Thread states and transitions

16.1.1   Thread States

In the simple Tortoise program, we saw that a thread can go through a number of states. When the "start" method is called, the Thread is ready to run, but not necessarily actually running. It must be scheduled to run by the Java runtime, depending on what may be happening with other threads at the time. Once the thread is running it can be put to sleep, which is one of several ways that a thread can be put into a non-runnable state. If it wakes up from sleeping, it can resume running. Eventually, it stops and dies. Figure 16.1 shows the various states that a thread can be in during its lifetime. We will look at some of the other features of the lifecycle, including "yield", "wait" and "notify" in the following sections.

16.2   Running Multiple Threads

Using the syntax described in the first example, we can create an object of a class derived from Thread and set it running. It is a simple step to move from there to a program that has more than one thread, that is, which is multithreaded (though, as we will see later, it is a more complex task to try to coordinate the activities of separate threads).

The key aspect of this example is declaring multiple thread objects. The main reason for starting with a tortoise in the first example was to use it as a basis for this program, TheTortoiseAndTheHare, where the tortoise and the hare are represented by separate but concurrent threads.

You will no doubt be familiar with the fable about the race between the tortoise and the hare, where the hare was so overconfident of victory that he fell asleep halfway through the race and lost as a result. This program simulates that race by sending the hare's thread to sleep for rather a long time. The Hare class extends Thread and contains a "run" method that slows the journey of the hare with a very long sleep between the top of the hill and the finish line.

```
package com.foundjava.chapter16;

public class Hare extends Thread
{
  public Hare(String name)
  {
    super(name);
  }

// the 'run' method displays the journey of the hare
  @Override
  public void run()
  {
    System.out.println(getName() + " has started racing");
// a short time to get to the oak tree...
    try
    {
      Thread.sleep(1000);
    }
    catch (InterruptedException e)
    {
      System.out.println("Interrupted");
    }
    System.out.println(getName() +
      " has passed the oak tree");
// a short time to get to the top of the hill
    try
    {
      Thread.sleep(1000);
```

```
    }
    catch (InterruptedException e)
    {
      System.out.println("Interrupted");
    }
    System.out.println(getName() +
      " is at the top of the hill (and has fallen asleep)");
// falls asleep for a long time
    try
    {
      Thread.sleep(20000);
    }
    catch (InterruptedException e)
    {
      System.out.println("Interrupted");


      }
    // gets to the end (after the tortoise, probably)
        System.out.println(getName() + " has finished!");
      }
    }
```

The tortoise takes longer as a rule to get between landmarks but does not fall asleep on the final stretch so gets to the end quicker overall. This is a different class from the previous Tortoise, so is called RacingTortoise.

```java
package com.foundjava.chapter16;

public class RacingTortoise extends Thread
{
  public RacingTortoise(String name)
  {
    super(name);
  }
// 'run' displays the journey of the tortoise
  @Override
  public void run()
  {
// slow but steady progress to the oak tree
    System.out.println(getName() + " has started racing");
    try
    {
      Thread.sleep(5000);
    } catch (InterruptedException e)
    {
      System.out.println("Interrupted");
    }
    System.out.println(getName() +
      " has passed the oak tree");
// slow but steady progress to the top of the hill
    try
    {
      Thread.sleep(5000);
    } catch (InterruptedException e)
    {
      System.out.println("Interrupted");
    }
    System.out.println(getName() +
      " is at the top of the hill");
// slow but steady progress to the checkered flag
```

```
    try
    {
      Thread.sleep(5000);
    } catch (InterruptedException e)
    {
      System.out.println("Interrupted");
    }
    System.out.println(getName() + " has finished!");
  }
}
```

In TheTortoiseAndTheHare, both animals start at (more or less) the same time, but the tortoise wins.

```
package com.foundjava.chapter16;

public class TheTortoiseAndTheHare
{
  public static void main(String[] args)
  {
// create two separate thread objects (a tortoise and a hare)
    Hare racingHare = new Hare("Hare");
    RacingTortoise racingTortoise = new
      RacingTortoise("Tortoise");
// start them both racing
    racingHare.start();
    racingTortoise.start();
  }
}
```

The story unfolds slowly at runtime:

```
Tortoise has started racing
Hare has started racing
Hare has passed the oak tree
Hare is at the top of the hill (and has fallen asleep)
Tortoise has passed the oak tree
Tortoise is at the top of the hill
Tortoise has finished!
Hare has finished!
```

Exercise 16.1

The race between the tortoise and the hare was rigged from the start. Write a class called RaceHorse that inherits from Thread and jumps fences between randomly generated sleeps. After a horse has jumped five fences it passes the finishing line. Use the constructor to set the name of the horse. Create a Steeplechase class that starts several horses running (but do not bet real money on the winner).

16.3 Thread Priority

We have seen from the previous example that a program can have more than one thread running at the same time. One issue that arises is what happens if two threads want to access the same program resources at the same time. Multithreading appears to be handling different tasks in parallel, but in fact the system is invisibly choosing between them so there is potential for conflict. Different Java implementations can have different ways of handling two threads competing for the same resource, but the programmer also has some influence. Among other techniques, different threads can be provided with different priorities, allowing a high-priority thread to request more access to processing time than a low-priority thread.

16.3.1 Setting Thread Priority

In the next example program, we compare the priority of bees and a bear when accessing a honeycomb. Since a bear is much larger than a bee and impervious to stings, it has a higher priority for eating honeycomb.

The bees in this code are what is known as a "selfish" thread, since they never choose to move to a non-runnable state by, for example, going to sleep. Given the chance they will spend all their time buzzing round the honeycomb. However, as we will see, the bees will be given a lower thread priority than the bear. The "if" statement in the "run" method here is only for formatting the output, which just prints a lot of "z's" to the console.

```
package com.foundjava.chapter16;

public class Bees extends Thread
{
// the bees buzz around their honey all the time, but can be
// interrupted by the bear who has a higher priority
```

```
@Override
  public void run()
  {
    for (int i = 0; i < 20000; i++)
    {
      System.out.print("z");
      if(i%100 == 0)
      {
        System.out.println();
      }
    }
  }
}
```

The bear is also a thread but spends more time asleep than looking for honey. However, it does occasionally wake up and go looking for lunch.

```
package com.foundjava.chapter16;

public class Bear extends Thread
{
  @Override
  public void run()
  {
// the bear sleeps at first
    try
    {
      Thread.sleep(50);
    } catch (InterruptedException e)
    {
      System.out.println("Interrupted");
    }
// when it wakes up, it goes straight for the honey.
// because it has a higher priority than the bees,
// they must stop until the bear has finished
    System.out.println("Mmmmmm, honey, yum yum!");
  }
}
```

One way of the bear getting access to the honey is by setting its priority to be much higher (though this is dependent on the operating system being preemptive to give the bear a time slice).

We can set the relative priorities of different threads using the "setPriority" method. This takes an integer parameter in the range 1 (low)–10 (high). There are also three priority constants defined in the Thread class, MIN_PRIORITY (1), MAX_PRIORITY (10) and NORM_PRIORITY (5, the default).

In the "BearBeesAndHoney" class, the priorities of the bear and bee threads are set, and the threads are started. The bees are given minimum priority and the bear is given maximum priority, so in resource competition with the bear, the bees should have to give way to the bear at some point.

```
package com.foundjava.chapter16;

public class BearBeesAndHoney
{
   public static void main(String[] args)
   {
// the bees have minimum priority
      Bees honeyBees = new Bees();
      honeyBees.setPriority(Thread.MIN_PRIORITY);
// the bear has maximum priority
      Bear hungryBear = new Bear();
      hungryBear.setPriority(Thread.MAX_PRIORITY);
      honeyBees.start();
      hungryBear.start();
   }
}
```

The output from this program is rather unpredictable, depending on the relative speed of the "for" loop and the way that a particular platform manages its threads. Suffice to say that at some point the bear should get its nose in the honey. You may need to change the bear's sleep time and/or the number of times the loop goes around to get this type of result.

```
zzzzzzzzzzzzzzzzzzzzzzzzzzzzzzzzzzzzzzzzzzzzzzzzzzzzzzzzzzzzzzzzzzz
zzzzzzzzzzzzzzzzzzzzzzzzzzzzzzzzzzzzzzzzzzzzzzzzzzzzzzzzzzzzzzzzzzz
zzzzzzzzzzzzzzzzzzzzzzzzzzzzzzzzzzzzzzzzzzzzzzzzzzzzzzzzzzzzzzzzzzz
zzzzzzzzzzzzzzzzzzzzzzzzzzzzzzzzzzzzzzzzzzzzzzzzzzzzzzzzzzzzzzzzzzz
zzzzzzzzzzzzzzzzzzzzzzzzzzzzzzzzzzzzzzzzzzzzzzzzzzzzzzzzzzzzzzzzzzz
zzzzzzzzzzzzzzzzzzzzzzzzzzzzzzzzzzzzzzzzzzzzzzzzzzzzzzzzzzzzzzzzzzz
zzzzzzzzzzzzzzzzzzzzzzzzzzzzzzzzzzzzzzzzzzzzzzzzzzzzzzzzzzzzzzzzzzz
zzzzzzzzzzzzzzzzzzzzzzzzzzzzzzzzzzzzzzzzzzzzzzzzzzzzzzzzzzzzzzzzzzz
zzzzzzzzzzzzzzzzzzzzzzzzzzzzzzzzzzzzzzzzzzzzzzzzzzzzzzzzzzzzzzzzzzz
zzzzzzzzzzzzzzzzzzzzzzzzzzzzzzzzzzzzzzzzzzzzzzzzzzzzzzzzzzzzzzzzzzz
zzzzzzzzzzzzzzzzzzzzzzzzzzzzzzzzzzzzzzzzMmmmmm, honey, yum yum!
zzzzzzzzzzzzzzzzzzzzzzzzzzzzzzzzzzzzzzzzzzzz etc...
```

Exercise 16.2
Modify the Steeplechase class so that one horse has maximum priority, and the others have minimum priority. Is this enough to ensure that the maximum priority horse always wins the race?

16.3.2 Yielding

Hoping that you can preempt a selfish thread by the rather brute force method of setting priorities is not the most elegant or reliable of options. A better approach would be to make the thread less selfish. The "sleep" method is one way of doing this, but is not necessarily the best option either, since threads may be sleeping when they could quite usefully be running. An alternative approach is to make a thread "yield", which as Fig. 16.1 shows, takes the thread back into its runnable state, where it can be scheduled to run again as soon as is practicable. The static "yield" method is a hint to Java's thread scheduler that the current thread is willing to give other threads the chance to access a processor (though it does not force this to happen). The following class provides a less selfish "run" method, which yields after every 100 iterations of the "for" loop. These bees could give the bear a chance at the honey even if both threads have the same priority.

```java
package com.foundjava.chapter16;

public class YieldingBees extends Thread
{
  @Override
  public void run()
  {
    for (int i = 0; i < 20000; i++)
    {
      System.out.print("z");
      if(i%100 == 0)
      {
        System.out.println();
        Thread.yield();
      }
    }
  }
}
```

Note
Since "yield" is only a hint to the thread scheduler, it should not be relied upon as a mechanism to guarantee that another thread can access processing resources.

16.4   Implementing the Runnable Interface

The previous examples have used subclasses of Thread, but in a single inheritance language like Java this can be very restrictive. An alternative approach is to implement the Runnable interface, leaving your own classes free to extend classes other than Thread. In the next example, we will use the Runnable interface to create threaded objects that are in an inheritance hierarchy. The Runnable interface declares a single method called "run". We can use this method to run an object as a thread without affecting its ability to inherit from a superclass. To help to visualize multiple threads executing concurrently, this program uses simple graphical images of several flying machines, flying in different directions and at different speeds. Figure 16.2 shows the classes in the hierarchy, implementing the Runnable interface.

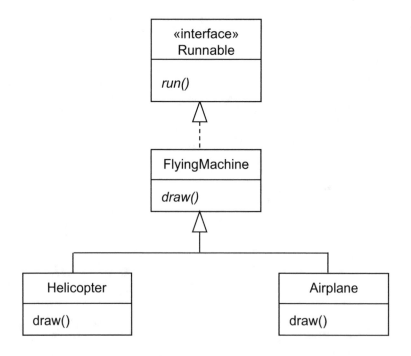

Fig. 16.2 Classes in an inheritance hierarchy implementing the Runnable interface

There are several differences between writing a class that inherits from Thread and one that implements the Runnable interface. First, of course, we use "implements Runnable" rather than "extends Thread" on the class declaration, as in this FlyingMachine class:

```
public abstract class FlyingMachine implements Runnable
```

The value of using the interface becomes more obvious when we look at the subclasses of FlyingMachine; Helicopter and Airplane:

```
public class Helicopter extends FlyingMachine
        implements Runnable
```

```
public class Airplane extends FlyingMachine
        implements Runnable
```

These classes are free to inherit from FlyingMachine since they do not need to inherit from Thread.

A Runnable class needs its own Thread object. In this example, the FlyingMachine class has a Thread declared as a private field.

```
private Thread thread;
```

This thread is created in the constructor, by passing the Runnable object (this FlyingMachine) as the parameter to the thread's own constructor:

```
thread = new Thread(this);
```

When a class inherits from Thread, it inherits all the Thread methods such as "start". In contrast, the Runnable interface only has the single "run" method. All other thread methods, such as "start" need to be invoked on the Thread object, for example,

```
thread.start();
```

The rest of the code in the class relates to what a FlyingMachine does while its thread is running, namely, moving across the screen. The animation is very crude: a FlyingMachine is moved by drawing over its current image in the background color to erase it, moving it along in the appropriate direction and then redrawing it in the foreground color. The background color can be returned from the graphical container hosting the application by using the "getBackground" method:

```
backgroundColor = container.getBackground();
```

Note

The graphical aspects of this example are not important. They are only used to visualize the threads

The four possible directions an airplane can travel in are north, south, east and west, so movement is limited to changing the current x- or y-values of the airplane's position:

```
switch(getDirection())
{
// East
  case 1: x++; break;
// South
  case 2: y++; break;
// West
  case 3: x--; break;
// North
  case 4: y--;
}
```

Here is the complete FlyingMachine class, apart from the getters and setters for the fields, which are omitted here as they have no particularly interesting features. Note the abstract "draw" method declared in the superclass but implemented in the subclasses.

```
package com.foundjava.chapter16;
import java.awt.Color;
import java.awt.Container;
import java.awt.Graphics;

public abstract class FlyingMachine implements Runnable
{
// attributes to record the position, direction and
// speed of the plane
  private int x;
  private int y;
  private int direction;
  private int speed;
// a reference to the containing Frame or Panel
  private Container container;
// a Thread in which to run
  private Thread thread;
// a java.awt.Graphics reference to enable drawing
```

```
// on the background
  Graphics graphics;

// the constructor initializes the attributes and starts the
// thread running
  public FlyingMachine(int startX, int startY, int direction,
    int speed, Container panel)
  {
    setX(startX);
    setY(startY);
    setDirection(direction);
    setSpeed(speed);
    setContainer(panel);
    setGraphics(panel.getGraphics());
// create a new Thread for 'this' object
    thread = new Thread(this);
// start it running
    thread.start();
  }

// getters and setters also added but not shown here

// this method runs the thread
  public void run()
  {
// run the thread while the plane is within a given area of
// the window
    while (getX() > 0 && getX() < getContainer().getWidth()
        && getY() > 0
        && getY() < getContainer().getHeight()) {
      try {
// pause for a time relative to the speed of the plane
        Thread.sleep(100 / speed);
// erase the current image by drawing over it
// in the background color
        draw(getContainer().getBackground());
  // move the plane in the appropriate direction
        switch (getDirection()) {
  // East
          case 1:
          x++;
          break;
  // South
          case 2:
```

```
              y++;
              break;
  // West
          case 3:
              x--;
              break;
  // North
          case 4:
              y--;
          }
  // redraw the plane in its new position
          draw(Color.black);
      }
      catch (InterruptedException e)
      {
          System.out.println("Interrupted");
      }
    }
    getGraphics().dispose();
  }
  public abstract void draw(Color col);
}
```

The "draw" method, which is implemented polymorphically in the two concrete subclasses, uses a java.awt.geom.AffineTransform to draw the flying machine's shape at the appropriate angle. To quote from the Javadoc,

> The AffineTransform class represents a 2D affine transform that performs a linear mapping from 2D coordinates to other 2D coordinates that preserves the "straightness" and "parallelness" of lines. Affine transformations can be constructed using sequences of translations, scales, flips, rotations, and shears.

Basically, an AffineTransform can perform quite sophisticated transformations of 2D shapes. Rotating a shape by 90° (quadrant rotation) is a pretty simple task for this class, and it has a special instance to do this, accessed via the "getQuadrantRotationInstance" factory method.

In the "draw" method, "this" flying machine is being drawn. Its own position is passed to the getQuadrantRotationInstance method to specify which quadrant the plane is to be drawn in. The quadrant values are 0–3, whereas the direction values are 1–4, so we subtract 1 from the position value to get the right quadrant value. The other values are the current x- and y-coordinates of the plane.

```
AffineTransform transform =
    AffineTransform.getQuadrantRotateInstance
        (getDirection()-1, getX(), getY());
```

The AffineTransform object has a "transform" method that takes two arrays, the first is the original set of x- and y-coordinates and the second is the result of rotating those coordinates. In our example an array called "values" holds the coordinates of the plane facing east, and an array called "result" is used to contain the transformed coordinates. As well as the two arrays, the "transform" method takes as parameters the required offset in the arrays (we just start at zero) and the number of points being transformed (this will be six for the Airplane, since we are drawing three lines, and eight for the Helicopter, which consists of four lines).

Figure 16.3 shows the relative coordinates being used for the two different flying machines.

Fig. 16.3 The relative coordinates used to draw the representations of the Airplane (above) and Helicopter (below) classes

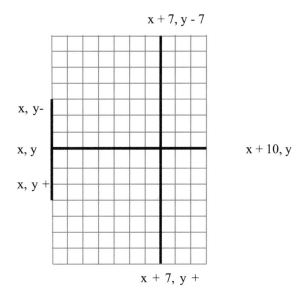

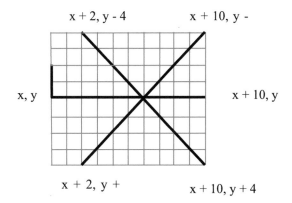

Since the result is an array of doubles we have to cast each coordinate from the "result" array to an int to draw the shape, since the "drawLine" method of the Graphics class requires four integer parameters (the x- and y-coordinates of each end of the line). Here is the "draw" method for the "Airplane" class. You should be able to see the coordinates from Fig. 16.3 being set in the "values" array.

```
@Override
public void draw(Color col)
{
// set the drawing color
  getGraphics().setColor(col);
// draw the plane in the current position.
//for each direction the shape will be rotated.
  double[] values = { getX(), getY(), getX() + 10, getY(),
    getX() + 7, getY() - 7, getX() + 7, getY() + 7, getX(),
    getY() + 3, getX(), getY() - 3 };
  double[] result = new double[12];
  AffineTransform transform =
    AffineTransform.getQuadrantRotateInstance(
      getDirection() - 1, getX(), getY());
  transform.transform(values, 0, result, 0, 6);
  getGraphics().drawLine((int) result[0], (int) result[1],
    (int) result[2], (int) result[3]);
  getGraphics().drawLine((int) result[4], (int) result[5],
    (int) result[6], (int) result[7]);
  getGraphics().drawLine((int) result[8], (int) result[9],
    (int) result[10], (int) result[11]);
}
```

The "draw" method for the Helicopter class is similar but has more coordinates.

```
@Override
public void draw(Color col)
{
// set the drawing color
  getGraphics().setColor(col);
// draw the plane in the current position.
// for each direction the shape will be rotated.
  double[] values = { getX(), getY(), getX() + 10, getY(),
    getX(), getY(), getX(), getY() - 2, getX() + 2,
    getY() - 4, getX() + 10, getY() + 4, getX() + 2,
```

```
    getY() + 4, getX() + 10, getY() - 4 };
double[] result = new double[16];
AffineTransform transform =
  AffineTransform.getQuadrantRotateInstance(
    getDirection() - 1, getX(), getY());
  transform.transform(values, 0, result, 0, 8);
  getGraphics().drawLine((int) result[0],
    (int) result[1],(int) result[2], (int) result[3]);
  getGraphics().drawLine((int) result[4],
    (int) result[5],(int) result[6], (int) result[7]);
  getGraphics().drawLine((int) result[8],
    (int) result[9],(int) result[10], (int) result[11]);
  getGraphics().drawLine((int) result[12],
    (int) result[13],(int) result[14], (int) result[15]);
}
```

The FlyingMachine class represents an object with a single thread of control within it. We can write a multithreaded program by creating several of these objects. The RadarPanel class creates four FlyingMachine subclass objects, initializing them to travel in four different directions and at four different speeds:

```
new Airplane(100, 100, 1, 2, this);
new Airplane(400, 150, 2, 1, this);
new Helicopter(200, 50, 3, 4, this);
new Helicopter(300, 350, 4, 1, this);
```

As soon as their constructors are called, each of the FlyingMachines starts its own thread. Note that we create the objects in the "paint" method of Radar Panel rather than in a constructor. This is because the component ("this") passed to the constructor of each FlyingMachine is not available until after the RadarPanel's own constructor has executed. A boolean field called "started" is used to check if we are visiting the "paint" method for the first time:

```
if(!started)
```

This is necessary because otherwise every time "paint" is called (by resizing or minimizing and maximizing the window), we would create four new FlyingMachines. The airplanes and helicopters run their threads until they reach the boundaries of the window when they will stop. This is the complete RadarPanel class:

```
package com.foundjava.chapter16;

import java.awt.Graphics;
import javax.swing.JPanel;
```

```
// to create a drawing area for the window,
// we create a subclass of JPanel
class RadarPanel extends JPanel
{
  private boolean started = false;

// the 'paint' method draws the screen
  @Override
  public void paint(Graphics g)
  {
    if (!started)
    {
// create some flying objects, each running in a different
// direction and at a different speed
      new Airplane(100, 100, 1, 2, this);
      new Airplane(400, 150, 2, 1, this);
      new Helicopter(200, 50, 3, 4, this);
      new Helicopter(300, 350, 4, 1, this);
      started = true;
    }
  }
}
```

The Radar class creates a Swing JFrame, adds the RadarPanel to it, configures the frame and makes it visible.

```
package com.foundjava.chapter16;

import javax.swing.JFrame;

public class Radar extends JFrame
{
  public static void main(String[] args)
  {
    JFrame radarWindow = new JFrame();
    RadarPanel panel = new RadarPanel();
    radarWindow.add(panel);
    radarWindow.setTitle("Air Traffic Radar");
    radarWindow.setBounds(0, 0, 500, 400);
    radarWindow.setDefaultCloseOperation
      (JFrame.EXIT_ON_CLOSE);
    radarWindow.setVisible(true);
  }
```

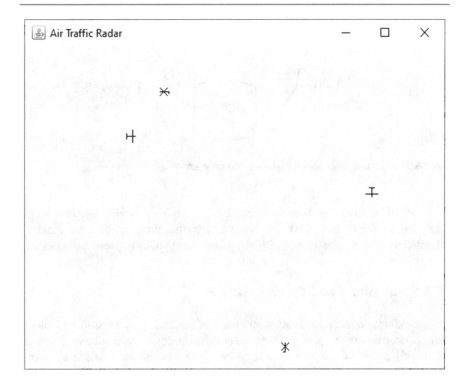

Fig. 16.4   Representations or aircraft running in different threads on the RadarPanel

Figure 16.4 shows the RadarPanel in a JFrame soon after the threads have begun to run.

16.5   Synchronizing Threads

Although we have seen several examples that used multiple threads running at the same time, we have not so far attempted to coordinate the activities of these different threads. Multithreading becomes more useful when we run multiple threads that can work together, rather than only working independently. This can, however, begin to get complex. With multithreaded code we often need to control multiple access to shared parts of the system. Figure 16.5 shows the type of problem that often arises in multithreaded programs. We have two threads, each trying to access the same resource concurrently (in this case a Deque). In cases like this, we need to make sure that both threads can manipulate the top of the queue without getting in each other's way.

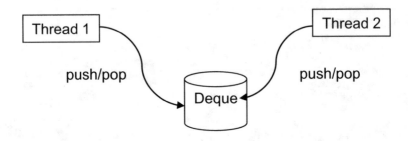

Fig. 16.5 Multiple threads needing access to the same resource

Fortunately, Java has been developed from the very beginning with multi-threading in mind, and there are some keywords, along with some methods inherited by all Java classes from Object, that support multiple thread management.

16.5.1 Monitors and Synchronization

Where multiple threads are used, some parts of the code may need to be isolated from concurrent thread access. Some mechanism needs to be available to ensure that multiple threads can take turns to access these parts of the code one at a time, blocking threads and notifying them when the resource becomes available. A section of code that can do this is known as a monitor. A monitor represents a shared resource that needs to be thread safe (i.e. protected from access by multiple concurrent threads). The "synchronized" keyword can be used to indicate code that needs to be single threaded. Any method can be synchronized.

```
public synchronized double[] getResults()
```

In Java, any object with one or more synchronized methods is a monitor. Alternatively, we can simply mark a block of code as synchronized, rather than a complete method. A monitor object (which can be "this") needs to be passed as an argument to the block.

```
synchronized(object)
{
  // code here
}
```

16.5.2 "wait", "notify" and "notifyAll"

All Java objects are thread aware, and inherit the "wait", "notify" and "notifyAll" methods from the Object class. In synchronized code, "wait" and "notify" can be

Table 16.1 Overloaded versions of the "wait" method from the Object class

Wait method	Effect
`void wait()`	Causes the current thread to wait until another thread notifies it to be able to run again
`void wait(long timeout)`	Like wait, but has a millisecond time-out
`void wait(long timeout, int nanos)`	Like wait, but has a nanosecond time-out added to the millisecond time-out

used to manage multiple thread access. "wait" methods block threads, and a waiting object can be released by "notify" methods. These methods can only be used inside synchronized code. If you try to use them in non-synchronized code you will get an IllegalMonitorStateException. There are three overloaded versions of the "wait" method (Table 16.1).

"wait" methods should always be called in a loop, to ensure that when the thread is ready to run, the correct conditions are in place. If they are not, it must wait again.

If threads are waiting, then they need to be notified when it may be possible for them to resume running. There are two methods that allow a monitor to notify waiting threads.

```
void notify()
```

Wakes up a single thread that is waiting on this object's monitor.

```
void notifyAll()
```

Wakes up all threads that are waiting on this object's monitor.

If "notifyAll" is called, it will be up to the thread scheduler in the Java runtime to decide which thread gets to run.

16.6 Synchronized Code Example

In the next example, we demonstrate how two separate threads can be synchronized so that one will wait to receive data from the other when it is notified that the data is ready. There are two classes in this example, Analyzer and Sensor, both of which are subclasses of Thread. The Sensor simulates a device that makes occasional readings from the environment (we simulate this in the class by generating random numbers). The Analyzer needs to retrieve data from the sensor once it has generated 10 readings (Fig. 16.6). Using thread synchronization in the Sensor class, we can make the Analyzer wait until 10 results are available, then notify it.

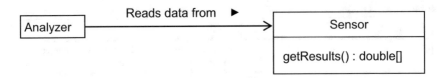

Fig. 16.6 Two threads that need to be synchronized so that one can receive data from the other

16.6.1   The Sensor Class

The Sensor contains an array that will fill up with ten readings before the data is made available to the Analyzer. Threads may cache object fields for optimization. However, if an object field is cached and accessed by multiple threads, this may leave the object in an inconsistent state. To avoid this, you can mark fields as "volatile", which prevents the threads from caching this field. The array in the Sensor class is therefore marked as "volatile".

```
private volatile double[] results = new double[10];
```

The Sensor also has an "index" field which is used to keep track of the current number of readings. Since this is not shared with other threads it does not need to be volatile.

```
private int index = 0;
```

In the synchronized "getResults" method, we force other threads to wait until there are enough results.

```
public synchronized double[] getResults()
{
    if (!ready) {
        try {
            wait();
        } catch (InterruptedException e) {
            e.printStackTrace();
        }
    }
    return results;
}
```

In the other synchronized method, "addResults", the waiting thread is notified as soon as the number of results equals ten. This method is called each time a result is added to the array.

```
public synchronized void addResult(double result)
{
  results[index] = result;
  if (index == MAX_READINGS - 1)
  {
    ready = true;
    notify();
    ready = false;
    index = 0;
  }
  else
  {
    index++;
  }
}
```

This is the complete Sensor class. The "run" method contains an endless loop that generates a random number every 200 ms. This is added to the array in the "addResult" method, which checks the current number of results to see if waiting threads should be notified.

```
package com.foundjava.chapter16;

public class Sensor extends Thread
{
  public static final int MAX_READINGS = 10;
  private volatile double[] results =
    new double[MAX_READINGS];
  private volatile int index = 0;
  private boolean ready = false;

  public synchronized double[] getResults()
  {
    if (!ready)
    {
      try
      {
```

```
      wait();
    }
    catch (InterruptedException e)
    {
      e.printStackTrace();
    }
  }
  return results;
}

public synchronized void addResult(double result)
{
  results[index] = result;
  if (index == MAX_READINGS - 1)
  {
    ready = true;
    notify();
    double myresult = 0.0;
    for (int i = 0; i < results.length; i++)
    {
      myresult += results[i];
    }
    System.out.println("Sensor Result: " + myresult);
    ready = false;
    index = 0;
  }
  else
  {
    index++;
  }
}

public void run()
{
  while (true)
  {
    try
    {
      Thread.sleep(200);
    }
    catch (InterruptedException e)
    {
      e.printStackTrace();
    }
```

```
    addResult(Math.round(Math.random() * 10));
  }
 }
}
```

16.6.2   The Analyzer Class

The Analyzer is the waiting Thread. In its constructor it creates an instance of the Sensor class and starts it running. The "run" method calls the "getResults" method of the Sensor, which will make it wait until it is notified. Once the method returns, the 10 values are added together to produce a result.

```
package com.foundjava.chapter16;

public class Analyzer extends Thread
{
  private Sensor dataSource;

  public Analyzer(Sensor sensor)
  {
    dataSource = sensor;
    dataSource.start();
  }

  public void run()
  {
    while (true)
    {
      double[] data = dataSource.getResults();
      double result = 0.0;
      for (int i = 0; i < data.length; i++)
      {
        result += data[i];
      }
      System.out.println("Result: " + result);
    }
  }
```

```
public static void main(String[] args)
{
  Analyzer sensorDataAnalyzer = new Analyzer(new Sensor());
  sensorDataAnalyzer.start();
}
}
```

The output will be a series of values that get printed to the console every couple of seconds, something like the following. The program will only end if you terminate it (in Eclipse you can do this by clicking on the red square on the tool bar of the output console tab).

```
Result: 57.0
Result: 42.0
Result: 57.0
Result: 55.0
Result: 60.0
Result: 42.0
Result: 44.0
Result: 46.0
```

Exercise 16.3

- Create three classes; Buffer, DataSource and Display.
  - A Buffer object can only store one integer at a time.
  - A DataSource object should start a thread that counts from zero and stores each value in a Buffer object.
  - A Display object should create a thread that keeps reading values from the Buffer object and printing them on the console.
- Manage the thread access so that each number is displayed on the console only once.
- The Buffer class needs to have some synchronized code that makes the DataSource and Display objects wait until their threads can have access, and then notifies them when it is ready.

16.7   Concurrent Collections

The "java.util.concurrent" package contains several collection classes that are designed to be accessed by multiple threads. The collection classes we looked at in Chap. 12 (apart from the legacy classes such as Vector) are not synchronized (single threaded) so would allow access to multiple threads. This is not always ideal, so we might wish to control multithreaded access to our collections. We can manually write code to synchronize a collection so that it only allows one thread at a time, but synchronized collections prevent concurrent access via a single lock, which gives poor scalability. Where multiple threads are expected to access a collection object, it is normally preferable to use one of the concurrent collection classes. A concurrent collection is thread-safe, but not governed by a single exclusion lock. One example of a concurrent collection class from the java.util.concurrent package is ConcurrentLinkedQueue, which is an efficient, scalable, thread-safe, non-blocking first-in-first-out (FIFO) queue. A more interesting class is the ArrayBlockingQueue, which implements the BlockingQueue interface, representing a fixed size queue where threads may be blocked if, for example, they try to add elements when the queue is full (the capacity of the queue is fixed by a constructor argument). The BlockingQueue interface provides four sets of methods that give you options about what policy you want to apply to the generic operation of inserting, removing or examining queue elements. The four policies, if an operation cannot be performed immediately, are as follows:

1. An exception is thrown.
2. A special value is returned (this may be either "null" or "false", depending on the operation).
3. The current thread is blocked indefinitely.
4. The current thread is blocked but only up to given maximum time limit.

Table 16.2 shows the methods that are used to insert, remove or examine elements, depending on which policy you want to follow.

In cases where you want to manage concurrent thread access to data structures, it is preferable to use classes from the java.util.concurrent package rather than coding the thread management code yourself.

Table 16.2 The methods of the BlockingQueue interface that implement different blocking policies

Action	Throws exception	Special value	Blocks	Times out
Insert	add()	offer(E)	put(E)	offer(E, time, unit)
Remove	remove()	poll()	take()	poll(time, unit)
Examine	element()	peek()	not applicable	

16.8   Summary

In this chapter we have looked at threads, using both inheritance from the Thread class, and implementing the Runnable interface. We saw the various states that a thread can be in during its lifetime (ready, running, non-runnable and dead). Code examples illustrated how multiple threads can be run concurrently, and how they can be put to sleep for certain periods of time. We saw how different priorities can be assigned to separate threads, and how to make threads less selfish by asking them to yield to other threads. Syntax differences between inheriting from the Thread class and implementing the Runnable interface were explained. A code example showed applying the Runnable interface with graphical objects to visualize how multiple threads can operate concurrently within an inheritance hierarchy. We saw how the Object class provides some methods; "wait", "notify" and "notifyAll", which enable threads to avoid concurrent access to certain parts of code, known as "monitors", marked by the "synchronized" keyword. We concluded the chapter with a brief introduction to the concurrent collections in the "java.util.concurrent" package.

Building GUIs with the JFC Swing Library

17

Graphical User Interface (GUI) libraries have many common characteristics. They provide interaction through a WIMP (Windows Icons Menus and Pointers) interface, with WYSIWYG (what you see is what you get) presentation. They enable a common look and feel across different applications, making it easy for users to switch between them and reducing the learning time for a new application that uses the same GUI library. Window appearance, including control components and menu placement, is consistent across multiple programs.

GUI programming has in the past been a complex task, but object-oriented languages have made coding easier because visual UI components have corresponding objects. Figure 17.1 shows how the visual components of a simple login window are represented directly by classes from the Java Swing library in the underlying code. There are three text labels (using the JLabel class), two text fields (using the JTextField class) and three buttons (using the JButton class). The UML diagram shows that the relationships between the underlying objects closely reflect the physical structure of the visual components.

Java has three generations of UI framework; the Abstract Windowing Toolkit (AWT), which was a simple general-purpose multi-platform windowing library introduced with the first version of Java, Swing, which was developed as a much more sophisticated code-based UI framework, and JavaFX, which was originally intended to replace Swing with a framework that could use either code-based or XML configuration.

The AWT was a very basic set of GUI components that enabled the creation of rather crude user interfaces in Java. It was written in only six weeks using the simplest possible techniques, building on the existing native windowing systems of the various platforms that the Java VM ran on, and wrapping them in a thin layer of Java. This means that although it did work across different platforms, it was not very consistent, and worked on a "lowest common denominator" basis; it included only those components that existed in a similar fashion on all platforms.

As soon as developers began using Java, they found that the AWT was not sufficient for commercial systems, and other GUI libraries began to appear on the

© Springer Nature Switzerland AG 2020
D. Parsons, *Foundational Java*, Texts in Computer Science,
https://doi.org/10.1007/978-3-030-54518-5_17

Fig. 17.1 The mapping between visual components and underlying objects

market. To avoid the market fragmenting into a range of nonstandard Java GUI libraries, Sun developed the Java Foundation Classes (JFC), a comprehensive set of cross-platform GUI components and services including graphical libraries, accessibility and drag and drop support, first introduced with version 1.2 of the JDK. A core part of the JFC was the "Swing" class library. This was based on one of the commercial Java libraries, the Internet Foundation Classes (IFC) from Netscape, and provided a fully featured set of classes for building Java graphical interfaces.

Although Swing provides far more functionality than the AWT, it is not an entirely separate library, in fact it is important to understand much of the AWT in order to write Swing programs. Some parts of the AWT framework have been updated to be used as part of Swing: some high-level classes, the event model and some utility classes. Swing components also ultimately inherit from core AWT components. Therefore, we need to learn some aspects of the AWT as well as Swing.

JavaFX was first released in 2008 with the intention to provide a more flexible and platform agnostic UI tool that could provide rich clients across multiple platforms, including mobile. However, the trajectory of Java as a language has moved away from developing new rich client applications, with most Java installations running as back end processing. As a result, JavaFX has never really gained a high profile, though it continues to be developed and used for new Java UI development. Given that there is still a large installed base of Swing UI applications in use, it is useful for Java developers to know something about both frameworks. This chapter focuses on Swing.

17.1   Components, Containers and Frames

In Swing, components are the objects that allow the user to interact with a graphical user interface. These include several different "controls" (buttons, menus, text fields, etc.) A container is a component that can contain other components. Examples of containers include the JFrame (which displays a window with title bar, frame and window control buttons) and the JPanel (which is just an area without

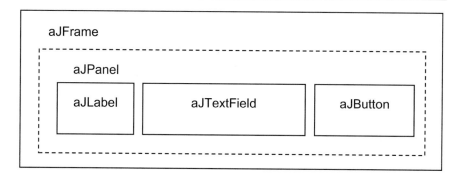

Fig. 17.2 Components and containers in parent-child relationships

any frame or buttons). Most of the Swing components have names beginning with "J" to differentiate them from older AWT components with similar names. For example, AWT has a "Button" class whereas Swing has a "JButton".

Containers hold one or more components in parent-child relationships. In Fig. 17.2, "aJPanel" is the parent (container) of "aJLabel", "aJTextField" and "aJButton". "aJFrame" is the parent of "aJPanel" and "aJFrame" has no parent (a frame is a top-level component that cannot be contained).

Figure 17.3 shows an inheritance hierarchy of some of the more fundamental classes in the UI libraries. AWT classes are in the java.awt package, and Swing classes in the javax.swing package. Both packages appear in the "java.desktop" module. The Swing package name is a java extension package ("javax") rather than a core package ("java"). Component (an abstract class) and Container (a Component that can contain other Components) are at the top of hierarchy. Swing components inherit from JComponent which itself is a subclass of Container. Swing dialogs and frames inherit from their AWT equivalents.

Swing components inherit some basic behavior from their superclasses. For example, components can be added to and removed from containers using the "add" and "remove" methods. Containers also have an optional layout manager, which controls the size and location of child components. There will be a default layout manager applied, which will vary depending on the type of container, but this can be changed (or removed) using the "setLayout" method.

17.2 Creating a Main Window Frame

Most graphical user interfaces are based on a main window *frame* within which other objects appear. In Swing, a frame is represented by the "javax.swing.JFrame" class. In the first example program, we create a main application window containing no other components. We will need to import the JFrame class from the javax.swing

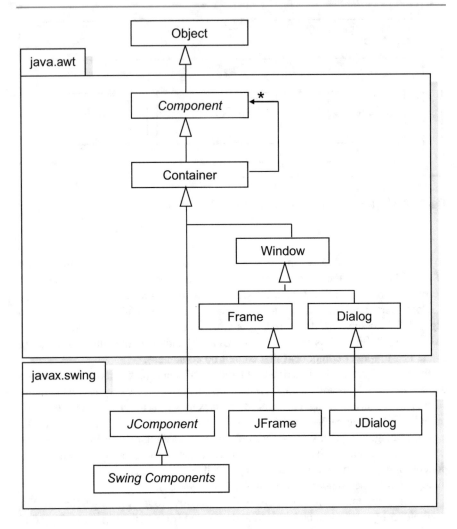

Fig. 17.3 An inheritance hierarchy of some of the fundamental AWT and Swing component and container classes

package, but no other Swing classes. To configure and show this frame, there are several methods called in the "main" method. We saw some of this code in Chaps. 8 and 16, but this time we will explain things in more detail.

17.2.1 Setting the JFrame's Title

We can pass the frame's title to the constructor, as in this example:

```
JFrame frame = new JFrame("My JFrame");
```

Or we can set it separately using the "setTitle" method.

```
frame.setTitle("My JFrame");
```

17.2.2 Selecting the JFrame's Closing Behavior

The setDefaultCloseOperation method defines what to do when the user attempts to close the frame. The javax.swing.WindowConstants interface specifies four options, also available via the JFrame class, which implements this interface. These options are:

DO_NOTHING_ON_CLOSE	
HIDE_ON_CLOSE	(the default)
DISPOSE_ON_CLOSE	(the best option unless applied to the main frame)
EXIT_ON_CLOSE	(implemented directly in JFrame)

If you do not set the close operation and use the default (HIDE_ON_CLOSE), closing the window leaves it running but invisible. This example uses EXIT_ON_CLOSE.

```
frame.setDefaultCloseOperation(JFrame.EXIT_ON_CLOSE);
```

This close operation should only be used on a main application window, since it will end the whole application. Any other windows that may appear within the application should be set to use DISPOSE_ON_CLOSE.

17.2.3 Sizing the JFrame

The "setBounds" method sets the initial position and dimensions of the frame so that when it appears it is not just a title bar and buttons. The first two parameters specify the top left-hand corner position of the JFrame, where the top left-hand corner of the screen is 0,0 (so setting these parameters to zero means that the frame will appear in the top left-hand corner of the screen). The other parameters define the initial width and height of the frame (in pixels), respectively.

```
frame.setBounds(0, 0, 500, 200);
```

An alternative option to setting the initial size of a frame is to call the "pack" method, which will size the frame to fit the components inside it.

```
frame.pack();
```

17.2.4   Showing the JFrame

The "setVisible" method takes a boolean parameter that can show or hide the frame. Passing it "true" will make the frame visible.

```
frame.setVisible(true);
```

Here is the complete example.

```
package com.foundjava.chapter17;
import javax.swing.JFrame;

public class SwingFrame
{
  public static void main(String[] args)
  {
    JFrame frame = new JFrame("My JFrame");
    frame.setDefaultCloseOperation(JFrame.EXIT_ON_CLOSE);
    frame.setBounds(0, 0, 500, 200); // or frame.pack();
    frame.setVisible(true);
  }
}
```

Figure 17.4 shows what the JFrame looks like when the class is run. It can be moved, resized, minimized, maximized and closed.

Fig. 17.4 The sized JFrame created by running the Swing Frame class

17.3 Swing Component Classes

A window on its own is of little use, so we need to add components to it to provide some functionality. These are some of the commonly used components.

- JLabel
- JTextField (single line of text that can be edited)
- JTextArea class (javax.swing) (multiple lines of text that can be edited)
- JButton
- JCheckbox (individual)
- JRadioButton (usually as part of a ButtonGroup)
- JComboBox

Figure 17.5 shows some of the Swing components in their hierarchy as subclasses of "JComponent". There are many other classes not included here but all share the fields and methods inherited from JComponent (and from Component, further up the hierarchy).

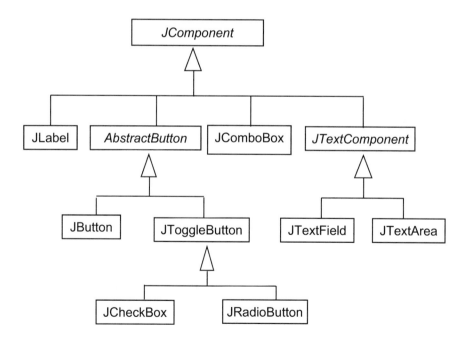

Fig. 17.5 Some of the Swing component classes that inherit from JComponent

17.3.1   The JLabel Class

JLabels are very simple because they are just text labels, mostly used to assist the readability of a GUI. Although an empty label can be constructed, a more commonly used form of the constructor sets the text of the label:

```
JLabel textLabel = new JLabel("Component label");
```

The default alignment for the text is against the leading edge (i.e. left aligned). Another version of the constructor can set the alignment using a second parameter. A set of Swing alignment values are defined as public static fields of the SwingConstants interface. Those normally used with JLabels are LEFT, RIGHT or CENTER. For example, to create a centered label we would pass CENTER as the second parameter:

```
JLabel centeredLabel =
    new JLabel("I am a label", SwingConstants.CENTER);
```

17.3.2   Adding Components to a Frame

Once created, component objects need to be added to the frame. This can be done in a "main" method, but this approach will not be very useful as our frames begin to require more functionality. Therefore we will need to start creating subclasses of JFrame with their own application specific behaviors.

Once we have created a subclass of JFrame, we can add components to it, usually in the constructor, though they can also be added and removed dynamically in other methods. Components are added to Containers using the "add" method, which takes as its parameter any Component object. For example, this code creates a label and adds it to the parent frame

```
JLabel myLabel = new JLabel ("Hello");
add(myLabel);
```

Note
The "add" method sometimes takes a slightly different form, depending on the layout manager being used to format the components on the screen.

Components are not, in fact, added directly to the JFrame. Rather, they are added to its content pane. A JFrame contains a JRootPane which is the content pane of the frame. This can be accessed using the "getContentPane" method, and we can add components to the content pane.

```
JFrame frame = new JFrame();
Container container = frame.getContentPane();
container.add(new JLabel("Hello"));
```

However, there are also convenience methods on the JFrame itself that enable you to add components via the JFrame without having to explicitly refer to the content pane.

```
frame.add(new JLabel("Hello"));
```

Actually, it is a bit more complex than this in terms of the various components that make up a JFrame, but we do not need to look any deeper at this stage. The following class, LabelFrame, is a subclass of JFrame that has a single JLabel added to it in the constructor. The "main" method displays the LabelFrame.

```
package com.foundjava.chapter17;

import javax.swing.JFrame;
import javax.swing.JLabel;
import static javax.swing.SwingConstants.*;

public class LabelFrame extends JFrame
{
  private JLabel label;

  public LabelFrame(String title)
  {
    super(title);
    label = new JLabel("I am a label", CENTER) ;
    add(label);
  }
  public static void main(String[] args)
  {
    LabelFrame frame = new LabelFrame("Label Frame");
    frame.setDefaultCloseOperation(EXIT_ON_CLOSE);
    frame.pack();
    frame.setVisible(true);
  }
}
```

Figure 17.6 shows the frame as it appears when made visible, with the frame packed around the label.

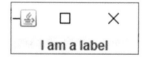

Fig. 17.6 A JLabel displayed in a JFrame

In this example we added a single label to a frame. If you try to add another label to the same frame using the "add" method, you will find that only the second label appears. This is because of the default layout manager used with frames. We will return to explain this is in a later section, however, for the next few examples, we will remove this layout manager to enable us to add components at specific locations within the frame.

Note
You will get the following warning from Eclipse on this class: "The serializable class LabelFrame does not declare a static final serialVersionUID field of type long". You will get this warning on many of the examples and exercises in this chapter. This is not important if you do not plan to Serialize objects of these classes. If you do want to Serialize them, then add a version number field like this (be sure to increment the version number if the class is changed).

```
private static final long serialVersionUID = 1L;
```

However, if you do not plan to Serialize any of these classes and just want the warning to go away, add the following annotation above any classes that give the warning:

```
@SuppressWarnings("serial")
```

Whenever you suppress a warning, add a comment above the line to explain why you are doing so.

17.3.3   Manually Positioning and Sizing Components

A JFrame object will have a default layout manager of the BorderLayout class. We will look at layout managers later, but for the moment we will use the methods of JComponent to manually position some components in a frame, To do this we first need to remove the default layout manager by passing "null" to the frame's "setLayout" method:

```
setLayout(null);
```

This allows us to add components without the layout manager positioning and sizing them automatically. The advantage of this is that we can precisely set the size and position of our components. The downside is that we lose the automatic resize behavior of layout managers. When you run the code from this example you will see that when the window resizes, the components maintain their size and position. First, however, we will look at some of the common methods of Component, and introduce a couple of new component types, the JTextField and the JButton.

17.3.4 Common Methods of Component and JComponent

All subclasses of Component inherit common methods. These include the following methods to control the position and/or size of a component.

```
public void setLocation(Point p)
public void setSize(Dimension d)
public void setSize(int width, int height)
public void setBounds(int x, int y, int width, int height)
public void setBounds(Rectangle r)
```

You will be familiar with the java.awt.Point class from previous chapters. The java.awt.Dimension class represents a rectangular area with a height and width (but does not specify a location). When positioning and sizing components, we can either perform these two tasks separately using "setLocation" and "setSize" or do both together using "setBounds". We have already used one version the "set-Bounds" method with a JFrame (which ultimately inherits from Component). As well as this version, which takes four integer parameters, there is another version that takes a java.awt.Rectangle as a parameter, which also sets the position, height and width.

Components can also be hidden or made visible using the "setVisible" method.

```
void setVisible(boolean)
```

and they can also be enabled or disabled.

```
void setEnabled(boolean)
```

Some methods of JComponent are unique to that class, and not present in the Component class. One example is the "setToolTip" method, which can be used to control what gets displayed when the mouse hovers over that component.

```
void setToolTip(String s)
```

There are many other methods, but we will start with an example that demonstrates a few of these. To make the example a bit more interesting we will introduce two more component types, the JTextField and the JButton.

17.3.5 The JTextField Class

A JTextField allows text to be typed in and edited. There is a default constructor with no parameters that will set the JTextField's initial width to zero columns.

```
JTextField textField = new JTextField();
```

An alternative constructor allows the number of text columns in the field to be specified, which is a better option when we start to use layout managers.

```
JTextField textField = new JTextField(20);
```

17.3.6 The JButton Class

JButtons are very simple objects because their only behavior is to be pressed. The JButton class has two constructors, one that creates a blank button and another one that creates a button with a text label. This, for example, creates a button with the label "Press Me!"

```
JButton button = new JButton("Press Me!");
```

17.3.6.1 Placing Components Using "SetBounds"

In the following example, a JLabel, a JTextField and a JButton are added to a frame, and have their position, width and height set using the "setBounds" method.

```
label.setBounds(10, 20, 300, 50);
textField.setBounds(110, 30, 200, 30);
  button.setBounds(110,70,100,30);
```

To demonstrate some of the other Component methods, the text field's tool tip is also set, and the button is disabled.

```
textField.setToolTipText("Enter some text here");
button.setEnabled(false);
```

Note that the button has no behavior associated with it in this example, so pressing it would not have any effect, even if it was enabled. This is the complete class:

```java
package com.foundjava.chapter17;

import javax.swing.JButton;
import javax.swing.JFrame;
import javax.swing.JLabel;
import javax.swing.JTextField;

public class NoLayout extends JFrame
{
  private JLabel label;
  private JTextField textField;
  private JButton button;

  public NoLayout()
  {
// turn off the default layout manager
    setLayout(null);
// create the components
    label = new JLabel("Enter some text");
    textField = new JTextField(20);
    textField.setToolTipText("Enter some text here");
    button = new JButton("Press Me!");
    button.setEnabled(false);
// add them to the window
    add(label);
    add(textField);

    add(button);
// manually position and size them
    label.setBounds(10, 20, 300, 50);
    textField.setBounds(110, 30, 200, 30);
    button.setBounds(110,70,100,30);
  }

  public static void main(String[] args)
  {
    NoLayout window = new NoLayout();
    window.setTitle("Manually Positioned Components");
    window.setBounds(200, 170, 500, 200);
    window.setVisible(true);
  }
}
```

Figure 17.7 shows the window in action. The button is disabled and the tool tip for the text field is currently visible.

Exercise 17.1

- Develop the previous example so that it becomes a login window, with one field to enter a username and another to enter a password.

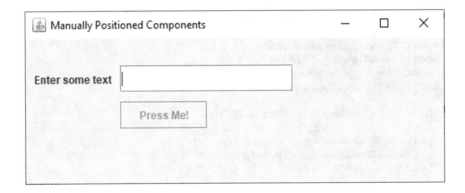

Fig. 17.7 Components manually positioned within a window

- The password entry field should be an object of the JPasswordField class, rather than a JTextField
- Provide appropriate labels for the fields
- Change the text on the button to "Log In", and position the components manually within the frame.
- Instead of using "setBounds", try using "setLocation" and "setSize" to place the components in the frame.

17.4   Colors, Fonts and Icons

When configuring components to be added to containers, we often want to make some changes to the default fonts and colors. Colors and Fonts can be used to configure Components using the following methods.

```
void setBackground(Color c)
void setForeground(Color c)
void setFont(Font f)
```

17.4.1   Setting Colors

The java.awt.Color class represents a Color object that can be passed to components to change their foreground and/or background colors. The java.awt.Font class provides the information needed to map the underlying characters of text data to the *glyphs* (shapes) that display them.

Thirteen standard colors are available through static final fields in the Color class (BLACK, BLUE, CYAN, DARKGRAY, GRAY, GREEN, LIGHTGRAY,

MAGENTA, ORANGE, PINK, RED, WHITE and YELLOW). For backward compatibility reasons these fields are specified in both upper and lower case so you can use either, for example,

```
Color.darkGray
```

Or

```
Color.DARK_GRAY
```

Since the usual naming convention for constants is to use upper case, the upper case versions are preferable. Other colors can be created by passing combinations of red, green and blue (RGB) values to a Color constructor method, with each value in the range 0–255.

```
new Color(n,n,n);
```

Color objects are immutable once created. The following code fragment shows the foreground and background colors of a JLabel being set, using two different ways of adding a Color: one using a standard constant and one using a Color object created using RGB values. The JLabel is an unusual component in that we cannot set the background without first setting the "opaque" property to "true". By default, labels are not opaque, so setting their background color has no visible effect.

```
JLabel label = new JLabel("Name:");
label.setOpaque(true);
label.setForeground(Color.darkGray);
label.setBackground(new Color(150, 210, 190));
```

Figure 17.8 shows the label in a frame, with its foreground and background colors set.

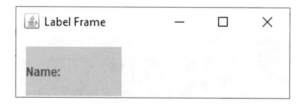

Fig. 17.8 A label with foreground and background colors set (the label has an opaque background)

17.4.2   Setting Fonts

The default text font was used by the components in our previous examples, but this can be changed using Font objects. A Font represents a character font that can be applied to text features of components. The Font constructor takes three parameters: the name of the font, the character style and the size. The font name can be either a logical name (portable generic font) or an actual font name available on the current system. The possible logical font names are Serif, SansSerif, Monospaced, Dialog, DialogInput and Symbol. Java maps logical font names to platform font families but the actual fonts will vary depending on the environment. You can get a String array of available font names from a GraphicsEnvironment object, using the "getAvailableFontFamilyNames" method. To get the GraphicsEnvironment object you use the static factory method "getLocalGraphicsEnvironment". This short example demonstrates the syntax:

```
package com.foundjava.chapter17;
import java.awt.GraphicsEnvironment;

public class ListFonts
{
  public static void main(String[] args)
  {
    GraphicsEnvironment env =
      GraphicsEnvironment.getLocalGraphicsEnvironment();
    String[] fontnames = env.getAvailableFontFamilyNames();
    System.out.println("Fonts available in this system:\n");
    for (int i = 0; i < fontnames.length; i++)
    {
      System.out.println(fontnames[i]);
    }
  }
}
```

You could get a very long list of fonts, which might begin something like this:

```
Fonts available in this system:

Agency FB
Algerian
Anonymous
Arial
Arial Black
Arial Narrow
Arial Rounded MT Bold
Bahnschrift
Baskerville Old Face
...etc.
```

17.4.3 Font Style and Size

The possible font styles, which can be passed as the second parameter to the Font constructor, are defined by the constants Font.BOLD, Font.ITALIC and Font. PLAIN. The BOLD and ITALIC styles can be combined using the "|" operator (i.e. Font.BOLD|Font.ITALIC). The third constructor parameter represents the font size in points. This example creates a 12-point, bold Helvetica font:

```
new Font("Helvetica", Font.BOLD, 12);
```

This example creates an italic sans serif font of size 20:

```
new Font("SansSerif", Font.ITALIC, 20);
```

This creates a 10 point, bold and italic Courier font:

```
new Font("Courier", Font.BOLD|Font.ITALIC, 10);
```

In this code fragment, a JTextField has both its Colors and its Font set

```
JTextField field = new JTextField();
field.setBackground(Color.BLACK);
field.setForeground(Color.WHITE);
field.setFont
    (new Font("Courier", Font.ITALIC | Font.BOLD, 20));
```

Figure 17.9 shows what this JTextField looks like when displayed in a frame.

Fig. 17.9 A JTextField with its Colors and Font changed from the default settings

17.4.4   Icons on Labels and Buttons

As well as being able to display text, the AbstractButton and JLabel classes both
have an "icon" property. This property is also inherited by subclasses of
AbstractButton such as JCheckBox, JMenuItem, JButton and JRadioButton. Text
can be oriented on any side of the image or on top of it, using the "horizon-
talTextPosition" and "verticalTextPosition" properties. Here, a JButton is constructed that takes an "ImageIcon" object as its second parameter, and the
ImageIcon is passed the name of an image file. For the image file to be found with
no file path added to the ImageIcon constructor the image needs to be added to the
root of the project in Eclipse. The position of the text on the button is set using
Swing constants and its font is also set.

```
JButton button = new JButton
    ("Foundational Java", new ImageIcon("Java.png"));
button.setHorizontalTextPosition(SwingConstants.CENTER);
button.setVerticalTextPosition(SwingConstants.TOP);
button.setFont(new Font("helvetica", Font.PLAIN ,40));
button.setForeground(Color.RED);
```

Figure 17.10 shows the button with its text and icon.

Fig. 17.10 A JButton with an ImageIcon added and its text (in 40-point Helvetica font)
positioned at the top and center of the button

Exercise 17.2
Change the Colors and Fonts of the components you added to a frame in Exercise
17.1. Include a change to the background color of the JFrame's content pane.

17.5   Some Additional Components

So far we have seen labels, text fields and buttons being added to containers. Here,
we will briefly introduce a few more of the commonly used controls. We also
introduce the JPanel and show how to change the look and feel of the UI.

17.5.1   JTextArea

A JTextArea is similar to a JTextField except that it can have multiple rows and
columns. There are several constructors, but probably the most useful allows you to
set the number of rows and columns:

```
public JTextArea(int rows, int columns)
```

JTextAreas are simple text entry components. More sophisticated multiline text
editing can be performed with JTextPanes or JEditorPanes.

17.5.2   CheckBoxes and Radio Buttons

Both JCheckBox and JRadioButton have the same superclass (JToggleButton) so
they can do pretty much the same things. However, there are general conventions
that a checkbox is a square box that can be checked or unchecked and is independent of any other checkboxes. In contrast, a radio button is a round box that
usually appears as part of a group of radio buttons, where only one of these can be
checked at any one time.

The idea of a radio button is that a radio can only be tuned to one
wavelength/station at a time, so it does not make sense for the user to be allowed to
check more than one of these buttons. In contrast, checkboxes are used where the
user can choose a selection of possibilities in combination. To stretch the radio
metaphor further, we might select any combination of "woofer", "subwoofer" and
"tweeter" simultaneously.

Checkboxes are created using the JCheckBox class. They are usually instantiated
with text labels as parameters, because it is not very helpful to have an unlabeled
checkbox:

```
JCheckBox check = new JCheckbox("Tick me");
```

We might use an alternative constructor that also initializes the state of the checkbox using a boolean argument after the text label. This example would initially check the box:

```
JCheckBox mailCheck = new JCheckBox("Don't send me stuff",
    true);
```

(Setting the argument value to "false" would create an unchecked box, which is the default).

To create radio buttons, we use the JRadioButton class. It is common practice to select one radio button in a group to be selected by default, for example:

```
JRadioButton radio1 = new JRadioButton("Radio 1", true);
JRadioButton radio2 = new JRadioButton("Radio 2");
```

However, as it stands these radio buttons are not in a group and will behave independently, like checkboxes. To put radio boxes into a group so that only one can be selected at any one time we must create a ButtonGroup object:

```
ButtonGroup buttons = new ButtonGroup();
```

Any number of radio buttons can then be added to this group.

```
buttons.add(radio1);
buttons.add(radio2);
```

Only one of the radio buttons added to this group can be selected at any one time.

17.5.3 JComboBox

A JComboBox displays a single item (the currently selected item) with a button that allows us to drop down a list of other items. The simplest JComboBox constructor takes no parameters:

```
JComboBox dropDownList = new JComboBox();
```

Once a JComboBox object has been created we could, for example, add Strings to it using the "addItem" method

```
dropDownList.addItem("cucumber");
```

Note
This is a rather simplistic approach and does not handle the problem of duplicate Strings being added—see the Javadoc for other options).

JComboBox objects are most often used to display drop down lists of String data; however, they can display other data if you provide your own implementation of the ListCellRenderer interface.

17.5.4 JSlider

This component is included as an example of one of the less standard Swing components. All the other components we have looked at so far (buttons, text fields, labels, etc.) are common across different UIs and were therefore included (in different forms) in the original AWT component library. However, Swing is not dependent on the native UI components so includes a much broader range of UI options. The JSlider represents a slider control that can be used for many different tasks, for example, controlling the volume of sound media or the zoom level of images. JSliders can be configured to be vertical or horizontal, can show labels or tick marks and be made to click to tick marks. The zero arguments constructor creates a horizontal slider with the range 0–100 and an initial value of 50.

```
JSlider sliderControl = new JSlider();
```

17.5.5 JPanel

A JPanel is a lightweight container that is used inside other containers. A common use for JPanels is to divide up the area of a frame using one of the layout managers and add different panels to different areas. Then each panel can host its own subset of components. We might, for example, create a JPanel, add components to it, and then add the JPanel to a JFrame:

```
JFrame frame = new JFrame();
JPanel panel = new JPanel();
JTextField textField = new JTextField(20);
JButton button = new JButton("Press me!");
panel.add(textField);
panel.add(button);
frame.add(panel);
```

17.6 Setting the Look and Feel

Swing emulates the look and feel of different platforms. The default is the "cross platform" look and feel. However, you can also set the look and feel to match the local system or apply the "motif" look and feel. You can change the setting dynamically by using the static "setLookAndFeel" method of the UIManager class, which requires as a parameter the class name of the look and feel. Two of these are supplied by built-in methods of the UIManager. The system look and feel can be retrieved from the "getSystemLookAndFeelClassName" method.

```
UIManager.setLookAndFeel
    (UIManager.getSystemLookAndFeelClassName());
```

Similarly, the default cross-platform look and feel class name can be returned from the "getCrossPlatformLookAndFeelClassName" method.

```
UIManager.setLookAndFeel
    (UIManager.getCrossPlatformLookAndFeelClassName());
```

Any other look and feel class will have to be explicitly specified by its class name, for example, the "motif" look and feel:

```
UIManager.setLookAndFeel
    ("com.sun.java.swing.plaf.motif.MotifLookAndFeel");
```

Rather a lot of exceptions can be thrown by this code, so there are several catch blocks required.

```
try {
  UIManager.setLookAndFeel
    ("com.sun.java.swing.plaf.motif.MotifLookAndFeel");
} catch (ClassNotFoundException e) {
  e.printStackTrace();
} catch (InstantiationException e) {
  e.printStackTrace();
} catch (IllegalAccessException e) {
  e.printStackTrace();
} catch (UnsupportedLookAndFeelException e) {
  e.printStackTrace();
}
```

If the look and feel is changed, then the "updateUI" method should be called on all Swing components to ensure that they update correctly. Figure 17.11 shows the example from Fig. 17.7 with the "motif" look and feel applied.

Exercise 17.3

- Add components of the JTextField and JComboBox classes to a frame.
- Add one JCheckBox and two JRadioButtons in a single ButtonGroup.Position the components using "setLocation" and "setSize" or "setBounds".
- Set the look and feel to use the system look and feel.

Exercise 17.4

Modify your solution to Exercise 17.3 so that your components are added to a JPanel rather than directly to a JFrame, then add the JPanel to the JFrame. Remove all your "setLocation" and/or "setBounds" methods. You should find that the components are automatically organized within the window. This is because of the layout manager used with JPanels, as explained in the next section. Note that if the text field does not have its size set then it is not given any space on the panel.

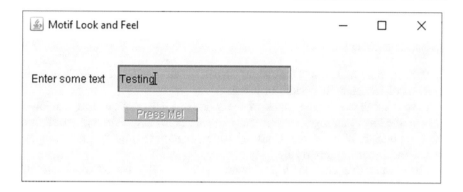

Fig. 17.11 Components set to use the "motif" look and feel

17.7   Layout Managers

As we have seen from previous examples, components can be placed manually within a frame using the "setBounds" method. We must size and position the components by hand, and they appear exactly how we place them. The problem with this approach is that the components do not resize. If the frame is resized, the components will stay the same size and in the same position. To some extent, we can control this by stopping the user from resizing the window, calling the JFrame's "setResizeable" method, which takes a boolean argument.

```
setResizable(false); // prevents a frame from being resized
```

However, there are other issues with manually positioning and sizing components; for example, if a window is displayed at a different resolution the components will not redraw properly. Java programs should be platform independent, but window components can be highly platform dependent; for example, font sizes can change with different video drivers. To make Java UIs more flexible and adaptive to their context, Swing containers can use layout managers to handle variable- sized components.

Layout managers are used to place the components according to some standard pattern, optionally with some additional constraints. Rather than having to position each component individually in a window, we can use a layout manager to apply a general pattern to the layout of the components. When a component is added to a container, the container uses the layout manager to position it within the container's visual space. The Component class provides methods to give the layout manager information about their minimum, preferred and maximum display sizes.

```
getMinimumSize()
getPreferredSize()
getMaximumSize()
```

Each of these returns a "Dimension" object, which specifies a component's size in terms of its height and width in pixels.

Layout managers handle much of the work of GUI creation. If a window is resized, the layout manager automatically calculates the new sizes and positions of the components. If any components are added or removed, the others are repositioned and resized appropriately.

There were five different layout managers in AWT, most of which are still commonly used.

- FlowLayout
- BorderLayout
- GridLayout
- CardLayout
- GridBagLayout

Many more have been added with, and since, Swing, including

- BoxLayout
- ScrollPaneLayout
- ViewportLayout
- SpringLayout

In this section we will introduce the two layout managers that are used by default by JFrames and JPanels the BorderLayout and the FlowLayout, and another simple layout manager, the GridLayout.

17.7.1 BorderLayout

The BorderLayout is the default layout manager for a JFrame's content pane and arranges components along each edge of the container, laying out up to four components at the points of the compass (North, South, East, West) with a fifth component residing in the center. The locations of these areas are indicated by static final fields of the BorderLayout class called NORTH, SOUTH, EAST, WEST and CENTER. Components are resized according to the pattern, with any extra space given to the CENTER component. You cannot have more than five components added to a BorderLayout, but you can have fewer. The other components will fill the available space.

When adding components to a BorderLayout, the second parameter to the "add" method is used to specify which of the five areas of the layout manager is to be used to host the component, for example,

```
frame.add(new JButton("North"), BorderLayout.NORTH);
```

Note

Using the standard "add" method without a second parameter always adds the component to the center of a BorderLayout manager.

In the following example, five buttons are added to a JFrame, positioning them in the five areas of the layout manager.

```
JFrame frame = new JFrame();
// Use add(Component, Object) method instead of add(Component)
frame.add(new JButton("North"), BorderLayout.NORTH);
frame.add(new JButton("South"), BorderLayout.SOUTH);
frame.add(new JButton("Center"), BorderLayout.CENTER);
frame.add(new JButton("East"), BorderLayout.EAST);
frame.add(new JButton("West"), BorderLayout.WEST);
frame.pack();
frame.setDefaultCloseOperation(JFrame.EXIT_ON_CLOSE);
frame.setVisible(true);
```

Figure 17.12 shows the buttons in the frame.

Resizing the frame will cause the components to also resize, with most of the additional space being taken up by the center component (Fig. 17.13).

17.7.1.1 BorderLayout Constraints

By default, the components in a BorderLayout have no spacing between them. This can be configured if required using additional parameters to the layout manager constructor. This means that the layout manager must be explicitly constructed and set to override the default settings. The first parameter represents the horizontal gap, the second the vertical gap (these can also be set after the layout manager has been constructed, using the "setHgap" and "setVgap" methods).

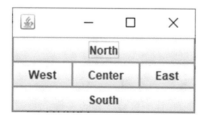

Fig. 17.12 The buttons in the frame packed to their minimum sizes

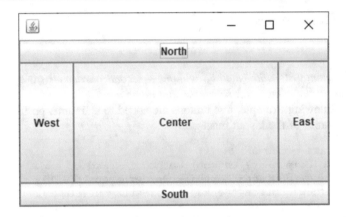

Fig. 17.13 The buttons in the frame automatically resized by the layout manager as the JFrame is enlarged

To apply a non-default BorderLayout to a JFrame we need to call the "setLayout" method, along with the constructor. This example sets a BorderLayout with a horizontal gap of 5 pixels and a vertical gap of 10 pixels:

```
setLayout(new BorderLayout(5, 10));
```

The following example shows a JFrame subclass that has its BorderLayout explicitly set, with horizontal and vertical gaps between components. Components are then added to each of the five regions of the layout. These components are two radio buttons in a button group, two buttons, and a text field that has its "editable" property set to false, so that it acts more like a label (but with a different default appearance).

```
package com.foundjava.chapter17;

import java.awt.BorderLayout;
import javax.swing.ButtonGroup;
import javax.swing.JButton;
import javax.swing.JFrame;
import javax.swing.JRadioButton;
import javax.swing.JTextField;

public class BorderLayoutWindow extends JFrame
{
  public BorderLayoutWindow()
  {
    setLayout(new BorderLayout(5,10));
    JTextField textField = new JTextField("Now Playing....",
30);
    textField.setEditable(false);
    JButton onButton = new JButton("On");
    JButton offButton = new JButton("Off");


    ButtonGroup radioButtons = new ButtonGroup();
    JRadioButton shuffle = new JRadioButton("Shuffle", true);
    JRadioButton continuous = new JRadioButton("Continuous");
    radioButtons.add(shuffle);
    radioButtons.add(continuous);
 // add all the components to the window
    add(BorderLayout.CENTER, textField);
    add(BorderLayout.NORTH, shuffle);
    add(BorderLayout.WEST, onButton);
    add(BorderLayout.EAST, offButton);
    add(BorderLayout.SOUTH, continuous);
  }

  public static void main(String[] args)
  {
    BorderLayoutWindow window = new BorderLayoutWindow();
    window.setTitle("Border Layout Window");
    window.pack();
    window.setVisible(true);
  }
}
```

Figure 17.14 shows the resulting window, with spacing between the components.

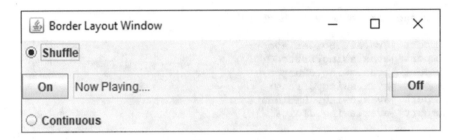

Fig. 17.14 Components added to a BorderLayout with horizontal and vertical spacing applied

17.7.2 FlowLayout

The simplest layout manager is the FlowLayout, which lays the components out like text; left to right, wrapping onto the next line where necessary. Like text, the layout can be left, right or center justified. By default, the FlowLayout will use center alignment, with horizontal and vertical gaps of five pixels. Components are given their preferred size and are not resized, just rearranged if the frame changes.

The FlowLayout is the default layout manager for JPanels. In the following examples we are going to use a subclass of JPanel to contain our components. Unlike the BorderLayout, we are not constrained to five regions, so more than five components are added to the MusicPlayerPanel in this example: a label, a text field, two buttons, a checkbox, two radio buttons and an instance of the JSlider class. When the panel is displayed in a frame, the components will appear in the sequence in which they were added, ordered left to right and top to bottom within the panel.

```
package com.foundjava.chapter17;
import javax.swing.ButtonGroup;
import javax.swing.JButton;
import javax.swing.JCheckBox;
import javax.swing.JLabel;
import javax.swing.JPanel;
import javax.swing.JRadioButton;
import javax.swing.JSlider;
import javax.swing.JTextField;

public class MusicPlayerPanel extends JPanel
{
  public MusicPlayerPanel()
  {
    JLabel textLabel = new JLabel("Volume");
    JTextField textField = new JTextField
      ("Now Playing....", 30);
    textField.setEditable(false);
    JSlider volume = new JSlider();
    JButton onButton = new JButton("On");
    JButton offButton = new JButton("Off");
    JCheckBox lockCheck = new JCheckBox("Lock");
    ButtonGroup radioButtons = new ButtonGroup();
    JRadioButton shuffle = new JRadioButton("Shuffle", true);
    JRadioButton continuous = new JRadioButton("Continuous");
    radioButtons.add(shuffle);
    radioButtons.add(continuous);

        // add all the components to the panel
            add(textField);
            add(lockCheck);
            add(onButton);

    add(offButton);
    add(shuffle);
    add(continuous);
    add(textLabel);
    add(volume);
  }
}
```

17.7.2.1 Adding a FlowLayout JPanel to a JFrame

It may seem from previous examples that the BorderLayout is too restrictive to be of much use, since it only has five regions that can contain components. However, any of these regions can contain panels, since JPanel is a subclass of JComponent. In the next example, we add a MusicPlayerPanel to a JFrame (the "add" method will add the panel to the central region of the layout).

```
MusicPlayerPanel playerPanel = new MusicPlayerPanel();
add(playerPanel);
```

Because MusicPlayerPanel is a subclass of JPanel, its default layout manager is of course a FlowLayout. Adding the panel to frame means that we are adding a component with a FlowLayout to one region of a BorderLayout.

Although in this example we will only add one panel to one region of the layout, other components or panels can be added to any or all of the remaining regions of the BorderLayout. In the next chapter we will use this technique to combine multiple panels together in the same frame.

In the following example, an instance of the MusicPlayerPanel is created in a frame's constructor, then added to the frame's content pane.

```
package com.foundava.chapter17;
import javax.swing.JFrame;

public class FlowLayoutWindow extends JFrame
{
  public FlowLayoutWindow()
  {
    MusicPlayerPanel playerPanel = new MusicPlayerPanel();
    add(playerPanel);
  }

  public static void main(String[] args)


  {
    FlowLayoutWindow window = new FlowLayoutWindow();
    window.setTitle("FlowLayout example");
    window.setBounds(0, 0, 520, 130);
    window.setDefaultCloseOperation(JFrame.EXIT_ON_CLOSE);
    window.setVisible(true);
  }
}
```

The output is shown in Fig. 17.15.

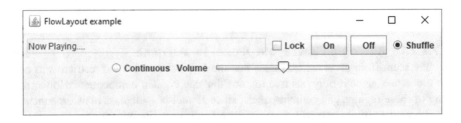

Fig. 17.15 Components in a FlowLayout with the default alignment (center aligned)

17.7.3   FlowLayout Constraints

As with theBorderLayout, the horizontal and vertical gaps between components in a FlowLayout can be set by constructors, or by "set" methods. In addition, the alignment can be changed (e.g. to the left or the right). To change the default layout manager of the panel, we call the "setLayout" method on the JPanel object. This example uses a parameterized constructor to set the alignment to the left, with a horizontal gap of 10 and a vertical gap of 20.

```
MusicPlayerPanel playerPanel = new MusicPlayerPanel();
playerPanel.setLayout(new FlowLayout(FlowLayout.LEFT, 10, 20));
add(playerPanel);
```

Figure 17.16 shows the effect of this change to the layout manager.

17.7.4   GridLayout

The GridLayout is rather like the FlowLayout in that the components are laid out left to right and top to bottom in the sequence that they are added to the container. However, we can specify the number of rows or columns that we want to have. The components will resize to fit these rows and columns.

The next class uses the same panel of components as the FlowLayout example, but in this case uses the GridLayout layout manager. Using a GridLayout is very simple. The constructor has two integer parameters that allow us to specify the number of rows or columns that we want. If the first parameter is non-zero, then the layout will organize the components using that number of rows. If we leave the first parameter (the number of rows) as zero, then the layout will use the second (columns) parameter instead. This example will use two columns with an automatic setting for the number of rows:

```
playerPanel.setLayout(new GridLayout(0, 2));
```

Further parameters can be added to set the horizontal and vertical gaps, for example,

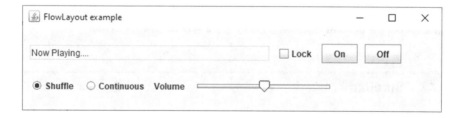

Fig. 17.16 Components in a FlowLayout (left aligned with horizontal and vertical gaps between components)

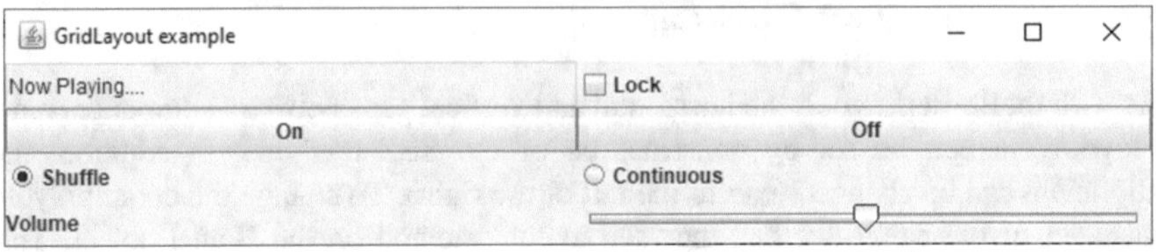

Fig. 17.17 Components in a GridLayout with two columns

```
playerPanel.setLayout(new GridLayout(0, 2, 5, 5));
```

This is the complete GridLayoutWindow class:

```
package com.foundjava.chapter17;

import java.awt.GridLayout;
import javax.swing.JFrame;

public class GridLayoutWindow extends JFrame
{
  public GridLayoutWindow()
  {
    MusicPlayerPanel playerPanel = new MusicPlayerPanel();
    playerPanel.setLayout(new GridLayout(0, 2));
    add(playerPanel);
  }

  public static void main(String[] args)
  {
    GridLayoutWindow window = new GridLayoutWindow();
    window.setTitle("GridLayout example");
    window.pack();
    window.setDefaultCloseOperation(JFrame.EXIT_ON_CLOSE);
    window.setVisible(true);
  }
}
```

The window will look like the one in Fig. 17.17, with the components organized into two columns.

Exercise 17.5
Change the panel from Exercise 17.4 to use a 4 column GridLayout.

17.8 Summary

In this chapter we have looked at various aspects of using Java to create graphical user interfaces. These have included Components (the objects that we interact with such as buttons and checkboxes) and Containers (components that can contain other components such as frames and panels). We have seen several Component types, including labels, buttons, radio buttons, text fields and combo boxes. We have also seen how these components can be configured in terms of their positions, sizes, colors and fonts. We have demonstrated how the look and feel of the whole application can be changed to be cross platform, native or "motif" style. We have introduced two ways of managing the layout of components in a container; either specifying their positions manually or using automatic layout managers. The layout managers we have looked at are the BorderLayout (the default layout manager for JFrames) the FlowLayout (the default layout manager for JPanels) and the GridLayout. We have also seen that JPanels can be used to host components and that these panels can be added to frames. In our code examples, we have only looked at how to make UI components appear on the screen, not how to respond to UI events with our own code. In the next chapter we will look at how we can handle component events to add underlying code to the UI.

Event-Driven Programming

18

In the previous chapter we looked at how components could be created, configured and arranged inside a container such as a JFrame. However, none of the components in the examples were able to process any events from the user. In this chapter, we will see how to write code that can respond to events such as buttons being pressed, text fields being changed and the movements of the mouse.

As soon as we write a program with a graphical user interface, we are providing an environment in which various events may occur: the user may press a button, or type into a text field and press Enter, or click on a radio button, or close a window or any of a thousand other possibilities. Which events may actually occur, and in which order they happen, is largely unpredictable. This means we must write event-driven code that is ready to respond appropriately to the various events that may be triggered by the user's actions.

18.1 Event Listeners

We can respond to events in the user interface by adding *listener* objects. There can be multiple listeners for each event. The job of these listeners is to be registered with a source of possible events and be notified when these events occur. A listener must implement the appropriate type of interface for the events that it is listening for. When an event does occur (or, as we say, is *fired*), an object representing that event is passed to a special event handler method of any objects that are listening for that event. This event object will contain information about what happened. For example, the mouse may have been clicked on part of the screen, in which case the event object would inform any listeners about the location of the mouse when the button click occurred. Figure 18.1 shows the basic concepts. "anObject" can fire events, and listener objects are added to its collection of listeners. If an event is fired, all the listeners are sent an event object that contains information about the event.

© Springer Nature Switzerland AG 2020
D. Parsons, *Foundational Java*, Texts in Computer Science,
https://doi.org/10.1007/978-3-030-54518-5_18

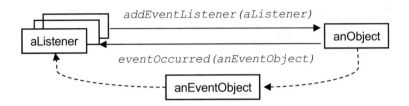

Fig. 18.1 Listeners are registered with objects that trigger events, and event objects are sent to listeners when those events are fired

18.2   Event Classes

There are many different types of event, and these are represented by various classes in a hierarchy that spans several packages. Each class represents a type of event. Figure 18.2 shows a very small part of the hierarchy with examples from both AWT and Swing. Later in this chapter we will see examples of these event objects being used in response to events in the user interface.

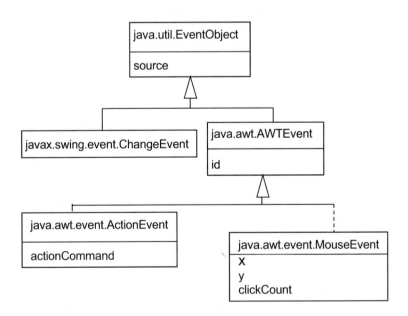

Fig. 18.2 A small part of the Event class hierarchy, showing the various packages in which event objects occur. The dotted line is intended to indicate that AWTEvent is an ancestor of MouseEvent, not an immediate superclass

18.3   EventListener Interfaces

For each EventObject type there are one or more event listener interfaces defined. Each interface declares methods which must be implemented by listeners to handle specific events. For example, the ActionListener interface declares the method "actionPerformed," which handles an ActionEvent, while the MouseListener declares several methods and handles MouseEvents.

18.3.1   A JButton ActionListener

For the first example we will implement an ActionListener. The ActionListener interface is very simple; it only declares the "actionPerformed" method, which receives an ActionEvent object when it is invoked (Fig. 18.3).

There are many components that can fire an ActionEvent, but perhaps the most commonly used is the JButton, which fires ActionEvents when it is pressed. Figure 18.4 shows how an object that implements the ActionListener interface can register with a JButton via the "addActionListener" method. This ActionListener will have its "actionPerformed" method invoked each time the button is pressed.

To implement the ActionListener interface we must create a class that provides a suitable implementation of the "actionPerformed" method. This can vary enormously across different ActionListener implementations since the context of the ActionListener is very application dependent. For example, what happens when you press a button depends entirely on the context. With this in mind, the following is just one possible example of how an ActionListener attached to a button might be implemented. However, it does represent a very generic action (closing a JFrame) so could potentially be reused in multiple applications.

The following example shows how to use a button press event to trigger the closing of a frame. A frame can be shut down using the "dispose" method, so we need to trigger this method in the ActionListener. In addition, the listener needs to have a reference to the frame that it is supposed to be closing. A simple option is to pass this to the constructor of the listener. The following class (CloseButtonListener) implements ActionListener, and the constructor takes a reference to a JFrame object. When the action event occurs, and the "actionPerformed" method is invoked, the JFrame is disposed of.

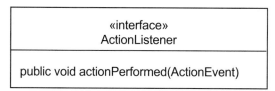

Fig. 18.3 The ActionListener interface

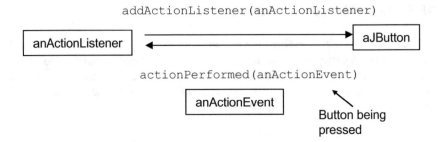

Fig. 18.4 The methods and event objects involved in listening for the ActionEvents triggered by a JButton

```
public class CloseButtonListener implements ActionListener
{
  private JFrame target;
  public CloseButtonListener(JFrame aFrame)
  {
    target = aFrame;
  }
  public void actionPerformed(ActionEvent event)
  {
    target.dispose();
  }
}
```

Now that we have a listener class, we need to make it possible for an object of this class to register itself as a listener to a JButton For each set of events that a particular source generates there is a method of the form "addXXXListener (EventListener)", where the "XXX" is the listener type. For an ActionListener, then, the method is called "addActionListener" (a JButton inherits this method from the AbstractButton class).

```
//javax.swing.AbstractButton method
public void addActionListener(ActionListener);
```

18.3.2   Adding a Listener

In this code, we create a JButton as the source of the event, then add an instance of CloseButtonListener to it. A reference to the JFrame ("frame") is passed to the constructor.

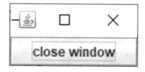

Fig. 18.5 The "close window" button, which has an ActionListener to close its frame

```
package com.foundjava.chapter18;
import javax.swing.JButton;
import javax.swing.JFrame;

public class CloseableWindow
{
  public static void main(String[] args)
  {
    JFrame frame = new JFrame();
    JButton closeButton = new JButton("close window");
    closeButton.addActionListener
      (new CloseButtonListener(frame));
    frame.add(closeButton);
    frame.pack();
    frame.setDefaultCloseOperation(JFrame.EXIT_ON_CLOSE);
    frame.setVisible(true);
  }
}
```

Figure 18.5 shows how the frame appears when the program is run. When the "close window" button is pressed, the window closes.

18.4 Multiple Action and Focus Listeners

Event sources and listeners form many-to-many relationships. Multiple listeners can listen to the same event from the same source, and one listener can listen for events from multiple sources. In the next example we will use multiple JTextFields to trigger multiple events and register multiple listeners. JTextFields, like all components, can trigger many different types of event. In this example we will demonstrate both ActionEvents and FocusEvents being fired by JTextFields. In a JTextField, focus events occur when the field gains or loses focus (a text field has focus when its text cursor is active). An action event is triggered by pressing Enter when the JTextField has focus.

The various classes in this example demonstrate how the same FocusListener is used with two different JTextFields, and how both a FocusListener and an ActionListener are applied to a single JTextField. Figure 18.6 shows a simple frame that contains two labels, two text fields and a button in a GridLayout (actually there are three labels; a blank label has been added as the fifth component to move the button to the right-hand column of the layout).

In this frame, both the text fields will have the same focus listener. This listener will change the background from white to yellow when the text field has focus, and back to white again when it loses focus (the first TextField will automatically have focus when the frame is first made visible). In addition, the second text field will have an ActionListener. This listener will check if the value typed into the field can be parsed as an integer. If it can, the background will turn green; if it cannot the background will turn red.

First, here is the TextFieldFocusListener. This implements the FocusListener interface, which declares the methods "focusGained" and "focusLost." The implementation of these methods changes the background color of the JTextField that is being listened to. Unlike the previous example we do not pass any objects as arguments to the listener's constructor. Instead, we use the event object that is passed to each method as an argument. By using the "getSource" method of this event object, we can get access to the text field that originally fired the focus event. This works well for this type of listener, where the object being listened to is also the object that we want to interact with. In cases where it is another object that we need to interact with (such as in the previous example, where a button fired the event but we needed to interact with a frame), navigating from the event object is a less straightforward approach.

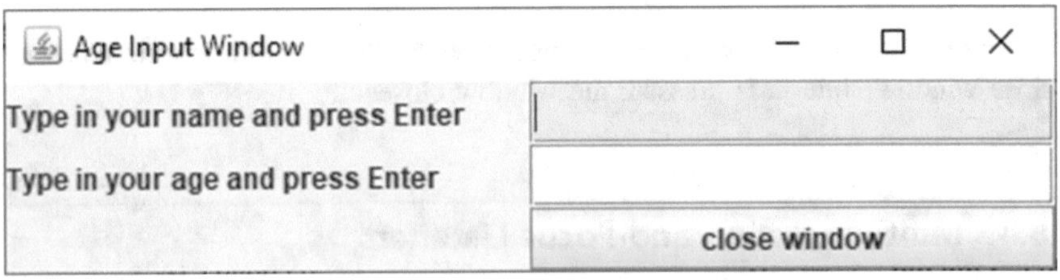

Fig. 18.6 A FocusListener indicating that a TextField has focus by changing the background color from white to yellow

```java
package com.foundjava.chapter18;

import java.awt.Color;
import java.awt.event.FocusEvent;
import java.awt.event.FocusListener;
import javax.swing.JTextField;

public class TextFieldFocusListener implements FocusListener
{
  @Override
  public void focusGained(FocusEvent e)
  {
    JTextField field = (JTextField)e.getSource();
    field.setBackground(Color.YELLOW);
  }

  @Override
  public void focusLost(FocusEvent e)
  {
    JTextField field = (JTextField)e.getSource();
    field.setBackground(Color.WHITE);
  }
}
```

The other listener in this example is an ActionListener to be applied to the second text field. This ActionListener gets the event source JTextField that is supposed to receive a value representing a person's age and changes the background according to whether the text can be converted to an integer or not. In our example, text that cannot be parsed by the "Integer.parseInt" method causes the text field background to turn red. Values that can be parsed turn it green.

```java
package com.foundjava.chapter18;

import java.awt.Color;
import java.awt.event.ActionEvent;
import java.awt.event.ActionListener;
import javax.swing.JTextField;

public class NumberValidationListener
    implements ActionListener
{
  @Override
  public void actionPerformed(ActionEvent e)
```

```
  {
    JTextField field = (JTextField) e.getSource();
    if (isValidAge(field.getText()))
    {
      field.setBackground(Color.GREEN);
    }
    else
    {
      field.setBackground(Color.RED);
    }
  }

    private boolean isValidAge(String ageValue)
    {
      try
      {
        Integer.parseInt(ageValue);
        return true;
      }
      catch (NumberFormatException e)
      {
        return false;
      }
    }
  }
```

The following class applies these listeners to various components.

```
package com.foundjava.chapter18;

import java.awt.GridLayout;

import javax.swing.JButton;
import javax.swing.JFrame;
import javax.swing.JLabel;
import javax.swing.JTextField;

public class AgeInputWindow extends JFrame
{
  public AgeInputWindow()
  {
    setLayout(new GridLayout(3,0));
    JButton closeButton = new JButton("close window");
  // add an action listener to a button to close the window
    closeButton.addActionListener
      (new CloseButtonListener(this));
    JTextField nameField = new JTextField(20);
    JTextField ageField = new JTextField(20);
```

```
// add an action listener to the 'age' field to validate it
  ageField.addActionListener
    (new NumberValidationListener());

// add a focus listener to both text fields
  TextFieldFocusListener focusListener =
  new TextFieldFocusListener();
  nameField.addFocusListener(focusListener);
  ageField.addFocusListener(focusListener);

  // add the components to the frame
    add(new JLabel("Type in your name and press Enter"));
    add(nameField);
    add(new JLabel("Type in your age and press Enter"));
    add(ageField);
    add(new JLabel());
    add(closeButton);
  }

  public static void main(String[] args)
  {
    AgeInputWindow window = new AgeInputWindow();
    window.setTitle("Age Input Window");
    window.pack();
    window.setDefaultCloseOperation(EXIT_ON_CLOSE);
    window.setVisible(true);
  }
}
```

Figure 18.7 shows the text field when a non-numeric character has been typed in and the Enter key has been pressed (the background will turn red).

Figure 18.8 shows the same field with a valid integer entered (the background will turn green).

Exercise 18.1

Write a simple GUI using a JFrame that contains a text field, a combo box and a button. When the button is pressed, the current contents of the text box should be added to the combo box.

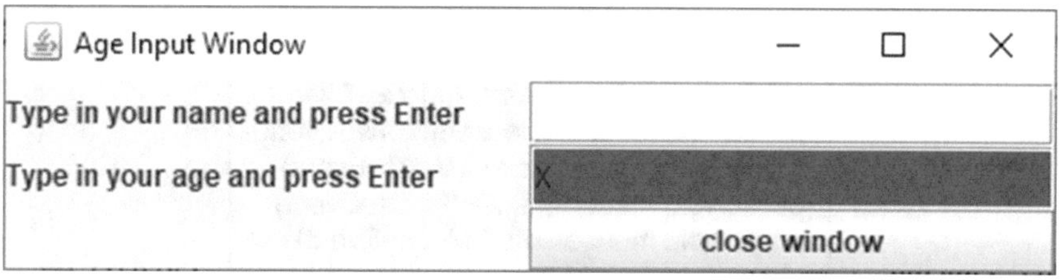

Fig. 18.7 The FocusListener changing the background of the text field to red if the value cannot be parsed to an integer

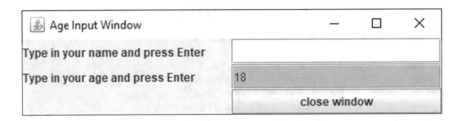

Fig. 18.8 A valid integer in the text field causing the listener to change the background to green

Exercise 18.2
Add a second button to your JFrame that will close the frame when it is pressed.

18.5 Responding to Mouse Events

There are different kinds of mouse events. Some are associated with the movement of the mouse, and some are associated with the mouse buttons or the mouse wheel. To further complicate matters, we sometimes need to know if the mouse is being moved while a button is being held down, so that we can drag or draw on components. To handle the various mouse events there are several different Listener interfaces, two of which we will introduce here; the MouseListener interface, which concerns itself with mouse button presses, and when the mouse pointer crosses the bounds of a component, and the MouseMotionListener interface, which allows us to monitor the movement of the mouse, and whether a mouse button is being held down while the mouse is moving.

Figure 18.9 shows the methods of the MouseListener interface. The "mouseEntered" and "mouseExited" events are triggered by the mouse moving in or out of the area covered by a component. The other three methods relate to the mouse buttons. "mousePressed" is triggered by a button being pressed down, and

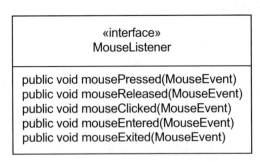

Fig. 18.9 The MouseListener interface

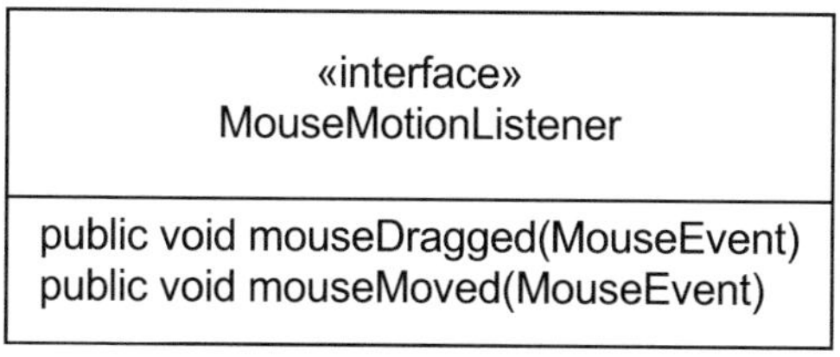

```
                ┌──────────────────────────────────────────────┐
                │                 «interface»                  │
                │            MouseMotionListener               │
                ├──────────────────────────────────────────────┤
                │  public void mouseDragged(MouseEvent)        │
                │  public void mouseMoved(MouseEvent)          │
                └──────────────────────────────────────────────┘
```

Fig. 18.10 The MouseMotionListener interface

"mouseReleased" is triggered when the button goes back up again. The "mouse-Clicked" event occurs after a mouse button has been both pressed and released. It is unlikely that you would want to respond to all three. In most cases we either want to know when the mouse has been clicked or track the press and release events (e.g. to draw a line or drag an object between two positions).

In addition, we can trace the motions of the mouse, either moving (no button pressed) or dragging (a button being pressed down), by implementing the MouseMotionListener interface (Fig. 18.10).

18.5.1 Mouse Listener Events

The next example demonstrates the mouse events captured by a MouseListener. It is not a particularly useful program but shows how the various mouse events are triggered. Like the first example, the constructor to the listener takes a JFrame as a parameter, enabling the listener to call methods of its host frame. The "mouse-Pressed" method is implemented to get the position of the mouse when it is clicked. This is very easy to do, since the MouseEvent object passed as a parameter contains a Point object representing the position of the mouse when one of its buttons was pressed. Once the position has been retrieved from the Point's "x" and "y" fields, this information is used to write the x- and y-coordinates as a String of text at that position in the frame, using the "drawString" method of the frame's Graphics object ("drawString" takes three parameters, the text to be drawn and the "x" and "y" positions of the text on the component). The Graphics object used to draw on the frame is acquired from JFrame's "getGraphics" method.

```
position = event.getPoint();
frame.getGraphics().drawString(position.x + "," + position.y,
        position.x, position.y);
```

The other methods are very simple. To demonstrate the "mouseClicked" and "mouseReleased" events, Strings are written to standard output. To demonstrate the "mouseEntered" and "mouseExited" methods, the background color is switched between white and light gray depending on whether the mouse has moved in or out of the frame.

```java
package com.foundjava.chapter18;
import java.awt.Color;
import java.awt.Point;
import java.awt.event.MouseEvent;
import java.awt.event.MouseListener;

import javax.swing.JFrame;

public class MyMouseListener implements MouseListener
{
  private Point position;
  private JFrame frame;
  public MyMouseListener (JFrame frame)
  {
    this.frame  = frame;
  }
  @Override
  public void mousePressed(MouseEvent event)
  {
    position = event.getPoint();
    frame.getGraphics().drawString(position.x + "," +
        position.y, position.x, position.y);
  }
  @Override
  public void mouseClicked(MouseEvent e)
  {
    System.out.println("clicked");
  }
  @Override
  public void mouseReleased(MouseEvent e)
  {
    System.out.println("released");
  }
  @Override
  public void mouseEntered(MouseEvent e)
  {
    frame.getContentPane().setBackground(Color.WHITE);
  }
  @Override
  public void mouseExited(MouseEvent e)
  {
    frame.getContentPane().setBackground(Color.LIGHT_GRAY);
  }
}
```

The MouseListenerWindow, to which "MyMouseListener" is applied, is very simple.

```
import javax.swing.JFrame;

public class MouseListenerWindow
{
  public static void main(String[] args)
  {
    JFrame frame = new JFrame();
    frame.addMouseListener(new MyMouseListener(frame));
    frame.setBounds(100,100,500,500);
    frame.setDefaultCloseOperation(JFrame.EXIT_ON_CLOSE);
    frame.setVisible(true);
  }
}
```

Figure 18.11 shows the state of the application after a mouse button has been pressed at various positions within the bounds of the frame. These graphical strings

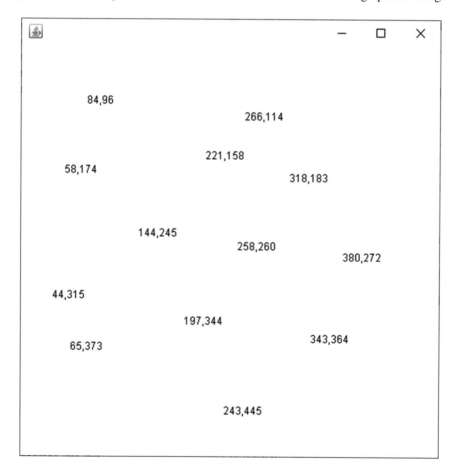

Fig. 18.11 The MouseListenerWindow after the mouse has been pressed several times within the bounds of the frame

are erased by the redrawn background color if the mouse is moved outside the current frame.

18.5.2 Mouse Motion Events

The next example is similar to the last one, but this time demonstrates the MouseMotionListener interface. Here, we implement the MouseMotionListener in the DrawMouseListener class. Only the "mouseDragged" method has been given a meaningful implementation. The other method, "mouseMoved" is empty. In the "mouseDragged" method, we retrieve the current mouse position (as we did in the previous example) and draw a filled rectangle (a square) at the current location. As long as either mouse button is held down when the mouse is moved, mouseDragged events will continue to be fired, and the method will keep drawing filled squares at its current position, so as the mouse is moved a continuous line will be drawn.

```java
package com.foundjava.chapter18;
import java.awt.Point;
import java.awt.event.MouseEvent;
import java.awt.event.MouseMotionListener;
import javax.swing.JFrame;

public class DrawMouseListener implements MouseMotionListener
{
  private Point position;
  private JFrame frame;

  public DrawMouseListener (JFrame frame)
  {
    this.frame  = frame;
  }

  @Override
  public void mouseDragged(MouseEvent e)
  {
    position = e.getPoint();
    frame.getGraphics().fillRect
      (position.x, position.y, 5, 5);
  }

  @Override
  public void mouseMoved(MouseEvent e)
  {
    // empty implementation
  }
}
```

The MouseDrawWindow class simply creates a frame and registers the MouseMotionListener with it.

```
package com.foundjava.chapter18;

import javax.swing.JFrame;

public class MouseDrawWindow
{
  public static void main(String[] args)
  {
    JFrame frame = new JFrame("Mouse Draw Window");
    frame.addMouseMotionListener(new          DrawMouseListen-
er(frame));
    frame.setBounds(100,100,500,500);
    frame.setDefaultCloseOperation(JFrame.EXIT_ON_CLOSE);
    frame.setVisible(true);
  }
}
```

Figure 18.12 shows the window if the mouse has been dragged with a mouse button held down.

Exercise 18.3
Write a program that draws a line between two points within a frame. Implement a subclass of MouseListener that captures "mouseClicked" events and draw a line between two consecutive mouse clicks. Use the "drawLine" method of the Graphics class; this method draws a line, using the current color, between the points (x1, y1) and (x2, y2).

```
drawLine(int x1, int y1, int x2, int y2)
```

Exercise 18.4
In the previous exercise, you had to create a class to implement the MouseListener interface, which meant implementing all six methods, even though only one was needed for that program. An alternative to implementing MouseListener is to extend the MouseAdapter class. This is a class that itself implements MouseListener with empty methods. This means that you only need to override the methods you are interested in.

Create a subclass of MouseAdapter that overrides the mouseClicked event in the same way as your previous MouseListener class. Modify the program you wrote for the previous exercise so that it uses your new class rather than the previous MouseListener.

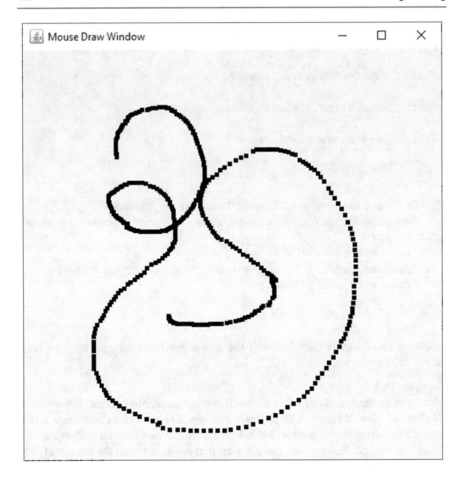

Fig. 18.12 Using a MouseMotionListener to draw when the mouse is dragged

18.6   Event Handlers as Inner Classes

In our previous examples we have written our event handlers as separate public classes. In some cases, this can make a lot of sense. For example, the listener that can be attached to a button in order to close a frame is a very generic action that could be reused in multiple applications, therefore having it as a separate reusable class is appropriate. In other cases, however, having a separate public class to handle events is less useful since many event handlers are very closely tied to a specific application and could not sensibly be used elsewhere. One way of addressing this issue would be to make some event handlers non-public classes within a package. This would limit their visibility outside the application within which the listeners are designed to be used. There is, however, another issue with having event handlers as separate classes, which is that we often find ourselves having to pass various objects between the event handlers and the objects they interact with. In some previous examples we have passed objects to event handler constructors to ensure that they could successfully interact with other objects. A more elegant solution is to write event handlers as *inner classes*, inside the classes that they interact with, giving them more direct access to those classes and other components declared inside them. There are various ways in which this can be done, which we will explore in the next example.

18.6.1   Implementing a DieListener

Back in Chap. 6 we created a Die class that was able to be "rolled" and return an integer in the range 1–6. Suppose that we want to create a UI application that will display the value of a rolled die when a button is pressed. This means we need to write an implementation of ActionListenerfor the button that can roll a Die and present the resulting value on a UI component. In our example this component will be a JLabel. Here is an example of how we might write such a listener in the style that we have been using so far. We would need to give the event handler access to both the instance of the Die, and the JLabel, for it to update the label with the value of the Die.

```java
package com.foundjava.chapter18;

import java.awt.event.ActionEvent;
import java.awt.event.ActionListener;
import javax.swing.JLabel;

import com.foundjava.chapter6.Die;

public class DieListener implements ActionListener
{
  private Die die;
  JLabel dieScore;

  public DieListener(Die die, JLabel dieScore)
  {
    this.die = die;
    this.dieScore = dieScore;
  }

  @Override
  public void actionPerformed(ActionEvent e)
  {
    dieScore.setText(String.valueOf(die.getRoll()));
  }
}
```

The following DieWindow class adds a DieListener to its button and passes references to the Die and the JLabel to the listener.

```java
package com.foundjava.chapter18;

import java.awt.BorderLayout;
import java.awt.Font;
import javax.swing.JButton;
import javax.swing.JFrame;
import javax.swing.JLabel;
import static javax.swing.SwingConstants;
import com.foundjava.chapter6.Die;

public class DieWindow1 extends JFrame
{
  JButton rollButton = new JButton("Roll Die");
  JLabel dieScore = new JLabel("",CENTER);
  Die die = new Die();

  public DieWindow1()
  {
    dieScore.setFont(new Font("Serif", Font.PLAIN, 40));
    add(rollButton, BorderLayout.SOUTH);
    add(dieScore);
    rollButton.addActionListener
      (new DieListener(die, dieScore));
  }

  public static void main(String[] args)
  {
    DieWindow1 dieWindow = new DieWindow1();
    dieWindow.setBounds(200, 200, 200, 200);
    dieWindow.setDefaultCloseOperation(EXIT_ON_CLOSE);
    dieWindow.setVisible(true);
  }
}
```

Figure 18.13 shows the application running, with a randomly generated Die value shown in the label area of the frame in response to the event handler attached to the "Roll Die" button.

Fig. 18.13   The value of a Die displayed in response to a button event handler

18.6.2   Inner Classes

While it is perfectly functional, this passing around of references is unnecessary if we take a different approach to the event handler, which is to create it as an *inner class*. An inner class is declared within the body of another class, which gives it direct access to all the fields and methods of that enclosing class. The revised version of the DieWindow class that follows no longer uses an external listener class. Instead, it includes an inner class. This inner class is declared in the body of the DieWindow class. The whole class declaration, including the definition of the "actionPerformed" method, appears here. Being inside the DieWindow class, it has direct access to the "die" and "dieScore" fields.

```
class DieListener implements ActionListener
{
  public void actionPerformed(ActionEvent e)
  {
    dieScore.setText(String.valueOf(die.getRoll()));
  }
}
```

The only other change to the DieWindow class is in the constructor. When it creates the DieListener it is no longer using an external listener class, so there is no need to pass parameter references around between objects. The inner class can directly access the Die and the JLabel because it belongs to the same class.

```
public DieWindow2()

{
  dieScore.setFont(new Font("Serif", Font.PLAIN, 40));
  add(rollButton, BorderLayout.SOUTH);
  add(dieScore);
  rollButton.addActionListener(new DieListener());
}
```

18.6.3   Local Inner Classes

An inner class can be used to create instances in any methods within the class, since its visibility is at the level of the class. Sometimes this is useful, as we might want to create different listener instances for different components within the class. In other cases, this requirement may not be relevant, and a listener might only be required within the scope of a single method. In cases like these, we can take a slightly different approach and use a *local inner class*. This is declared within the body of a method, and only has visibility within that method. In this example, the local class is declared within the body of the constructor. Instead of declaring a class with name that could be used in other parts of the enclosing class, all we do here is give a local variable name to an implementation of the ActionListener interface. The local name ("dieListener") is then used to apply the listener to the button in the same method. The "dieListener" would have no visibility outside this method so could not be used elsewhere but could be used multiple times in this method. Note the final semicolon; the declaration of the local inner class is created as a single statement.

```
public DieWindow3()
{
  dieScore.setFont(new Font("Serif", Font.PLAIN, 40));
  add(rollButton, BorderLayout.SOUTH);
  add(dieScore);
  ActionListener dieListener = new ActionListener() {
    public void actionPerformed(ActionEvent e)
    {
      dieScore.setText(String.valueOf(die.getRoll()));
    }
  };
  rollButton.addActionListener(dieListener);
}
```

18.6.4   Anonymous Inner Classes

Finally, there is one more approach that we can take which is to use an *anonymous inner class*. In this case, there is not even a local variable name being used to refer to the listener. Instead, the ActionListener implementation is applied directly to a component (in this case the "rollButton") using the "addActionListener" method. The parameter to this method is an implementation of the ActionListener interface that is anonymous (it has no class name and no reference name). Note the final parenthesis, which is the closing parenthesis of the parameter list of the addActionListener method, and the semicolon that terminates the whole statement. Note that, with this approach, the listener can only be applied to a single component.

```
public DieWindow4() {
  dieScore.setFont(new Font("Serif", Font.PLAIN, 40));
  add(rollButton, BorderLayout.SOUTH);
  add(dieScore);
  rollButton.addActionListener(new ActionListener() {
      public void actionPerformed(ActionEvent e)
      {
        dieScore.setText(String.valueOf(die.getRoll()));
      }
    });
}
```

18.6.5   Lambda Expressions as Event Handlers

It will probably come as no surprise to you that we can also implement event handlers using lambda expressions, since many of the event handler method signatures are specified in interfaces that have one abstract method.

For our final version of the event handler for the Die class, we can use the following lambda expression. Since the ActionListener only has the abstract method "actionPerformed", this can be inferred as the method being implemented by the lambda expression.

```
rollButton.addActionListener
    (e -> dieScore.setText(String.valueOf(die.getRoll())));
```

Here is the whole constructor. This example goes a long way to showing the value of lambda expressions in simplifying code.

Table 18.1 Event handler class types, their visibility and reusability

Type of event handler class	Visibility	Level of reusability
Separate class	Public	Across different applications
Inner class	Within a class (like a field)	In any method of the class (e.g. multiple handler objects of the same class can be created and applied to multiple components in different methods)
Local inner class	Within a method (locally named, like a local variable)	In the same method of the class (e.g. the same handler object can be applied to multiple components in the same method)
Anonymous inner class	Within a method (no local name)	A single instance of the handler class can be used with a single component
Lambda expression	Within a method (no named event handler method)	The lambda expression is applied directly to the component

```
public DieWindow5()
{
   dieScore.setFont(new Font("Serif", Font.PLAIN, 40));
   add(rollButton, BorderLayout.SOUTH);
   add(dieScore);
   rollButton.addActionListener
      (e -> dieScore.setText(String.valueOf(die.getRoll())));
}
```

In summary, there are several different ways of writing event handlers, varying the visibility and reusability of the various classes. As the requirements for visibility and reusability lessen, we are better able to encapsulate the event handlers within their enclosing classes. In situations where an event handler can be reused across multiple applications, writing a separate event handler class is the best solution. If an event handler is for one application only then some form of inner class is a better option, but lambda expressions are probably the way to go if you want the shortest and simplest code. Table 18.1 shows the various types of event handler class, their visibility and their levels of reusability.

18.7 JPanel Subclasses and Multi-panel Layouts

In the last chapter we saw that JPanels can be added to a frame. However, simply adding instances of the existing JPanel class is not always flexible enough for building interfaces, and sometimes we need panels that have application-specific roles. The next example gives some indication of how this can be done by adding subclasses of JPanel to a JFrame.

Previous examples have also used some simple layout managers, but these are quite restrictive in the layout options they provide. One way of overcoming these restrictions is to use separate parts of a JFrame's layout manager to host different panels that have their own layouts.

We can define any number of subclasses of JPanel to manage different components or display graphical outputs. In this example, two separate subclasses (ScaledImagePanel and ImageControlPanel) are defined. ScaledImagePanel displays a scalable image, while ImageControlPanel contains JSlider components to set the horizontal and vertical scale of the image. By using subclasses, we can add extra functionality to the panels.

The ScaledImagePanel maintains properties (fields, with getters and setters) for the height and width of the image, and for the image filename. The "set" methods for the image height and width, as well as setting the values of the fields, also call "repaint" to redisplay the image:

```
public void setImageHeight(int height)
{
  imageHeight = height;
  repaint();
}

public void setImageWidth(int width)
{
  imageWidth = width;
  repaint();
}
```

The constructor sets the image filename from its parameter argument, using a "set" method.

```
public ScaledImagePanel(String imageFilename)
{
  setImageFilename(imageFilename);
}

public void setImageFilename(String imageFilename)
{
  this.imageFilename = imageFilename;
}
```

The "getImageFilename" method is used in the "getImage" method, which gets an instance of the java.awt.Toolkit from the "getDefaultToolkit" factory method. This Toolkit object can create a java.awt.Image object from a suitable file.

```
public String getImageFilename()
{
    return imageFilename;
}

public Image getImage()
{
    Toolkit kit = Toolkit.getDefaultToolkit();
    return kit.getImage(getImageFilename());
}
```

The "paint" method displays the scaled image by first clearing the background by drawing a filled rectangle over the panel in the background color, and then calling "drawImage" on the graphics object. The final parameter to this method is an object that implements the ImageObserver interface. Swing components automatically implement this interface, so we are simply passing "this" panel to the method so that it can be informed of image draw events.

```
public void paint(Graphics g)
{
    g.fillRect(0, 0, this.getWidth(), this.getHeight());
    g.drawImage(getImage(), 0, 0, getImageWidth(),
        getImageHeight(), this);
}
```

These various methods of the ScaledImagePanel class demonstrate one of the advantages of subclassing, namely, that we can add new methods to our panels. This is the complete class.

```java
package com.foundjava.chapter18;

import java.awt.Graphics;
import java.awt.Image;
import java.awt.Toolkit;
import javax.swing.JPanel;

class ScaledImagePanel extends JPanel
{
  private int imageHeight = 1000;
  private int imageWidth = 1000;
  private String imageFilename;

  public ScaledImagePanel(String imageFilename)
  {
    setImageFilename(imageFilename);
  }
  public void setImageFilename(String imageFilename)
  {
    this.imageFilename = imageFilename;
  }

  public String getImageFilename()
  {
    return imageFilename;
  }

  public Image getImage()
  {
    Toolkit kit = Toolkit.getDefaultToolkit();
    return kit.getImage(getImageFilename());
  }

  public void setImageHeight(int height)
  {
    imageHeight = height;
    repaint();
  }
```

```
  public void setImageWidth(int width)
  {
    imageWidth = width;
    repaint();
  }

  public int getImageHeight()
  {
    return imageHeight;
  }

  public int getImageWidth()
  {
    return imageWidth;
  }

// paint displays the scaled image
  public void paint(Graphics g)
  {
// clear the background
    g.fillRect(0, 0, this.getWidth(), this.getHeight());

// display the image scaled
    g.drawImage(getImage(), 0, 0, getImageWidth(),
      getImageHeight(), this);
  }
}
```

The other panel, ImageControlPanel, contains two JSliders that the user can control to change the width and height of the scaled image. The ControlPanel is passed a reference to the ScaledImagePanel in its constructor so that it can send messages to it. Again, we can see that subclassing allows us to customize the panel, in this case by providing a specialized constructor.

The key event handling aspect of this class is the JSliders' listener. The movement of a JSlider triggers ChangeEvents, captured in the "stateChanged" method of the ChangeListener interface. In this case, a local inner class is used; since the event handling is similar, we can combine the two possible responses within a single event handler by checking the event source. Then the same local event handler can be added to the two sliders. Because this example uses the same event handler code for two different objects it is not ideal for a lambda expression, since we would have to add the same expression to each object.

```
ChangeListener sliderListener = new ChangeListener()
{
  @Override
  public void stateChanged(ChangeEvent e)
  {
    if(e.getSource().equals(heightSlider))
    {
      scaledImagePanel.setImageHeight
        (heightSlider.getValue());
    }
    else
    {
      scaledImagePanel.setImageWidth(widthSlider.getValue());
    }
  }
};

heightSlider.addChangeListener(sliderListener);
widthSlider.addChangeListener(sliderListener);
```

This panel uses a GridLayout to position the components, with two rows:

```
ImageControlPanel(ScaledImagePanel panel)
{
  GridLayout layout = new GridLayout(2, 0);
  setLayout(layout);
//etc.
```

When the components have been added to the panel, the initial size of the image is set using the initial values of the sliders (in this example they have both been set at 500 pixels).

```
scaledImagePanel.setImageHeight(heightSlider.getValue());
scaledImagePanel.setImageWidth(widthSlider.getValue());
```

Here is the complete ImageControlPanel class. All of the implementations are in the constructor, with the ChangeListener added as a local inner class and applied to both sliders.

```java
package com.foundjava.chapter18;

import java.awt.GridLayout;

import javax.swing.JLabel;
import javax.swing.JPanel;
import javax.swing.JSlider;
import javax.swing.event.ChangeEvent;
import javax.swing.event.ChangeListener;

public class ImageControlPanel extends JPanel
{
  private JLabel heightLabel = new JLabel("Image Height:");
  private JLabel widthLabel = new JLabel("Image Width:");
  private JSlider heightSlider = new JSlider(0, 1000, 500);
  private JSlider widthSlider = new JSlider(0, 1000, 500);
// a reference to the other panel so it can be updated
  private ScaledImagePanel scaledImagePanel;

// constructor receives a reference to the scaled image panel
  ImageControlPanel(ScaledImagePanel panel) {
    GridLayout layout = new GridLayout(2, 0);
    setLayout(layout);
    scaledImagePanel = panel;
    add(heightLabel);
    add(widthLabel);
    add(heightSlider);
    add(widthSlider);
    scaledImagePanel.setImageHeight(heightSlider.getValue());

      scaledImagePanel.setImageWidth(widthSlider.getValue());
```

```
// local inner class
   ChangeListener sliderListener = new ChangeListener()
   {
     @Override
     public void stateChanged(ChangeEvent e)
     {
       if(e.getSource().equals(heightSlider))
       {
         scaledImagePanel.setImageHeight
           (heightSlider.getValue());
       }
       else
       {
         scaledImagePanel.setImageWidth
           (widthSlider.getValue());
       }
     }
   };
// same listener applied to both sliders
   heightSlider.addChangeListener(sliderListener);
   widthSlider.addChangeListener(sliderListener);
  }
}
```

Now the two subclasses of JPanel are defined, they can be added to the following ImageScaler class that provides a host JFrame. The main frame constructor simply adds objects of the two specialized panels that are initially sized using the "setBounds" method. The ImageControlPanel is added to the North region of the JFrame's BorderLayout and the ScaledImagePanel added to the Center (which will expand to fill the unused regions).

The filename is passed to the ImageScaler's constructor. This is the complete class.

```
package com.foundjava.chapter18;

import java.awt.BorderLayout;
import javax.swing.JFrame;

public class ImageScaler extends JFrame
{
   private ImageControlPanel controlPanel;
private ScaledImagePanel scaledImagePanel;

public ImageScaler(String imageFilename)
{
   setLayout(new BorderLayout());
   scaledImagePanel = new ScaledImagePanel(imageFilename);
   controlPanel = new ImageControlPanel(scaledImagePanel);
   controlPanel.setBounds(0, 20, 400, 80);
   scaledImagePanel.setBounds(0, 100, 500, 500);
   add(controlPanel, BorderLayout.NORTH);
   add(scaledImagePanel, BorderLayout.CENTER);
}

public static void main(String[] args)
{
   ImageScaler scaler = new ImageScaler("Duke-Guitar.png");
   scaler.setTitle("Image Scaler");
   scaler.setBounds(0, 0, 500, 500);
   scaler.setDefaultCloseOperation(JFrame.EXIT_ON_CLOSE);
   scaler.setVisible(true);
}
}
```

Figure 18.14 shows the output from the program in its initial state. Moving either of the sliders will change the height or the width of the image.

18.7.1   The GridBagLayout

Before looking at further aspects of event handling, we will take a brief detour through another of the layout managers, the GridBagLayout. The most sophisticated of the original AWT layout managers, it is used in conjunction with "GridBagConstraints" objects to give maximum control over how components are arranged on an underlying grid. Unlike a standard GridLayout, the GridBagLayout allows components to span multiple rows and columns, to be repositioned within a cell of the grid, to be resized and to be spaced apart. We can also weight the relative sizes of components against each other. This example gives some idea of how this

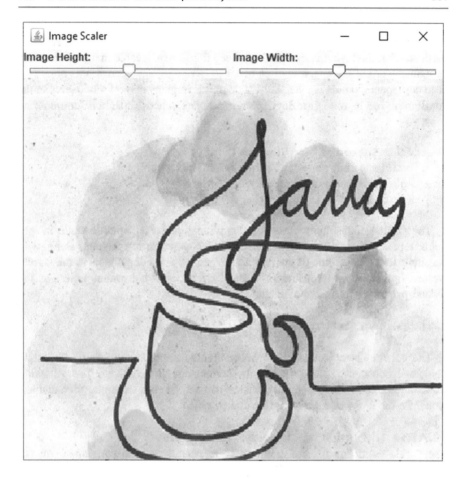

Fig. 18.14 The ImageScaler, showing the scale of an image on one panel controlled by Swing components (in a GridLayout) on a separate panel. Both panels are added to the frame's BorderLayout

layout manager can be used, but there are many ways in which its features can be applied to create flexible and sophisticated user interfaces.

One reason for using a GridBagLayout is to enable us to use a single layout manager in a frame. Dividing up the frame into separate panels can be useful but in some cases it increases the complexity of inter-component communication, as references must be passed between various panels. After we have introduced the basic mechanics of organizing a GridBagLayout, we will return to the image scaling example and see how we might re-implement it using a GridBagLayout.

A GridBagLayout has two aspects. First, it comprises the layout grid, on which components are positioned using x- and y-coordinates, starting at 0, 0 for the top left-hand cell of the grid. Second, the way that each component is managed inside the cells of the grid is specified by a GridBagConstraints object. As well as declaring a layout manager, then, we also declare at least one constraints object.

Although it is possible to use the same constraints object for more than one component, it makes it difficult to ensure that all the settings are appropriate, particularly if the layout is modified. To keep things manageable in all but the most straightforward of layouts, it is often better to have a separate constraints object for each component, which is what we will do in this implementation. For example, the "onButton" has its own GridBagConstraints object called "onButtonContraints":

```
// a button
JButton onButton = new JButton("On");
// a constraints object to use with this button
GridBagConstraints onButtonConstraints =
    new GridBagConstraints();
```

The GridBagConstraints class consists almost entirely of public static integer fields representing various characteristics of a component's layout, along with constants for setting some of their values. When we add components to the layout, we can optionally add constraints to them by giving a constraints object as the second parameter to the "add" method.

```
add(onButton, onButtonConstraints);
```

The constraints object needs to be configured appropriately, using its public fields and constants, before we add the component to the layout. The following subsections outline the constraints that we can set. In each example, "constraints" would be the name of a GridBagConstraints object.

18.7.1.1 The "gridx" and "gridy" Constraints
The "gridx" and "gridy" constraints set the position of the component on the underlying grid. The top left cell of the grid is 0, 0:

```
constraints.gridx = 0;
constraints.gridy = 0;
```

18.7.1.2 The "gridwidth" and "gridheight" Constraints
The "gridwidth" and "gridheight" constraints specify the width and height of a component in the layout by the number of rows or columns that they occupy. We can use these values to make components span multiple rows and/or columns. As one alternative to providing the exact number of columns, one of the available constants for these fields is "REMAINDER" which causes the component to take up the rest of the current row or column, for example,

```
constraints.gridwidth = GridBagConstraints.REMAINDER;
```

18.7.1.3   The "fill" Constraint

The "fill" constraint defines how a component fills the available space within its cell. All components have a preferred size, which is how they display by default. If this leads to unused space we can alter this by filling. We can set the "fill" value to NONE, HORIZONTAL, VERTICAL or BOTH, for example,

```
constraints.fill = GridBagConstraints.HORIZONTAL;
```

18.7.1.4   The "insets" Constraint

The "insets" constraint is an object of the Insets class that is used to represent the margins around a component. It has four public fields that can be set: "top", "left", "bottom" and "right". This example sets the "right" and "left" insets by accessing individual fields:

```
constraints.insets.left = 10;
constraints.insets.right = 10;
```

Alternatively, we can set all the insets using the constructor of the Insets class (the parameters are in the order top, left, bottom and right):

```
constraints.insets = new Insets(4, 4, 4, 4);
```

18.7.1.5   The "ipadx" and "ipady" Constraints

Unlike insets, which add extra space around the outside of a component, the padding constraints ("ipadx" and "ipady") increase the size of the component itself. The following example would increase the height of a component by 10 pixels and its width by 20:

```
constraints.ipadx = 20;
constraints.ipady = 10;
```

18.7.1.6   The "anchor" Constraint

The "anchor" constraint controls the position of the component within its cell, provided it does not already fill the cell. The default position is in the center, but we can place the component at any of the following "compass points": CENTER, NORTH, NORTHEAST, EAST, SOUTHEAST, SOUTH, SOUTHWEST, WEST and NORTHWEST, for example,

```
constraints.anchor = GridBagConstraints.NORTH;
```

18.7.1.7   The "weightx" and "weighty" Constraints

The "weightx" and "weighty" constraints enable components to adjust themselves within the frame relative to each other. The simplest thing is to weight one component only. This should be a component that looks sensible when it is enlarged. A text area is a good candidate, for example. If only one component is to be weighted, then the weight value chosen is not important, as long as it is a non-negative value, for example,

```
constraints.weightx = 1;
constraints.weighty = 1;
```

If more than one component is to be weighted, then the weight values are relative, for example, if we had two components on one row we could give one a "weightx" value of 6 and the other a "weightx" value of 4. This would result in the first component taking 60% of the available horizontal space and the second component taking 40%.

In this program, we will apply examples of all these constraints to a simple window. Figure 18.15 shows how the components will be laid out on the underlying grid, and where the constraints will be applied.

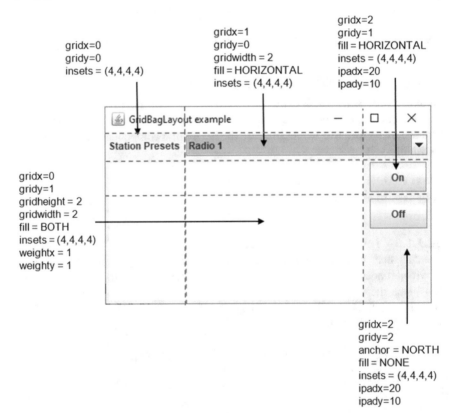

Fig. 18.15 Components laid out on a GridBagLayout with their constraints. The dotted lines indicate the underlying grid

This is the complete class. It uses separate GridBagConstraints objects for each component. Among other things it shows how components can span rows and columns within the grid.

```java
package com.foundjava.chapter18;

import java.awt.GridBagConstraints;
import java.awt.GridBagLayout;
import java.awt.Insets;
import javax.swing.JButton;
import javax.swing.JComboBox;
import javax.swing.JFrame;
import javax.swing.JLabel;
import javax.swing.JTextArea;
public class GridBagWindow extends JFrame
{
  public GridBagWindow() {
    setLayout(new GridBagLayout());
    JLabel textLabel = new JLabel("Station Presets");
    JComboBox presets = new JComboBox();
    presets.addItem("Radio 1");
    presets.addItem("Radio 2");
    presets.addItem("Radio 3");
    presets.addItem("Radio 4");
    JTextArea textArea = new JTextArea();
    JButton onButton = new JButton("On");
    JButton offButton = new JButton("Off");
// add all the components. each has its own constraints
// the text label constraints are position and insets
    GridBagConstraints textLabelConstraints =
      new GridBagConstraints();
    textLabelConstraints.gridx = 0;
    textLabelConstraints.gridy = 0;
    textLabelConstraints.insets = new Insets(4, 4, 4, 4);
    add(textLabel, textLabelConstraints);
// the JComboBox constraints are position, insets, spanning
// two columns and filling those columns horizontally
    GridBagConstraints presetsConstraints =
      new GridBagConstraints();
    presetsConstraints.gridx = 1;
    presetsConstraints.gridy = 0;
    presetsConstraints.insets = new Insets(4, 4, 4, 4);
    presetsConstraints.gridwidth = 2;
    presetsConstraints.fill = GridBagConstraints.HORIZONTAL;
    add(presets, presetsConstraints);
```

```
// the text area constraints are position, insets, spanning
// two columns and two rows and filling both rows and
// columns. this component is also given a weighting to help
// adjust all components to the frame
    GridBagConstraints textAreaConstraints =
      new GridBagConstraints();
    textAreaConstraints.gridx = 0;
    textAreaConstraints.gridy = 1;
    textAreaConstraints.insets = new Insets(4, 4, 4, 4);
    textAreaConstraints.gridwidth = 2;
    textAreaConstraints.gridheight = 2;
    textAreaConstraints.fill = GridBagConstraints.BOTH;
    textAreaConstraints.weightx = 1.0;
    textAreaConstraints.weighty = 1.0;
    add(textArea, textAreaConstraints);
// the constraints on the buttons are position,
// insets and padding.
    GridBagConstraints onButtonConstraints =
      new GridBagConstraints();
    onButtonConstraints.gridx = 2;
    onButtonConstraints.gridy = 1;
    onButtonConstraints.insets = new Insets(4, 4, 4, 4);
    onButtonConstraints.ipadx = 20;
    onButtonConstraints.ipady = 10;
    add(onButton, onButtonConstraints);
// in addition, the 'off' button is anchored to the
// top (north) of its cell
    GridBagConstraints offButtonConstraints =
      new GridBagConstraints();
    offButtonConstraints.gridx = 2;
    offButtonConstraints.gridy = 2;
    offButtonConstraints.anchor = GridBagConstraints.NORTH;
    offButtonConstraints.insets = new Insets(4, 4, 4, 4);
    offButtonConstraints.ipadx = 20;
    offButtonConstraints.ipady = 10;
    add(offButton, offButtonConstraints);
  }
  public static void main(String[] args)
  {
    GridBagWindow window = new GridBagWindow();
    window.setTitle("GridBagLayout example");
    window.pack();
      window.setDefaultCloseOperation(EXIT_ON_CLOSE);
    window.setVisible(true);
  }
}
```

If you resize the window by dragging its borders, you should see that GridBagLayouts provide good resizing behavior, allowing the weighted components to take up the slack without disrupting other components. An example of the resizing behavior of this layout is shown in Fig. 18.16.

As an example of applying a GridBagLayout, the following class applies a GridBagLayout to the scaled image example that we saw earlier, when we used two separate panels. Here, all the components are laid out using a GridBagLayout. The components are the same as in the previous version, apart from one of the sliders, which is given vertical orientation, using an additional parameter to the constructor.

```
private JSlider heightSlider =
    new JSlider(SwingConstants.VERTICAL, 0, 1000, 400);
```

To ensure that the vertical slider changes the height of the picture in the same direction as the slider control, we invert its values using the "setInverted" method (setting it to "true"):

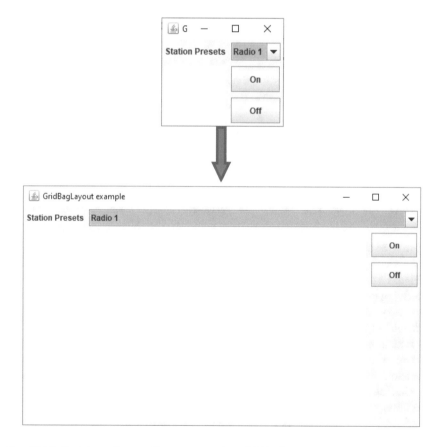

Fig. 18.16 Resizing a Frame with components in a GridBagLayout

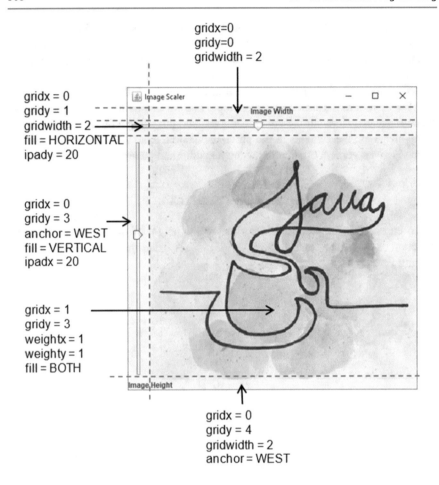

gridx=0
gridy=0
gridwidth = 2

gridx = 0
gridy = 1
gridwidth = 2
fill = HORIZONTAL
ipady = 20

gridx = 0
gridy = 3
anchor = WEST
fill = VERTICAL
ipadx = 20

gridx = 1
gridy = 3
weightx = 1
weighty = 1
fill = BOTH

gridx = 0
gridy = 4
gridwidth = 2
anchor = WEST

Fig. 18.17 The ScaledImagePanel and other components arranged using a GridBagLayout

```
heightSlider.setInverted(true);
```

Figure 18.17 shows how the layout is managed, with dotted lines showing the underlying grid. The two sliders have been given additional padding to increase the space they take up, and they have fill settings to ensure they fill the available horizontal or vertical space. The ScaledImagePanel fills in both directions to take up any remaining space in the frame.

Here is the GridBagScaler class which replaces the ImageControlPanel and ImageScaler classes from our earlier example (the ScaledImagePanel is reused as is). One advantage of using the GridBagLayout, apart from its presentational flexibility, is that we no longer have to coordinate communication between two different panels. All the components in the GridBagLayout are visible to each other.

```java
package com.foundjava.chapter18;

import java.awt.GridBagConstraints;
import java.awt.GridBagLayout;

import javax.swing.JFrame;
import javax.swing.JLabel;
import javax.swing.JSlider;
import javax.swing.SwingConstants;
import javax.swing.event.ChangeEvent;
import javax.swing.event.ChangeListener;

public class GridBagScaler extends JFrame
{
  private ScaledImagePanel scaledImagePanel;
  private JLabel heightLabel = new JLabel("Image Height");
  private JLabel widthLabel = new JLabel("Image Width");
  private JSlider heightSlider =
    new JSlider(SwingConstants.VERTICAL, 0, 1000, 400);
  private JSlider widthSlider = new JSlider(0, 1000, 400);

  GridBagScaler(String imageFilename)
  {
  // set up the GruidBagLayout
    setLayout(new GridBagLayout());
    scaledImagePanel = new ScaledImagePanel(imageFilename);

    GridBagConstraints widthLabelConstraints =
      new GridBagConstraints();
    widthLabelConstraints.gridx = 0;
    widthLabelConstraints.gridy = 0;
    widthLabelConstraints.gridwidth = 2;

    GridBagConstraints widthSliderConstraints =
      new GridBagConstraints();
    widthSliderConstraints.gridx = 0;
    widthSliderConstraints.gridy = 1;
    widthSliderConstraints.gridwidth = 2;
    widthSliderConstraints.fill =
      GridBagConstraints.HORIZONTAL;
    widthSliderConstraints.ipady = 20;
```

```
GridBagConstraints heightLabelConstraints =
   new GridBagConstraints();
heightLabelConstraints.gridx = 0;
heightLabelConstraints.gridy = 4;
heightLabelConstraints.gridwidth = 2;
heightLabelConstraints.anchor = GridBagConstraints.WEST;

GridBagConstraints heightSliderConstraints =
   new GridBagConstraints();
heightSliderConstraints.gridx = 0;
heightSliderConstraints.gridy = 3;
heightSliderConstraints.anchor = GridBagConstraints.WEST;
heightSliderConstraints.fill =
   GridBagConstraints.VERTICAL;
heightSliderConstraints.ipadx = 20;

GridBagConstraints scaledImagePanelConstraints =
   new GridBagConstraints();
scaledImagePanelConstraints.gridx = 1;
scaledImagePanelConstraints.gridy = 3;
scaledImagePanelConstraints.weightx = 1.0;
scaledImagePanelConstraints.weighty = 1.0;
scaledImagePanelConstraints.fill =
   GridBagConstraints.BOTH;

// add the components to the layout
  add(heightLabel, heightLabelConstraints);
  add(widthLabel, widthLabelConstraints);
  add(heightSlider, heightSliderConstraints);
  add(widthSlider, widthSliderConstraints);
  add(scaledImagePanel, scaledImagePanelConstraints);
  scaledImagePanel.setImageHeight(heightSlider.getValue());
  scaledImagePanel.setImageWidth(widthSlider.getValue());

  ChangeListener sliderListener = new ChangeListener()
  {
    @Override
    public void stateChanged(ChangeEvent e)
```

```
      {
        if(e.getSource().equals(heightSlider))
        {
          scaledImagePanel.setImageHeight
            (heightSlider.getValue());
        }
        else
        {
          scaledImagePanel.setImageWidth

            (widthSlider.getValue());
        }
    }
  };
  // add the ChangeListener to both sliders
    heightSlider.addChangeListener(sliderListener);
    widthSlider.addChangeListener(sliderListener);

  // Invert the vertical slider so it changes the size of
  // the picture in the same direction as the slider
    heightSlider.setInverted(true);
  }

  public static void main(String[] args)
  {
    GridBagScaler scaler =
      new GridBagScaler("javacup_small.jpg");
    scaler.setTitle("Image Scaler");
    scaler.setBounds(500,500,500,500);
    scaler.setDefaultCloseOperation(EXIT_ON_CLOSE);
    scaler.setVisible(true);
  }
}
```

Exercise 18.5
Modify your answer to Exercise 17.5 by applying a GridBagLayout to the panel.
Give each component an appropriate GridBagConstraints object.

18.8 Separating the "Model" from the "View"

The next example introduces an important design issue in programs with a graphical interface, namely, the separation of the "model" (the underlying data in a program) from the "view" (the GUI that the user sees). In previous GUI programs, the code was almost entirely embedded in the visual components of the interface, but in larger programs we need to separate out the underlying program from its interface. That way we can develop, and test, programs and interfaces separately and make them more independent and maintainable.

This example represents a table of distances between major international cities of the type often seen presented as a grid in atlases. What is interesting about this type of data is that it is represented in a triangular array. This is where only half of the two-dimensional table of values is needed, since the other half would simply repeat these values. In this table, the distance between, for example, Beijing and Cairo, is identical to the distance between Cairo and Beijing, so there is no point storing the same data twice. Table 18.2 shows the table of distances that we will be using in this example.

The important point is that the underlying model of the distances should be implemented using a separate class with its own methods, not be part of the graphical classes used for the user interface. The view should send messages to the underlying model object and get the necessary data for display. With this layered architecture of model and view, the same model can be used for multiple views, and the model can be tested separately from the view.

Table 18.2 A table of distances in miles between various cities

Beijing	645								
Cairo	1,029	4,695							
Cape Town	7,329	8,044	4,479						
London	1,138	5,070	2,183	5,987					
Mumbai	7,040	2,957	2,710	5,105	4,476				
New York	8,815	6,842	5,618	7,799	3,471	7,807			
Rio de Janeiro	7,635	1,076	6,140	3,775	5,750	8,338	4,803		
Sydney	1,342	5,545	8,958	6,856	10,558	6,306	9,934	8,412	
Tokyo	5,474	1,307	5,957	9,156	5,956	4,194	6,755	11,532	4,842
	Auckland	Beijing	Cairo	Cape Town	London	Mumbai	New York	Rio de Janeiro	Sydney

18.8.1 The Model Class: FlightDistances

The FlightDistances class is the underlying model that contains data about the distances (in miles) between cities. The names of ten cities are held in a static final array of Strings.

```
private static final String[] cities = {"Auckland", "Beijing",
  "Cairo", "Cape Town", "London", "Mumbai", "New York",
    "Rio de Janeiro", "Sydney", "Tokyo"};
```

Client code can access this array via the static "getCities" method.

```
public static String[] getCities()
{
  return cities;
}
```

Marking an array as "final" means that its reference cannot be assigned to a different array, but it does not prevent the data in the array from being changed. This is similar to the unmodifiable collections we looked at in Chap. 12.

The class uses a static final two-dimensional array of integers to hold the distance data. A two-dimensional array (as we briefly introduced back in Chap. 3) can be thought of as having both rows and columns and is declared by using two sets of square brackets rather than one:

```
private static final int[][] distanceTable;
```

There are ten cities in the distance table, so they can be represented by integers in the range zero to nine. The array is therefore created with both dimensions of size ten:

```
distanceTable = new int[10][10];
```

The distance data is put into the array using a static block, as described below.

Note
Using an array is appropriate here because we are working with a small amount of static data (the distances between cities do not change). In an application requiring more dynamic data, we would probably use a collection of collections to represent data in two dimensions.

To find out the distance between two cities, the "getDistance" method is passed two integers representing the origin and destination of the journey and returns the distance between them. This is achieved by using the argument values to access a particular element in the array, for example,

```
return distanceTable[origin][destination];
```

All the fields and methods of the FlightDistances class are static because it provides a fixed set of data and does not require different objects with different states. Since classes with only static methods will not need a constructor, we need somewhere else to put initialization code. This can be done using a static code block. This is simply a code block marked with the "static" keyword. Any code included within this block will be executed as soon as the class is loaded.

```
// the static block creates the array and fills it with data
static
{
//etc.
```

The "getDistance" method returns the distance between two cities, given index values in the range 0–9. Since the triangular array is only half filled with data, the method checks to see if the source index is lower than the destination index. If this is not the case, the values need to be switched so that the correct half of the array is used for the lookup.

```
if (origin < destination)
{
  return distanceTable[origin][destination];
}
else
{
  return distanceTable[destination][origin];
}
```

There is also the possibility that one or both arguments might be out of range. If this is the case, a "try...catch" block will catch the ArrayIndexOutOfBoundsException and return −1 to the caller. It also writes a message to standard error output (this will not affect any UI component that might use this class).

```
try
{
  ...
}
// out of bounds indexes return -1
catch (ArrayIndexOutOfBoundsException e)
{
  System.err.println("Invalid origin or destination index "
  + origin + " or " + destination);
  return -1;
}
```

Here is the complete FlightDistances class, which is mostly data being put into the array. Because this is the underlying model for the program, it does not contain any UI components. The way that the data is being put into the array has been done rather laboriously here so that the code comments can help you see how the triangular array is being constructed.

```java
package com.foundjava.chapter18;

public class FlightDistances
{
  private static String[] cities = { "Auckland", "Beijing",
    "Cairo","Cape Town", "London", "Mumbai", "New York",
    "Rio de Janeiro","Sydney", "Tokyo" };
// declare a two-dimensional array of integers
  private static int[][] distanceTable;

// the static block creates the array and fills it with data
  static
  {
// create a 10 by 10 array
    distanceTable = new int[10][10];
// where the two indexes are the same, the distance is zero
// because the origin and destination are the same city
    for (int i = 0; i < 10; i++) {
      distanceTable[i][i] = 0;
    }
// create the data as a triangular array
// (only half the array needs to be populated)
    distanceTable[0][1] = 6455; // Auckland <-> Beijing
    distanceTable[0][2] = 10298;// Auckland <-> Cairo
    distanceTable[0][3] = 7329; // Auckland <-> Cape Town
    distanceTable[0][4] = 11389;// Auckland <-> London
    distanceTable[0][5] = 7640; // Auckland <-> Mumbai
    distanceTable[0][6] = 8815; // Auckland <-> New York
    distanceTable[0][7] = 7635; // Auckland <-> Rio
    distanceTable[0][8] = 1342; // Auckland <-> Sydney
    distanceTable[0][9] = 5474; // Auckland <-> Tokyo

    distanceTable[1][2] = 4695; // Beijing <-> Cairo
    distanceTable[1][3] = 8044; // Beijing <-> Cape Town
    distanceTable[1][4] = 5070; // Beijing <-> London
    distanceTable[1][5] = 2957; // Beijing <-> Mumbai
    distanceTable[1][6] = 6842; // Beijing <-> New York
    distanceTable[1][7] = 10764;// Beijing <-> Rio de Janeiro
    distanceTable[1][8] = 5545; // Beijing <-> Sydney
    distanceTable[1][9] = 1307; // Beijing <-> Tokyo
```

```
    distanceTable[2][3] = 4479;  // Cairo <-> Cape Town
    distanceTable[2][4] = 2183;  // Cairo <-> London
    distanceTable[2][5] = 2710;  // Cairo <-> Mumbai
    distanceTable[2][6] = 5618;  // Cairo <-> New York
    distanceTable[2][7] = 6140;  // Cairo <-> Rio de Janeiro
    distanceTable[2][8] = 8958;  // Cairo <-> Sydney
    distanceTable[2][9] = 5957;  // Cairo <-> Tokyo

    distanceTable[3][4] = 5987;  // Cape Town <-> London
    distanceTable[3][5] = 5105;  // Cape Town <-> Mumbai
    distanceTable[3][6] = 7799;  // Cape Town <-> New York
    distanceTable[3][7] = 3775;  // Cape Town <-> Rio
    distanceTable[3][8] = 6856;  // Cape Town <-> Sydney
    distanceTable[3][9] = 9156;  // Cape Town <-> Tokyo
    distanceTable[4][5] = 4476;  // London <-> Mumbai
    distanceTable[4][6] = 3471;  // London <-> New York
    distanceTable[4][7] = 5750;  // London <-> Rio de Janeiro
    distanceTable[4][8] = 10558; // London <-> Sydney
    distanceTable[4][9] = 5956;  // London <-> Tokyo

    distanceTable[5][6] = 7807;  // Mumbai <-> New York
    distanceTable[5][7] = 8338;  // Mumbai <-> Rio de Janeiro
    distanceTable[5][8] = 6306;  // Mumbai <-> Sydney
    distanceTable[5][9] = 4194;  // Mumbai <-> Tokyo

    distanceTable[6][7] = 4803;  // New York <-> Rio de Janeiro
    distanceTable[6][8] = 9934;  // New York <-> Sydney
    distanceTable[6][9] = 6755;  // New York <-> Tokyo

    distanceTable[7][8] = 8412;  // Rio de Janeiro <-> Sydney
    distanceTable[7][9] = 11532; // Rio de Janeiro <-> Tokyo

    distanceTable[8][9] = 4842;  // Sydney <-> Tokyo
    }

// given integers to represent airports in the table,
// this method returns the distance between them
    public static int getDistance(int origin, int destination)
```

```
    {
      try
      {
        if (origin < destination)
        {
          return distanceTable[origin][destination];
        }
        else
        {
          return distanceTable[destination][origin];
        }
      }
// out of bounds indexes return -1
      catch (ArrayIndexOutOfBoundsException e)
      {
        System.out.println
          ("Invalid origin or destination index " + origin
          + " or " + destination);
        return -1;
      }
    }

  public static String[] getCities()
  {
    return cities;
  }
}
```

The main concept in this example is that the underlying implementation code is separate from the user interface. This means that it can be tested separately before a UI is added. The following JUnit test case demonstrates some simple test methods that partially exercise the code. This is not by any means an exhaustive set of tests, but covers some of the key features:

- Testing that if the origin and destination are the same then zero is returned.
- Testing a known distance between a valid origin and destination against the distance value returned by the method.
- Testing that the same distance is returned if the indexes of the origin and destination are switched.
- Testing that any out of range integer parameter results in −1 being returned.
- Testing that the array of city names is not null.
- Testing a valid city name index against its expected city name.

No doubt you can think of many other tests that could usefully be applied. Here is the test code with these initial tests in place (the FlightDistances class above passes all these tests).

```java
package com.foundjava.chapter18;

import static org.junit.jupiter.api.Assertions.assertEquals;
import static org.junit.jupiter.api.Assertions.assertNotNull;
import org.junit.jupiter.api.Test;

public class DistancesTestCase
{
  @Test
  public void testGetZeroDistance()
  {
    int distance = FlightDistances.getDistance(0, 0);
    assertEquals(0, distance);
  }

  @Test
  public void testGetValidDistance()
  {
    int distance = FlightDistances.getDistance(1, 2);
    assertEquals(4695, distance);
  }

  @Test
  public void testGetValidDistanceHigherFirstIndex()
  {
    int distance = FlightDistances.getDistance(2, 1);
    assertEquals(4695, distance);
  }

  @Test
  public void testInvalidIndex()
  {
    int distance = FlightDistances.getDistance(10, 1);
    assertEquals(-1, distance);
  }

  @Test
  public void testGetCitiesArray()
```

```
  {
     String[] cities = FlightDistances.getCities();
     assertNotNull(cities);
  }

  @Test
  public void testGetCities()
  {
     String[] cities = FlightDistances.getCities();
     assertEquals("Tokyo", cities[9]);
  }
}
```

18.8.2   The View Class: DistanceViewer

Once we have a properly implemented and tested model, we can add a UI. The DistanceViewer class provides the graphical user interface to the system, using two JComboBox objects: one for the name of the city of origin and one for the destination. Note that since a JComboBox can contain different types of element, we need to specify the element type as "String" for this example.

```
private JComboBox<String> fromCity;
private JComboBox<String> toCity;
```

The city names are added to these combo boxes using the String array returned from the FlightDistances class.

```
String[] cities = FlightDistances.getCities();
fromCity = new JComboBox<String>(cities);
toCity = new JComboBox<String>(cities);
```

Like other component actions in previous examples, changing the selection in a JComboBox fires an ActionEvent, so we need an ActionListener to handle these events. To find the distance, the chosen city values need to be returned from the two JComboBoxes. This is achieved using the "getSelectedIndex" method, which returns the index of the selected string. Since the index values start at zero, they will match the zero-indexed array in our FlightDistances class. This means that we can use the values retrieved from the combo boxes directly as parameters to another method, "showDistance", which retrieves the relevant distance from the underlying model and updates the view. As in the previous example, we have not used a lambda expression because we are reusing the same implementation in two places.

```
ActionListener cityListener = new ActionListener() {
  public void actionPerformed(ActionEvent e)
  {
    showDistance(fromCity.getSelectedIndex(),
      toCity.getSelectedIndex());
  }
};
```

The "showDistance" method gets the distance from the "getDistance" method of the FlightDistances class, then sets the text of the "resultLabel". The separate use of the "measureString" will be useful in a later exercise, where we allow the display to be shown in either kilometers or miles. It also has the side effect of applying String concatenation to the integer "distance" value, which would otherwise have to be cast from integer to String to be set as the text of a JLabel.

```
private void showDistance(int fromCity, int toCity)
{
  int distance = FlightDistances.getDistance
    (fromCity, toCity);
  String measureString = " miles";
  resultLabel.setText(distance + measureString);
}
```

This is the complete DistanceViewer class. It uses a GridBagLayout to arrange the components.

```java
package com.foundjava.chapter18;

import java.awt.GridBagConstraints;
import java.awt.GridBagLayout;
import java.awt.event.ActionEvent;
import java.awt.event.ActionListener;
import javax.swing.JComboBox;
import javax.swing.JFrame;
import javax.swing.JLabel;

public class DistanceViewer extends JFrame
{
  private JComboBox fromCity;
  private JComboBox toCity;
// text label for dynamic update
  private JLabel resultLabel;

  public DistanceViewer() {
    String[] cities = FlightDistances.getCities();
    fromCity = new JComboBox(cities);
    toCity = new JComboBox(cities);

    ActionListener cityListener = new ActionListener() {
      public void actionPerformed(ActionEvent e)
      {
        showDistance(fromCity.getSelectedIndex(),
        toCity.getSelectedIndex());
      }
    };
    fromCity.addActionListener(cityListener);
    toCity.addActionListener(cityListener);

    setLayout(new GridBagLayout());
      GridBagConstraints line2Constraints =
        new GridBagConstraints();
      line2Constraints.gridy = 1;
      GridBagConstraints labelConstraints =
        new GridBagConstraints();
      labelConstraints.gridwidth = 3;
```

```
// create the text labels for the choices
   JLabel fromLabel = new JLabel("From:");
   JLabel toLabel = new JLabel("To:");
// create and add the text label for the result
   JLabel distanceLabel = new JLabel
     ("The distance between the cities is");
// create a text label to display the result
   resultLabel = new JLabel("0");

// add these components to the frame
   add(distanceLabel, labelConstraints);
   add(resultLabel);
   add(fromLabel, line2Constraints);
   add(fromCity, line2Constraints);
   add(toLabel, line2Constraints);
   add(toCity, line2Constraints);
 }

 private void showDistance(int fromCity, int toCity)
 {
   int distance = FlightDistances.getDistance
     (fromCity, toCity);
   String measureString = " miles";
   resultLabel.setText(Integer.toString(distance) +
     measureString);
 }

 public static void main(String[] args)
 {
   DistanceViewer viewer = new DistanceViewer();
   viewer.setTitle("Mileage table between major cities");
   viewer.setDefaultCloseOperation(EXIT_ON_CLOSE);
   viewer.setBounds(100, 100, 500, 150);
   viewer.setVisible(true);
 }
}
```

Figure 18.18 shows the distance viewer giving the distance between New York and Tokyo.

Exercise 18.6

- Modify the DistanceViewer so that it allows the user to choose between displaying the distances in either miles or kilometers, using two radio buttons in a button group.

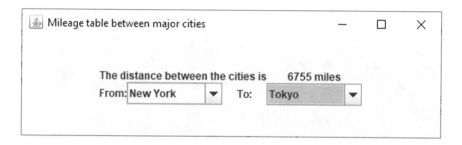

Fig. 18.18 The distance viewer application in use

- Use the radio button ActionEvents to change the way that the distance is displayed.
- The conversion between miles and kilometers should use the following formula: 1 mile = 1.60934 km.

18.9   Summary

Building on the previous chapter, which covered how to make UI components appear on the screen, this chapter explained how component events can be handled to add underlying code to the UI. It outlined the features of Java that can manage events being fired from various components and mouse actions. Various types of event and event listeners were introduced, including ActionEvents, MouseEvents and ChangeEvents. Different ways of writing event listeners were described, namely, public classes, inner classes, local inner classes, anonymous inner classes and lambda expressions. We saw how each of these approaches has its own characteristics that make it appropriate for a specific context. The GridBagLayout was used to demonstrate how flexible component layouts can be built to reduce the communication overhead of alternative approaches such as using multiple panels. Finally, the chapter looked at the importance of separating the underlying data model from the view, so that the model can be separately tested before having a UI added and can be reused independently of the user interface.

Dialogs and Menus, Models and Views

19

In a typical application, you want to give some information to, or get some information from, the user in different contexts. Dialogs provide pop-up windows that can provide focused modes of interaction for an application. Dialogs can be either modal or modeless; modal dialogs prevent the user from doing anything in the dialog's parent application until the dialog has been dismissed. With a modeless dialog, the user can work in other windows of the application without dismissing the dialog.

A dialog is dependent on the parent window from where it was launched. When that parent window is minimized, maximized or destroyed, its dependent dialogs follow. The parent window of a dialog must be an instance of JFrame (or a subclass).

19.1 Predefined Dialogs in Swing

Swing provides some predefined types of dialog that have generic uses across many applications, such as message boxes, and dialogs for navigating the file system and choosing colors. This section provides a brief introduction to these dialogs.

19.1.1 Message Box Dialogs Using JOptionPane

The simplest Swing dialogs are created using the JOptionPane class, which supports the creation of modal dialogs that handle simple interactions with the user. There are three types of dialog that can be created using a JOptionPane (as shown in Table 19.1).

The three generic types of dialog can all be configured in a variety of ways, and a generic option dialog can be created with characteristics of all three types. Instances of the dialog types can be created using various overloaded static methods of the

© Springer Nature Switzerland AG 2020
D. Parsons, *Foundational Java*, Texts in Computer Science,
https://doi.org/10.1007/978-3-030-54518-5_19

Table 19.1 Types of dialog created by the JOptionPane class

Dialog type	Description
Message dialog	Tell the user about something that has happened
Confirm dialog	Asks a confirming question, like yes/no/cancel
Input dialog	Prompt for some input from the user

JOptionPane class. For example, to show a simple message dialog with an "OK" button, you can use one of the "JOptionPane.showMessageDialog" methods. The following simple program shows examples of the three basic types of dialogs being created with their various "show…" methods. This is just a syntax example to show how the JOptionPane can be used to create different dialogs, so does not have any specific context. Normally, a dialog would be launched from a host Component, which would be passed as the first parameter to the "showConfirmDialog" and "showInputDialog" methods. However, a dialog can be launched directly without a host component, by using a null reference, as we do in this example. These dialogs appear using their default settings.

```
package com.foundjava.chapter19;

import javax.swing.JFrame;
import javax.swing.JOptionPane;

public class OptionPanes extends JFrame
{
  public static void main(String[] args)
  {
    JOptionPane.showMessageDialog(null, "Hello!");
    JOptionPane.showConfirmDialog(null, "Are you sure?");
    JOptionPane.showInputDialog
        (null, "Please enter something");
  }
}
```

Figure 19.1 shows the three dialogs, which will appear one after the other.

Confirmation and input dialogs both return values to the code that calls them, so the application can respond to the user's selections or data entry. The JOption-Pane's messages, title, icons, buttons, etc., can all be configured in a variety of combinations. Later in this chapter we will see some JOptionPanes being used in the context of other examples.

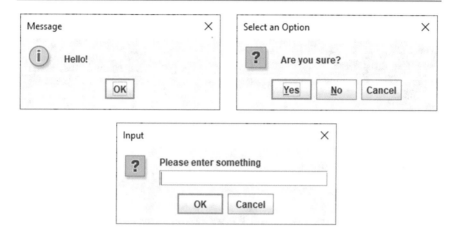

Fig. 19.1 Message dialogs from the JOptionPane class

19.1.2   File Chooser Dialogs Using JFileChooser

A very generic dialog that can be used across many different applications is a file chooser dialog that can be used for loading and saving files. Swing provides the JFileChooser class to create dialogs for navigating the file system and selecting files. Objects of this class can be configured as either "open" or "save" dialogs using the "showOpenDialog" or "showSaveDialog" methods. There is also a "showDialog" method that can be used to create a dialog that has a customized message on the dialog's "approve" button, rather than the standard "Open" or "Save" (e.g. you might have a "Run Application" button).

To use a file chooser dialog, first create a JFileChooser, then pass the parent container as a parameter to the chosen "show…" method. Once the dialog has been closed, use the other methods to retrieve the resulting file information. The following code fragment shows a "file open" dialog being created. If the value returned from the "show…" method approves the action, then we retrieve the name of the chosen file from the dialog.

```
JFileChooser chooser = new JFileChooser();
int returnVal = chooser.showOpenDialog(container);
if(returnVal == JFileChooser.APPROVE_OPTION)
{
  String filename =
    chooser.getSelectedFile().getName();
}
```

We can then use the file handling syntax covered in Chap. 13 to interact with the selected file. Figure 19.2 is a generic example that shows how file dialogs will

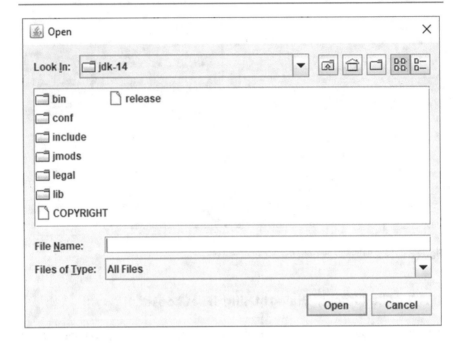

Fig. 19.2 A JFileChooser dialog configured with a generic title and button label

appear (other configurations of the dialog look much the same but will have different titles and button labels, such as "Save").

Exercise 19.1

- Write a subclass of JFrame that will display an "open file" dialog when a button is pressed
- When the file dialog is closed, pop-up a message box that displays the name of the selected file.

19.1.3 Color Chooser Dialogs Using JColorChooser

Another of the predefined Swing dialogs is the JColorChooser. This is a component that can be easily reused in any application that needs to enable users to select colors. We can interact with a JColorChooser to change the foreground or background colors of other components. To demonstrate the basic functionality of a JColorChooser, the following example consists of a color chooser, a button and a panel. When the button is pressed, the panel will be repainted in the color currently selected by the color chooser. To do this, we create a (lambda expression) listener for the button that gets the currently selected color from the color chooser with the "getColor" method then changes the current color of the panel using "setBackground".

```
colorButton.addActionListener
(e -> colorPanel.setBackground(colorChooser.getColor()));
```

The rest of the code is simple, laying out the three components on a BorderLayout. We use the simplest form of the JColorChooser constructor, which takes no arguments. This is the complete program:

```
package com.foundjava.chapter19;
import javax.swing.*;
import java.awt.*;
import java.awt.event.*;

public class ColorChooserWindow extends JFrame
{
  private JColorChooser colorChooser;
  private JButton colorButton;
  private JPanel colorPanel;

  public ColorChooserWindow(String title) {
    super(title);
    setLayout(new BorderLayout());

    colorChooser = new JColorChooser();
    colorPanel = new JPanel();
    colorButton = new JButton("Change Color");
    colorButton.addActionListener(e ->
        colorPanel.setBackground(colorChooser.getColor()));
    add(colorChooser, BorderLayout.NORTH);
    add(colorPanel, BorderLayout.CENTER);
    add(colorButton, BorderLayout.SOUTH);
  }

  public static void main(String[] args)
  {
    ColorChooserWindow window = new
      ColorChooserWindow("Color Chooser");
    window.setBounds(0, 0, 500, 600);
    window.setDefaultCloseOperation(EXIT_ON_CLOSE);
    window.setVisible(true);
  }
}
```

Figure 19.3 shows the color chooser with one of its tabbed panes selected. Each one has a different way of selecting the color.

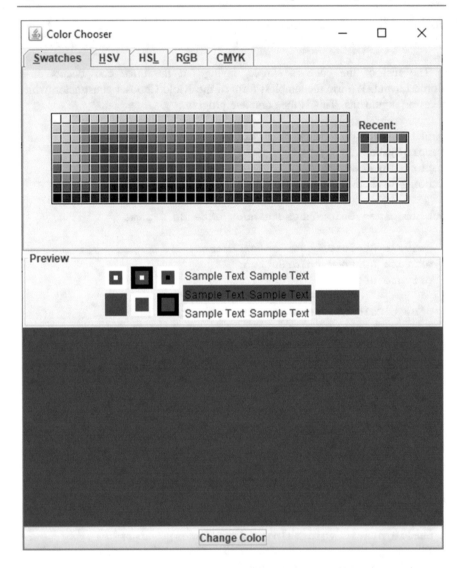

Fig. 19.3   The JColorChooser with one of its tabbed panes selected

19.2   Custom Dialogs with JDialog

So far we have been looking at some of the generic dialog types that are predefined in Swing, but applications will also need all kinds of dialogs customized to the requirements of those applications. These customized dialogs can be created by using specialized subclasses of the JDialog class. These dialogs can have complex sets of components and event listeners, just like frames. A full discussion of custom dialogs is far beyond the scope of this book, so the following example is just intended to give a brief introduction to some of the basics of creating a custom dialog.

The example dialog that will be introduced here is designed to allow the user to enter three items of data that can be used with the "drawString" method of the Graphics class. This method has three arguments: the text to be drawn (a String) and the x and y positions of the text (integers). To make it easy to pass these values from a dialog to the component that draws the String, a value object will be useful. A value object represents a field that is more complex than a simple data type, encapsulating more than one value (like a date does, for example, or a "money" object that contains both a value and a currency). The following class acts as a value object to encapsulate the three values needed to draw a graphical string, with JavaBean style properties.

```java
package com.foundjava.chapter19;

public class StringData
{
  private String text;
  private int x;
  private int y;

  public String getText()
  {
    return text;
  }
  public void setText(String text)
  {
    this.text = text;
  }
  public int getX()
  {
    return x;
  }
  public void setX(int x)
  {
```

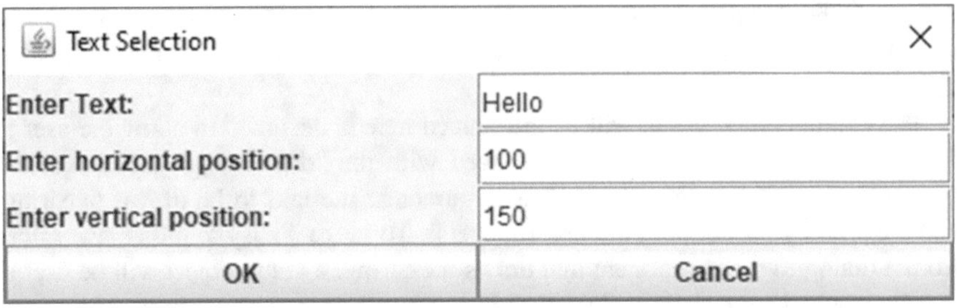

⚜ Text Selection	✕
Enter Text:	Hello
Enter horizontal position:	100
Enter vertical position:	150
OK	Cancel

Fig. 19.4 A dialog to enter the text and position values for a graphical string

```
    this.x = x;
  }
  public int getY()
  {
    return y;
  }
  public void setY(int y)
  {
    this.y = y;
  }
}
```

Now we can create a dialog that can populate one of these objects and pass it back to the calling object. Figure 19.4 shows what the dialog will look like for this example, using a simple GridView layout manager. The user can type in the text, along with the X and Y positions.

The class used to create this dialog extends JDialog.

```
public class DrawStringDialog extends JDialog
```

The dialog's constructor has the host JFrame passed to it and passes this to the superclass constructor along with a Boolean that sets the modality for the dialog ("true" means modal).

```
public DrawStringDialog(JFrame owner)
{
// set the owning frame and make the dialog modal
  super(owner, true);
```

The main part of the dialog's functionality is contained in the event listener for the button. If the "OK" button is pressed then the data from the three text fields is put into a StringData object. This code includes some exception handling where the x- and y-values are converted from Strings into integers.

```
if(event.getSource() == okButton)
{
  stringData.setText(textField.getText());
  try
  {
    stringData.setX(Integer.parseInt(xField.getText()));
    stringData.setY(Integer.parseInt(yField.getText()));
  }
  catch(NumberFormatException e)
// etc…
```

This is the complete DrawStringDialog class

```
package com.foundjava.chapter19;
import java.awt.GridLayout;
import java.awt.event.ActionEvent;
import java.awt.event.ActionListener;
import javax.swing.JButton;
import javax.swing.JDialog;
import javax.swing.JFrame;
import javax.swing.JLabel;
import javax.swing.JTextField;

public class DrawStringDialog extends JDialog
{
// visual components
  private JLabel textLabel = new JLabel("Enter Text: ");
  private JLabel xLabel =
      new JLabel("Enter horizontal position: ");
  private JLabel yLabel =
      new JLabel("Enter vertical position: ");
  private JTextField textField = new JTextField(20);
  private JTextField xField = new JTextField(20);
  private JTextField yField = new JTextField(20);
  private JButton okButton = new JButton("OK");
  private JButton cancelButton = new JButton("Cancel");
// value object to store the text and position of the string
  private StringData stringData = new StringData();

  public DrawStringDialog(JFrame owner)
  {
// set the owning frame and make the dialog modal
      super(owner, true);
```

```
    setTitle("Text Selection");
    setLayout(new GridLayout(0, 2));
    add(textLabel);
    add(textField);
    add(xLabel);
    add(xField);
    add(yLabel);
    add(yField);
    add(okButton);
    add(cancelButton);
    pack();
    okButton.addActionListener(dialogListener);
    cancelButton.addActionListener(dialogListener);
    setDefaultCloseOperation(DISPOSE_ON_CLOSE);
  }

  ActionListener dialogListener = new ActionListener() {
  public void actionPerformed(ActionEvent event)
  {
    if(event. getSource() == okButton)
    {
      stringData.setText(textField.getText());
      try{
      stringData.setX(Integer.parseInt(xField.getText()));
      stringData.setY(Integer.parseInt(yField.getText()));
      }
      catch(NumberFormatException e)
      {
        e.printStackTrace();
      }
    }
    setVisible(false);
  }
};

public StringData showDialog()
{
  setVisible(true);
  return stringData;
}
}
```

Of course, having a Dialog class is only part of the story. We also need a host application that will launch the dialog and retrieve information from it. The following class, DrawStringFrame, contains a JPanel and a JButton. When the button is pressed, the event handler calls the "showData" method of the DrawStringDialog, using a reference ("this") to the parent JFrame. After the dialog closes, the StringData is retrieved as the value returned from the method. If the StringData returned from the dialog contains a String, the event handler adds the StringData object to a collection (called "strings") and then uses the data to draw all the strings in the collection on the screen by calling the "repaint" method.

```
button.addActionListener(e->
{
   DrawStringDialog stringDialog = new DrawStringDialog(this);
   StringData stringData = stringDialog.showDialog();
   if(stringData.getText() != null)
   {
      strings.add(stringData);
   }
   repaint();
});
```

As we saw in earlier examples, the "repaint" method triggers a call to "paint", which we can override. In the version of "paint" used here, we iterate through the collection of StringData objects and show them on the panel using the "drawString" method.

```
@Override
public void paint(Graphics g)
{
   super.paint(g);
   for(StringData i : strings)
   {
       String text = i.getText();
       int textX = i.getX();
       int textY = i.getY();
      g.drawString(text, textX, textY);
   }
}
```

This is the complete class.

```
package com.foundjava.chapter19;

import java.awt.BorderLayout;
import java.awt.Container;
import java.awt.Graphics;
```

```java
import java.util.ArrayList;
import java.util.Collection;

import javax.swing.JButton;
import javax.swing.JFrame;
import javax.swing.JPanel;

public class DrawStringFrame extends JFrame
{
  private JPanel drawingArea = new JPanel();
  private Collection<StringData> strings =
    new ArrayList<StringData>();

  public DrawStringFrame()
  {
    JButton button = new JButton("Press to Add Text");
    Container container = getContentPane();
    container.add(drawingArea, BorderLayout.CENTER);
    container.add(button, BorderLayout.SOUTH);
    button.addActionListener(e->
    {
      DrawStringDialog stringDialog =
        new DrawStringDialog(this);
      StringData stringData = stringDialog.showDialog();
      if(stringData.getText() != null)
      {
        strings.add(stringData);
      }
      repaint();
    });
  }

  @Override
  public void paint(Graphics g)
  {
    super.paint(g);
    for(StringData i : strings)
    {
    String text = i.getText();
    int textX = i.getX();
    int textY = i.getY();
    drawingArea.getGraphics().drawString
      String text = i.getText();
      int textX = i.getX();
```

```
        int textY = i.getY();
        g.drawString(text, textX, textY);
    }
}

public static void main(String[] args)
{
    DrawStringFrame frame = new DrawStringFrame();
    frame.setTitle("Graphical Strings");
    frame.setDefaultCloseOperation(EXIT_ON_CLOSE);
    frame.setBounds(100, 100, 500, 300);
    frame.setVisible(true);
}
}
```

When the class is run, the "Text Selection" dialog can be triggered multiple times by using the button added to the frame. Figure 19.5 shows the custom dialog being used to enter the details of a StringData object. A String from a previous invocation of the dialog can be seen in the panel that is added to the host frame.

Exercise 19.2

- Add a "size" field to the StringData class.
- Modify the "TextSelection" dialog to allow this value to be entered.
- Use this value to set the font size used when the string is drawn.

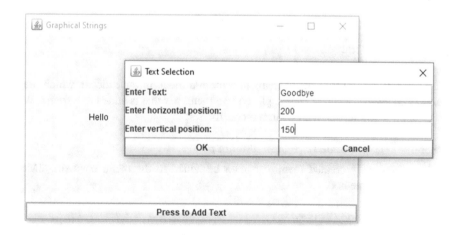

Fig. 19.5   The custom dialog being used to add graphical strings to a panel

19.3   Using Menus

Application frames frequently provide menus so that the user can select different courses of action while using the application. In this section we introduce menu bars, menus and menu items.

19.3.1   Adding a Menu to a Frame

To add a menu to a JFrame, we use three classes; JMenu, JMenuItem and JMenuBar. One of the JMenu constructors allows you to set the menu's text label, which will appear in the menu bar, for example.

```
JMenu fileMenu = new JMenu("File Menu");
```

A JMenuItem is one selection from a menu and is created using a constructor that takes the text label of the item as its parameter. As an example, we might create a menu for providing the basic file management functions that are common to many applications. In this simple example, we will assume there are four menu items. "New", "Open", "Save" and "Exit"

```
JMenuItem newItem = new JMenuItem("New");
JMenuItem openItem = new JMenuItem("Open");
JMenuItem saveItem = new JMenuItem("Save");
JMenuItem exitItem = new JMenuItem("Exit");
```

To add a JMenuItem to a menu, we use the "add" method of the JMenu object:

```
fileMenu.add(newItem);
fileMenu.add(openItem);
fileMenu.add(saveItem);
fileMenu.add(exitItem);
```

This will put the four menu items into the file menu in the order in which they have been added. A menu can be placed in a menu bar that is added to a frame. We can create a JMenuBar with a simple constructor:

```
JMenuBar mainMenuBar = new JMenuBar();
```

The previously created menu can then be added to the menu bar using JMenuBar's "add" method

```
mainMenuBar.add(fileMenu);
```

Finally, when the menu bar is complete, it can be added to the JFrame using the "setJMenuBar" method.

Fig. 19.6   The file menu added to a JFrame

```
setJMenuBar(mainMenuBar);
```
The menu items will now automatically appear when the menu is selected. Figure 19.6 shows the file menu as it appears in a Frame, when the menu's text label has been selected.

19.3.2   Menu Enhancement: Separators, Mnemonics and Accelerators

There are several enhancements that can be made to menus. In this section we will briefly cover separators, mnemonics and accelerators.

19.3.2.1   Menu Separators

A menu separator is simply a horizontal line that appears between groups of items in a menu, to put them into categories and make them easier to navigate. The "addSeparator" method of the JMenu class allows the separator to be added between menu items. In this example a separator is added between the "Save" and "Exit" items

```
fileMenu.add(newItem);
fileMenu.add(openItem);
fileMenu.add(saveItem);
fileMenu.addSeparator();
fileMenu.add(exitItem);
```

Figure 19.7 shows the effect of adding this separator at this position.

Fig. 19.7   A separator added to a menu

19.3.2.2 Mnemonics

Mnemonics allow a user to navigate menus and access menu items directly using the keyboard. When a mnemonic is added to a menu or menu item, one letter in the menu or menu item text is underlined. Menus that have a mnemonic added can be opened (in Windows) by typing the ALT key with the mnemonic letter. Once a menu is opened, a menu item can be accessed by typing the associated mnemonic letter. Mnemonics can be added using the "setMnemonic" method, which takes as its parameter the character to be used as the mnemonic (underlined in the menu). In the file menu example we have previously introduced, we might set the following mnemonic letters as being suitable for the four options we have defined. In this example there are no duplicates in the first letters of each menu item, so all the mnemonics use the first letter. In other cases (e.g. if we added a "Save As…" menu item so that two options both began with the letter "S"), we would have to use an alternative letter for one of the options.

```
newItem.setMnemonic('N');
openItem.setMnemonic('O');
saveItem.setMnemonic('S');
exitItem.setMnemonic('E');
```

Figure 19.8 shows the file menu when each menu item has these mnemonic characters defined.

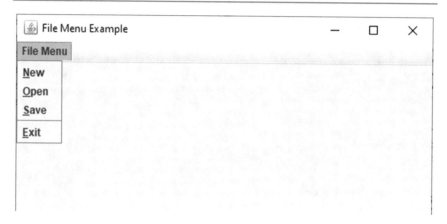

Fig. 19.8   Mnemonic characters added to menu items

19.3.2.3   Keyboard Accelerators

Keyboard accelerators allow you to create keyboard shortcuts for accessing menu items directly, without having to open the menu first. The key combination to use for the accelerator is shown beside the item in the menu. Menu items have an accelerator property of type Keystroke. The Keystroke object encapsulates the key that was pressed along with any modifiers (e.g. the Shift key, the CTRL key, etc.). The syntax is a little complex. The "getKeyStroke" method takes as its first parameter the key that will trigger the menu item. This character is expressed as a virtual key. A virtual key represents the character itself, as opposed to the physical position of the key on the keyboard, which will vary between locales. Each key on the keyboard has a matching virtual key code, defined as a public static field of the java.awt.event.KeyEvent class. These fields have names beginning with the prefix "VK_", followed by a code that represents the chosen key. For letters these can be the actual letter character. Therefore "KeyEvent.VK_S" simply refers to the "S" key.

The second parameter represents the other keys that are used in combination with the character key. These can be specified using public final fields of the ActionEvent class and combined using the bitwise OR operator ("|").

```
int modifiers =
    ActionEvent.SHIFT_MASK | ActionEvent.CTRL_MASK;
KeyStroke ks = KeyStroke.getKeyStroke
    (KeyEvent.VK_S, modifiers);
saveItem.setAccelerator(ks);
```

Fig. 19.9   An accelerator added to the "Save" item of a menu

Figure 19.9 shows the menu after the accelerator defined above has been added to the "Save" menu item.

19.3.3   MenuListeners

So far we have seen how we can add and configure menus and menu items. However, nothing will happen when we select a menu item unless we add an appropriate listener object to that item. As we did for some other controls in the last chapter, we must add ActionListeners. In this example we implement the listener as an inner class ("FileMenuListener") with a constructor that takes a reference to the parent frame.

```
class FileMenuListener implements ActionListener
{
  private JFrame frame;
  public FileMenuListener(JFrame parent)
  {
    frame = parent;
  }
//etc.
```

The MenuListener responds to different menu choices by getting the text label of the menu item from the "getActionCommand" method of the event object.

```
String command = e.getActionCommand();
```

The String returned from this method can then be used in selection statements to choose the appropriate course of action, for example,

```
if(command.equals("New"))
{
  int returnVal =
    chooser.showDialog(frame, "Create New File");
  if(returnVal == JFileChooser.APPROVE_OPTION)
  {
    // create new file...
```

When we add the ActionListeners to the MenuItems we use a FileMenuListener as the parameter along with the reference to the JFrame, as in this example where an action listener is added to the "New" menu item:

```
newItem.addActionListener(new FileMenuListener(this));
```

In the example that follows there is a frame that contains a menu and responds to menu items being selected. To keep the class reasonably small there is no actual file handling here. Instead, message dialogs are displayed using JOptionPanes to indicate the values being returned from the dialogs for the "New", "Open" and "Save" menu options. For the "Exit" menu item, a confirmation dialog is displayed. If the value returned from the dialog is "YES_OPTION", then the frame is closed. Since the default buttons for a confirmation dialog are "Yes", "No" and "Cancel" it is better to replace these with just "Yes" and "No" buttons for this context. We can set this using the "YES_NO" field from the JOptionPane as the fourth parameter to the "showConfirmDialog" method. This also requires us to set the third parameter, which is the title of the dialog.

```
int dialogOption = JOptionPane.showConfirmDialog
  (getContentPane(), "Are you sure you want to exit?",
    "Exit Application", JOptionPane.YES_NO_OPTION);
if (dialogOption == JOptionPane.YES_OPTION)
{
 frame.dispose();
}
```

This is the complete class.

```java
package com.foundjava.chapter19;
import java.awt.event.ActionEvent;
import java.awt.event.ActionListener;
import java.awt.event.KeyEvent;
import java.awt.event.WindowEvent;
import java.io.File;
import javax.swing.JFileChooser;
import javax.swing.JFrame;
import javax.swing.JMenu;
import javax.swing.JMenuBar;
import javax.swing.JMenuItem;
import javax.swing.JOptionPane;
import javax.swing.KeyStroke;

public class FileMenuFrame extends JFrame
{
  private JFileChooser chooser = new JFileChooser();
  private File currentFile;

  public FileMenuFrame()
  {
    JMenu fileMenu = new JMenu("File Menu");
    JMenuItem newItem = new JMenuItem("New");
    JMenuItem openItem = new JMenuItem("Open");
    JMenuItem saveItem = new JMenuItem("Save");
    JMenuItem exitItem = new JMenuItem("Exit");

    newItem.setMnemonic('N');
    openItem.setMnemonic('O');
    saveItem.setMnemonic('S');
    exitItem.setMnemonic('E');

    int modifiers =
      ActionEvent.SHIFT_MASK | ActionEvent.CTRL_MASK;
    KeyStroke ks = KeyStroke.getKeyStroke
      (KeyEvent.VK_S, modifiers);
    saveItem.setAccelerator(ks);

    fileMenu.add(newItem);
    fileMenu.add(openItem);
    fileMenu.add(saveItem);
    fileMenu.addSeparator();
    fileMenu.add(exitItem);
```

```java
JMenuBar mainMenuBar = new JMenuBar();
mainMenuBar.add(fileMenu);
setJMenuBar(mainMenuBar);

class FileMenuListener implements ActionListener
{
  private JFrame frame;

  public FileMenuListener(JFrame parent) {
    frame = parent;
  }

  public void actionPerformed(ActionEvent e)
  {
    String command = e.getActionCommand();
    if (command.equals("New")) {
      int returnVal = chooser.showDialog
        (frame, "Create New File");
      if (returnVal == JFileChooser.APPROVE_OPTION) {
// create new file
        currentFile = chooser.getSelectedFile();
        JOptionPane.showMessageDialog
          (frame, "New file " + currentFile);
      }
    }
    if (command.equals("Open")) {
      int returnVal = chooser.showOpenDialog(frame);
      if (returnVal == JFileChooser.APPROVE_OPTION) {
// open file
        currentFile = chooser.getSelectedFile();
        JOptionPane.showMessageDialog
          (frame, "Open file " + currentFile);
      }
    }
    if (command.equals("Save")) {
      int returnVal = chooser.showSaveDialog(frame);
      if (returnVal == JFileChooser.APPROVE_OPTION) {
// save file
        currentFile = chooser.getSelectedFile();
        JOptionPane.showMessageDialog
          (frame, "Save file " + currentFile);
      }
    }
```

```
        if (command.equals("Exit")) {
            int dialogOption = JOptionPane.showConfirmDialog
                (getContentPane(),
                    "Are you sure you want to exit?",
                    "Exit Application",
                    JOptionPane.YES_NO_OPTION);
            if (dialogOption == JOptionPane.YES_OPTION) {
                frame.dispose();
            }
        }
    }
  }
    newItem.addActionListener(new FileMenuListener(this));
    saveItem.addActionListener(new FileMenuListener(this));
    openItem.addActionListener(new FileMenuListener(this));
    exitItem.addActionListener(new FileMenuListener(this));
  }

  public static void main(String[] args)
  {
    FileMenuFrame menuFrame = new FileMenuFrame();
    menuFrame.setBounds(100, 100, 500, 500);
    menuFrame.setDefaultCloseOperation(EXIT_ON_CLOSE);
    menuFrame.setVisible(true);
  }
}
```

Running the program will show various file dialogs like those seen in Fig. 19.2. Figure 19.10 shows the confirmation dialog triggered by selecting the "Exit" menu item.

Exercise 19.3

- Create an application with a frame that hosts a "Color" menu.
- Add a few basic color choices to the menu.
- Include a field in the frame class that can store a reference to the Graphics object that it uses, with getter and setter methods.
- Set the value of this field after the frame has been constructed.
- Add a suitable event handler that will change the foreground color in response to the menu selection.
- Use the color when drawing on the panel using the mouse, as we did in Chap. 18 . You will need to access the Graphics reference from the frame.
- Add another option to the menu that will invoke a JColorChooser and use the value returned from that to set the drawing color. Invoke the JColorChooser as a modal dialog using the static "showDialog" method, e.g.

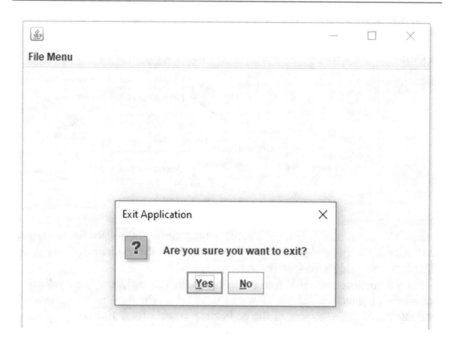

Fig. 19.10 A confirmation dialog triggered by a menu listener

```
Color col = JColorChooser.showDialog
(frame, "Choose Color", Color.WHITE);
```

19.4 Model View Controller in Swing Components

In Chap. 18 we saw that it was desirable to separate out the code that managed the user interface of an application from the underlying data model. We did this by building a non-graphical class to manage a table of distances, which was used by a separate graphical class for display. This is necessary in order to make our applications flexible and scalable, enabling us to have different views of the same model or perhaps different models for the same view. Several of the larger classes in the Swing library are very good examples of this approach, providing different related components for models and views by applying the Model View Controller (MVC) design pattern. Swing uses MVC to devolve various implementation responsibilities in UI components. The model maintains the domain-specific state information, while the view displays what the model layer represents. The job of the

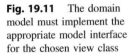 **Fig. 19.11**   The domain model must implement the appropriate model interface for the chosen view class

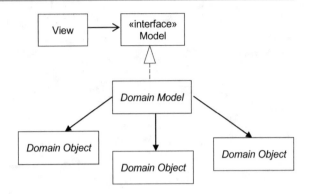

controller is to control the interaction between the user, the view and the model. In Swing, the view and controller responsibilities are encapsulated in the Swing components, so it is the separation of the view from the model that is most significant from a coding perspective.

For a domain-specific model to be plugged into standard view, the model must implement an interface that the view can work with. The implementing class will then interact with the objects of the underlying domain (Fig. 19.11).

Many Swing components need a separately coded model class. For example, JTextPane has a javax.swing.text.Document, and JTable has a javax.swing.table. TableModel. In this section we will look at some simple examples of creating models for both components.

19.4.1   Model and View in JTextPane Components

The JTextPane component provides some text management facilities that enable it to be used as a reasonably useful text editor and/or formatter. The "document" property, provided by an implementation of the javax.swing.text.Document interface, acts as the underlying model and defines the text and formatting. This formatting includes supporting multiple text fonts, sizes and styles within the same component, and multiple paragraph formats. It also provides automatic word wrapping.

The JTextPane class provides the view and the controller. Changes to the document model are immediately reflected in the view.

Fig. 19.12 Using a
JTextPane as a simple plain
text editor

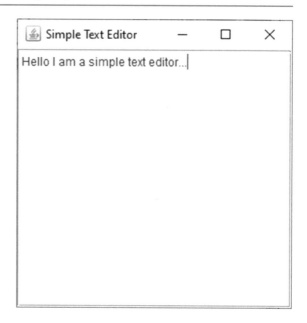

19.4.1.1   Adding a Document

Swing provides an AbstractDocument class that implements the Document interface, and concrete document classes that allow different types of document to be created (RTF, HTML). For this example, we will be using the DefaultStyledDocument class, which supports character and paragraph styles similar to Rich Text Format (RTF).

A document is added to a JTextPane using the "setDocument" method. The text pane needs to be added to a JScrollPane, which can then be added to the frame:

```
JTextPane textPane = new JTextPane();
Document document = new DefaultStyledDocument();
textPane.setDocument(document);
JScrollPane scroller = new JScrollPane(textPane);
getContentPane().add(scroller);
```

The following simple program creates a JTextPane and adds it to a JScrollPane and a frame. Since no formatting features have been applied, this window works like a very simple plain text editor.

```
package com.foundjava.chapter19;
```

```java
import javax.swing.JFrame;
import javax.swing.JScrollPane;
import javax.swing.JTextPane;
import javax.swing.text.DefaultStyledDocument;
import javax.swing.text.Document;

public class SimpleTextPane extends JFrame
{
  public SimpleTextPane()
  {
    JTextPane textPane = new JTextPane();
    Document document = new DefaultStyledDocument();
    textPane.setDocument(document);
    JScrollPane scroller = new JScrollPane(textPane);
    getContentPane().add(scroller);
  }

  public static void main(String[] args)
  {
    SimpleTextPane textPane = new SimpleTextPane();
    textPane.setTitle("Simple Text Editor");
    textPane.setBounds(100, 100, 300, 300);
    textPane.setDefaultCloseOperation(EXIT_ON_CLOSE);
    textPane.setVisible(true);
  }
}
```

Figure 19.12 shows the JTextPane in use, with some text entered. Text typed into the view automatically updates the underlying document model.

19.4.1.2 Text Styling with AttributeSets

Formatting of the text in a JTextPane can be done by applying attribute sets to the text. Swing includes a SimpleAttributeSet class that can be used for this, with a simple constructor.

```java
SimpleAttributeSet textStyle = new SimpleAttributeSet();
```

Each attribute set defines a set of formatting information such as font size, bold, underline and text color. Individual attributes are added to an attribute set using static "set" methods from the StyleConstants class. Here, for example, the attribute set is given a bold style (the second Boolean parameter specifies if we are adding or removing the style).

```java
StyleConstants.setBold(textStyle, true);
```

Once a SimpleAttributeSet is created, it can be applied to selected parts of the text in the styled document. The currently selected text can be returned from the TextPane using the "getSelectionStart" and "getSelectionEnd" methods.

```
int start = textPane.getSelectionStart();
int end = textPane.getSelectionEnd();
```

The text style can be applied to the document using the "setCharacterAttributes" method. The parameters to this method specify the character range to be formatted, the text style and a boolean parameter that specifies whether the new style replaces (or augments) the current style.

```
document.setCharacterAttributes(start, end - start,
    textStyle, false);
```

Here is the complete example of a text pane that allows some simple formatting of a document. Three text styles are created: bold, italic and plain. These are set inside an event handler that is triggered by three buttons (one for each type).

```
package com.foundjava.chapter19;

public class StringData
{
  private String text;
  private int x;
  private int y;

  public String getText()
  {
    return text;
  }
  public void setText(String text)
  {
    this.text = text;
  }
  public int getX()
  {
    return x;
  }
  public void setX(int x)
  {
```

```java
  JButton plainButton = new JButton("Plain");
  plainButton.addActionListener
    (new FormatButtonListener());
  JPanel panel = new JPanel();
  panel.add(boldButton);
  panel.add(italicButton);
  panel.add(plainButton);
  add(panel, BorderLayout.SOUTH);
  add(scroller);
 scroller.setVerticalScrollBarPolicy
  (JScrollPane.VERTICAL_SCROLLBAR_AS_NEEDED);
scroller.setHorizontalScrollBarPolicy
  (JScrollPane.HORIZONTAL_SCROLLBAR_AS_NEEDED);
  textPane.setDocument(new DefaultStyledDocument());
}

class FormatButtonListener implements ActionListener
{
  public void actionPerformed(ActionEvent e)
  {
    StyledDocument document =
      (StyledDocument) textPane.getDocument();
    int start = textPane.getSelectionStart();
    int end = textPane.getSelectionEnd();
    SimpleAttributeSet textStyle =
      new SimpleAttributeSet();
    if (e.getActionCommand().equals("Bold"))
    {
       StyleConstants.setBold(textStyle, true);
    }
    if (e.getActionCommand().equals("Italic"))
    {
      StyleConstants.setItalic(textStyle, true);
    }
    if (e.getActionCommand().equals("Plain"))
    {
      StyleConstants.setItalic(textStyle, false);
      StyleConstants.setBold(textStyle, false);
    }
    document.setCharacterAttributes(start, end - start,
      textStyle, false);
  }
}
```

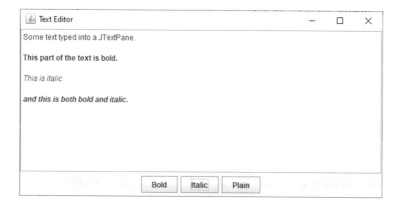

Fig. 19.13   Some text formatted in a text pane

```
public static void main(String[] args)
{
  FormattableTextPane textPane =
    new FormattableTextPane("Text Editor");
  textPane.setBounds(100, 100, 600, 600);
  textPane.setDefaultCloseOperation(EXIT_ON_CLOSE);
  textPane.setVisible(true);
}
}
```

Figure 19.13 shows the example text pane with some formatting applied to parts of the text.

19.4.1.3   Presenting Read-Only Text

Once the document is added it can be edited, though if required editing can be disabled so the TextPane can be used simply to present text rather than edit it, as in this example.

```
package com.foundjava.chapter19;
import java.awt.Container;
import javax.swing.JFrame;
import javax.swing.JScrollPane;
import javax.swing.JTextPane;
import javax.swing.text.BadLocationException;
import javax.swing.text.DefaultStyledDocument;
import javax.swing.text.Document;
```

```java
import javax.swing.text.SimpleAttributeSet;
import javax.swing.text.StyleConstants;

public class ReadOnlyTextPane extends JFrame
{
  public ReadOnlyTextPane()
  {
    super();
    JTextPane textPane = new JTextPane();
    textPane.setEditable(false);
    textPane.setDocument(buildDocument());
    JScrollPane scroller = new JScrollPane(textPane);
    getContentPane().add(scroller);
  }


  private Document buildDocument()
  {
    Document document = new DefaultStyledDocument();
    SimpleAttributeSet body = new SimpleAttributeSet();
    StyleConstants.setFontSize(body, 14);
    SimpleAttributeSet title = new SimpleAttributeSet();
    StyleConstants.setBold(title, true);
    StyleConstants.setFontSize(title, 18);
    try
    {
      document.insertString(document.getLength(),
        "It's an Object-Oriented World\n\n", title);
      document.insertString(document.getLength(), "A  Planet,
derived from HeavenlyBody theEarth, this object, this finite
state\n", body);
      document.insertString(document.getLength(), "machine ha-
sAir, hasWater, isBlue, universal behaviours; orbit(), ro-
tate().\n\n", body);
      document.insertString(document.getLength(), "A  generic
container for dynamically bound Life polymorphic of every
class,\n", body);
      document.insertString(document.getLength(), "specialis-
es, copies, generalises, objects responding to messages
passed.\n\n", body);
      document.insertString(document.getLength(), "Adam   and
Eve were our metadata, Eve part of Adam, the rib aggrega-
tion.\n", body);
```

```
     document.insertString(document.getLength(), "We inherit-
ed the earth, and the method of the serpent was knowledge,
anApple (its instantiation)\n\n", body);
     document.insertString(document.getLength(),  "Humanity's
metaclass knows our numbers, counting the transient human
race.\n", body);
     document.insertString(document.getLength(), "A kind of
Life, a part of persistence, the cosmic object data-
base.\n\n", body);
     document.insertString(document.getLength(), "Instantiat-
ed by the Big Constructor, destroyed, deleted, memory re-
claimed.\n", body);
     document.insertString(document.getLength(),      "Falling
from scope, garbage collected among billions of stars, un-
counted, unnamed.\n", body);
    }
    catch (BadLocationException exception)
    {
      exception.printStackTrace();
    }
    return document;
  }

  public static void main(String[] args)
  {
    ReadOnlyTextPane textPane = new ReadOnlyTextPane();
    textPane.setBounds(100, 100, 600, 600);
    textPane.setDefaultCloseOperation(EXIT_ON_CLOSE);
    textPane.setVisible(true);
  }
}
```

Figure 19.14 shows the read-only text in the text pane.

Exercise 19.4
The previous example showed a read-only document being displayed in a text pane.
Modify this code so that it can read the text data from a file.

- Use the CENTER and SOUTH areas of a BorderLayout to build a text file reading window.
- Add a button to a panel in the SOUTH area to invoke a JFileChooser to select a file.
- Add a JTextPane to the CENTER to display the contents of the selected file.
- In terms of reading a text file, remember that an InputStreamReader class can be used to open a text file for input. This object can then be passed to the constructor of a Buffered Reader object which has a "readLine" method for reading in a line of text from a file.

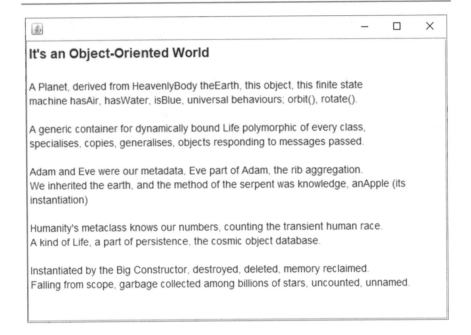

Fig. 19.14   A read-only document displayed and formatted in a text pane

19.4.2   Model and View in the JTable Component

In our final example we will look at the JTable component, which displays a graphical table based on a separate table model. The JTable needs to be populated with data, and this data comes from a separate data model object, which must implement the TableModel interface.

19.4.2.1   Implementing the TableModel Interface

The easiest way to provide a data model for a JTable is to subclass AbstractTableModel, in the "javax.swing.table" package, which provides default implementations for most of the methods in the TableModel interface, including event handling. To create a working subclass of AbstractTableModel you only need to implement these three methods:

```
public int getRowCount();
public int getColumnCount();
public Object getValueAt(int row, int column);
```

These methods inform the table how many rows and columns to draw, and what data goes in each cell. In our example, we will populate the table from a list of Modules taken from an example Course object.

Note
We will use the Course class from Chap. *12, which uses a Collection to manage its Modules.*

Our ModuleTableModel class, then, inherits from AbstractTableModel and has a Course field from which it will obtain its list of Modules (the CourseCreator will be a simple utility class that provides a Course object for test purposes).

```
public class CourseTableModel extends AbstractTableModel
{
   private Course course = CourseCreator.createCourse();
```

Of the three methods we need to override, "getColumnCount" is the simplest. Since we want to display the data from Module objects, we will have three columns to contain the module name, credit points and assessment data from each object.

```
public int getColumnCount()
{
   return 3;
}
```

"getRowCount" is also simple, since all Collections have a "size" method. We can use this to tell the table how many rows are required (one for each object).

```
public int getRowCount()
{
   return course.getModules().size();
}
```

Overriding "getColumnName", which has a default implementation in the AbstractTableModel class (using spreadsheet style titles; A, B, C, etc.), is again straightforward in principle, though there are various ways that we could implement it. We need to return a String that corresponds to the column index passed in as a parameter. In this implementation, we use a "switch" statement to return hard coded Strings. Note that returning directly from each case means that we do not need to worry about putting a break between the cases, since a return will always short circuit a method. There is also no default entry since the "return null" at the end serves the same purpose.

```
public String getColumnName(int column)
{
   switch (column) {
     case 0:
       return "Module Name";
     case 1:
       return "Credit Points";
     case 2:
       return "Assessment";
   }
   return null;
}
```

Implementing the "getValueAt" method is more complex since we have to deal with both rows and columns. The row and column positions are passed into the method as parameters, and we must return the data for the table cell at that position.

In our implementation, we first locate the correct object for the selected row number, using the "getModules" method that returns the collection, then get the individual module elements from the collection based on the row number.

```
Module m = course.getModules().get(row);
```

We then select the appropriate data from the object that matches the chosen column. Like the "getColumnName" method we use a switch statement with embedded returns.

```
switch (col)
{
  case 0:
    return m.getName();
  case 1:
    return m.getCreditPoints();
  case 2:
    return m.getAssessment();
}
return null;
```

Tables do not have to be "read only". We can set any (or all) of the cells, rows or columns to allow them to be edited, by returning "true" from the "isCellEditable" method. In this example, the "Assessment" column is made editable.

```
public boolean isCellEditable(int row, int column)
{
  if (column == findColumn("Assessment"))
  {
    return true;
  }
    ...
```

Editing a cell automatically triggers the "setValueAt" method, which in this example updates the assessment property of the selected Module

```
public void setValueAt(Object object, int row, int column)
{
  String assessment = (String) object;
  course.getModules().get(row).setAssessment(assessment);
}
```

Of course, allowing a table to be editable is the easy part. In a real application you would have to ensure that changes to the view are reflected in the underlying model. This is not too difficult to do, because the JTable has inbuilt support for event handling, but is not covered in this introductory example.

This is the complete CourseTableModel class.

```java
package com.foundjava.chapter19;

import javax.swing.table.AbstractTableModel;
import com.foundjava.chapter12.Course;
import com.foundjava.chapter12.Module;

public class CourseTableModel extends AbstractTableModel
{
  private Course course = CourseCreator.createCourse();
// override the default implementations of
// getColumnCount, getRowCount and getColumnName
  public int getColumnCount()
  {
    return 3;
  }

// the number of rows will be the number of
// objects in the list
  public int getRowCount()
  {
    return course.getModules().size();
  }

// for each cell, we get the data from the list
  public Object getValueAt(int row, int col)
  {
// the row number matches the position in the list
    Module m = course.getModules().get(row);
// each column displays a field from the module
    switch (col) {
      case 0:
        return m.getName();
      case 1:
        return m.getCreditPoints();
      case 2:
        return m.getAssessment();
    }
    return null;
  }

// column names match the fields of a Module
  public String getColumnName(int column)
  {
    switch (column) {
```

```
      case 0:
        return "Module Name";
      case 1:
        return "Credit Points";
      case 2:
        return "Assessment";
    }
    return null;
  }


// Make the Assessment editable
  public boolean isCellEditable(int row, int column)
  {
// Avoid hard-coding column numbers
    if (column == findColumn("Assessment"))
    {
      return true;
    }
    else
    {
      return false;
    }
  }


  public void setValueAt(Object object, int row, int column)
  {
// return if we are not changing the assessment column
    if (column != findColumn("Assessment"))
    {
      return;
    }
    String assessment = (String)object;
    course.getModules().get(row).setAssessment(assessment);
  }

  public Course getCourse()
  {
    return course;
  }
}
```

19.4.2.2   Creating a JTable View

Having built our underlying data model, we can now turn our attention to the view. This is fairly simple, since the Swing classes do all the actual work. In our example we create an instance of the CourseTableModel.

```
courseTable = new CourseTableModel();
```

We then create a visual JTable component, which needs to be associated with our table model (passed to the constructor).

```
JTable table = new JTable(courseTable);
```

All we need to do is add the JTable to a JScrollPane, and then add the scroll pane to the main window.

```
JScrollPane scrollpane = new JScrollPane(table);
Container container = getContentPane();
container.add(scrollpane);
```

This is the complete ModuleTable class

```
package com.foundjava.chapter19;

import javax.swing.*;
import javax.swing.table.JTableHeader;
import java.awt.*;

public class ModuleTable extends JFrame
{
// a reference to the data table model
  private CourseTableModel courseTable;

  public ModuleTable()
  {
    super();
    courseTable = new CourseTableModel();
// create the visual table using the table model as its data
    JTable table = new JTable(courseTable);
    this.setTitle(courseTable.getCourse().getName() +
      " course modules");
// add the table to a scroll pane
    JScrollPane scrollpane = new JScrollPane(table);
// add the scroll panel to the main content pane
    Container container = getContentPane();
    container.add(scrollpane);
```

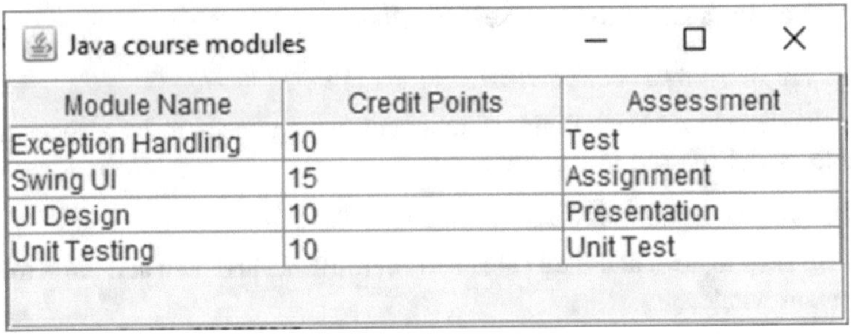

Module Name	Credit Points	Assessment
Exception Handling	10	Test
Swing UI	15	Assignment
UI Design	10	Presentation
Unit Testing	10	Unit Test

Fig. 19.15   Course module data displayed in a JTable

```
   }

   public static void main(String[] args)
   {
      ModuleTable window = new ModuleTable();
      window.setDefaultCloseOperation(EXIT_ON_CLOSE);
      window.setBounds(0,0,400,150);
      window.setVisible(true);
   }
}
```

Figure 19.15 shows the table displaying the data from the course modules

Exercise 19.6
Put the module table into a frame that contains other components that can display the details of the current course to which the modules belong.

Exercise 19.7
Use a JTable to display the data from a suitable table model relating to bank account transactions. Create some objects of the Transaction class from exercise 13.2 and use these in your table model.

19.5   Summary

Chapter 17 introduced the basic components and containers of a Java Swing User Interface (UI), and Chap. 18 introduced event-driven programming, enabling us to capture user events through UI components. However, in order to build usable applications with a UI we need to provide the basic components of a WIMP (Windows, Icons, Menus and Pointers) interface. Therefore, we began this chapter with an explanation of how to create dialogs, which provide richer options for interacting with the user through multiple windows and saw how to integrate them into a frame-based application. The initial examples demonstrated the use of some built-in Swing dialogs, such as the JOptionPane, and then progressed to creating custom dialogs based on the JDialog class. This was followed by an example of how to add menus to a Swing application, including the addition of separators, mnemonics and keyboard accelerators. The latter part of the chapter explored the Model View Controller architecture, which is an important aspect of some of the more sophisticated Swing components. Code examples introduced the separation of model and view in two components: the JTextPane and the JTable.

Java Web Servers and the HttpClient

20

In its early days, Java came to prominence because of Java Applets, running in web browsers, but the days of Applets are over, along with the later Java Web Start technology, which allowed desk top applications to be deployed over the web. These technologies were retired primarily due to security concerns, which led to increasingly limited support by web browsers, and were removed from the Java Standard Edition (Java SE) in 2018. At the same time, those components of Java Enterprise Edition (Java EE) that used to be included in the standard edition of Java were also removed, while Java EE itself became Jakarta EE after ownership was transferred from Oracle to the Eclipse Foundation. Since this is not a book about Java/Jakarta EE, you might wonder what there is to cover in a chapter about Java SE and the Web. In fact, there is still some link between them because 2018 also saw the introduction of the HttpClient class, which provides a mechanism for Java code to make an HTTP connection to a web server. Since testing out the HttpClient will require us to host some web resources to connect to, we will begin with a brief overview of web browsers, URLs and HTML.

Note
Attempting to use classes like "Applet" or JApplet" in Eclipse will come up with a warning that these classes have been "deprecated". They will appear in the editor with the class names struck through.

20.1 Web Browsers, URLs and HTML Pages

Web browser software (e.g. Chrome, Edge, Firefox, Safari, etc.) is designed to retrieve information from remote sites on the World Wide Web (WWW) using Uniform Resource Locators (URLs). Much of the information is made available in the form of Hypertext Markup Language (HTML) web pages.

© Springer Nature Switzerland AG 2020
D. Parsons, *Foundational Java*, Texts in Computer Science,
https://doi.org/10.1007/978-3-030-54518-5_20

20.1.1   URLs

A URL is basically the Internet address of a resource on a server and typically is written in three parts, the protocol, the server address and the name of the resource (including any path information). The terminology of some of the Java classes we look at uses the slightly broader term of Uniform Resource Identifier (URI) which defines the name of a resource but possibly not every aspect of its location. The distinction is not important at the level of the code we are using in this chapter.

20.1.1.1   The HTTP Protocol

The protocol prefix for web pages is "http://". This stands for "hypertext transfer protocol" and most URLs start this way. Indeed, this part is often omitted, because it is usually the browser's default protocol (though there are other web protocols such as the File Transfer Protocol (FTP)).

20.1.1.2   The Server Address

The server address usually begins with "www" (World Wide Web), followed by the name of the site and its "domain", which defines its category and may include its country code. Each of these is separated by a period (full stop). Take, for example, the following URL:

```
http://www.foundjava.com
```

"foundjava" is the name of the server site and "com" means a company. Common alternatives to "com" are "edu" for academic institutions and "org" for organizations. Many URLs are within a country domain, such as ".co.uk" or ".ac. nz". If you are running a test server on your local machine, the domain name becomes "localhost".

20.1.1.3   The Path and Resource Name

The final part of a URL can include the location (directory) and (optionally) name of the file at the site. For example (this is not a real web address):

```
http://www.mywebsite.com/docs/index.html
```

This looks for the file "index.html" in the "docs" directory. The file name will generally end in "html" (or sometimes just "htm") because it will usually be a file written in HTML (see below). If no filename is specified, "index.html" is often the server's default file name that it will send back to the browser. If no index file is present then a directory listing may be displayed instead, or an error page, depending on the server's configuration.

Increasingly, URLs that include the filename are being replaced by "clean URLs" or "slugs", where the URL has no filename but just ends in what looks like a folder but is a reference to the page. This type of URL is more robust to changing files on the server and works better with search engines. Here, for example, is the

URL of the Java source code on the "foundjava.com" website. Note that the page uses the slug "java-code" but this is not an HTML filename.

```
http://www.foundjava.com/java-code/
```

20.1.2 Hypertext Markup Language (HTML)

Web browsers display screens of information written using HTML. The browser takes the basic information stored in the HTML file and formats it appropriately using *tags* embedded into the text of the file. All HTML files begin with an <html> tag and end with </html>. Most HTML tags are terminated in this way, using a forward slash followed by the tag name. The following example is a very simple HTML file, showing additional tags for the page header (<head>, which can include a title <title>), the main body of the text (<body>) and some text. Header tags (such as <h1>) can be used to format the size of text. The <p> tag is used to specify paragraphs. The "DOCTYPE" at the top of the file specifies the version of HTML that is being used. This example uses HTML 5 (different DOCTYPES have different expectations about how the document should be structured).

```
<!DOCTYPE html>
<html>
  <head>
    <title>Foundational Java</title>
  </head>
  <body>
    <h1>Welcome to Foundational Java</h1>
    <p>
     This is the HTML content - can be read by the HTTPClient
    </p>
  </body>
</html>
```

You can create an HTML page as a file within Eclipse, which will recognize it by the file extension as a web page. Once it has been created, if you right click on the file and select "Open With", one of the options is "Web Browser". Figure 20.1 shows what the HTML file looks like when opened in the Eclipse Web browser. This file has been called "welcome.html" (we will be referring to this filename later).

Simple files can easily be written by hand, but for more complex pages it is better to use one of the many available HTML editing tools. Some simple HTML pages will be needed to deploy onto a server for the examples in this chapter. If you want to do more substantial work with Jakarta EE, it is recommended that you

Fig. 20.1 A simple HTML page opened in the Eclipse Web Browser

download the Eclipse IDE for Enterprise Java Developers which includes a range of editors for different types of file used in web development.

20.2   Setting Up a Tomcat Server

In this section we will cover the basics of deploying a web page to the Tomcat server. Tomcat is an open source Java application server that supports the Web application components of the Jakarta EE specification. These components can generate dynamic content (i.e. web pages that are generated dynamically by code running on the server). Application servers like Tomcat can also serve static content, such as pre-written HTML pages, through a built-in HTTP server.

20.2.1   Installing and Starting Tomcat

Tomcat can be downloaded in multiple formats, including a Windows installer, but in this chapter we will work through an example based on downloading a zipped archive, which can be extracted to a suitable location on your computer. Using this type of installation helps you to get a clearer view of how Tomcat runs and how it can be configured.

Tomcat can be downloaded from https://tomcat.apache.org/. The following sections assume that the zipped archive version has been downloaded and extracted to a folder called "apache-tomcat-10" on the "C:" drive of a Windows machine. In these examples version 10 of Tomcat is being used but the basic processes described have been common to many versions of Tomcat.

To start Tomcat, first navigate to the "bin" folder of the Tomcat installation directory. For example, if Tomcat has been installed into "C:\apache-tomcat-10", the "bin" folder will be immediately underneath this directory:

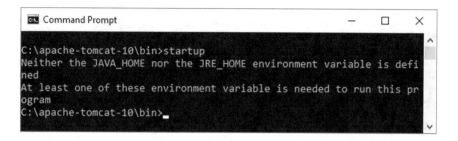

Fig. 20.2 The error message from the Tomcat application server if the JAVA_HOME environment variable has not been set

```
C:\apache-tomcat-10\bin
```

In the "bin" folder there will be a file called "startup" that can be used to start the server, either by running it from File Explorer or from the Command Prompt. The best way to start Tomcat so you can see what is happening is to open the Command Prompt and navigate to the "bin" folder of your Tomcat installation, Then type "startup" at the prompt. This way, if anything goes wrong, you can see the output in the Command Prompt. On first installation, startup will fail unless the JAVA_HOME environment variable has not been set to point to an installation of Java SE (Fig. 20.2).

As this error message shows, it is necessary to set the JAVA_HOME variable to indicate to Tomcat where Java is installed on your machine. The best way to do this is to use a plain text editor (such as the file editor in Eclipse) to create a file called "setev.bat", then add it to the "bin" folder of your Tomcat installation. The content of this text file would be something like (depending on where you have installed Java):

```
set JAVA_HOME=C:\Program Files\Java\jdk-14
```

Once your "setenv.bat" file has been added to the "bin" folder, running the startup script should result in a successful server start. You should see a separate "Tomcat" window appear, with some log messages (Fig. 20.3). Do not close this window, as this will stop the server.

20.2.2   The "localhost" URL and Port Number

When we run a test server on the local machine, we use the *loopback address*. This is IP address 127.0.0.1, which is also known as "localhost" (assuming the usual default setting on your machine). The HTTP server that is included with Tomcat runs by default on port 8080. Therefore, the URL that can be used to connect to the server running on the local machine is:

Fig. 20.3 Some startup messages from the Tomcat application server

```
http://localhost:8080
```

To check that Tomcat is running correctly, open a Web browser and direct it to this URL. You should see the default Tomcat server home page (Fig. 20.4).

A quick way to stop the server is simply close the command window in which it is running. A better approach, which enables Tomcat to shut down its threads in an orderly manner, is to run the "shutdown" file in the "bin" folder of your Tomcat installation.

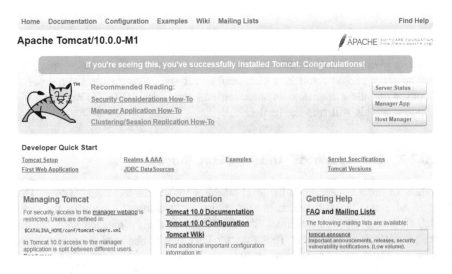

Fig. 20.4 The Tomcat server home page

20.3   Deploying a Web Application to Tomcat

Web applications are part of the Jakarta Enterprise Edition (Jakarta EE), which specifies some folders and files that are used to deploy Java web applications.

Static content (e.g. HTML files) can be put into the root of the folder structure (the "context root"). In addition, a Java web application may include a *deployment descriptor*, which is an XML file used to configure how the web server deploys the resources in the application. This file is called "web.xml", and it is put into a special folder called "WEB-INF".

Jakarta EE application components may be packaged in JAR file formats so that they can be easily deployed as a single unit. Although all the deployment units in Jakarta EE are JAR files, different extensions are used to identify their purpose. For example, a JAR file for a web application archive is given a ".war" extension. In the following sections we will put the required resources together as files in Eclipse, then deploy them to Tomcat using an Ant build file.

Note
At the time of writing, the most recent version of Java EE from Oracle was version 8 from 2017. With the 2019 release of Jakarta EE by the Eclipse Foundation, the version number remained the same (Jakarta EE 8), underlining that the Eclipse version is fully compatible with Java EE 8.

20.3.1   XML Deployment Descriptors

The "web.xml" deployment descriptor must be both well formed and valid XML so that its elements can be processed by the application server. An application server will usually validate any deployment descriptors when an application is deployed and cannot load the application if any of the descriptors are not valid. Depending on the version of the web application descriptor that is being used, there may be either a Document Type Definition (DTD) or an XML Schema available to validate deployment descriptors. The following example uses an XML Schema.

```
<?xml version="1.0" encoding="UTF-8"?>
<web-app version="3.1"
  xmlns="http://xmlns.jcp.org/xml/ns/javaee"
  xmlns:xsi="http://www.w3.org/2001/XMLSchema-instance"
  xsi:schemaLocation="http://xmlns.jcp.org/xml/ns/javaee
http://xmlns.jcp.org/xml/ns/javaee/web-app_3_1.xsd">
  ...
</web-app>
```

You can see from this schema that the root element is called "webapp". Inside this element may appear many nested elements, which must appear in the order specified by the XML Schema. Apart from the compulsory root element, all the other elements are either optional or may occur zero or more times. This means that the number of elements used in a valid "web.xml" deployment descriptor can vary a great deal between applications. You can create an XML deployment descriptor in Eclipse as a text file in the "src" folder (right click then choose "New" → "File").

A useful element to add is the "welcome-file-list". The role of this element is to configure the default page that will be served when a client connects to the URI of the Web application. The "welcome-file-list" element, if present, must contain at least one "welcome-file" entry, which is the name of the page that is served to the client if they do not request a specific resource. In our example, the default response will be the "welcome.html" page. Here is the complete "web.xml" page for this example.

```
<?xml version="1.0" encoding="UTF-8"?>
<web-app version="3.1"
  xmlns="http://xmlns.jcp.org/xml/ns/javaee"
  xmlns:xsi="http://www.w3.org/2001/XMLSchema-instance" .
  xsi:schemaLocation="http://xmlns.jcp.org/xml/ns/javaee
http://xmlns.jcp.org/xml/ns/javaee/web-app_3_1.xsd">
  <welcome-file-list>
    <welcome-file>welcome.html</welcome-file>
  </welcome-file-list>
</web-app>
```

The structure and data types of the XML file will be validated by the server using the XML Schema when the web application is deployed, and any error messages will appear in the server's output window (the one shown in Fig. 20.6). The actual content between the tags is not specified by the Schema (e.g. what constitutes a valid web page name). This information will, however, be processed by the application server when it tries to deploy the application. This means that even an XML document that is valid according to the Schema may have errors in its content that prevent the application from deploying properly.

20.3.2 Deploying to the Server

So far our web application involves two files that must be deployed in a specific folder structure. In order to get it running on Tomcat we must create a web archive and deploy it to the "webapps" folder of the server. This is easily done using Ant. In fact, there is a special "war" task in Ant, designed to create a web archive. We can also use Ant to deploy the web application by copying the ".war" file to the server's deployment folder.

20.3.2.1 Deploying the WAR File with Ant

In this section we will look at an Ant build file that will create the necessary working folders that we will use to assemble our Web application. It will then add the HTML page to the context root (the top-level folder in the "war" file) while the web application deployment descriptor ("web.xml") is placed in a "WEB-INF" folder.

Much of the build file used in this example uses tasks that should be familiar from Chap. 14. First, a series of properties are set for various folders and file names, including the deployment folder for Tomcat web applications.

```
<project name="webap" default="copy-war" basedir=".">
  <property name="deployfolder" value="c:\webapp" />
  <property name="sourcefolder"
    value="${deployfolder}\sources" />
  <property name="configfolder"
    value="${deployfolder}\config" />
  <property name="webapp"
    value="${deployfolder}\foundjava.war" />
<property name="tomcat-deploy"
    value="C:\apache-tomcat-10\webapps" />
```

The purposes of these various files and folders are as follows:

- deployfolder

The root folder for the various deployment files, which will also be used as the build destination folder for the web archive

- sourcefolder

This folder will contain files that need to be in the root folder of the web application, in this case the "welcome.html" file

- configfolder

This folder will contain the "web.xml" file

- webapp

This specifies the file name of the web application to be built ("foundjava.war")

- tomcat-deploy

The deployment folder for the Tomcat web server (this is called "webapps" in the Tomcat installation)

The "prepare" target simply creates the required folders and copies files into them from the Eclipse source folders. The "createwar" target uses the "war" task to create a web archive. The "destfile" attribute is the web application to be created, and the "webxml" attribute is the location of the "web.xml" file. When it creates the WAR file, this task will put the "web.xml" file in a WEB-INF folder inside the archive. All the files specified in the "fileset" will also be added to the archive.

```
<!-- build the war file -->
<target name="createwar" depends="prepare">
  <war destfile="${webapp}"
       webxml="${configfolder}/web.xml" >
    <fileset dir="${sourcefolder}"/>
  </war>
</target>
```

The final target, "copy-war", simply copies the war file to the web server's deployment folder, where it will be automatically (re)deployed. Here is the complete build.xml file:

```
<project name="webap" default="copy-war" basedir=".">
  <property name="deployfolder" value="c:\webapp" />
  <property name="sourcefolder"
    value="${deployfolder}\sources" />
  <property name="configfolder"
    value="${deployfolder}\config" />
```

```
<property name="webapp"
  value="${deployfolder}\foundjava.war" />
<property name="tomcat-deploy"
  value="C:\apache-tomcat-10\webapps" />

<target name="prepare"
    description="create output folders for the build">
    <delete dir="${deployfolder}" />
  <mkdir dir="${deployfolder}" />
  <mkdir dir="${sourcefolder}" />
  <mkdir dir="${configfolder}" />
  <copy file="welcome.html" todir="${sourcefolder}"/>
  <copy file="web.xml" todir="${configfolder}"/>
</target>

<!-- build the war file -->
<target name="createwar" depends="prepare">
  <war destfile="${webapp}"
    webxml="${configfolder}/web.xml" >
    <fileset dir="${sourcefolder}"/>
  </war>
</target>

<!-- copy the war file to the Tomcat server -->
<target name="copy-war" depends="createwar">
  <copy file="${webapp}" todir="${tomcat-deploy}" />
</target>

</project>
```

Running the Ant batch file will process this file using the default target ("copy-war"). You should see output like that shown in Fig. 20.5.

You can see from this output that the WAR file is built, and then it is deployed to the server. Since this build script hot deploys to Tomcat, you should find that your web application has been rebuilt and redeployed.

The application will be deployed using the name of the WAR file as the name of the web application. In this example, then, the web application will be called "foundjava". Once the web application has been deployed and the server is running, the application will be available to browser clients using the following URL (assuming a local test server):

```
http://localhost:8080/foundjava
```

Because "welcome.html" is specified in the "web.xml" deployment descriptor as the default welcome file, this page should appear in the browser without needing to

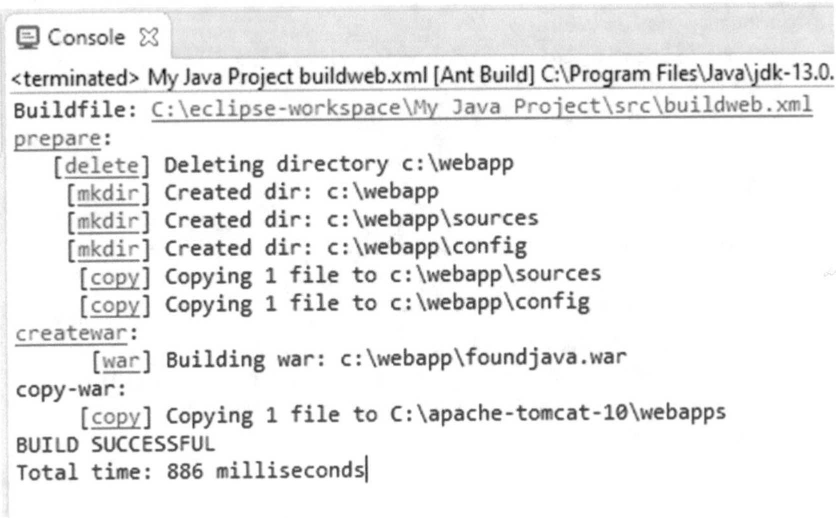

```
Console ⌗
<terminated> My Java Project buildweb.xml [Ant Build] C:\Program Files\Java\jdk-13.0.
Buildfile: C:\eclipse-workspace\My Java Project\src\buildweb.xml
prepare:
    [delete] Deleting directory c:\webapp
    [mkdir] Created dir: c:\webapp
    [mkdir] Created dir: c:\webapp\sources
    [mkdir] Created dir: c:\webapp\config
    [copy] Copying 1 file to c:\webapp\sources
    [copy] Copying 1 file to c:\webapp\config
createwar:
    [war] Building war: c:\webapp\foundjava.war
copy-war:
    [copy] Copying 1 file to C:\apache-tomcat-10\webapps
BUILD SUCCESSFUL
Total time: 886 milliseconds
```

Fig. 20.5 The output from the build file that creates and deploys the web application archive

be specifically requested. However, we could alternatively invoke it directly like this.

```
http://localhost:8080/foundjava/welcome.html
```

Figure 20.6 shows what the page looks like in Chrome. Note the URI of the page in the address bar.

Exercise 20.1
Download and install Tomcat. Add a "setenv.bat" file to the "bin" folder of the Tomcat installation that sets the value of the JAVA_HOME environment variable. Check that you can start the server from the Command Prompt and view the Tomcat home page by opening a browser on http://localhost:8080.

← → C ⌂   ⓘ localhost:8080/foundjava/

Welcome to Foundational Java

This is the HTML content - can be read by the HTTPClient

Fig. 20.6 The "welcome.html" page in Chrome, downloaded from the local Tomcat server

Exercise 20.2
Create a short HTML file and an XML deployment descriptor in the "src" folder of your Eclipse project. Create an Ant build file to deploy these resources in a "war" file to the "webapps" folder of your server. Check that the webapp deploys successfully and connects to the web page using the name of your web-app.

20.4   The HttpClient Class

Now that we have a web server up and running, we can finally look at the java.net. http.HttpClient class and see how it can enable a Java program to make an HTTP connection to a server. The HttpClient, which was introduced with Java 11, has a complex set of configuration options and methods, so in this chapter we will only touch the surface of its capabilities. It can make a connection to a server either synchronously (blocking) or asynchronously (unblocking). The examples in this chapter use asynchronous connections. The code structure is like that of the collection streams that we looked at in Chap. 12, again based on underlying lambda expressions.

In this short example of using the HttpClient to make an asynchronous connection, there are two parts to the code: creating an HTTP request to send to the server, then receiving the HTTP response and doing something with it. The first step is to create an HTTPClient object using the static "newHttpClient" method of the HttpClient class.

```
HttpClient client = HttpClient.newHttpClient();
```

In a separate step, creating the request is done via the HttpClient.Builder interface with the "uri" and "build" methods of the builder being chained together to create the HttpRequest.

```
HttpRequest request = HttpRequest.newBuilder()
  .uri(URI.create("http://localhost:8080/foundjava/"))
  .build();
```

Now that we have an HttpClient object and an HttpRequest object, we can use the two together to send the request to the server and get a response.

Getting the response uses the HttpClient, sending an asynchronous request (using the "sendAsync" method) and defining a BodyHandler to be used for the response. The BodyHandlers interface can create different types of BodyHandler from its methods. The "ofString" method creates a BodyHandler that will handle the body of the response as a String. The "sendAsync" method returns a "CompletableFuture" object, to which the "thenApply", "thenAccept" and "join" methods are chained as the asynchronous processes complete.

The "thenAccept" method executes when the body is available, and in this case sends it to the "println" method of "System.out"

```
client.sendAsync(request, BodyHandlers.ofString())
  .thenApply(HttpResponse::body)
  .thenAccept(System.out::println)
  .join();
```

Here is a class that puts the HttpClient code into a static method so it can be reused. A URI is passed in as a parameter argument and a String is returned, comprising the body of the web resource. Note that instead of printing out the String returned from the response, it is appended to a StringBuffer, which is then converted to a String and returned.

```
package com.foundjava.chapter20;

import java.net.URI;
import java.net.http.HttpClient;
import java.net.http.HttpRequest;
import java.net.http.HttpResponse;
import java.net.http.HttpResponse.BodyHandlers;

public class HTTPSourceReader {
  public static String getHTTPString(String uri)
  {
    StringBuffer htmlText = new StringBuffer();
    HttpClient client = HttpClient.newHttpClient();
    HttpRequest request = HttpRequest.newBuilder()
      .uri(URI.create(uri))
      .build();
    client.sendAsync(request, BodyHandlers.ofString())
      .thenApply(HttpResponse::body)
      .thenAccept(htmlText::append)
      .join();
    return htmlText.toString();
  }
}
```

We can check that this works using the following class, which passes in the URL of the webapp running on Tomcat. However, any URL can be passed into the "getHttpString" method.

```
package com.foundjava.chapter20;

public class HttpSourceReaderRunner {
  public static void main(String[] args) {
    String htmlString = HttpSourceReader.getHttpString
     ("http://localhost:8080/foundjava/");
    System.out.println(htmlString);
  }
}
```

Connecting to the example web application running on Tomcat, the output from the program is simply the source of the HTML page.

```
<!DOCTYPE html>
<html>
 <head>
  <title>Foundational Java</title>
 </head>
 <body>
  <h1>Welcome to Foundational Java</h1>
  <p>
   This is the HTML content - can be read by the HTTPClient
  </p>
 </body>
</html>
```

20.4.1   Reading HTML into a Swing HTMLEditorKit

So, what can a piece of Java code do with some data that it has read from an HTTP connection? If it is an HTML file that has been read, then one possible option is to display it in a client-side application using an HTMLEditorKit, which can be put into a suitable Swing pane, such as a JEditorPane. JEditorPane is the superclass of JTextPane, which we saw in the last chapter. Since we do not require the text formatting tools of JTextPane for handling HTML code, a JEditorPane is sufficient for this task.

The next example should look mostly familiar to you from previous chapters. A JFrame is created, and a JEditorPane is added to it. Then the HTMLEditorKit is added to the pane and a document suitable for HTML is added. The JEditorPane is then put into the center of a BorderLayout and a scrollbar is added to the pane. All that remains is to call the "getHttpString" method to read an HTML page from the server and this can be added to the pane. It will then be displayed and is able to be edited (note that editing can be disabled by using "setEditable(false)"). With further development, this sort of editor pane could be used to update web pages that could then be redeployed to the server.

```java
package com.foundjava.chapter20;

import java.awt.BorderLayout;
import javax.swing.JEditorPane;
import javax.swing.JFrame;
import javax.swing.JScrollPane;
import javax.swing.text.Document;
import javax.swing.text.html.HTMLEditorKit;

public class HTMLWindow extends JFrame
{
  public HTMLWindow(String title)
  {
    super(title);
    // add a JEditorPane
    // (will allow the text content to be edited)
    JEditorPane htmlPane = new JEditorPane();

    // add an HTML editor kit
    HTMLEditorKit kit = new HTMLEditorKit();
    htmlPane.setEditorKit(kit);

    // create a document from the HTMLEditorKit an
    // add it the the JEditorPane
    Document document = kit.createDefaultDocument();
    htmlPane.setDocument(document);

  htmlPane.setLayout(new BorderLayout());
  getContentPane().add(htmlPane, BorderLayout.CENTER);
  getContentPane().add(new JScrollPane(htmlPane));

  // read some HTML from a URI
  String htmlString = HttpSourceReader.getHttpString
    ("http://localhost:8080/foundjava/");
  htmlPane.setText(htmlString);
  // uncomment this line to make the text read-only
  // htmlPane.setEditable(false);
  }

  public static void main(String[] args)
  {
      HTMLWindow window = new HTMLWindow("HTML Viewer");
      window.setBounds(0, 0, 500, 600);
      window.setDefaultCloseOperation(EXIT_ON_CLOSE);
      window.setVisible(true);
  }
}
```

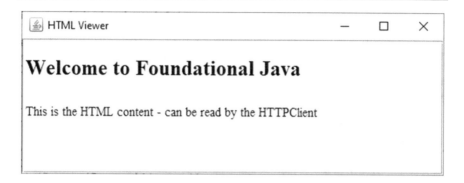

Figure 20.7 shows the HTML document rendered in the HTMLEditorKit. If the JEditorPane has been set to "editable" then the HTML can be edited in the pane.

20.4.2   Reading JSON Web Services

As well as hosting web pages such as the one we have been working with in the examples so far in this chapter, the web also acts as the platform for many other services. These services come in many forms and use a range of protocols, but a common approach is to use RESTful web services. Representational state transfer (REST) is not a specific protocol, rather it is an architectural style of services used over HTTP. A common way of implementing these services is to provide them using JavaScript Object Notation (JSON), which consists of text-based documents that structure data using attribute-value pairs and arrays. A web service will provide an API that can be used to assemble HTTP requests for making queries against the service, returning a JSON response.

A very common type of web service is a weather service, where the service can be queried for a specific set of weather information based on various parameters. The next example will use the "OpenWeather" service, which provides free access to weather data through several different APIs. The one we will use in the next example is the JSON version of the "current weather data" API, which provides current weather data for one location.

Note
To use the API you will have to first set up an account to access an API key that you can use with calls to the service.

API calls to the server have simple formats, such as this one that requests the weather using the name of a city (the version number might vary—check the current API on the OpenWeather website for details):

```
api.openweathermap.org/data/2.5/weather?
   q={city name}&appid={api key}
```

For example, to query the weather in London, and adding the "units" property to get the temperature in Centigrade (the default is Kelvin), we could use the following call (your own API key would need to be added at the end):

```
http://api.openweathermap.org/data/2.5/weather?q=London&units
=metric&appid=...
```

If you put this API call into the address bar of a browser, the returned data would look something like Fig. 20.8:

The curly braces contain sets of attribute-value pairs, which may be nested inside each other. The square brackets indicate an array. In Fig. 20.8, "weather" is an array, though in this example it is an array with only one element.

20.4.2.1 Processing a JSON Web Service with the HttpClient and JSON.simple

Unfortunately, there is currently no standard Java library for parsing JSON, but there are several third-party tools available. The one used in this example is JSON. simple which, as the name suggests, provides an easy to use Java library for handling JSON. You will need to download the "json.simple.jar" file to a suitable folder on your machine. For download information, see https://cliftonlabs.github.io/json-simple/

Once the JAR file has been downloaded, add it to the modulepath of your project using the "Java Build Path" for your project (Fig. 20.9).

Once the JAR file is on the modulepath, we can use the JSON.simple classes alongside the HttpClient to read JSON data from the weather service and parse it on the client. The next example uses the following classes from JSON.simple:

```
import org.json.simple.JSONArray;
import org.json.simple.JSONObject;
import org.json.simple.parser.JSONParser;
import org.json.simple.parser.ParseException;
```

The first step in the parsing process, after using our existing HttpSourceReader to read the JSON data from the server as a String, is to get an instance of JSONParser.

```
JSONParser jsonParser = new JSONParser();
```

Then we can convert the String data into a JSONObject so it can be processed.

{"coord":{"lon":-0.13,"lat":51.51},"weather":[{"id":801,"main":"Clouds","description":"few
clouds","icon":"02d"}],"base":"stations","main":
{"temp":7.06,"feels_like":5.03,"temp_min":3.89,"temp_max":10.56,"pressure":1030,"humidity":70}
,"visibility":10000,"wind":{"speed":0.5},"clouds":{"all":24},"dt":1586244659,"sys":
{"type":1,"id":1414,"country":"GB","sunrise":1586236880,"sunset":1586285000},"timezone":3600,"
id":2643743,"name":"London","cod":200}

Fig. 20.8 Weather data in JSON format returned from the OpenWeather web service

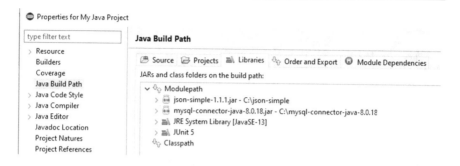

Fig. 20.9 Adding the json.simple.jar file to the modulepath in Eclipse

```
JSONObject jsonData =
    (JSONObject)jsonParser.parse(jsonString.toString());
```

It is easy to access a value in a JSON object using the attribute name as an argument to the "get" method. For example, if we look for the "name" attribute, it will return the city name as the value (you can see this attribute-value pair toward the end of the JSON data in Fig. 20.8).

```
System.out.println("\nCity: " + jsonData.get("name"));
```

Handling array data means setting up a loop that can iterate through each element of the array (although in this case we know there is only one element). We retrieve a JSONArray from the main JSONObject, then access each JSONObject inside the "weather" array:

```
JSONArray jsonWeatherData =
    (JSONArray) jsonData.get("weather");
JSONObject jsonWeather = null;
// Loop through the "weather" array
for(int i=0; i<jsonWeatherData.size(); i++)
{
  jsonWeather = (JSONObject)jsonWeatherData.get(i);
// etc.
```

Here is the complete class:

```java
package com.foundjava.chapter20;

import org.json.simple.JSONArray;
import org.json.simple.JSONObject;
import org.json.simple.parser.JSONParser;
import org.json.simple.parser.ParseException;

public class WeatherClient
{
  public static void main(String[] args)
  {
    String jsonString = HttpSourceReader.getHttpString
      ("http://api.openweathermap.org/data/2.5/
         weather?q=london&units=metric&appid=your key");
    JSONParser parse = new JSONParser();
    try
    {
      JSONObject jsonData =

        (JSONObject)parse.parse(jsonString.toString());
      System.out.println("\nCity: " + jsonData.get("name"));
      JSONObject jsonMain = (JSONObject)jsonData.get("main");
      System.out.println("\nTemperature (Celsius): "
        + (jsonMain.get("temp")));
      JSONArray jsonWeatherData =
        (JSONArray) jsonData.get("weather");
      JSONObject jsonWeather = null;
      // Loop through the "weather" array
      for(int i=0; i<jsonWeatherData.size(); i++)
      {
        // Get the data from the array elements
        // using the index number
        jsonWeather = (JSONObject)jsonWeatherData.get(i);
        System.out.println
          ("\nMain: " + jsonWeather.get("main"));
        System.out.println
          ("Description: " +jsonWeather.get("description"));
      }
    }
    catch(ParseException e)
    {
      e.printStackTrace();
    }
  }
}
```

Here is an example output from running the code. London is unsurprisingly cold and cloudy.

```
City: London

Temperature (Celsius): 9.17

Main: Clouds
Description: few clouds
```

Exercise 20.3
Using the HttpSourceReader to read JSON data from the OpenWeather web service, create a Swing frame that displays selected parts of the weather data.

20.5 Summary

In this chapter we have looked at setting up a web server using the Tomcat Jakarta EE application server. We saw how Tomcat can be installed from a downloaded archive and started from the command prompt to make it easy to see what is going on when the server starts. We saw how a configuration file needs to be added to the server's "bin" folder to ensure that it can locate a Java installation on startup. We then went through the process of creating and deploying a web application, containing an HTML page and a "web.xml" deployment descriptor, packaged into a "war" archive using an Ant build file. Our coverage then looked at the Java HttpClient class and how it can be used to connect to a web server and download data to be processed locally on the client. Examples covered both connecting to an HTML page and presenting it in an editable window and reading weather data from a JSON web service.

Index

© Springer Nature Switzerland AG 2020
D. Parsons, *Foundational Java*, Texts in Computer Science,
https://doi.org/10.1007/978-3-030-54518-5

Printed in the United States
by Baker & Taylor Publisher Services